THE VAMPIRE
GOES TO COLLEGE

THE VAMPIRE GOES TO COLLEGE

Essays on Teaching with the Undead

Edited by Lisa A. Nevárez

Foreword by Sam George

McFarland & Company, Inc., Publishers
Jefferson, North Carolina, and London

LIBRARY OF CONGRESS CATALOGUING-IN-PUBLICATION DATA

The Vampire Goes to College : Essays on Teaching
with the Undead / edited by Lisa A. Nevárez ;
foreword by Sam George.
p.   cm.
Includes bibliographical references and index.

ISBN 978-0-7864-7554-4
softcover : acid free paper ∞

1. Vampires in literature.   2. Literature—Study and teaching.
3. Vampire films—History and criticism.   4. Popular
literature—History and criticism—Theory, etc.
I. Nevárez, Lisa, editor of compilation.
PN61.V36 2014   807.1'1—dc23   2013041034

BRITISH LIBRARY CATALOGUING DATA ARE AVAILABLE

On the cover: Youthful vampire (iStockphoto/Thinkstock)

Manufactured in the United States of America

*McFarland & Company, Inc., Publishers
Box 611, Jefferson, North Carolina 28640
www.mcfarlandpub.com*

For Isabella and Sebastian:
You have my undying love.

Acknowledgments

This book has been inspired by the wonderful conversations I've had with so many individuals, be they at meetings of the Popular Culture Association or at the grocery store (yes, really!). A love for vampires can make its way from academic gatherings to other venues quite readily.

I extend an enormous thank you to my faculty colleagues at Siena College, and to the administrators and staff, who have helped this volume come to fruition through their support for conference travel, reassigned time, and assistance with assembling the manuscript. Thank you to librarian Catherine Crohan, who worked with my "vamps" in the Honors seminar I taught, "The Vampire." To the seminar "vamps"—thank you for a rewarding semester!

And, especially, I extend my heartfelt thanks to my fellow faculty in the Siena College English Department. Their support has been invaluable, and I've enjoyed sharing snippets of the vampire project with them in the halls of Kiernan.

Thank you, so much, to Rachel Stein for her gracious mentoring throughout this entire project, from its origins as an idea I was batting about in our shared office to its present life as a book.

My family has been a lifeline. Thank you to my parents, and to Christine, Mike, and Julia, for their support and understanding. I am grateful for your tolerance levels when a conversation has devolved (again) into one centered on the Undead.

Words cannot adequately capture the extent of my gratitude to my husband, Charles. He fielded oh-so-many one-sided "conversations" about The Book and, as always, has been my strongest supporter.

I dedicate this book to my two fabulous children, Isabella and Sebastian. My love for you is eternal.

Table of Contents

Foreword

Sam George

Since their animation out of folk materials in the nineteenth century, by Polidori, as Varney and in LeFanu and Stoker, vampires have been continually reborn in modern culture. They have stalked texts from Marx's image of the leeching capitalist to the multifarious incarnations in contemporary fictions in print and on screen. They have enacted a host of anxieties and desires, shifting shape as the culture they are brought to life in itself changes form. More recently, their less charismatic undead cousins, zombies, have been dug up in droves to represent various fears and crises in contemporary culture. It is surprising then, given the recent vogue for vampires and all things undead, that there has never until now been a book that explores the teaching of vampire studies in colleges and universities.

When, in the late 1970s, Sir Christopher Frayling was researching his book *Vampyres: Lord Byron to Count Dracula* in the reading room of the British Museum, Gothic studies hadn't yet entered the academy and vampires were not considered an appropriate topic for academic research. If you visit the British Library nowadays, you might not find anyone who is not studying the Gothic! Back then, Frayling was the first to invite vampires into the academy, having just been given access to the newly discovered *Dracula* notebooks (Stoker's lost research notes for the novel). The rigor and sheer scope of his research can be seen to have initiated the critical study of vampire texts. This collection, with its focus on teaching the undead, builds upon, but in some ways moves away from, the now conventional "Gothic studies" approach in that the vampire, following Frayling, forms its own tradition and discipline.

Seminal works by Nina Auerbach and Ken Gelder in the twentieth century have paved the way for this collection, which continues to document the interest in vampires within academic circles, now responding to more recent developments. Today, Gothic courses are embraced, but vampire studies still require explanation.[1] Bringing vampires into the curriculum has proved controversial. When I set up the first vampire Master's degree course in the U.K. in 2010 as part of the "Open Graves, Open Minds Vampires and the Undead in Modern Culture" project, news stories emerged that we were reacting against the Americanization of the genre, developing a vampire degree, and eating food out of coffins (this part was true at least!).[2] There have been detractors and scoffers, though these have not been without humor.[3] The project continues to explore the vampire in all its vicissitudes.[4] It has been amusing, but it has also provoked interesting debates about the canon and the study of popular literature in universities.[5] This new collection on teaching the vampire is essential to these debates. It skillfully communicates the significance of studying the representation of the vampire, the richness of such research, and the lively discussions that inevitably ensue.

Frayling identified the dominant archetypal vampires as they emerge in fiction: the Byronic vampire (or "Satanic Lord"), the Fatal Woman, the Unseen Force, the Folkloric Vampire, the "camp" vampire, and vampire as creative force.[6] Another strand has since developed — the vampire with a conscience. The scholars here are fortunate in being the first to comment on teaching this new sympathetic vampire as it appears in the twenty-first century. For some, it has meant the adulteration of the power of the Gothic and the emphasis on paranormal romance (a new genre in itself) between human beings and sparkly, vegetarian revenants, and this has led to a clash of genres and a "Gothic romanced."[7] The new vampire, however, and its parallel generic hybridity, invites new and interesting approaches to undead/Gothic studies.

The range of essays herein is wide, and all the ambivalences of the humanized vampire, who still bears traces of his or her monstrous otherness, are revealed in an educational context. Here otherness (race, ethnicity, gender, sexuality) is made to connect to the student's own experiences of diversity or alterity in the classroom (and more broadly), and important pedagogical strategies for teaching and reading the vampire are openly discussed and shared. These include ideas for putting together a vampire syllabus, including the pairing of texts for study, ways of approaching young adult readers and pertinent themes for analysis, together with new and innovative learning and teaching provisions such as blogs and role playing games that are certain to engage even the most reluctant student. The book is remarkable for its international engagement, embracing vampire studies in the United States and in Europe, and in its breadth and scope, exploring both canonical and popular texts and encouraging an interdisciplinary approach, involving literature, film, education and cultural studies. At the end of the twentieth century Nina Auerbach recalled that "vampirism is wearing down and vampires need a long restorative sleep."[8] How wrong she was! This book celebrates first-hand and with some panache their awakening in the classroom in the twenty-first century.

Notes

1. The "Open Graves, Open Minds: Vampires and the Undead in Modern Culture" project has sought to take up this mantle, initiating vampire conferences and symposia in universities and developing vampire studies in literature at the Master's level in the U.K. The research project itself was launched in 2010; it relates the undead in literature, art, and other media to questions concerning gender, technology, consumption, and social change. Based at the University of Hertfordshire, it has provided an interdisciplinary forum for the development of innovative and creative research into vampires, examining these creatures in all their various manifestations and cultural forms.

2. See, for example, Paul Casciato, "Bringing vampires back home — to Britain," *Reuters*, 6 April 2010, http://uk.reuters.com/article/2010/04/06/uk-britain-university-vampires-idUKTRE6352NP20100406; "University Rejects 'Americanisation' of Vampires," *NPR*, 7 April 2010, www.npr.org/templates/story/story.php?storyId=125660207; Karon Liu, "Bloody Hell: Brits Complain Yanks Are Stealing Their Vampires," *Toronto Life*, 7 May 2010, www.torontolife.com/daily/hype/the-american-invasion/2010/05/07/bloody-hell-brits-complain-yanks-are-stealing-their-vampires/; "Robert Pattinson, Kristen Stewart on Coffin Boffin Syllabus," *STV Entertainment News*, 7 April 2010, http://entertainment.stv.tv/showbiz/168301-robert-pattinson-kristen-stewart-on-coffin-boffin-syllabus; Mark Byrne, "Vampire Lit Gets Its Scholarly Due," *Galleycat*, www.mediabistro.com/galleycat/vampire-lit-gets-its-scholarly-due_b11462; Chanel Lee, "Wanna Study Edward Cullen," *Howstuffworks*, 9 April 2010, blogs.howstuffworks.com/2010/04/09/wanna-study-edward-cullen-and-eric-northman-head-to-england/.

3. "Listen up, Lestat lovers: The University of Hertfordshire in England will be offering a master's degree in vampire lit, apparently the only one of its kind in the world. We imagine that the program, which begins

this September, will cover all the bloodsucking basics, from Nosferatu to *Twilight* and of course Anne Rice. Extra credit for anyone who scores an interview with a vampire." *Globe and Mail*, 6 April 2010, www.the-globeandmail.com/life/style/tori-spellingvampire-uobama-jeans-wear/article1529173/.

4. We now have a website to track that research and provide OGOM news: www.opengravesopenminds.com.

5. See Simon Midgley, "Counting on Dracula," *The Times*, 16 March 2011, p. 7, for example.

6. Sir Christopher Frayling, *Vampyres: Lord Byron to Count Dracula* (London: Faber, 1988), p. 62.

7. In Fred Botting's phrase; see *Gothic Romanced: Consumption, Gender and Technology in Contemporary Fictions* (London: Routledge, 2008).

8. Nina Auerbach, *Our Vampires, Ourselves* (Chicago: University of Chicago Press, 1995), p. 192.

Sam George, Ph.D., is a senior lecturer in literature at the University of Hertfordshire. She is the co-editor (with Bill Hughes) of *Open Graves, Open Minds: Representations of Vampires and the Undead from the Enlightenment to the Present Day*. She completed a special edition of *Gothic Studies* on vampires and is a frequent commentator appearing in *The Guardian*, *The Times* (London), and *The Wall Street Journal*.

Introduction

Lisa A. Nevárez

From the fanged and frightening revenant, to the sparkling Cullen clan, to Count Chocula cereal: really, what isn't to like about the vampire? He or she can scare the socks off a victim yet can even be used — in a humorous way — to sell products. The year 2013 brought television viewers two vampire commercials: one with a vampire family in a Nutrigrain cereal bar commercial, the other in a Geico insurance commercial that featured a thirsty vampire at a blood drive. The vampire is a flexible creature in today's culture, and we can — and do— use the vampire to frighten trick-or-treaters at Halloween or, yes, to sell breakfast foods and insurance.

Malleable as they are, vampires coexist quite nicely with academia and its professoriate. Vampire "texts," which include literature as well as film and other media, certainly hold their own in any conversation about the Gothic, as Sam George's foreword attests. In the Western literary tradition, John Polidori's "The Vampyre," the Victorian *Varney the Vampire*, J. Sheridan LeFanu's *Carmilla*, and Bram Stoker's *Dracula* form the "classics" of the vampire canon. Moving into the twentieth century, Stephen King and, especially, Anne Rice have crafted vampire novels that have withstood a few decades of readers. And now, in the twenty-first century, it remains to be seen how Stephenie Meyer's popular *Twilight* saga will fare. With all of the above texts, one can readily track down corresponding monographs, essays, chapters, conference presentations, and all sorts of exciting academic discourse entirely focused on the vampire.

There exists a tantalizing intersection between these academic points of focus and what academics do when they aren't writing, researching, or presenting — which is teaching. After all, our students are the ultimate barometers of popular culture consumerism in all its myriad forms. Many of us have used popular culture examples into our classrooms as a means of livening up a lecture, and of demonstrating to students just how enduring a "text" can be. At the very least, I have the utmost conviction that several of us— myself included — use popular film adaptations to illustrate the above "endurance test." A prime example can be found in the numerous productions inspired by Jane Austen, from updated — and different — settings in *Bride and Prejudice* (from *Pride and Prejudice*) and *Clueless* (from *Emma*), that incite fruitful classroom conversation.

When it comes to popular culture and vampires, undergraduates are well-versed in nuanced distinctions between *True Blood* and *The Vampire Diaries* and can carry on extensive conversations on such topics, at least in my experience. And a few can even weigh in on the now plentiful Jane Austen/vampire novels out there such as *Mr. Darcy, Vampyre* by Amanda Grange and *Jane Bites Back* by Michael Thomas Ford. In all this lies a valuable link between "us" (the professors) and "them" (the students). We seek to engage students on their own terrain by utilizing popular culture in various ways. The figure of the vampire is a notable example of an exciting way to catch students at their most eager and to share with them the manifold ways academics discourse about that very figure.

Although the vampire may seem a potential victim of postmortem rigor mortis, he or she in fact provides a pliable model with regard to theme and context. That is, the vampire can serve as a vehicle for exploring difference and Otherness, and race and ethnicity, and sexuality and gender. With his or her lengthy "lifespan," the vampire allows us to connect disparate eras and centuries, both within one work and with a comparative approach. With the vampire emerging in print, online, and on the movie and television screens, not to mention role-playing games (RPGs), one can readily discuss different media types as well.

The goal of this collection is to celebrate the plentiful ways instructors are engaging with the figure of the vampire in the classroom. To that end, individuals have stepped forward to share syllabi, writing prompts, essay topics, and text pairings, among other useful items. The field of vampire studies is a community, with "homes" in George's "Open Graves, Open Minds" project, as mentioned in her foreword, and across the Atlantic in the Popular Culture Association, and in numerous other enclaves worldwide.

An enduring challenge instructors who wish to teach the vampire face is not only situating the vampire in an historical context, but querying what makes the vampire a legitimate focus of scholarly and pedagogical inquiry. "Part I: Teaching the Historical Vampire" opens with an essay by Sue Weaver Schopf, who takes the reader through the challenges she faced in offering her course "The Vampire in Literature and Film" at Harvard's Division of Continuing Education. It garnered some media attention, and she shares with the reader how she structured it and poses questions that are asked in many of these essays, such as how we account for the longevity of the vampire in such disparate national and geographical settings, not to mention across different belief systems. Next is Heide Crawford's essay, which traces the figure of the vampire from its 18th-century Central European background and considers how to present that important historical information in the classroom, making it accessible to students. Rounding out the first part is Lisa Lampert-Weissig's essay on historicizing the vampire in different time periods. She similarly discusses the vampire against a backdrop of central Europe at the start of her classes and in this essay, but then shifts the focus to 20th- and 21st-century America. She transitions to Southern California in particular, and converses about films such as *Blacula* in the context of race riots and the HBO series *True Blood*, which she situates against the issue of same-sex marriage.

"Part II: Teaching the Diverse Vampire" includes essays that discuss Otherness, in terms of race, ethnicity, and sexuality. U. Melissa Anyiwo offers the reader an outline of her First Year Seminar class, "Being Human: Life Through the Eyes of Outsiders and the Undead," in which she discusses the "body" of the vampire as a means of exploring concepts of differences, race in particular, and how to present these ideas to first year students. Crystal Boson similarly discusses the "Undead of Color" in her presentation of a course outline designed to incorporate conversations about racial difference, via film and literature, through theoretical approaches such as postcolonialism. Two other essays present the vampire through the lens of queer studies. Seri I. Luangphinith describes her course devoted to Otherness and concentrates on the creative work her students produced and how this course, and its ensuing conversations on social alterity, led to a means of assessing various types of diversity at her institution. Concluding this part is Jean R. Hillabold's essay focusing on homoeroticism in Anne Rice's *Interview with the Vampire*, which she pairs with a parallel discussion of Oscar Wilde's *The Picture of Dorian Gray*. As she reads them, the central characters in both texts convey a focus on beauty and monstrosity.

Following these conversations on Otherness is "Part III: Writing the Vampire," which features essays focused on a theme that runs through many of the essays in this collection beyond this particular part. Amy Hodges presents her use of the *Twilight* saga as a means of teaching writing in a first-year composition course, and at the same time discusses how the students can analyze concepts such as "highbrow" and "lowbrow" literature. Neena Cinquino also discusses writing, but emphasizes writing in a course engineered for science students. She presents not only the role of scientific inquiry in texts such as *Dracula*, but also translates that into writing exercises for the classroom. Wrapping up this part is the essay by Vicky Gilpin about writing in the community college classroom. She leads the reader through a series of assignments geared toward encouraging the nontraditional student to engage in conversations about the vampire as a means of developing writing and analytic skills.

"Part IV: Teaching the Textual Vampire" presents text pairings and thematic threads that an instructor could use. Alissa Burger offers a possible classroom text pairing with *Dracula* and Stephen King's *'Salem's Lot* and shares some techniques such as "mapping" that facilitate this sustained textual comparison. The *Twilight* saga appears again in Heather Duerre Humann's essay on teaching those four novels against a backdrop of nineteenth-century canonical texts. This then leads to conversations on the evolution of the "canon" and exercises on forging links to Meyer's contemporary, non-canonical novels. Murray Leeder defines "text" more broadly and takes the reader through his work in a film studies class on teaching three film versions of *Dracula*. Students have the opportunity to learn about genre convention and genre evolution while analyzing this cinematic portrayal of the vampire through *Nosferatu* (1922), *Dracula* (1931), and *Horror of Dracula* (1958). The fourth essay in this part is Alisha M. Chambers' tracing of the theme of religion in a selection of vampire texts, such as *Marked* by P.C. and Kristin Cast and *The Last Vampire* by Christopher Pike. She engages Christian, Hindu, and Native American (Cherokee) belief systems in her analyses of these vampire texts for the classroom. The American college classroom transitions to a Polish learning environment in the next essay, by Michał Wolski. He presents a means of connecting the vampire to canonical Polish literature, and in so doing provides a model for others interested in forging links to national literatures that perhaps may fall outside of Western Europe. He then discusses the role-playing game *Vampire: The Masquerade* and its function in engaging the student learner, both in Poland and in other nations. In this case, "text" shifts to yet another type of medium.

"Part V: Engaging the Student," presents specific learning contexts that an instructor may be using. The first essay, by Candace R. Benefiel and Catherine Coker, shares their experience in teaching a vampire-themed First Year Seminar course. Their inclusion of fan fiction and fan practices offers a unique angle on catching the attention of the first-year student. Online learning and "inquiry-guided learning" form the focus of the next essay, by Anne Daugherty and Jerri L. Miller. They also present models for digital storytelling, all to the end of engaging the student taking an online course on the vampire. In another classroom context, Leslie Ormandy presents two models of community college classrooms at 100-level and 200-level classes. She offers several classroom exercises and text recommendations for those interested in pursuing a discussion of the vampire in this setting. Rita Turner outlines yet another medium for presenting the vampire, this time in a media and cultural studies course. She employs critical media and cultural theory in unpacking the figure of the vampire and touches on themes that run throughout this collection, such as the vampire as a marginalized figure. The final essay is my own, and in it I share my experience with teaching the vampire in an Honors seminar. In particular, I provide the reader with a discussion of my use of blogging as both a research tool and a means of encouraging conversation in a different context.

The time is right for this collection: after all, the vampire is never "dead." In fact, the figure of the vampire is emerging in exciting new ways in the classroom. This collection of essays seeks to foster collaboration and dialogue across different disciplines, and to serve as a collective resource for those who do, or wish to, teach the vampire. It is our responsibility as instructors to dust off the cobwebs from the coffin and crack open the lid to welcome — again, or for the first time — the Undead.

"Legitimizing" Vampire Fiction as an Area of Literary Study

Sue Weaver Schopf

When I first proposed teaching "The Vampire in Literature and Film" in 2010 in Harvard's Division of Continuing Education, I needed to convince some of my colleagues that this would be a legitimate scholarly inquiry rather than simply a lightweight course responding to a pop culture fad. In fact, I came in for quite a bit of teasing for "abandoning" the canonical 19th- and early 20th-century literature I normally teach and taking up what were assumed to be works of little or no artistic merit or cultural significance. Some of the greatest skepticism came from colleagues who also teach literature — something for which I was unprepared, given that Harvard offers an undergraduate concentration in folklore and mythology and occasional courses in Gothic literature. Encouragement came, however, from two senior colleagues who teach in other disciplines. One is a well-known historian of religion and Mesoamerican anthropology; the other is a professor of visual and environmental studies who teaches a course in fantasy and simulation. Both noted the frequent occurrence of the vampire figure in their fields and said that my course would be an interesting addition to the curriculum.

In contrast to these mixed attitudes inside the University, I encountered unbridled enthusiasm from the general public. With the announcement that the course would be available both live in Cambridge and online, I received letters and emails from some remarkable people (e.g., a physician in England, a career naval officer stationed off the coast of Southeast Asia, a historian teaching in the Midwest, a dancer in the South of France) who "confessed" (as they put it) to a love of vampire literature, which they felt they had never been able to acknowledge to others for fear of being ridiculed! I heard from several high school teachers and college instructors who told me about their own attempts to propose a course in vampire literature, only to have their idea rejected; they were elated that they could now tell their department chairs that such a course was being offered at Harvard. Students were especially enthusiastic. Nearly 200 enrolled in the course (about 75 percent of them women); and since it was being offered in the Extension School, the students ranged in age from 17 to 75 and included full-time undergraduates, part-time graduate students, and non-credit students composed of retirees, practicing lawyers and physicians, teachers, librarians, musicians, and Harvard staff members, among others. This diverse audience fell into two categories: self-declared fans of vampire fiction and those who were curious about the prevalence of the vampire in contemporary culture but had read little or none of the literature.

Chatter about the course ended up on several websites, including those of some authors of vampire fiction whose works we would be reading in the course and the Penguin website, which noted that I was using four of their titles in the class. I was also contacted by the *Times* of London, National Public Radio, the *Boston Globe* and many other publications, as well as MTV.com. In the interviews that followed, the principal question asked was, "How *do* you account for the ongoing fascination with vampires?" And from those who had been secret readers of vampire fiction, the chief response was, "Wonderful! At last vampire literature can come out of the closet!" The level of attention was perhaps even more surprising than my colleagues' skepticism since my course was certainly not the first of its kind to be offered at a university. Prior to these experiences, I hadn't considered the possibility that a course in vampire literature might still be considered "controversial" or unworthy of academic study. After all, this is the great age of cultural studies, and the class-oriented distinction between "highbrow" and "lowbrow" art has all but disappeared. If genres such as science fiction, detective fiction, and fantasy have been welcomed into college curricula, why not vampire literature, which has a very different — and much older — pedigree? All I knew was that in my 30 years of teaching, I had never received such a response to a course before it began. But it was a clear signal that a great many people are interested in this literature and are looking for an academic setting in which to engage in intelligent discussion about it.

Perhaps many English departments across the country remain skeptical about the literary value of this genre, even as a plethora of scholarly books and articles, works of fiction, films and television series continue to appear and gain increasing traction in the marketplace. Without sacrificing the obvious fun and excitement that draws readers to vampire literature, I wanted my course to demonstrate this subgenre's interesting ancestry and to provide students with multiple strategies for identifying each work's connections with that past, as well as its responsiveness to the social anxieties of the age. And for the benefit of our doubting colleagues, I also sought to demonstrate how a study of vampire literature can be framed using a number of other indisputably "serious," widely-accepted disciplines to illuminate it.

The extensive research and preparation for the course included anthropological, mythic-folkloric, psychoanalytical, and historical writings on the vampire legend. Gender and genre studies and film histories also provided part of the framework. Therefore, the course opened with a detailed discussion of these diverse approaches, which established the 3000-year history of this legend and provided background context for the course's principal questions: How do we account for the longevity and evolution of the vampire figure across time, geographies, nations, and belief systems? With what fears, fantasies, and social realities does it connect? How do authors of vampire fiction incorporate vestiges of a recognizable vampire tradition yet refresh the genre by simultaneously rewriting it?

I began with a review of the extensive writings of anthropologists and folklorists, who have posited numerous explanations for the emergence and continuity of the legend in pagan cultures. Although exhibiting features and behaviors that differ somewhat from the conception of the modern European vampire, blood-drinking demons occur in the legends of ancient Persia, Assyria, and Mesopotamia (including Babylonia, Akkadia, and Sumer), as well as in the Sanskrit folklore of India. They are found in Hebrew demonology, Egyptian, Greek, and Roman mythology. Later versions of the legend are found in parts of Africa and South America, Southeast Asia, and especially in the Slavic countries of Eastern Europe. Many of my students believed the legend to begin with Bram Stoker or with the *Dracula* films of the 1930s. They also thought the legend came exclusively from Transylvania or Hungary (assumptions widely shared by the general public). The students were surprised at its ancient lineage — and by the interpretations of anthropologists and folklorists seeking to account for the widespread belief in a vampire-like creature. These explanations derive from a complex of several commonly shared ideas within pagan, polytheistic cultures: belief in an active spirit world, an afterlife, fear and worship of the dead; the ascribing of misfortune to the agency of supernatural entities; lack of understanding about symptoms of disease, causes of human and animal deaths, stages in the decomposition of the dead body; superstitions regarding the anagogic properties of blood and the apotropaic power of certain acts or materials. Although many scholarly sources are available that provide both comparative accounts of the vampire legend and analyses of the beliefs associated with individual countries or regions (Summers, Barber, Melton, Perkowski, Lawson), I found the collection of essays edited by Alan Dundes, *The Vampire: A Casebook*, a model of critical approaches to the subject, particularly since the contributors come from the fields of Slavic studies, history, linguistics, anthropology, forensic science, and psychiatry.

One of the most interesting essays is the translation and structural analysis by Jan Louis Perkowski of nineteen field-collected Romanian accounts of encounters with vampires, which he examines for their similarities and differences. They share much in common with other accounts of vampires — both ancient and modern. For example, (1) one most often becomes a vampire at death, but the potential causes range from the evil nature of the deceased to an animal walking over the body before burial; (2) attacks frequently occur on family members and animals; (3) vampires sometimes drink milk as well as blood; (4) descriptions of eating, biting, sucking, and having sex with the victim are common; (5) the vampire typically rises from the grave and attacks at night; (6) the dead are presumed to be thirsty (death being associated with dryness); (7) killing the vampire is achievable primarily through burning the corpse, decapitating it, and driving a stake through the heart, as all of these mechanisms eliminate any possibility of renewal by taking fluid from a victim; (8) protective talismans include garlic, hawthorn, wild rose, and millet seeds, among others; and (9) a deceased person is thought to be a vampire if decomposition of the body is delayed and several other physical attributes of the corpse are evident (blood, a ruddy complexion, bloating of the body).

Since many of these beliefs are typically associated with pagan cultures, the fact that the vampire figure continues into early and later Christian culture raises some provocative questions. (The Catholic Church, for example, acknowledged the existence of vampires in 1215 at the Fourth Lateran Council in Rome.) Did certain doctrines or practices within the Greek Orthodox and Roman Catholic churches contribute to the continuing belief in the existence of vampires? Anthropological research suggests they did. Many of the ancient superstitions and folkloric traditions regarding the origins and activities of vampires, in addition to the effective counteragents that one could use against them, continue well into early modern culture, even as some of these beliefs are refitted to Christian narratives. Ernest Jones states,

> The reasons why a spirit is prevented from resting in peace and forced to wander to and fro against his will may lie in his destiny, in his own misdeeds or in interference on the part of those left behind him. The Roman Catholic Church has elaborated this group into a complete dogma; masses are said for those in purgatory ["The Vampire" 114].

Disagreements between the Greek and Roman Churches resulted in conflicting interpretations related to heresy, decomposition, and vampirism, but each in its own way kept the belief in vampires alive:

Unfortunately the Greek Orthodox Church — it is said in a spirit of opposition to the Roman Catholic pronouncement that the bodies of saints do not decompose — supported the dogma that it is the bodies of wicked, unholy, and especially excommunicated, persons which do not decompose. Just as the Roman Catholic Church taught that heretics could be turned into Were-wolves, the Greek Orthodox Church taught that heretics became Vampires after death [Jones, "The Vampire" 103].

Further illuminating the anthropological studies is the large body of psychoanalytical writing on the vampire. In these works we find deeper explanations for why a figure of such historicity continues to play a role in the dreams, fears, and fantasies of much later societies and why this particular monster, unlike most others, though menacing and deadly, is also highly erotic. Two psychologists in my class were unaware that analysts such as Sigmund Freud, Richard von Krafft-Ebing, Havelock Ellis, Carl Jung, Ernest Jones, and Melanie Klein had ever mentioned vampires, much less theorized about the psychic disturbances that manifest themselves as vampire fantasies and visitations from supernatural entities. Freud and Jones argue that the figure of the vampire, like all manifestations of the supernatural, represents the externalization of repressed feelings of guilt, love, and hate, which are projected onto another. In the case of the vampire, this "other" is a corpse, often a deceased spouse or relation, about whom the survivor has experienced a host of ambivalent feelings, including anger and a possibly unconscious wish that the person would die (thus engendering guilt), along with a post-mortem desire for the return of the deceased, often accompanied by erotic dreams. These desires give rise to the fantasy that the dead will return either to take revenge on the living or to attempt to reenter the mortal life, which, presumably, he or she regrets losing.

The vampire can also represent other repressed antisocial impulses and unconventional sexual desires. While both Freud and Jones trace the earliest origin of these repressed feelings to infantile incestuous wishes, both also explore mankind's complicated relationship to death, which begins in the earliest stages of civilization. Coincident with the idea of a soul that is separate from the body is the notion of immortality, a concept that emerges in response to the unthinkable possibility of one's own death. A key notion of Freud's, useful to understanding our attraction to the vampire figure, is found in *Beyond the Pleasure Principle* in which he states that man is in a constant source of conflict between two equally compelling instincts: the life drive (*eros*) and the death drive (later referred to as *thanatos* by his analyst-secretary, Paul Federn). Another of Jones's essays, "Psycho-Analysis and Anthropology," draws from the work of anthropologists who see self-preservation as the most powerful motivating force in primitive societies and beyond. The many rites, customs, and legends within these societies that focus on how to prolong or restore life and youth and to ensure immortality again remind us of an essential element bound up with the character of the vampire: the lure of immortality. Blood, of course, symbolizing the very essence of life, plays a key role in many such rituals and is obviously central to the vampire legend. In *Totem and Taboo*, Freud emphasizes the totemic significance of blood, which can include a horror of it, the giving of it as a gift in a sacrificial act, as well as the consumption of it in order to incorporate the life force of the victim (animal or human) into oneself. Montague Summers states:

> Since Dr. Havelock Ellis has acutely remarked that "there is scarcely any natural object with so profoundly an emotional an effect as blood," it is easy to understand how nearly blood is connected with the sexual manifestations, and how distinctly erotic and provocative the sight or even the thought of blood almost inevitably proves [188].

All of these ideas, when brought together, provide important clues as to why the vampire figure summons up such deeply embedded associations in human consciousness that combine both attraction and repulsion.

For Carl Jung, the vampire is an ancient and a powerful archetype, part of the collective unconscious of both sexes, representing the Shadow or that unrecognized part of the self that, as Freud suggested, contains our repressed wishes and most shameful antisocial impulses (Shanahan). Another essential element in vampirism is sucking and biting, which involve both pleasure and pain. Krafft-Ebing in *Psychopathia Sexualis* (129), Ellis in *Studies in the Psychology of Sex* (126), and Klein in *The Psychoanalysis of Children* (179) have related these aspects of vampirism to the oral sadism stage of infantile development when the pleasure of sucking at the mother's breast is replaced by the sadistic pleasure of biting. According to Klein, yet another set of anxieties and repressed feelings occurs when the mother withdraws her breast from the newly weaned child, ranging from a sense of deprivation to acute anger, which may result in aggression toward the breast—that is, a wish to bite (185–186). The linkage among these psychological phenomena and the focus on the female breast in vampire narratives, the mixture of pleasure and pain associated with the vampire's "kiss," the motif of the vampire's hunger and need of vital fluids, and the mingling of erotic desire with violence constitute another provocative cluster of circumstances that shed light on our complex response to the vampire.

Jung's theory of archetypes and Freud's analysis of imaginative literature likewise help to explain why stories that represent such encounters with the dark side of consciousness so completely engage the reader's attention. Comparing the writing of imaginative literature to dreaming and "fantasying," Freud writes:

> The motive forces of fantasies are unsatisfied wishes, and every single fantasy is the fulfillment of a wish, a correction of unsatisfying reality.... They are either ambitious wishes ... or they are erotic ones.... If the meaning of our dreams usually remains obscure to us ... it is because of the circumstance that at night there also arise in us wishes of which we are ashamed; these we must conceal from ourselves, and they have consequently been repressed, pushed into the unconscious. Repressed wishes of this sort ... are only allowed to come to expression in a very distorted form ["Creative Writers and Daydreaming" 713–714].

The creative writer often draws from folk psychology, myths, legends, fairy tales, which may themselves represent "distorted vestiges of the wishful fantasies of whole nations..." (715). The many stories from mythology, for example, featuring sexual encounters between mortals and immortals—used countless times in the history of literature—fall into this category. If such fantasies were disclosed directly, we might feel repelled. But the writer, through sheer artistry, overcomes this feeling of repulsion in us, "and our actual enjoyment of an imaginative work proceeds from a liberation of tensions in our minds ... thenceforward to enjoy our own daydreams without self-reproach or shame" (716). Thus, our attraction to vampire literature can be partly explained by the writer's ability to provide the reader with a safe "space" in which to engage vicariously in forbidden fantasies and transgressive conduct. Freud's notion of the "uncanny" (derived in part from the interesting relation between the words *unheimlich* and *heimlich*) also sheds light on the durability of the vampire in the historical imagination and thus its ongoing attraction as a literary subject. He defines the uncanny as "that species of the frightening that goes back to what was once well known and had long been familiar" but was "estranged from [the psyche] only through being repressed" ("The Uncanny" 124, 148). Freud further notes that for many people, the acme of the uncanny is represented by anything to do with death, dead bodies, revenants, spirits and ghosts.... Yet in hardly any other sphere has our thinking and feeling changed so little since primitive times or the old been so well preserved, under a thin veneer, as in our relation to death.... Since nearly all of us still think no differently from savages on this subject, it is not surprising that the primitive fear of the dead is still so potent in us and ready to manifest itself if given any encouragement. Moreover, it is probably still informed by the old idea that whoever dies becomes the enemy of the survivor, intent upon carrying him off with him to share his new existence [148–149].

Although Freud is speaking of fear of the dead here, his statement is easily applied to the *un-dead*, which likewise return from the grave to disturb the living.

After establishing the anthropological and psychoanalytical interpretations of the vampire legend, I next introduced the class to some of the historical records and scholarly inquiries produced during the 17th and 18th centuries, ostensibly documenting "personal attacks" by vampires and wider outbreaks of vampiric activity within particular communities. These accounts provided opportunities for discussing the history of medicine, the limits of science in interpreting deviations from an assumed norm, and the problem of verification even when events are reported by reputable individuals. Such narratives also demonstrate how folkloric memory supported by "eye-witness testimony" further cemented belief in supernatural entities, even as the Age of Reason and modern science were advancing. Drawing these elements together for students heightened the drama in Stoker's *Dracula*, which brilliantly dramatizes the struggle between belief and disbelief, between superstition and science (notably illustrated in Van Helsing's challenge to Dr. Seward "To believe in things you cannot," Williams 309).

Because many of the French, German, and Slavic primary sources remain untranslated, one is grateful for the availability of texts such as Paul Rycaut's *State of the Greek and Armenian Churches* (1679), *Travels of 3 English Gentlemen from Venice to Hamburg, Being the Grand Tour of Germany in the Year 1734* (both in electronic versions), and the excellent translations of portions of Romanian historical documents and stories from *Ion Creanga* provided by Agnes Murgoci and N. I Dumitrascu, all of which include recorded accounts of interactions with vampires and the dire consequences to local villages from these attacks. Along with excerpts from Dom Augustin Calmet's influential treatise, *Dissertations sur les apparitions et sur les revenants et les vampires* (1746), also available online, these selections gave students a sense of the seriousness and even urgency that characterized the struggle to come to terms with events that seemed to defy rational explanation. Especially surprising to students was the fact that exhumations of persons suspected of being vampires were taking place here in New England as late as the 1890s — the case of nineteen-year-old Mercy Brown of Exeter, Rhode Island, being the most famous (Bell). My purpose was not to lead students to "believe" in vampires but to understand how a powerful legend that spanned millennia and appeared to be supported by modern historical "evidence" became a compelling subject precisely when it did in 18th- and 19th-century literature, when questions surrounding the existence of vampires had not yet been fully extinguished by science. Furthermore, these accounts reinforce one of the major structural features of much vampire literature: namely, how the process of "discovery" of the vampire is often delayed or impeded by the conflict between belief and disbelief.

With the anthropological, mythic-folkloric, psychoanalytical, and historical bases of the vampire legend established, the course then turned to its literary representation. We began with the classic texts of Coleridge, Byron, Polidori, LeFanu, and Stoker — the writers who established the basic components of the vampire tale and who drew from some of the legends and historical accounts presented above. Examining these literary lines of descent against this broader "genealogical" background of the vampire underscored two important points I wished to make about vampire literature: first, that it is always dialogic and inter-textual in nature (Bakhtin, Kristeva, Barthes); second, that authors may incorporate some of the accepted conventions of a literary genre but thwart others in order to expand the boundaries of the genre (Jauss). The vampiric "dialogue" that evolves from Coleridge to Byron to Polidori to LeFanu and Stoker perfectly demonstrates this kind of literary rela-tionship, which provided the authors with a fascinating character type on which to build but also an opportunity to foreground their private and public anxieties related to class, money, sexuality, power, and difference and to project these onto the vampire figure. For instructors, this exchange and development makes it likewise possible to demonstrate how quickly the vampire becomes a symbolic figure representing what every era fears most — whether that be female sexuality, disease, or exploitation by the wealthy outsider (Gordon and Hollinger, Auerbach). When later authors such as Tom Holland (*Lord of the Dead*), Elizabeth Kostova (*The Historian*), and Carlos Fuentes (*Vlad*) directly connect their works with these predecessors, they do so by producing a combination of echoes and distortions. A similar kind of echoing and distorting occurs in many of the works produced after Anne Rice completely reverses the tradition by introducing "the sensitive vampire," who is hungry for community, finds the killing of humans disagreeable, and who paves the way for the courtliness of Edward and the domesticity of the Cullen family in Stephenie Meyer's *Twilight* novels. Students enjoyed "connecting the dots," so to speak, becoming sufficiently familiar with a group of vampire novels that they could discern the continuities with earlier works, vestiges of the folkloric traditions, and deviations that kept the genre from becoming stale.

We explored a fairly representative selection of vampire fiction in the course, although after finding The Vampire Library (http://www.vampirelibrary.com/) and learning that nearly 1600 works of vampire fiction exist, deciding on what constituted "a representative selection" for a 15-week course was the greatest challenge. In addition to the works named above, we also read Laurell K. Hamilton's *Guilty Pleasures*, Charlaine Harris's *Dead Until Dark*, Kim Harrison's *Dead Witch Walking*, John Ajvide Lindqvist's *Let the Right One In*, Rachel Caine's *Glass Houses*, and Seth Grahame-Smith's *Abraham Lincoln: Vampire Hunter*. These were chosen specifically because of their clever blending of genres, fresh re-envision-ing of the vampire story, and diverse audiences for which they were intended. We had begun by discussing the conventions of the more traditional types of genre fiction: the Gothic, detective, and romance novel. By the end of the course, we had explored some of the edgy contemporary hybrids including urban fantasy, paranormal romance, the literary mash-up, and the faux history — a real lesson in the creative reworking of genre. Gender, as well as genre, figured in our discussions since vampire literature, from the beginning, presents women not simply as victims but as sources of power.

From a structural and thematic perspective, several of the later novels present an alter-nate reality in which the uneasy co-existence with vampires is a given. They live in the open with humans. This device derails the traditional plot structure involving the characters' unawareness of the existence of vampires, the ultimate "discovery" of the vampire's identity, and the need to destroy the vampire. Instead, contemporary works of vampire fiction take the reader into the world of crime, school bullying, political maneuvering, parental neglect, racial discrimination, incest, alcoholism, and inter-species coupling. Often the humans are more monstrous than the vampires — part of the domestication of the vampire that began with Anne Rice's works. Nonetheless, traces of the folkloric traditions remain, even if they have been redefined: vampires still have certain limitations, can be made and destroyed only in specific ways, must have blood to survive (even if it is artificial blood in some instances), and definitely have sex with partners of diverse orientations. Plenty of these new vampires are still evil and predatory. But the reader is asked to distinguish between the good and the bad and to see the fallacy in overgeneralizing about an entire class of beings (Charlaine Harris's *Southern Vampire Series*, set in Bon Temps, Louisiana, is especially adept at using vampires to explore racial and gender discrimination). Some of the men in the class were not too keen on the kinder, gentler vampire types, arguing that they are not at all like "real vampires." But several of their classmates reminded them that there *are* no "real vampires," that they exist *only* in "versions" of themselves, and that even in some of the folktales, vampires rose from the grave and went straight to visit their wives; and in the early vampire stories, a desire for friendship and intimacy was clearly evident. Making the cleverest pun of the year, a student wrote that, both in these early narratives and in many contemporary works, the vampire-human relationships were often much more than "one-bite stands."

Because film has shaped so many students' conceptions of the vampire, I made 24 vampire films available for after-class viewing, beginning with F. W. Murnau's *Nosferatu* (1922) and ending with Michael and Peter Spierig's *Daybreakers* (2010). Vampire film histories (Silver and Ursini) and online compilations (http://public.wsu.edu/~delahoyd/vampire films.html; http://www.geocities.ws/fvaresi/film.htm) revealed that nearly 600 vampire-themed films and television series had been made. My "evolutionary" approach to the literature was equally applicable to the development of the vampire film, which likewise carried the stamp of elements derived from folklore and from literature but which also engaged in the same kind of "dialogue" with its filmic predecessors. I particularly wanted the students to notice how the many representations of the vampire had changed over time and how films, like the literature, reflected the social concerns of the period, often using the vampire as a metaphor to express them. These issues were central to my choices.

The several versions of the Dracula story as presented by Hammer Films, with Christopher Lee's indelible stamp on the role, illustrated how each succeeding film departed further and further from the Stoker novel. (Since most people hadn't read the Stoker novel prior to the class but had seen some of the films, they were now a bit shocked at the disservice that had been done to the brilliantly constructed novel and could see how it had been trivialized.) However, one of the Hammer Films, *The Brides of Dracula* (1960), did include a particularly Freudian moment when the handsome Baron Meinster (the re-named Dracula figure) vampirizes his own mother. A film version of Stoker's novel actually closest to it turned out *not* to be Francis Ford Coppola's self-titled *Bram Stoker's Dracula* (1992) but the 1977 BBC version, *Count Dracula*, with Louis Jourdan in the title role, which both adheres to the plot and retains some of the actual dialogue from the novel. Though giving a superbly understated performance, Louis Jourdan is altogether too handsome for the role, but his power over the innocent Mina (played by the enchanting Judy Bowker) is rendered more credible. With a minimum of special effects, this version manages to capture more of the genuine horror in Stoker's novel than other films with their grand CGI effects and buckets of blood.

The production values of Roy Ward Baker's *The Vampire Lovers* (1970), one of the few attempts to dramatize LeFanu's *Carmilla,* were consistent with Hammer's usual stable of horror films, but it did — perhaps coincidentally — succeed in foregrounding the breast imagery found in LeFanu's story. Like *The Brides of Dracula*, the film curiously resonates with the psychoanalytical interpretations that connect the vampire fantasy with the repressed desire for and violence upon the mother's breast. Other films based on novels we were reading included Neil Jordan's *Interview with the Vampire* (1994), which faithfully retains the framing device of the novel and the first-person narration, and episodes 1 and 2 of the HBO *True Blood* series, based on Harris's *Dead Until Dark*, and a great example of how writing that merely suggests erotic inter-species couplings can be given a full 3-D treatment on a cable network. Unlike *True Blood*, Catherine Hardwicke's PG-13–rated *Twilight* (2008) captured the sexual tension in Bella and Edward's romance, heightened all the more by the vampire's determined restraint, while the lean script managed to conceal much of the weakness of Meyer's writing. The fact that the novels had sold 116 million copies and the box office receipts for the films at that point had brought in $1.8 billion led to some interesting discussions about what students believed the appeal of the *Twilight* series to be, given the fact that the writing itself did not measure up to the quality of the other works on the reading list. Somehow, the story — and the films — managed to tap into a number of the deep-seated fantasies for which the work of the anthropologists, folklorists, and psychoanalysts had prepared us: the mortal-immortal union, eternal youth and beauty, unchanging love, death as only a threshold to be crossed before obtaining immortality.

Louis de Pointe du Lac and Edward Cullen are not the only sensitive vampires: in a 1979 remake of *Nosferatu*, German Expressionist filmmaker Werner Herzog has his lonely vampire (memorably played by Klaus Kinski) lament at the bedside of Lucy, "The absence of love is the most abject pain." In Frank Langella's portrayal of Dracula, in John Badham's 1979 film, the vampire is a romantic figure, solitary, very sexy, and longing for a bride that will be his companion in eternity. (The dance sequences in the film are certainly a new addition to the vampire's courtship ritual.) Even the hybrid vampire, Blade, based on the comic book series, possesses an unusual kind of moral sense and chooses to protect the human world from vampires and their familiars.

The most disturbing novel that we read was Lindqvist's *Let the Right One In*, because of the realistic portrayal of bullying and its psychological effect on Oskar, the young victim; the obliviousness of his divorced parents to his suffering; the dependency of the child vampire, Eli, on the adult, Håkan, who murders others and drains their blood for her and who also happens to be a pedophile; and, finally, because of the horrifying manner in which the twelve-year-old "Elias" became "Eli." Despite two almost back-to-back film versions being made in 2008 and 2010 (one Swedish, one American), students were surprised that both elected to omit Eli's backstory and Håkan's sexual deviance. We agreed that we had come to an interesting moment in films when the vampire was less frightening to behold than the perversity of humans. Other films we viewed similarly used the vampire as a metaphor for the social concerns of the time: the vampires in *The Lost Boys* and *Near Dark* (both 1987) roam in gangs and form surrogate family units; the vampire's thirst for blood and the human's thirst for violence are likened to drug addiction in Abel Ferrara's *The Addiction* (1995); a future world dominated by vampires that have exhausted the supply of humans and their blood in *Daybreakers* reminds the audience of a world threatened by food and energy shortages.

The proliferation of vampire films and the growth and sales of vampire fiction in recent years raised other provocative questions that we discussed. In 2009, as I was commencing my research for the course, six of the ten works on the *New York Times* Best Seller list in the Children–Young Adult category were vampire-themed books. Publishers reported the sales of the most popular series—*Blood Coven* by Mari Mancusi, *Blue Bloods* by Melissa De La Cruz, *The Chronicles of Vladimir Tod* by Heather Brewer, *Evernight* by Claudia Gray, *House of Night* by P.C. and Kristen Cast, *The Immortals* by Alyson Noel, *The Morganville Vampires* by Rachel Caine, *Night World* and *The Vampire Diaries* by L.J. Smith, *Vampire Academy* by Richelle Mead, *Vampire Kisses* by Ellen Schreiber, and of course the *Twilight* saga by Stephenie Meyer—were literally keeping bookstores and the publishing industry afloat. Since then, series clearly aimed at the adult market such as Guillermo del Toro and Chuck Hogan's *The Strain Trilogy* and Justin Cronin's *The Passage* and *The Twelve* (with the final volume in the trilogy forthcoming), along with many others, clearly indicate that the interest in fiction of this kind cuts across time and age groups. Data such as these lead us back to important issues related to the social and psychological function of art and, specifically, to the function of horror and the ways in which it continues to tap into our deepest fears and longings.

While vampire literature can certainly be taught as a fascinating subgenre in its own right, independent of all the critical approaches that I chose to employ, for my own purposes it was important to present this body of work as a serious academic subject to my students and colleagues, underscoring the historicity of the legend and the depth of analysis given it by scholar-researchers in other respected fields. The novels selected for study afforded us abundant opportunities to examine the social concerns embedded within the vampire narrative, the diversity of forms that writers employ, and the challenge that each succeeding generation of authors and filmmakers must confront as they set out to create anew. The questions we sought to answer at the beginning of the course we had successfully answered by the end. I learned a great deal in the process, and my students left the class asking when there would be a "Vampires, Part Two" with an entirely new reading list. The sequel is currently in development. Since the course ended, I have been invited to give a number of guest lectures on this subject, and the most gratifying comments—frequently heard at the conclusion of each one—begin with the words, "I never knew before...."

References

Adams, Hazard, ed. *Critical Theory Since Plato*, rev. ed. Fort Worth: Harcourt Brace Jovanovich College, 1992. Print.

Adams, Hazard, and Leroy Searle, eds. *Critical Theory Since 1965*. Tallahassee: Florida State University Press, 1986.

The Addiction. Dir. Abel Ferrara. Perf. Lili Taylor and Christopher Walken. 1995. Film.

Auerbach, Nina. *Our Vampires, Ourselves*. Chicago: University of Chicago Press, 1995. Print.

Bakhtin, Mikhail M. *The Dialogic Imagination*. Ed. Michael Holquist. Trans. Caryl Emerson and Michael Holquist. Austin: University of Texas Press, 1981. Print.

Barber, Paul. "Forensic Pathology and the European Vampire." Dundes 109–142.

_____. *Vampires, Burial, and Death*. New Haven: Yale University Press, 2010. Print.

Barthes, Roland. "The Death of the Author." 1968. Adams 1130–1133.

Bell, Michael. *Food for the Dead: On the Trail of New England's Vampires*. Middletown, CT: Wesleyan University Press, 2001. Print.

Blade Trinity. Dir. David Goyer. Perf. Wesley Snipes, Jessica Biel, Dominic Purcell, Ryan Reynolds, and Parker Posey. 2004. Film.

Bram Stoker's Dracula. Dir. Francis Ford Coppola. Perf. Gary Oldman, Wynona Ryder, Anthony Hopkins, and Keanu Reeves. 1992. Film.

Buffy the Vampire Slayer. Season 5 (2000). Episode 1: "Buffy vs. Dracula." Dir. Joss Whedon. Perf. Sarah Michelle Gellar. W. B. Television Network. 2006. DVD.

Caine, Rachel. *The Morganville Vampires*. *Glass Houses* and *The Dead Girls' Dance*. 2006. 2007. New York: New American Library, 2009. Print.

Čajkanović, Veselin. "The Killing of a Vampire." Dundes 72–84.

Calmet, Dom Augustin. *The Phantom World: The History and Philosophy of Spirits, Apparitions, &c. &c.*, vol. 2: *Dissertation* on *the Ghosts Who Return to Earth Bodily, the Excommunicated, the Oupires or Vampires, Vroucolacas, etc.*, 2d ed. 1751. Ed. and trans. Henry Christmas. Philadelphia: A. Hart, 1850. *Project Gutenberg.* Web. 11 January 2013.

Count Dracula. Dir. Philip Saville. Perf. Louis Jourdan, Frank Finlay, and Judi Bowker. 1977. Film.

Daybreakers. Dir. Michael and Peter Spierig. Perf. Ethan Hawke, Willem Dafoe, and Sam Neill. 2010. Film.

Dracula. Dir. John Badham. Perf. Frank Langella, Laurence Olivier, and Kate Nelligan. 1979. Film.

Dracula. Dir. Tod Browning. Perf. Bela Lugosi. 1931. Film.

du Boulay, Juliette. "The Greek Vampire: A Study of Cyclic Symbolism in Marriage and Death." Dundes 85–108.

Duda, Heather. *The Monster Hunter in Modern Popular Culture.* Jefferson, NC: McFarland, 2008. Print.

Dundes, Alan. "The Vampire as Bloodthirsty Revenant: A Psychoanalytic Post Mortem." Dundes 159–175.

_____, ed. *The Vampire: A Casebook.* Madison: University of Wisconsin Press, 1998. Print.

Eclipse. Dir. David Slade. 2010. Film.

Ellis, Havelock. *Studies in the Psychology of Sex*, vol. 3. Philadelphia: F. A. Davis, 1928. Print.

Filmography. Web. http://www.geocities.ws/fvaresi/film.htm.

Florescu, Radu, and Raymond McNally. *Dracula: Prince of Many Faces: His Life and His Times.* Boston: Little, Brown, 1989. Print.

Freud, Sigmund. "Beyond the Pleasure Principle." 1920. *The Freud Reader.* Ed. Peter Gay. 1989. New York: W. W. Norton, 1995. 594–626. Print.

_____. "Creative Writers and Daydreaming." 1908. Adams 712–716.

_____. *Totem and Taboo: Some Points of Agreement Between the Mental Lives of Savages and Neurotics.* 1913. Trans. and ed. James Strachey. New York: W. W. Norton, 1989. Print.

_____. "The Uncanny." 1919. Trans. David Mclintock. *The Uncanny with an Introduction by Hugh Haughton.* Ed. Adam Phillips. New York: Penguin, 2003. 121–162. Print.

Geary, Robert. "'Carmilla' and the Gothic Legacy: Victorian Transformations of Supernatural Horror." Heldreth and Pharr 19–30.

Gelder, Ken. "Ethnic Vampires: Transylvania and Beyond." Gelder 1–23.

_____. *Reading the Vampire.* New York: Routledge, 1994. Print.

_____. "Vampires and the Uncanny: LeFanu's 'Carmilla.'" Gelder 42–64.

Gordon, Joan. "Sharper than a Serpent's Tooth: The Vampire in Search of Its Mother." Gordon and Hollinger 45–55.

Gordon, Joan, and Veronica Hollinger, eds. *Blood Read: The Vampire as Metaphor in Contemporary Culture.* Philadelphia: University of Pennsylvania Press, 1997. Print.

Grahame-Smith, Seth. *Abraham Lincoln: Vampire Hunter.* New York: Grand Central, 2010. Print.

Gravett, Sandra. *From Twilight to Breaking Dawn: Religious Themes in the Twilight Saga.* St. Louis: Chalice Press, 2010. Print.

Halberstam, Judith. *Skin Shows: Gothic Horror and the Technology of Monsters.* Durham: Duke University Press, 1995. Print.

Hamilton, Laurell. *Guilty Pleasures.* 1993. New York: Jove, 2002. Print.

Harris, Charlaine. *Dead Until Dark.* 2001. New York: Ace, 2008. Print.

Harrison, Kim. *Dead Witch Walking.* New York: HarperCollins, 2004.

Heldreth, Leonard, and Mary Pharr, eds. *The Blood Is the Life: Vampires in Literature.* Bowling Green: Bowling Green State University Press, 1999. Print.

Holland, Tom. *Lord of the Dead: The Secret History of Byron.* New York: Pocket Books, 1995. Print.

Holmes, Trevor. "Coming Out of the Coffin: Gay Males and Queer Goths in Contemporary Vampire Fiction." Gordon and Hollinger 169–188.

Holte, James Craig, ed. *The Fantastic Vampire: Studies in the Children of the Night: Selected Essays from the Eighteenth International Conference on the Fantastic in the Arts.* 1997. Westport, CT: Greenwood Press, 2002. Print.

Horror of Dracula. Dir. Terence Fisher. Perf. Christopher Lee and Peter Cushing. 1958. Film.

The Hunger. Dir. Tony Scott. Perf. David Bowie, Catherine Deneuve, and Susan Sarandon. 1983. Film.

Interview with the Vampire. Dir. Neil Jordan. Perf. Tom Cruise and Brad Pitt. 1994. Film.

Jaffé, Philip, and Frank DiCataldo. "Clinical Vampirism: Blending Myth and Reality." Dundes 143–158.

Jauss, Hans Robert. "Literary History as a Challenge to Literary Theory." 1967. *Critical Theory Since 1965.* Adams and Searle. 164–183.

Jung, C. G. *Civilization in Transition*, vol. 10. *The Collected Works of C. G. Jung*, 2d ed. Princeton: Princeton University Press, 1966. Print. 21 vols.

_____. *Mysterium Coniunctionis: Inquiry into the Separation and Synthesis of Psychic Opposites in Alchemy*, vol. 14. *The Collected Works of C. G. Jung*, 2d ed. Princeton: Princeton University Press, 1996. Print. 21 vols.

Klein, Melanie. *The Psychoanalysis of Children*. New York: Grove, 1960. Print.

Kostova, Elizabeth. *The Historian*. New York: Back Bay Books, 2005. Print.

Krafft-Ebing, Richard von. *Psychopathia Sexualis*. New York: Pioneer, 1953. Print.

Krauss, Friedrich. "South Slavic Countermeasures against Vampires." Dundes 67–71.

Kristeva, Julia. *Desire in Language: A Semiotic Approach to Literature and Art*. New York: Columbia University Press, 1980.

Latham, Rob. "Consuming Youth: The Lost Boys Cruise Mallworld." Gordon and Hollinger 129–147.

Lawson, J.C. *Modern Greek Folklore and Ancient Greek Religion*. Cambridge: Cambridge University Press, 1910.

Let Me In. Dir. Matt Reeves. Perf. Kodi Smit-McPhee, Chloe Moretz, and Richard Jenkins. 2010. Film.

Let the Right One In. Dir. Tomas Alfredson. Perf. Kare Hedebrant and Lena Leandersson. 2008. Film.

Lindqvist, John. *Let the Right One In*. Trans. Ebba Segerberg. New York: Thomas Dunne, 2007. Print. Rpt. of *Låt den Rätte Komma In*. 2004.

Lorrah, Jean. "Dracula Meets the New Woman." Heldreth and Pharr 31–42.

The Lost Boys. Dir. Joel Schumacher. Perf. Kiefer Sutherland and Jason Patric. 1987. Film.

Melton, J. Gordon. *The Vampire Book: The Encyclopedia of the Undead*. Detroit: Visible Ink Press, 1994. Print.

Meyer, Stephenie. *Twilight*. 2005. New York: Little, Brown, 2006. Print.

Murgoci, Agnes. "The Vampire in Roumania." Dundes 3–11.

Near Dark. Dir. Kathryn Bigelow. Perf. Adrian Pasdar, Jenny Wright, and Bill Paxton. 1987. Film.

Nelson, Victoria. *Gothicka: Vampire Heroes, Human Gods, and the New Supernatural*. Cambridge: Harvard University Press, 2012. Print.

New Moon. Dir. Chris Weitz. 2009. Film.

Nixon, Nicola. "When Hollywood Sucks, or, Hungry Girls, Lost Boys, and Vampirism in the Age of Reagan." Gordon and Hollinger 115–128.

Nosferatu. Dir. Werner Herzog. Perf. Klaus Kinski and Isabelle Adjani. 1979. Film.

Nosferatu. Dir. F. W. Murnau. Perf. Max Schreck. 1922. Film.

Oldys, William, and John Malham, eds. "The Travels of Three English Gentlemen." *The Harleian Miscellany or, a Collection of Scarce, Curious, and Entertaining Pamphlets and Tracts, as Well in Manuscript as in Print, Found in the Late Earl of Oxford's Library, Interspersed with Historical, Political, and Critical Notes*, vol. XI. 218–328. London: Robert Dutton, 1810. *Google Book Search*. Web. 11 January 2013.

Overstreet, Deborah Wilson. *Not Your Mother's Vampire: Vampires in Young Adult Fiction*. Lanham, MD: Scarecrow Press, 2006. Print.

Perkowski, Jan. "The Romanian Folkloric Vampire." Dundes 35–46.

Pharr, Mary. "Vampiric Appetite in *I Am Legend*, '*Salem's Lot*, and *The Hunger*." Heldreth and Pharr 93–104.

Queen of the Damned. Dir. Michael Rymer. Perf. Aaliyah and Stuart Townsend. 2002. Film.

Rice, Anne. *Interview with the Vampire*. 1976. New York: Ballantine, 1997. Print.

Rickels, Laurence. *The Vampire Lectures*. Minneapolis: University of Minnesota Press, 1999. Print.

Rycaut, Paul. *The Present State of the Greek and Armenian Churches, Anno Christi 1678 Written at the Command of His Majesty by Paul Ricaut*. London, 1679. Early English Text Society. Web.

Shanahan, Margaret L. "Psychological Perspectives on Vampire Mythology." Melton 492–501.

Silver, Alain, and James Ursini. *The Vampire Film: From* Nosferatu *to* Interview with the Vampire, 3d ed. New York: Limelight Editions, 1997. Print.

_____. *The Vampire Film: From* Nosferatu *to* Twilight, 4th ed. New York: Limelight Editions, 2010. Print.

Summers, Montague. *Vampires and Vampirism*. Mineola, NY: Dover, 2005. Print. Rpt. of *The Vampire: His Kith and Kin*. 1929.

Taylor, Joules. *Vampires*. London: Octopus Publishing, 2009. Print.

Telotte, J. P. "A Parasitic Perspective: Romantic Participation and Polidori's *The Vampyre*." Heldreth and Pharr 9–18.

Tomc, Sandra. "Dieting and Damnation: Anne Rice's *Interview with the Vampire*." Gordon and Hollinger 95–113.

True Blood. Season 1 (2008). Episodes 1–2. Dir. Alan Ball. Perf. Stephen Moyer and Anna Paquin. HBO Home Video. 2009. DVD.

Twilight. Dir. Catherine Hardwicke. Perf. Robert Pattinson, Kristen Stewart, and Taylor Lautner. 2008. Film.

Vampire Filmography. Web. http://public.wsu.edu/~delahoyd/vampirefilms.html.

The Vampire Library. Web. http://www.vampirelibrary.com/.

The Vampire Lovers. Dir. Roy Ward Baker. Perf. Peter Cushing. Hammer Films, 1970. Film.

Williams, Anne, ed. *Three Vampire Tales: Complete Texts with Introduction, Historical Context, Critical Essays*. Boston: Wadsworth, 2003. Print. New Riverside Editions.

Wilson, Katharina. "The History of the Word *Vampire*." Dundes 12–34.

Wood, Martin. "New Life for an Old Tradition: Anne Rice and Vampire Literature." Heldreth and Pharr 59–78.

"But why do they have fangs?"
The Cultural History of the
Vampire as a Teaching Strategy
in the Literature Classroom

Heide Crawford

In an age of paranormal teen romance novels such as the popular *Twilight* series by Stephenie Meyer, it is a bit daunting to be confronted with the task of teaching a course on the vampire in literature under the general course heading "German Popular Culture." I expected that most students would not associate the literary vampire with Germany or German literature, but an understanding of the literary vampire's roots in German literature is, in fact, essential for an understanding of the modern vampire in literature and film and my challenge as an instructor was to make this history lesson not only interesting and informative, but compelling and, most importantly, relevant to the students' understanding of today's imaginations of the vampire.

This course was a general education course, in which students enrolled for Humanities credit at the Ohio State University. I taught this class for two consecutive quarters— Fall quarter 2010 and Winter quarter 2011, and the enrollment was 22 and 24 students, respectively. As I walked to class on the first day of the Fall quarter 2010, I wondered how receptive students would be for a course that focused on the evolution of the literary vampire figure from Central European folklore to poetry and prose of the eighteenth and nineteenth centuries. The full title of the course was "German Literature and Popular Culture: The Vampire in German Literature and Film," so I was not surprised to learn that students expected to read more modern works than those we covered in class. In fact, the works we read either initiated the popular culture surrounding the vampire figure in the eighteenth century or they were published at the height of the pan–European "vampire craze" in the nineteenth century and even pre-dated most of the more well-known vampire stories by British authors such as John Polidori ("The Vampyre"; 1819), J. Sheridan LeFanu (*Carmilla*; 1872) and Bram Stoker (*Dracula*; 1897).

In an effort to reflect the pop culture focus of the course, it was necessary to not only read and discuss popular vampire literature and view the German vampire films *Nosferatu: A Symphony of Horror* (1922; Friedrich Wilhelm Murnau) and Werner Herzog's 1979 tribute to Murnau's film, *Nosferatu: The Vampyre,* but also to show how the vampire became a popular culture phenomenon in the eighteenth century German literature that introduced the vampire as a literary figure. To better understand our modern perceptions of the vampire, we started on the first day of class with a word association game about the vampire. Consistently, students mentioned vampire characteristics, such as fangs, blood-sucking and shape-changing, which are features of modern vampire literature and film since Bram Stoker's *Dracula* and not the original Central European folklore. This exercise caused at least one student to wonder, "But why do they have fangs?" And so, as a class, we realized that we wanted answers to these questions about the common traits of the vampire, why they have these traits and what their different traits mean for the stories in which they appear and the culture that created them.

Our attempt in this course to uncover the meaning behind the various images of the vampire presented to us in literature and film and how these common traits developed began with an exploration of the history of the vampire in Central European folklore that ultimately led to its adaptation in creative literature. In this course, I emphasized that an understanding of the earliest known Central European folklore, the earliest known vampire literature from eighteenth-century Germany and the earliest characteristics of the vampire facilitate an understanding of the many different uses of the vampire figure in subsequent centuries and literary cultures leading up to and including contemporary vampire fiction. From our discussions in class, I found that a solid understanding of the historical development of the vampire from Central European folklore to its use in the earliest literature helped students understand more modern metaphorical uses of the vampire as a unique monster that reflects the fears and anxieties of the culture for which it was written.

To this end, we began by reading some of the most popular Central European folklore that influenced the first German authors of popular vampire poetry in the eighteenth century. Our source for the folklore and for detailed analysis of the characteristics of the earliest known Central European vampire folklore was Paul Barber's book *Vampires, Burial and Death: Folklore and Reality* (2010). After discussing the vampire from folklore, we proceeded in chronological order by reading the first works by eighteenth century German authors that feature the vampire as a main character in English translation. These included the first known vampire poem, "The Vampire" (1748) by Heinrich August Ossenfelder, "Lenore" (1774) by Gottfried August Bürger, and "The Bride of Corinth" (1797) by Johann Wolfgang von Goethe. We then read some of the most popular works of vampire prose form the nineteenth century: "The Love-Charm" (1812) by Ludwig Tieck; "Wake Not the Dead!" (1823) by Ernst Benjamin Salomo Raupach; "The Mysterious Stranger" (1847) by Karl Adolf von Wachsmann; and *Dracula* (1897) by Bram Stoker.[1] We concluded the course by viewing Murnau's and Herzog's *Nosferatu* films and by reading and discussing the ideas about the metaphorical significance of the monster in literature expressed by Jeffrey Jerome Cohen in the introduction to his book *Monster Theory: Reading Culture* (1996) and how this theory connects with our discussions of the vampire in the German works we read and in the films we viewed.

In a typical class period, students worked in small groups or with a partner to discuss and record in worksheets aspects of the texts they read and the vampire figures in these texts, i.e., his or her appearance, demeanor and the likely metaphoric significance for the work. After they had spent approximately 10 minutes working together, we discussed their findings as a class. Instead of lecturing first and having students respond with their ideas after I had discussed theoretical concepts, my approach was more akin to the "backward design"[2] approach to instruction, whereby I determined a learning goal for the class period and the course, and designed activities and worksheets that were intended to aid the students in reaching that goal. For example, when we met in class to discuss the first known vampire poem, Heinrich August Ossenfelder's poem "Der Vampir" (The Vampire; 1748), my goal was for the students to make connections between the vampire folklore we had studied previously and this first attempt to use the vampire as a literary figure. I asked the students to refer to the information they had collected in the worksheet comparing folklore stories (Fig. 1) and compare the literary vampire in Ossenfelder's poem with the vampire figures in the folklore accounts. The students noticed the important similarities, such as the setting in Hungary, but they also noticed important differences that made the vampire a literary figure. For example, they noticed that the poem was told from the vampire's perspective and they noticed that blood sucking was a metaphor for dangerous seduction in the poem.

Before we started reading the folklore, I provided the students with an introduction to the historical background of the vampire in German literature as it became adapted from Central European folklore in the mid-eighteenth century. Despite my focus on "backward design" for the majority of the course, I believed it was necessary for students to have some understanding of the history that set the stage for vampire folklore and later, the literary vampire. The style I chose for this "history lesson" was an informal lecture format during one class period, i.e., approximately 50 minutes with time at the end and during the presentation for questions and comments. This lecture included a power point presentation with the most important facts in bullet points and some images. I will summarize the most important points here.

Historical Background

During the first decades of the eighteenth century, poets, scientists and philosophers in Germany and in other Western European countries tried to come to terms with the vampire phenomenon that Austrian occupying forces in Central Europe had relayed to the West. In 1716, the Ottoman Turks declared war on the Habsburgs after they had succeeded in driving the Venetians out of Peloponnesus and the Aegean archipelago and after the Habsburg Emperor Charles VI (1685–1740) had formed an alliance with the Venetians. On July 21, 1718, at Passarowitz in Serbia peace was restored among Turkey, Austria and Venice. As a result of the Peace of Passarowitz, the Habsburgs were able to keep their conquests in the Banat, eastern Slovenia, northern Serbia and western Wallachia and they were able to recover South Hungary. The Turks kept their conquests in Venice and Greece. Occupying forces from the Austrian armies remained in the areas acquired by the Habsburgs until 1739 and Charles VI commissioned them to record their observations of local customs and submit their reports to the court in Vienna.

The Emperor took great interest in the stories of vampire superstition in these reports and funded expeditions into these areas by doctors, clergy, scientists and other officials, charging them with the task of documenting the alleged incidents of vampirism in his newly acquired territories and collecting stories of vampires from the corpus of local folklore. Commanding officers stationed in Serbia repeatedly received orders from the Emperor to investigate reports of vampirism in Serbian villages and dutifully sent their reports back for review. These reports mark the earliest documented sources of information on the Central European vampire superstition that were later available to poets in the West. The growing interest in the stories of vampirism in Serbia was not, however, restricted to the court in Vienna; Charles VI circulated the reports among other ruling houses of the Empire.

Once published, these Central European vampire stories inspired debate in Western Europe among philosophers, poets, and scientists on the possibility of the actual existence of vampires. In 1728, the German theologian and academic Michael Ranft wrote what is still recognized today as one of the first and most thorough historical reports on vampirism in Europe, an essay bearing the rather colorful title *On the Chewing and Smacking by the Dead in Their Graves*. In 1734, he published an expanded edition of his treatise. In keeping with the times, Ranft wrote his report in what he called a rationalist manner in contrast to what he considered the emotional and enthusiastic styles of his contemporaries. While his colleagues' reports were intended to comply with Enlightenment methodology, in Ranft's assessment they remained mostly unscientific. Ranft's report is more in compliance with the philosophy and methodology of the Enlightenment because he seeks answers to the vampire phenomenon in nature.

Charles VI's interest in stories of vampirism from his newly acquired territories in the Balkans followed by his daughter Maria Theresa's efforts to ban practices associated with this superstition and the persecution of witches in Hungary resulted in a general association of Hungary with the vampire by Western Europeans (Klaniczay 179). Although Central European vampire beliefs were essentially Greek and Slavic in origin, the most popular stories and reports that were circulating through Europe in the first half of the eighteenth century placed the vampire in Hungary and other neighboring countries, such as Romania. This connection between Hungary and the vampire becomes particularly apparent in the image of the vampire in the German poetry that introduced this monster into literature, most obviously when the poets name specific towns or geographic landmarks in these regions. The literary vampires in these early German poems and prose works also exhibit distinct characteristics that are primarily reminiscent of the vampires from the Central European stories, rather than Germany's own folklore, emphasizing their popular appeal at the time.

In an effort to attract, retain and entertain readers, editors of popular journals were eager to publish the vampire stories from Central Europe. The first magazine to publish a report about the vampire superstition in Serbia was the *Wienerisches Diarium* (Viennese Diarium). The article appeared in the July 21, 1725, issue of the magazine under the title "Copy of an Essay from the Gradisk District," identifying it as the story about a suspected vampire named Peter Plogojowitz that *Kameralprovisor* (military chaplain) Frombald had written and submitted to court administrators in Vienna (Schroeder 41 and 77). In fact, popular Western European print media functioned as a direct link between the Central European vampire stories and the first literary vampire when the first vampire poem was published in a scientific magazine in response to an article on the Central European vampire stories. In 1748, Christlob Mylius, the editor of the popular science magazine *Der Naturforscher* (The Natural Scientist), was planning to publish an article on the vampire stories from Central Europe that had been collected for Charles VI ("The 125th Letter from the Jewish Letters"). It was his practice in his publication to follow each scientific article with a poem that reflected the article's theme, so he invited his friend, the German poet Heinrich August Ossenfelder, to write a poem that reflected the theme of the article on vampires. With the publication of his short poem, "Der Vampir" (The Vampire), Ossenfelder barely escaped complete obscurity and he is now recognized as the first known poet to have adapted the vampire from folklore for creative literature. What is unique and important about Mylius' scientific publication in 1748 is that it effectively marks the introduction of the vampire into literature through scientific inquiry and investigation by way of popular media.

Central European Vampire Folklore

In an effort to understand the Central European vampire folklore that captured the fascination of western Europeans and the characteristics of these vampires, we read some of the most popular vampire folklore stories ("Peter Plogojowitz," "The Shoemaker of Silesia," "Visum et repertum/Arnod Paole" and "Vrykolakas") published in Paul Barber's book and made our own folklore comparisons based on the information in the chapters of Barber's book devoted to the folklore stories. I designed the following folklore comparison table for the students to fill out after they had read the folklore stories.

FIG. 1. FOLKLORE COMPARISON TABLE

Features of Comparison	Peter Plogojowitz	Shoemaker of Silesia	Visum et repertum (Arnod Paole)	Vrykolakas
Geographic origin				
Character in life				
Basis for suspicion as a revenant				
Method of attack				
Appearance upon exhumation				
Method of destroying revenant				
Other important features of comparison				

This folklore comparison table became a useful tool when we read the first known vampire poetry and prose works in our course. A close examination of the Central European folklore that attracted German poets revealed to students the different types of vampire tales and diverse images of the vampire figures that are at the root of the many traits we associate with the literary vampire today. As we worked on the folklore comparisons, based on what students observed as they read the folklore in conjunction with what we read in Barber's book, we were able to make several observations about the folklore, including important similarities and differences that facilitated an understanding of later vampire poetry and prose works. I will summarize these findings here.

As we read the vampire folktales, we recorded in the worksheet (Fig. 1) details about the images of the vampire in the Central European folklore that informed German poets. Students remarked that the tales varied somewhat depending on the country from which the folklore originated. The students concluded that the culturally-based differences among the stories called attention to this monster's complexity, but also its malleable nature, a useful trait for story-telling purposes.

After comparing notes, students noted that most vampire folktales follow one of two common folkloric tale types. One is that a person from a village dies and is buried properly. Shortly thereafter family members and others die unexpectedly and inexplicably. The first to die becomes the scapegoat for the deaths following his. He is accused of returning to kill members of his family or community by sapping or draining their energy and leaving them pale or weak and apparently devoid of blood to die shortly thereafter. Although the alleged incidents of "vampirism" were instead epidemics of illness in the community, the inexplicable nature of the illness, combined with the local superstitions, often led villagers to scapegoat the first to die. In preliterate societies such as these, which lack an understanding of physiology, pathology and immunology, how does one account for disease and death? Death is blamed on the dead. And epidemics are blamed on the first to die — an unintended understanding of contagion.

A second common tale type is that the future revenant who dies violently, either by murder or suicide, returns to haunt others in the community. Sometimes people die and he is blamed for the haunting or the deaths. In many of the stories that belong to this tale type, the suspected vampire was not well-liked when alive because he was of a generally malevolent nature. If the person who died violently and was disliked as a mortal was well-known, then it seems natural that people might identify him as a monster and ascribe mischievous behavior in the community to his malicious behavior when alive.

Common to stories from both tale types is that the townspeople exhume and examine the body of the accused revenant, noting in particular that the body appears fresh with evident growth of hair and nails, despite the fact that it had been buried for weeks or months. The body looked more alive than dead to the people who exhumed it because of their lack of knowledge of the decomposition process.[3] After making these key observations and after the presiding authorities had determined that the exhumed body was in fact a vampire, it became necessary to "kill" the revenant either by decapitation, staking, burning or any combination of these according to local belief and practice. Usually any unexplained deaths ceased after the revenant was destroyed.

Another observation students made about the folkloric vampire was that most often the vampire was male and he had a zombie-like demeanor or a ghost-like appearance as a revenant. Although folkloric vampires may exhibit ghost-like qualities, they should not be confused with ghosts, which are disembodied spirits. Vampires in folklore and literature appear in corporeal form to the humans they seek out, not as ethereal spirits. Usually, the vampire revenant from folklore does not suck blood or kill and he returns to haunt his own community or relatives— not strangers. This imagery shows, then, that a vampire is not as easily defined as one might expect. In fact, one significant development of the literary vampire in the eighteenth century, which can be traced to its diverse portrayals in the folklore from Central Europe, is that the vampire becomes as complex a creature as regular mortals are; it becomes a human-seeming monster with personality, passion and purpose. Its monstrous nature, however, connects it metaphorically to the more sinister side of the human condition and the culture it lives in or invades.

The Vampire in Prose

After familiarizing ourselves with the history of the vampire in German literature, the folklore that inspired German authors and the first vampire poetry, we proceeded to read some of the first German vampire prose works. I will summarize here some of the information I provided as background information for the works themselves and information from our class discussions of these early prose works.

Ludwig Tieck wrote the first known prose work with a vampire theme in 1811 as part of his fairy-tale collection, *Phantasus*, which was first published in two volumes in 1812, several years before John Polidori published the first British vampire story "The Vampyre" in 1819. This story, "The Love-Charm," belongs to Tieck's *Stadtmärchen* (city fairy-tales), which are also the first such city fairy-tales in German literature.

In his story, Tieck combines obvious elements from vampire literature, especially in the appearance and demeanors of vampires (pallor, bright red lips, unnatural stiffness, licking blood from the victim's neck) with Black Magic. When I asked students if there was a vampire in this story, they had two responses: either the protagonist himself, Emil, was the vampire because of his obsession with a young woman, or his love interest was the vampire because of her evil nature (Black Magic; human sacrifice to perform love magic on Emil) and her outward appearance (extreme pallor contrasted with red lips). Some students argued that she was a witch and not a vampire because of the Black Magic she performed in the story. This observation was especially exciting for me, because it segued nicely into a discussion about the historical connection between vampirism and witchcraft.

Though this connection may not be immediately clear, the roots of vampirism and witchcraft in European cultural and folklore history have been linked since ancient times. Many pagan religions had vampire figures among their demonic beings that also demonstrated similarities to the *lamia* of Ancient Greece (Melton 685). The demonization of witches and the connection that was made soon afterward to vampirism defined both as evils that opposed the Church. As such, they could be resisted and controlled with the assistance of sacred and blessed objects, such as the crucifix, the Eucharist wafer and Holy Water (688). And if these monsters were women who killed children, they were all the more evil.

Though Tieck did not employ any outwardly obvious characteristics of the contemporary fictional vampire in his story, such as a corpse that rises from the grave to torment or kill loved ones, he made an important historical connection between the demonization of witchcraft and the demonization of vampirism when he brought the two together in the image of the witch/vampire bride in his story "The Love-Charm." This suggests knowledge of the history of the persecution of witches. Moreover, Tieck used the vampire in his story as the embodiment of such societal anxieties and fears as infanticide, anonymity in the big city and the unawareness of a person's true nature.

Ernst Benjamin Salomo Raupach was a very prolific playwright, having produced for the Berlin Court Theater a total of 98 plays between 1820 and 1842, most of which were historical dramas and 21 of which were never published (Goedeke 657–658). His primary goal in writing dramatic works was to rid the German theater of foreign influences, especially from France, and bring German plays back to the German theater. In his vampire fairy-tale "Wake Not the Dead!" Raupach enhances the image of the female vampire by combining the common motifs of the dead lover returning with those of sorcery, necromancy, the danger of unbridled longing and lust for the deceased, and of course infanticide. The overriding themes that Raupach connects with his female vampire figure and with the protagonist's, Walter's, desire for her in this story are the social taboos of necrophilia, adultery and bigamy (Hock 110) that are evident in Walter's actions from the very beginning: "Frequently of a night, instead of retiring to his consort's chamber, he repaired to Brunhilda's grave, where he murmured forth in discontent, saying, 'Wilt thou sleep forever?'" (Haining 96), and when he exclaims to the sorcerer, "Aye, but not in the cold grave: she shall rather rest on this bosom which burns with eagerness to clasp her" (99), his necrophilic desires are even more blatant. Walter is punished most severely for his infractions when his vampire mistress kills his children.

Raupach's story introduces important and very new and modern elements to the image of the vampire figure in the early nineteenth century. Brunhilda focuses her attacks on children and adolescents in an effort to restore her own youthful energy and if Walter dies before she is killed, she will continue to kill men. Moreover, the image of Brunhilda as a vampire seductress who repeatedly feeds on children or young people predates J. Sheridan LeFanu's vampire Carmilla in his novella *Carmilla* (1872) and Bram Stoker's vampire Lucy in *Dracula* (1897). Especially Brunhilda's method of attack is a new trait of the literary vampire at this time. She anaesthetizes her victims with her breath of violets, putting them into a deep sleep, and then she feeds on them. Though she sucks the blood from their breasts, as is common for vampires from Central European folklore, she does not kill them immediately. Her victims fade away over time, gradually losing their energy and youthful appearance until they finally die. This is a common trait among vampires in British literature later in the nineteenth century, especially in Stoker's *Dracula*, and it has been connected metaphorically to diseases such as consumption, cancer and pulmonary tuberculosis. From the standpoint of building a suspenseful narrative around the vampire figure, such a gradual wasting away of the victim produces a dramatic effect, especially at a time in the late nineteenth century when disease featured quite prominently in literature.

Furthermore, Raupach's vampire has very modern metaphoric value as an entity that embodies social anxieties and fears, a theory of the monster's role in literature that Jeffrey Jerome Cohen addresses in his book *Monster Theory: Reading Culture* (1996). Brunhilda is beautiful and desirable as a woman, but she is also the corruptive force that destroys the peaceful family unit Walter has with his wife Swanhilda and his children. In this story, the vampire's body functions metaphorically as a repository for common societal fears about the destruction of the family connected with adultery or even bigamy that may end in divorce and a metaphoric death of the family line, especially evident in the children's deaths in the story. Walter's desire for Brunhilda is also centered completely on the passion and excitement he remembers from the early days of their marriage. Though he remembers the controlling and manipulative aspects of her personality that developed later in their marriage, his decision to ignore this in favor of once again experiencing physical love with the reanimated corpse of his wife is irrational. In this story, the social ill represented by the vampire is that unbridled passion is dangerous and unnatural and it can destroy otherwise strong social units, such as the family.

Dracula

Our modern perception of the vampire has been formed much like a mosaic from an accumulation of images and metaphoric uses that have been passed down first through regional folklore and then from poet to poet and from artist to artist. The most famous vampire of fiction, Dracula, has been formed and greatly influenced by false associations with a historical Dracula. There is evidence in Bram Stoker's notes for his novel that he borrowed the name "Dracula" for his vampire from a historical "Voivode [military commander] Dracula," which Stoker discovered during his research at Whitby Library. There is no evidence that Stoker was, in fact, referring to the historical Romanian Prince Dracula, also known as Vlad Tepes or Vlad the Impaler from Wallachia (1431–1476),[4] notorious for his habit of impaling his enemies' bodies in an effort to deter further aggressors.[5] This has been a common misperception that very likely stems from confusing the names of the

Voivode Dracula with Prince Dracula (Vlad Tepes). The only documented connection between Stoker's Dracula and a historical Voivode Dracula is in Stoker's use of the name, very likely because it means the devil, a more appropriate and creative choice of a name than Stoker's original name for his vampire: Count Wampyre (Miller 187–188). Hence, the most famous literary vampire, Dracula, though localized in Central Europe, does not have its origins in the vampire folklore of the Balkans as do the original vampires from the earliest German poems, but rather in the name of a historical figure from this region that had nothing to do with vampirism.

During our class discussions of the characteristics exhibited by Dracula, his identity as an aristocrat from an old noble family in Eastern Europe and the general theme of colonialism in Stoker's novel, students were immediately reminded of strikingly similar themes in the 1847 story "The Mysterious Stranger" by Karl Adolf von Wachsmann, which they recorded in a worksheet that included a table prompting them to compare characters and aspects of the story, the vampires and their victims:

FIG. 2. CHARACTER AND STORY COMPARISON

	The Mysterious Stranger	Dracula
Vampire's appearance		
Vampire's character (also in life, if known)		
Primary victim's character	Franziska:	Lucy:
Primary victim's demise	Franziska:	Lucy:
Notes on first encounter with the vampire (encountered where and under what circumstances)		
Vampire's idiosyncrasies/ odd behavior		
Vampire's background/ family heritage		
Characteristics of the vampire hunter	Woislaw:	Van Helsing:
Destruction of the vampire		
Other notes of comparison		

In this story, a Habsburg family travels to eastern Hungary to take possession of a castle they recently inherited. As they travel through the forests of the Carpathian Mountains, accompanied by a local guide who is well-versed in local superstition, the party of travelers encounters a mysterious stranger, the knight Azzo von Klatka, who becomes especially attracted to Franziska, one of the young women in the party. After several of his visits with the family, during which he never eats or drinks, Franziska begins to weaken and grow ill. When the soldier Woislaw, Franziska's cousin Betrha's fiancé, returns from the wars against Napoleon in Russia the family is finally able to come to Franziska's aid. Armed with a strong understanding of regional superstition and the means by which one can fight the attack of a vampire, Woislaw is able to first identify Azzo as a vampire and he is able to plan how he and Franziska must work together to kill the vampire. Considering the many similarities between Dracula and the vampire knight Azzo in Wachsmann's story, the popularity of "The Mysterious Stranger" when it was first published and its international appeal after it was translated into English in 1860, students wondered if Stoker may have been inspired by this story.

Though it is generally understood that Stoker was inspired by LeFanu's story *Carmilla*, students were correct to wonder whether he may have also known of Wachsmann's story. I was pleasantly surprised to observe how the students in this course made such connections between *Dracula* and "The Mysterious Stranger." We had begun the course with close comparisons of shared and differing characteristics of the vampire in the early folklore stories and by the end of the course the students were using these skills to make connections between our prose works. And where they saw traits, such as shape-changing or pronounced fangs in later works and in film, which did not connect to the early folklore or the earliest vampire poetry and prose, students wondered what these new traits might mean for the particular story, whether there was any metaphorical significance. They wondered if Dracula's ability to shape-change reflected his desire to re-invent his identity for a new culture and a new era in Victorian London. Based on the students' final discussions of individual vampire traits and their likely metaphorical uses, I was convinced that an introduction to the historical background of the vampire in Central European folklore was essential to effectively teach the vampire in literature. In future courses that are not restricted to German literature, I will proceed in like fashion, but will expand the list of works to include Anne Rice's novel *Interview with a Vampire* (1976) and the first novel in Charlaine Harris's Sookie Stackhouse series, *Dead Until Dark* (2001).

Concluding Remarks

After teaching this course for two consecutive quarters at Ohio State University, I found that the teaching methodology I employed, combining some informal lecture where necessary, for example background history and background information on some of the authors, with a "backward design" and an inductive reasoning based, student-centered approach to teaching to be very effective. By the end of the semester, students had become skilled in organizing their observations of important characteristics and uses of the vampire in the literature and applying these observations to thorough analyses of the literature, which they demonstrated in exams and essays. Furthermore, and especially important for my goals for the course, through their careful analyses of individual stories and poems, students arrived at more universally applicable ideas about the literary vampire as a metaphor for a society's fears and anxieties, connecting directly with Jeffrey Jerome Cohen's "monster theory" in his book *Monster Theory: Reading Culture* and proving to me and each other that they had not only learned about the evolution of the vampire from folklore, but also about its place in literature and film. And much to my delight, students answered the question "But why do they have fangs?" by suggesting that Dracula's fangs might be a metaphor for dangerous sexual predators, much like the vampire in the first vampire poem by Ossenfelder.

Notes

1. Bram Stoker's novel *Dracula* is included in this course on the vampire in German literature because German film director F.W. Murnau's movie *Nosferatu: A Symphony of Horror* is based on Stoker's popular novel.

2. Grant Wiggins and Jay McTighe, "What Is Backward Design?" in *Understanding by Design*, 1st ed. (Upper Saddle River, NJ: Merrill Prentice Hall, 2001), pp. 7–19.

3. The apparent posthumous growth of hair and nails, which is in fact "a shedding of the nails, and loosening of the hair," is particularly noticeable, but is simply part of the natural decomposition process (Barber 106). The "fresh" appearance of the corpse is attributable to a phenomenon known as "skin slippage," the "sloughing away" of the upper skin layer to reveal skin that is not actually new, but rather "raw-looking" (109).

4. To be more specific, Prince Dracula was born in Transylvania, in a fortified German town called Schassburg or Sighisoara in Romania (McNally, *In Search*, 15).

5. McNally, *In Search*, 3. Though Dracula made wide use of impalement, it was not his innovation. Impalement was well-known in Asia and was practiced in Turkey during the Middle Ages (91).

Bibliography

Barber, Paul. *Vampires, Burial, and Death: Folklore and Reality*. New Haven: Yale University Press, 2010. Print.

Cohen, Jeffrey Jerome, ed. *Monster Theory: Reading Culture*. Minneapolis: University of Minnesota Press, 1996. Print.

Goedeke, Karl. *Grundrisz zur Geschichte der Deutschen Dichtung aus den Quellen von Karl Goedeke*, 2d ed., vols. 3, 4 and 8. Dresden: Verlag von L. Ehlermann, 1905. Print.

Haining, Peter, ed. *Gothic Tales of Terror. Volume Two: Classic Horror Stories from Europe and the United States*. Baltimore: Penguin, 1973. Print.

Hock, Stefan. *Die Vampyrsagen und ihre Verwertung in der deutschen Literatur*. Berlin: Verlag von Alexander Duncker, 1900. Print.

Klaniczay, Gábor. *The Uses of Supernatural Power: The Transformation of Popular Religion in Medieval and Early-Modern Europe*. Princeton: Princeton University Press, 1990. Print.

McNally, Raymond T., and Radu Florescu. *In Search of Dracula: The History of Dracula and Vampires*. New York: Houghton Mifflin, 1994. Print.

Melton, J. Gordon. *The Vampire Book: The Encyclopedia of the Undead*. Detroit: Visible Ink Press, 1994. Print.

Miller, Elizabeth. *Dracula: Sense and Nonsense*. Westcliff-on-Sea: Desert Island, 2000. Print.

Schroeder, Aribert. *Vampirismus: Seine Entwicklung vom Thema zum Motiv*. Frankfurt am Main: Akademische Verlagsgesellschaft, 1973. Print.

Wiggins, Grant, and Jay McTighe. *Understanding by Design*. Upper Saddle River, NJ: Merrill Prentice Hall, 2001. Print.

Taking Dracula's Pulse:
Historicizing the Vampire

Lisa Lampert-Weissig

Perhaps it's only fitting that my fondness for the Marxist critic Frederic Jameson's exhortation—"always historicize"—very likely cost me my big Hollywood break. Somehow a developer for film scripts had gotten hold of my name and wanted to discuss my research as possible film material. I was skeptical when I read his email, but I also grew up in L.A., so I gave the guy a call. As I suspected, he wasn't all that interested in most of my work on medieval literature, but there was one aspect of my research that sounded intriguing to him: vampires. I should have just cooked up a kung fu action flick about Erzsebet Báthory on the spot, but, instead, when he intoned, "Ah, the timeless creature, the vampire," I couldn't help myself. "Actually," I interjected, "the vampire is anything but timeless. Vampires are historically constructed creatures." Summoning up my best understandings of the work of Jeffrey Jerome Cohen and Nina Auerbach, I launched into a mini-lecture on the need to historicize the vampire.

Needless to say, I'm still waiting for my lucky break, but my insistence on historicizing has been good for my day job. I want to share here how my emphasis on historical and cultural contexts in my classes on vampire literature and film has led to some very successful discussions and student writing on the vampire, particularly in relation to questions of race and sexuality. My course is structured chronologically with Stoker's *Dracula* at its center. It is my contention that what has made the figure of Dracula a "timeless legend" is actually very much connected to history. Stoker took, I believe, the "pulse" of his time. His work distills anxieties about sexuality, technology, race and empire that were already present in European discourses about the vampire and presents them in ways that fit his particular place and moment, England in 1897. The themes that dominate *Dracula* continue to be with us, of course, and the class also looks at how writers and artists since Stoker have taken up these themes and how they continue to adapt them.[1] As Nina Auerbach has contended, "every generation creates and embraces its own vampires" (vii). In my class we look at how this embrace of the vampire has occurred from the very beginnings of this literary figure in the West—the so-called Vampire Epidemic of the 1730s—through to twenty-first century works like Octavia Butler's *Fledgling* and the television series *True Blood*.

Course enrollment has ranged from 40 to 100 students, which has impacted the types of assignments given. For lower enrollments, I have included a brief writing assignment for each class: a "thinksheet." For each class session, I post a list of study questions on the course website and then ask the students to respond to one of the questions in a one-half to one full page typed answer. The thinksheets form the starting point for discussion. The thinksheets are not graded on a letter scale. Each student begins with an "A" on his or her thinksheets (typically 20 percent of total grade). Students are allowed to miss one or two assignments and after that the "A" begins to erode. I comment extensively on the thinksheets. This allows me to dialogue with students and encourages them to take the assignment seriously: it's not "busy work." The fact that the individual thinksheets aren't assigned letter grades also allows students to simply "think" and explore ideas. If a student turns in a thinksheet that clearly doesn't fulfill the assignment (very short or extremely sloppy, for example), he or she is immediately notified in writing that the overall thinksheet grade depends on carrying out the assignment in good faith and is asked to meet with me in office hours if the problem persists.

The thinksheet question for my discussion of the Murnau and Herzog adaptations of *Dracula*, for example, is as follows.

In the conclusion to Stoker's *Dracula*, evil is defeated in a way strikingly different to the endings of the Murnau and Herzog films. In a paragraph discuss the changes in the conclusions and then write another paragraph arguing what you see as the significance of that change. How does it change our view of the overall story? of its depiction of evil? of its depiction of Dracula? (choosing one of these elements will suffice for the analysis).

At the larger range of course size, I have to drop this writing assignment and the course consists primarily of lecture. Even with the lecture format I still provide students with study questions posted on the course website and use small group "break-out" sessions in order to facilitate student engagement. For the larger lecture course I give a traditional in-class final examination with short-answer questions, ID terms and an essay question. The smaller classes have had a take-home final with a choice of essay questions designed written in about the same time as a three-hour traditional in-class exam. Since the smaller courses have thinksheets, I see less of a need to test whether or not students have done the course reading, as they must complete the reading to write the thinksheets. Therefore, overall, the lower enrollment classes have more writing, more discussion and less reliance on lecturing, although the course at all sizes is still structured to meet minimal departmental and campus-wide page requirements.

No matter what the enrollment, students write a 10–12 page research paper. In preparation for the paper, we have one lecture by our humanities librarian about research techniques and resources. Students are also required to submit pre-writing assignments: a bibliography created on Refworks (I will be switching to Zotero—an open source bibliography program — the next time I teach the course) and a one-page abstract that explains their thesis and approach. With half of our course readings originally in German and half originally in English, the course is designed to fulfill requirements for both our English Literature and German Studies students. Our handful of German studies students has special requirements for paper topics using German primary texts in the original; we make arrangements for German credit guidelines individually at the beginning of the course. To save on costs for the students I try to limit the number of books they need to purchase and rely heavily on our library's e-reserve for short works as well as on texts and translations available on the web.[2]

The students in the course have primarily been juniors and seniors, in part because of enrollment restrictions on upper-division courses. About half of the students have been majors from our Literature department and the rest have come from a very wide variety of majors, including many from science and engineering, which is not surprising given the emphasis on science on the UC San Diego campus. I have found that the thinksheet questions, lecture on library resources and the pre-assignments for the research paper have been extremely important in helping non-majors to understand disciplinary expectations for literary analysis.

My course begins where my research on vampires originally began: in the Middle Ages. Perhaps based on my own youthful encounters with Anne Rice's Lestat, before researching the vampire, I had always imagined that the literary vampire had its roots in my field of primary training, medieval literature, but this not the case. I begin my lectures with this misconception and we then consider the vampire within a pantheon of monsters, including the werewolf, wonderful examples of which can be found in medieval literature such as Marie de France's lai, "Bisclavret," or the romance narrative, *Guillaume de Palerne*. But despite a tantalizing reference to a *sanguissuga* [blood sucker] in William of Newburgh's *Historia rerum Anglicarum* [History of English Affairs] vampires do not burst on the literary scene until the eighteenth century.

The rest of my lecturing on these origins is then devoted to the historical context of this emergence and the so-called "Great Vampire Epidemic" of the 1730s. I draw upon the important folkloric and forensic research of Paul Barber in *Vampires, Burial and Death* (1988) and the provocative thesis of Erik Butler's *Metamorphoses of the Vampire* (2009) to look at how the vampire legend took hold in Western Europe. This requires that I provide the students with some background into both the Ottoman and Hapsburg empires and how the Peace of Passarowitz in 1718 led to Hapsburg military and medical personnel encountering the phenomenon of corpse exhumation and execution in response to plague among those native to parts of Serbia and Wallachia.[3]

I present the students with maps of the region as well as have them read translations of reports from Hapsburg officials that are readily accessible in Barber. These reports sent back by these officials of famous cases such as those of Arnod Paole (1732) and Peter Plogojowitz (1725) led to the true vampire epidemic, an epidemic of scientific and literary production in Western Europe. This rampant interest in vampires was fueled, Butler argues, not simply by curiosity, but by political anxiety: those in the West were disturbed and intrigued by native inhabitants of the Balkans carrying out vampire-killing rituals in defiance of Hapsburg officials. Butler's close readings of these reports demonstrate that the inhabitants of these Balkan villages were not simply acting on their own pre-scientific answers to natural phenomena of disease, burial, and decomposition (Barber). The Balkan peasants were also engaging in acts of political resistance against yet another invading empire, as Hapsburg domination of the region replaced that of the Ottomans. I ground this reading of the origins of the vampire in a very specific discussion of Western European views of the Balkans and the ways that these early discourses can be tied to discourses of race and ethnicity through representations of Ottoman/Hapsburg conflict as well as tensions between different Christian denominations. I also explain how the flurry of dissertations that followed these reports from the Balkans, such as Michael Ranft's *De Masticatione Mortuorum* (Leipzig, 1728) demonstrate intersections between political and early scientific discourses that continue in the vampire legend today. It is no accident, I argue, that the first piece of vampire literature, Heinrich August Ossenfelder's 1748 lyric "Der Vampir" appeared in the pages of *Der Naturforscher* [The Nature Researcher], a natural philosophy journal. I use a handout with my own translation of the lyric for the course; a good translation and the German original can be found in Crawford.

We read and analyze "Der Vampir" and continue on to the emergence of the vampire in a variety of German-language texts, reading Gottfried August Bürger's widely popular lyric "Lenore" (1773) in relation to the Seven Years' War (1754/56–63) and Goethe's "Braut von Korinth" [Bride of Corinth] (1797) within discourses of East and West and of religion, superstition, and the Enlightenment. We look at two short stories, "Wake Not the Dead!" (1800) (attributed to Tieck but likely by Raupach) and E.T.A. Hoffmann's "Aurelia" (1818).[4] These early vampire narratives introduce several important elements that remain with us throughout the course. Themes of sexuality and an Orientalist fascination with an exoticized East are deeply connected to the original sources of these literary productions, the reports of vampires from the Balkans.

Also running through these texts is a critical engagement with Christianity that can range from the negative references to pious mothers in "Der Vampir" and "Lenore" to the much more fully articulated critique on Christian sexual strictures in Goethe's poem. This Christian thematic also needs to be considered in relation to Enlightenment critiques of religion and superstition and to early scientific activity and discourses of the period. The first vampire poem, after all, appears in a journal about natural philosophy—early science—and we consider the ways that the vampire, as a being both living and dead, engaged those interested in questions of science. All of these themes, I try to show, can be found in the figure of the vampire and also come to shape racial representation in relation to this figure. We consider the question of intersectionality: what makes a human identity? (Crenshaw). And how can we think about this question in relation to a non-human being? How can thinking in this way help us to define the human?

After setting up the early German context for the literary vampire, we move on to the English literary vampire. Since there are so many non–Literature majors in the course, I give a further lecture on Romanticism and its role in English literary history. We then read Coleridge's "Christabel" (1797/1800) and Byron's "Giaour" (1813) as antecedents to Polidori's "The Vampyre" (1819).[5] We look at this text in relation to the intriguing story of its creation at Villa Diodati along with Mary Shelley's *Frankenstein* and then examine the currents of sexuality, Orientalism, and the development of an intimate relationship between Aubrey and Ruthven in the story. We read these in the context of its German and English textual antecedents and also carefully lay the groundwork for how these themes will be treated in later texts.

After reading Polidori we then turn to LeFanu's *Carmilla* (1872). Both texts depict homoerotic relationships between a vampire and a human, but in radically different ways. I present *Carmilla* as an important transition text between the early Romantic vampires we have been examining and Stoker's *Dracula*, for which it seems clearly to be a source. I also bring in here a mini-lecture on the Gothic tradition, which has been haunting the earlier texts we have examined, and consider this tradition in relation both to Romanticism and the vampire tradition. We pay special attention to the Styrian setting of *Carmilla*, reading it both in terms of the East/West tension between the Balkans and Europe that we have already seen, but also in the context of LeFanu's own Irish background. We consider depictions of sexuality and ethnic difference in relation to each other and to the scientific framing of the text within the papers of Dr. Hesselius. We then turn to examine LeFanu's portrayal of the attraction between Laura and Carmilla in relation to the stark contrast that they pose with the little-known German vampire short story, "Manor," written by Karl Heinrich Ulrichs (1825–95) in 1885.

Ulrichs' story is noteworthy because of its positive depiction of a homoerotic relationship between a vampire and a young man. Ulrich is himself a fascinating figure. Trained as a jurist, he openly advocated for rights for homosexuals at a time when homosexuality was illegal in a growing range of German-speaking territories, territories through which he himself had to move to escape persecution and imprisonment. Ulrichs eventually died in poverty in Italy, where he composed "Manor." Set in the Faero Islands, located halfway between Norway and Iceland, "Manor" eschews the typical Orientalist setting of the vampire tale, and the love story between boy and vampire unfolds in an entirely working-class milieu, a fishing village. The love between the two, which lasts beyond death, is also eventually accepted by the boy's mother, in another inversion of the typical role of the intervening mother, that goes back to Ossenfelder's "Der Vampir." We examine "Manor" within Ulrichs' own theory of homosexuality, "Uranism," and its components of Nordic myth, looking at "Manor" as a point of contrast against the dark and gothic representations of vampirism that dominate our course readings.

After Ulrichs, we turn to Stoker's *Dracula*, which is the fulcrum of the course. We read the novel as a kind of nodal point for the themes of science, religion, race, gender, and sexuality that we have been examining. We first focus in on *Dracula* as a novel of 1897 London, beginning with a look at the various locales that Stoker details in the novel, using graphics and maps. Drawing upon work by Bram Dijkstra and Elaine Showalter on fin-de-siècle culture, we consider the various elements of this culture that Stoker brings to the novel and the ways that Stoker makes thematics we examined in earlier texts "nineteenth century up-to-date with a vengeance" to reflect the concerns of 1897 England (Williams, 180).

Setting up this information for the students includes lecture materials on the relevance of the New Woman, the Wilde trial in 1895, the advent of technological advances that feature throughout the novel, and, as Stephen Arata has so convincingly demonstrated, a fear of Occidentalism that shapes the novel's representation of ethnicity and race. We examine Stoker's representation of Dracula and the region from which he comes in terms of late nineteenth-century views about the East and about race, including "sciences" such as Lombroso's phrenology. We read the novel as "taking the pulse" of late-nineteenth century England, tapping into the currents in vampire narrative that we have already examined and which will continue to influence vampire literature and film into the present day.

After completing *Dracula* we turn to two German film adaptations of Stoker's work, Friedrich Wilhelm Murnau's 1922 *Nosferatu: eine Symphonie des Grauens* and Werner Herzog's 1979 remake, *Nosferatu: Phantom der Nacht*.[6] We look at each film as an adaptation of Stoker's work considering how Murnau and Herzog transfer the film to specific German contexts. We first consider Murnau's film within the context of Weimar film and the specific political and cultural milieu of Germany after the First World War and significantly also after the Spanish influenza epidemic of 1918. What would it mean to an audience member in 1922 to witness the coming of a plague ship after the Spanish flu epidemic had wiped out millions? Prominent in our considerations are those readings of *Nosferatu* that see its depiction of Count Orlok as anti–Semitic and which also read the film in the context of the rise of National Socialism (Kracauer and Elsässer). We also do some frame-by-frame analysis of the work, considering the background to silent film and also the question of the monster himself — is he sympathetic?

We then turn to Herzog's remake, examining it, following the work of S.S. Prawer, as a post–Holocaust film. We look at the Count not as a possible figure for the Jew, but instead as a figure for evil and consider the ways in which the residents of Wismar can be viewed not as mere victims of the vampire, but as complicit in their own fates. Why does Jonathan decide to take on the assignment to Dracula's castle and how do his ambition and his restlessness contribute to his fate? When Jonathan himself becomes the new vampire, is this a radical change or a fulfillment of some element of his character?

We look specifically at the film in the context of the New German cinema and the way that many young filmmakers of Herzog's generation, born during or just after the era of National-Socialism, came to question the roles of their parents and grandparents in the atrocities of World War II and the Holocaust. Looking at the film as a post–Holocaust film, a reading inspired by S.S. Prawer, gives it a new dimension. The films striking opening shot of mummies takes on added meaning when considered against photographs taken at the liberation of Nazi concentration camps. We also follow Prawer in considering the way that the film borrows from German Romanticism. We go back to the elements of German and English Romanticism that we have already covered and then compare individual shots in the film to German Romantic paintings.

The most significant sequence here is the long segment in the film where Jonathan hikes the final stretch to Dracula's castle. We consider the role of the Wanderer in German Romanticism and examine Casper David Friedrich's "Wanderer Above the Sea of Fog" (1818) to consider how Herzog is drawing upon the German Romantic tradition (Casper and Linville). Herzog himself was a friend of the critic Lotte Eisner, who pioneered the readings of Murnau's film version in the context of German art history. We also note the soundtrack in this sequence, which employs the eerie two-chord chant by Popul Vuh that haunts the opening mummy sequence and which recurs in the film and then changes to the opening of Wagner's "Rheingold" as Jonathan reaches a mountain summit.

We consider the visual and audio references to German Romanticism in the context of German history. Herzog, following Murnau, moves the Dracula story to a German context, the Biedemeyer era. We consider this historical period in German history, one of relative peace, but also one that Thomas Mann thought was characterized by a "machtgeschütze Innerlichkeit," an ability to turn within to focus on hearth and home that was afforded by military strength (a situation I ask students to consider in relation to their own lives as contemporary U.S. citizens). Herzog stresses the bourgeois order of Lucy and Jonathan's home with details that echo Murnau's and he writes of this setting: "Hier ist die Welt in biedermeierlicher Ordnung" [Here the world is in Biedermeyer order] (Herzog, *Stroszek*, 79). We consider the significance of the German concept of "Kultur" as well as Germany's role as a cultural leader in the Romantic era. We then consider whether if, by drawing upon some of great masterworks of German cultural production, Herzog is implicitly questioning Germany's path. How did the nation that produced such art also produce such evil? And where does such evil come from? Is it, like Dracula, a figure from without—coming from the East? Who is the figure in the dark cape on the bridge in Wismar and what might this figure symbolize? Is there something within the characters and Wismar itself that draws the vampire?

We consider these questions also in relation to Stoker's *Dracula* and the figures of Lucy and Jonathan in the novel. We consider finally Hannah Arendt's concept of the "banality of evil" in relation to the Biedermeyer context of the film and German post–War consciousness. How does the transferring of the action from England at the height of Empire to this historical era in Germany change the representation of evil? What is the role of two historical contexts—Biedermeyer-era Germany and post–World War II Germany—in shaping the figure of the vampire? And, if the inhabitants of Wismar are perhaps complicit in allowing evil in their midst, how can such an interpretation of complicity with evil be seen in the post–War German context?

We then turn to read two texts that are explicit in their connections between vampires, blood, and race and that mark a bridge from European to American contexts, Hanns Heinz Ewers' 1921 novel *Vampir* and Octavia Butler's *Fledgling* (2005). Both writers attempt to shake up reader expectations by exploring taboo topics. Ewers (1871–1943) is a little-known but fascinating figure. An occultist and prolific and popular writer in pre–World War II Germany, he wrote *Vampir* as the final volume of his Frank Braun trilogy. Loosely autobiographical, *Vampir* is based on Ewers' time in the United States during World War I, where he agitated for the German cause and was briefly imprisoned for this work. The novel follows Frank Braun as he also works for the German cause during World War I, but focuses on his relationship with his half–Jewish lover, Lotte Lewi, and a mysterious ailment plaguing him. Frank experiences periodic episodes of debilitating weakness, the occurrence of which seems synced to his meetings with Lotte. He comes to suspect that Lotte is a vampire, draining him of strength, but at the novel's end he discovers that just the opposite is true. Frank himself is the vampire, his condition contracted through a bat bite while in the South Seas. Lotte has been offering her blood to him, out of love for him, but also out of devotion to the German cause. Her sacrifice enables his rhetorical efforts on behalf of the Fatherland.

Teaching *Vampir* poses numerous difficulties.[7] The German edition and its U.S. translation (1934) are both rare and the American edition is bowdlerized, cutting out passages depicting pedophilia, as well as Ewers' anti–American rhetoric, and his offensive racist language concerning people of color. The text is also far from a literary masterwork, but is worth teaching because of the explicit ways that it connects vampirism and early twentieth-century discourses of race. A self-proclaimed "philo–Semite," Ewers represents an interesting case of cognitive dissonance because he was also an early and ardent supporter of Hitler and Nazism. We examine the sections in *Vampir* that proclaim both the German and Jewish "races" as uniquely destined for combined glory, as inheritors of the glory of the twelve tribes of Israel and explore how Ewers' "philo-semitism" is merely the flipside of the anti–Semitism and racism that are the hallmarks of National-Socialism. A provocateur like Ewers might seem to be a target for Nazi persecution and, indeed, works like his *Fundvogel* (1928), which focuses on a transsexual, led to the banning of his writings and his own (self-contested) expulsion from the Nazi party. The racist hierarchy within which he views German-Jewish destiny, however, differs from Nazi racism in its embrace of certain kinds of Jews, but is also essentially in accord with it. We examine these issues through sections of the novel and through selections of some of Ewers' "philo–Semitic" writings. The vampire is central to Ewers' notion of race, since blood is the primary symbol of race for him and we examine the use of blood in the construction of the concept of race and in racist discourse.

Against this background we read Octavia Butler's *Fledgling* (2005), which begins with Shori, a character who awakens not knowing her true identity or even understanding the nature of her own being. Shori slowly comes to learn that she is part-human and part–Ina, the product of a genetic experiment begun by her Ina mothers. Ina have a different social structure than humans, with a communal and clan-structured society that also involves living in open, symbiotic relationships with humans that involve feeding, sex and intense emotional bonds. The humans and the Ina become dependent on one another, a co-dependence that mirrors addiction. The relationships between Ina and humans are also not entirely equal and Butler uses this imagined social picture to explore questions of social hierarchy, co-dependence, race, and slavery and their intertwined relationship in U.S. history. Butler challenges reader expectations by having Shori appear to be a black girl of around age 10 or 11, when she is actually 53 years old. We discuss the novel in relation to the slave narrative and the *Bildungsroman* and contrast the ways in which Butler and Ewers use themes of blood and vampirism to explore questions of race, racism, addiction, and sexuality in highly contrasting ways.

Butler's novel is our bridge from European to U.S. contexts. We shift back in time to examine *Blacula* (1972) and *Ganja and Hess* (1973). My approach to these films involves an opening lecture on the contexts of Blaxploitation film and how *Blacula* fits into this moment in film history with specific attention to representation of African Americans in film and to the shift in vampire films in the early seventies to the modern day begun by the commercially successful *Count Yorga, Vampire* (1970) and the television series, *Dark Shadows* (1966–71). We pay special attention to the opening of the film, which sets the story of Mamuwalde/Blacula within the history of slavery in the Americas, a contribution to the film introduced by the actor who plays Blacula, William Marshall. In the thinksheet for *Blacula*, students are asked to discuss how this opening shapes the film. While acknowledging that *Blacula* is a commercial film and intended as entertainment, we also consider the film within larger national discourses of race and specifically within the context of L.A. history.

This is an especially engaging part of the course for me because I was growing up in L.A. when *Blacula* was made, and for my students, the majority of whom are from Southern California, many from L.A. We look at *Blacula* as a Los Angeles film, focusing on the portrayal of the LAPD in the film, both in terms of the systemic racism depicted in the force and the choice to feature scenes of crowd control, curfew and officers in riot gear. I then introduce the historical context of the Watts Rebellion/Riots of August 1965, arguing that the depiction of race and racism in the film must be considered against this background. If Blaxploitation cinema was marketed to an African American audience, what would that target audience have made of the depiction of the LAPD in the film? Of Mamuwalde/Blacula as a tragic hero? Of the film's reference to the Black Panther party? We also turn again to the concept of intersectionality. How does the representation of Mamuwalde/Blacula intersect with the film's portrayal of female characters and with its homophobia? Following the work of Jenkins, Medovoi and Novotny, we look at these questions within the specific historical context of the Black Power movement, which is introduced to the students through lecture.

We then turn to the much less well-known film *Ganja and Hess*, which likely would not have been made if not for the commercial success of *Blacula*.[8] Director Bill Gunn was given backing to create another Blaxploitation feature, but what was created instead is a beautiful "art film" with a challenging narrative structure that explores race, racism, sexuality, Christianity and, especially, addiction, which is at the heart of the film. At the center of the film is Dr. Hess Green, played by Duane Jones, who is perhaps now best known for his role as Ben in George Romero's *Night of the Living Dead*. Green is wealthy, highly educated, and isolated from the black community. He becomes a vampire through an attack by his suicidal assistant, George Meda, who stabs him with an ancient African object contact with which leaves him addicted to blood. Hess then falls in love with Meda's wife, Ganja, who has come in search of her missing husband, marries her and turns her into a vampire. Hess's situation is characterized by his addiction and by his isolation from the rest of the black community. He lives in isolation on an estate in the wealthy, white enclave of Westchester County in New York, a home where he notes that he is the "only colored on the block." The movie contrasts him to his chauffeur, who is also the leader of a thriving

African American church. Hess eventually rejects the vampiric state and dies in the shadow of the cross. In considering *Ganja and Hess* we focus on mise-en-scène, cinematography and sound to examine how vampirism functions as a metaphor for addiction in the film and how through the use images of African and European art, of sound and of Christian imagery, Gunn explores questions of race and racism in the 1970s U.S.

From these early films we then turn to two works that students are often quite familiar with: *Blade* and the HBO series *True Blood*. We look at *Blade* as a story about race, miscegenation, and slavery, as Blade, like Shori in Butler's *Fledgling*, is a human-vampire hybrid. Is vampirism a metaphor for white identity in *Blade*? The film also features prominent yet rather obscure visual references to Asians and Asian-Americans. We explore the ways that the film's hero, Blade, comes to represent both a racial hybrid and a figure that is also a cyborg. Blade uses technology to fight vampires and to fight the vampire within himself, tying this element in the film directly back to Stoker's engagement with technology and science in *Dracula* and to the paradigms of race in that novel.

We end the course with the HBO series *True Blood*. Students view episode one of the first season of the show and also the special extras included on the boxed set of Season One, which includes mock advertisements for and against the "Vampire Rights Amendment" alluded to in the show and a "Mockumentary" about vampires after the "Great Revelation." These ads go along with various websites created by the show for the American Vampire League, a group that lobbies for vampire rights and the Fellowship of the Sun, a church devoted to the eradication of vampires. To study the series we look closely as well at the title sequence of the show, breaking down the images and discussing the ways in which they relate to the show's treatment of race, sexuality, religion and also notions of ecstatic experience. We then finally analyze *True Blood*, which premiered in September 2008, in relation to California's Proposition 8, the ballot measure designed to limit marriage in the state to only being legally valid between one man and one woman, which passed in November 2008. Prop 8, debate over which was extremely heated and public in California at the very time that *True Blood* premiered, seems to me and to my students to be a clear context for the series. I try, however, to keep our discussion away from reading *True Blood* as a simple analogy or allegory. Instead we focus on the question "Are vampire rights human rights?" This question, prompted by the special DVD features like the Vampire Rights Amendments ads, brings us to discussions of how society defines "the human," and "the citizen." How do legislators, jurists and individuals make decisions about who is entitled to civil and human rights and who is not?

The vampire, a liminal figure that is human and not-human, dead and yet living, provides a unique way for us to discuss these issues. The discussions have ranged to the questions of racial equality, immigration and rights for the LGBT community alluded to specifically in the series, and also questions of rights for those who have been convicted of crimes, specifically pedophiles, since vampires in the series are not strictly benevolent and can be dangerous. How does one determine the status of personhood and who should have the right to make such decisions?

We obviously don't find answers to these questions, but as one student remarked to me, the context of vampire narrative can create a "safe space" for students to speak about these issues. We are dealing with issues of identity and rights rather directly, but because the vampire is also a fictional creation, students can examine these questions through the characters and situations in the films and novels with a combination of engagement and distance that can allow for more open discourse. Throughout the course we also continually look back at earlier historical contexts in order to compare texts and contexts. How, for example, can we examine the "out of the coffin" themes of *True Blood* in connection to themes of homoeroticism in "Christabel," *Carmilla* and "Manor"? How do discourses of race in *True Blood* figure in comparison to how they appeared in earlier works such as Ewers' *Vampir* or *Blacula*?

This deep engagement with the vampire narrative and with its historical contexts has led to some extremely strong research papers. One very successful paper prompt asks students to compare Richard Matheson's 1954 *I Am Legend* with the 2007 film version starring Will Smith. Students use close analysis of the both the film and the novel as well as the historical contexts in which they are written. Matheson wrote his novel in the 1950s and set it in Compton, an area of Los Angeles that had a growing African American population at that time.[9] The 2007 movie, which casts a wildly popular African American actor as its lead, changes the racial dynamics of the story, just as the film's setting in New York had to also have an impact on its post–9/11 audience. Students have gone in many directions with this comparison, including investigations of primary materials related to the Cold War context of the novel and detailed studies of the artwork featured in the 2007 film, but each approach tied the question of the vampire to a very specific historical moment to terrific results.

Another highly successful prompt asked students to think about the 1897 portrayal of technological innovations in *Dracula* in relation to Bekka Black's 2010 *iDrakula*, a novel created out of text messages, web searches and email exchanges that centers around the iPhone. Students considered the role of technology in each case and the way that this technology shaped the novels' characterization as well as their treatments of gender and race.

The final assignment for the class has varied. I have, for example, used a traditional exam format, with short answers, ID terms and essays in a three-hour in-class exam for my large lecture. In the classes with smaller enrollments, however, I don't feel a need to test the students on the readings because the thinksheet assignments force them to read and write about all reading assignments. In these classes I have asked students to write a take-home essay of 800 to 1000 words an op-ed style and these have produced some excellent essays. They are to pretend that the editor of a major newspaper has asked contacted them to explain the current popularity of vampires based on their wide readings in vampire literature. They are to present their own thesis about why they think vampires have such current popularity using some of the earlier work that we have read as a major part of their argument.

The prompt attempts to get students to present original ideas in a concise way while all the while asking them to demonstrate their knowledge of our readings and the contexts that produced them. The assignment allows students to consider their own historical moment in relation the past and helps them to see how the knowledge they have gained about historical representation can aid them in thinking about their own social contexts and considering the ways that the themes of race, gender and sexuality that run through vampire narrative can be more fully understood and appreciated in relation to historical contexts.

So this discussion of my class can perhaps best be seen as the somewhat ironic story of how the creature of the night has been good for my day job. Remembering to "always historicize" cost me my name in lights, but asking students to consider the figure of the vampire not as timeless, but as a creature constructed and reconstructed within history, has helped us to consider in productive ways some of the most challenging political and social issues of our own time.

Notes

1. These ideas are at the core of my book project, "Dracula's Pulse," which examines Stoker in light of early Latin and German works and as a source for contemporary vampire narrative.

2. In order to attempt to keep student costs low I have tried to use electronic reserves or resources available on the web whenever possible and have attempted to cite useful ones in my notes here.

3. A wonderful source on these early materials and current research on them is *Magia Posthuma*, the blog of Niels K. Peterson.

4. There are numerous early translations of "Lenore" that can be found on the web. I have assigned this one by Rossetti: http://en.wikisource.org/wiki/Lenore_%28Rossetti%29. A translation of Goethe's "Braut" can be found in Collins 136–142 as well as widely on the web. "Wake Not the Dead!" can be found at http://www.sff.net/people/doylemacdonald/l_wakeno.htm or in Frayling (165–190). "Aurelia" is also in Frayling (190–207).

5. I ask students to purchase the collection edited by Williams, which contains the Byron, Polidori, and Coleridge we read along with *Carmilla* and Stoker's *Dracula*.

6. Murnau's film is now widely available on the web, but I strongly recommend the Kino version listed in the bibliography. Herzog shot his film with an international cast in multiple languages. After learning that a couple of confused non–German-speaking freshmen experienced the double terror of accidently watching the entire film in German without subtitles, I now to take extra care to guide students carefully through the viewing options available through DVDs and the Web.

7. Useful sources on Ewers are Brandenburg, Knobloch, Kugel, and Wikoff. See also Lampert-Weissig, which contains further bibliography.

8. *Ganja and Hess* has a complicated production history. Diawara and Klotman and the additional materials on the 2006 DVD are especially helpful for preparing to teach the film.

9. The Compton setting has been especially meaningful to my current UCSD students in light of the racist "Compton Cookout" incident connected to our campus. This event and the various responses to it brought national attention to the problematic campus climate at UCSD and other UC schools. UCSD campus climate has been a significant component in our discussions in the vampire class and very likely has potential relevance on other campuses as well. On the "Compton Cookout" and its impact see Archibold.

Bibliography

Arata, Stephen D. "The Occidental Tourist: Dracula and the Anxiety of Reverse Colonization." *Victorian Studies* 33.4 (1990): 621–45. Print.

Archibold, Randal. "California Campus Sees Uneasy Race Relations." *New York Times*. 26 Feb. 2010. Web. 14 Feb. 2013.

Arendt, Hannah. *Eichmann in Jerusalem: A Report on the Banality of Evil*. New York: Viking, 1964. Print.

Auerbach, Nina. *Our Vampires, Ourselves*. Chicago: University of Chicago Press, 1995. Print.

Barber, Paul. *Vampires, Burial, and Death: Folklore and Reality*. New Haven: Yale University Press, 1988. Print.

Black, Bekka. *iDrakula*. Naperville, IL: Sourcebooks, 2010. Print.

Blacula. Dir. William Crain. Perf. William Marshall, Vonetta McGee. American International Pictures, 1972. Film.

Blade. Dir. Stephen Norrington. Perf. Wesley Snipes. New Line Cinemas, 1998. Film.

Brandenburg, Ulrike. *Hanns Heinz Ewers (1871–1943): Von Der Jahrhundertwende Zum Dritten Reich: Erzählungen, Dramen, Romane 1903–1932*. New York: Peter Lang, 2003. Print.

Butler, Erik. *Metamorphoses of the Vampire in Literature and Film: Cultural Transformations in Europe, 1732–1933*. Rochester: Camden House, 2010. Print.

Butler, Octavia E. *Fledgling: Novel*. New York: Seven Stories Press, 2005. Print.

Casper, Kent, and Susan Linville. "Romantic Inversions in Herzog's *Nosferatu*." *German Quarterly* 64.1 (1991): 17–24. Print.

Cohen, Jeffrey Jerome, ed. *Monster Theory*. Minneapolis: University of Minnesota Press, 1996. Print.

Collins, Margo, ed. *Before the Count: British Vampire Tales: 1732–1897*. Camarillo, CA: Zittaw Press, 2007. Print.

Count Yorga, Vampire. Dir. Robert Quarry. 1970. MGM Home Entertainment, 2004. DVD.

Crawford, Heide. "The Cultural-Historical Origins of the Literary Vampire in Germany." *Journal of Dracula Studies* 7 (2005): n. pag. Web. 14 Feb. 2013.

Crenshaw, Kimberlé W. "Mapping the Margins: Intersectionality, Identity Politics, and Violence against Women of Color." *Stanford Law Review* 43 (1991): 1241–1299. Print.

Diawara, Manthia, and Phyllis R. Klotman. "Ganja and Hess: Vampires, Sex, and Addictions." *Black American Literature Forum* 25 (1991): 299–314. Print.

Dijkstra, Bram. *Evil Sisters: The Threat of Female Sexuality and the Cult of Manhood*. New York: Alfred A. Knopf, 1996. Print.

_____. *Idols of Perversity: Fantasies of Feminine Evil in Fin-De-siècle Culture*. New York: Oxford University Press, 1986. Print.

Eisner, Lotte H. *The Haunted Screen: Expressionism in the German Cinema and the Influence of Max Reinhardt*. Berkeley: University of California Press, 2008. Print.

Elsässer, T. *Weimar Cinema and After: Germany's Historical Imaginary*. New York: Routledge, 2000. Print.

Ewers, Hanns Heinz. *Fundvogel: Die Geschichte einer Wandlung*. Berlin: Sieben Stäbe, 1928. Print.

_____. *Vampir: Ein Virwilderter Roman in Fetzen und Farben*. Berlin: Sieben Stäbe, 1928. Print.

Ewers, Hanns Heinz, and Fritz Sallagar (trans.). *Vampire*. New York: John Day, 1934. Print.

Frayling, Christopher. *Vampyres: Lord Byron to Count Dracula*. Boston: Faber and Faber, 1991. Print.

Ganja & Hess. Dir. Bill Gunn. Perf. Duane Jones. 1973. Image Entertainment, 2006. DVD.

Herzog, Werner. *Stroszek; Nosferatu: Zwei Filmerzählungen*. München: Hanser, 1979. Print.

_____, dir. *Nosferatu: Phantom der Nacht*. Perf. Klaus Kinski. 1979. Anchor Bay Entertainment, 2002. DVD.

I Am Legend. Dir. Francis Lawrence. Perf. Will Smith. Warner Home Video, 2008. DVD.

Jameson, Fredric. *Postmodernism, or, the Cultural Logic of Late Capitalism*. Durham: Duke University Press, 1991. Print.

Jenkins, Jerry Rafiki. "Blacula and the Question of Blackness." *Blaxploitation Revisited*. Ed. Eric Charles Pierson, Christine Acham, and Gerald R. Butters. Santa Barbara: Screening Noir, 2005. Print.

Knobloch, Marion. *Hanns Heinz Ewers: Bestseller-Autor in Kaiserreich und Weimarer Republik*. Marburg: Tectum, 2002. Print.

Kracauer, Siegfried. *From Caligari to Hitler: A Psychological History of the German Film*. 1947. New York: Noonday Press, 1959. Print.

Kugel, Wilfried. *Der Unverantwortliche: Das Leben des Hanns Heinz Ewers*. Düsseldorf: Grupello, 1992. Print.

Lampert-Weissig, Lisa. "The Vampire as Dark and Glorious Necessity in George Sylvester Viereck's *House of the Vampire* and Hanns Heinz Ewers' *Vampir*." *Open Graves, Open Minds: Representations of Vampires from Enlightenment to the Present Day*, eds. Sam George and Bill Hughes. Manchester: Manchester University Press, forthcoming 2013.

Novotny, Lawrence. "Fear of a Blaxploitation Monster: Blackness as Generic Revision in AIP's Blacula." *Film International* 7, no. 3 (2009): 14–26. Print.

Marie de France. *The Lais of Marie De France*. Trans. Glyn S. Burgess. New York: Penguin, 1986. Print.

Matheson, Richard. *I Am Legend*. 1954. Cutchogue, NY: Buccaneer Books, 1991. Print.

Medovoi, Leerom. "Theorizing Historicity, Or the Many Meanings of Blacula." *Screen* 39.1 (1998): 1–21. Print.

Murnau, F. W., dir. *Nosferatu, eine Symphonie des Grauens*. 1922. Kino International, 2007. DVD.

Night of the Living Dead. Dir. George A. Romero. Perf. Duane Jones. 1968. Elite Entertainment, 2002. DVD.

Peterson, Niels K. *Magia Posthuma*. n.d. Web. 2 Feb 2013.

Prawer, S. S. *Nosferatu — Phantom Der Nacht*. London: BFI, 2004. Print.

Ranft, Michael. *Traktat von dem Kauen und Schmatzen der Toten in Gräbern*. Diedorf Ubooks, 2006. Print.

Ryan, Alan. *The Penguin Book of Vampire Stories*. New York: Penguin, 1987. Print.

Sconduto, Leslie. *Guillaume de Palerne: An English Translation of the 12th Century French Verse Romance*. Jefferson, NC: McFarland, 2004. Print.

Shelley, Mary Wollstonecraft. *Frankenstein: Or, the Modern Prometheus*. 1831. Ed. J. Paul Hunter. New York: Norton, 2012. Print.

Showalter, Elaine. *Sexual Anarchy: Gender and Culture at the Fin de Siècle*. New York: Viking, 1990. Print.

True Blood: The Complete First Season. Dir. Alan Ball. Home Box Office. Warner Home Video, 2009. DVD.

Ulrichs, Karl Heinrich. "Manor." 1885. Trans. Hubert Kennedy. *Embracing the Dark*. Ed. Eric Garber. Boston: Alyson, 1991. 98–108. Print.

_____. *Matrosengeschichten und Gedichte: Ein Lesebuch*. 1885. Berlin: Rosa Winkel, 1998.

Wikoff, Karin Elizabeth. "Hanns Heinz Ewers' Vampir." MA thesis, Cornell, 1995. Print.

Williams, Anne, et al. *Three Vampire Tales*. Boston: Houghton Mifflin, 2003. Print.

Outside/In: Using Vampires to Explore Diversity and Alienation in a College Classroom

U. Melissa Anyiwo

"I thought we were going to learn about Twilight, *instead I now understand more about race than I ever thought possible"*— FYS student, Final Reflection, Fall 2011[1]

For the last thirty years issues of diversity and inclusion have become central to the teaching pedagogies and mission statements of many institutions of higher education. However, while we now recognize the centrality of exposing students to excluded groups in society, these discussions are often limited to "islands of excellence" in traditional programs such as African American or women's and gender studies (AAC&U, 2010). While the majority of U.S. college campuses remain predominantly white, discussions of excluded and oppressed minorities in such courses can often alienate those in the majority (white, male, upper-middle class, heterosexual, Christian), creating notions of blame or feelings of guilt, which can shut down dialogues before they really begin, thereby retarding learning. This essay explores one alternative avenue to such discussions through the infusion of diversity into a course not coded as such.

Curry College's First Year Studies Inquiry course "Being Human: Life Through the Eyes of Outsiders and the Undead" was an attempt to introduce predominantly white students to concepts of difference in ways that avoided frustrating analytical roadblocks.[2] This link, connected with a Writing Workshop course, focused on the ways that outsiders see the world, and how insiders alienate and ultimately absorb those who think, feel, or look differently. By focusing on vampires (and other forms of the (un)dead in Writing Workshop), students were able to examine the ways they have been indoctrinated into particularly American norms: how they see the world, how they evaluate and understand difference, how they react to and deal with such perceived differences, and how groups are assigned normative values that change over time. Both classes offered models of inclusive teaching by providing alternatives to traditional modes of minority content and ideas about difference without it being labeled or coded as such through a lens that, arguably, included everyone in the conversation.

This essay explicitly explores the uses of the vampire narrative in the classroom to expose students to the varieties of social construction and the absorption of the Outsider through the use of two of our three key readings, Polidori's "The Vampyre" (1819) and

45

Monica Jackson's "The Ultimate Diet" (2004), and mention of our third, Roy Thomas' graphic novel adaptation of Bram Stoker's *Dracula* (2010). By exploring the uses of each text, this essay demonstrates ways that students were able to explore notions of difference without becoming caught up in traditional dichotomies that more often than not retard learning. It also provides a tool to illustrate how the uses of non-traditional content can effectively help create engaged, socially aware, empathetic students. As one student reflected at the end of the semester, "All students should take first year seminar because I believe it expands your mind and makes you think in ways you have not before" (FYS student, Final Reflection, Fall 2011).

Constructing Identity

> *I thought I knew who I was when I got to Curry, or maybe I just didn't care.... I only knew people who were like me and I thought that was because of where I lived. Now I know I chose to ignore who I was and what made me this way. I like myself a whole lot more now and have lots of different friends from this class who I never would have talked to before. But I still don't want to be a vampire*— FYS student, Final Reflection, Fall 2011

As a child I loved to read. My mother, a Nigerian immigrant and former math teacher, still loves to highlight her perception of my perpetual oddity by relating endless tales of how I was always reading, in bed, under the bed, in the back of the car, in the dark with a torch. "She never spoke," she loves to say. "She was always just reading!" Yet, despite my love of the written word, I never once saw myself in the works I consumed. I was a lower-middle class black girl with divorced Nigerian immigrant parents. Girls like me were not the subjects of British literature, nor did people like me write Brit lit. It, like most Western literature, was as white and exclusive as can be. Non-whites were the outsiders, the monsters on the fringes, or the exotic terrors of dark continents who needed to be destroyed or at least commodified and forcibly assimilated. In the 1970s, my formative years, few in Great Britain seemed to believe in such things as racism or the impact such attitudes have on children. Indeed the first song I remember hearing at public school was "10 Little Niggers," in which children who looked like me were systematically slaughtered for the enjoyment of a white audience. The first time I got in real trouble at that same school was when, consumed with shame-filled rage, I chased a boy around the playground for calling me a nigger.[3] It was no wonder that I lost myself in fantasy both in the pages of books and in my fathomless imagination. At eleven, my final year of primary school, my librarian solemnly handed me a worn copy of Bram Stoker's *Dracula* from a secret stash under her desk. "I think you'll enjoy this," she said to the little girl who spent her lunch times curled up on the dusty floor of the tiny library hiding in books, while the rest of the student body played outside. She was so right. While I'm sure most people who read *Dracula* identify with Jonathan Harker, or Mina Murray, I encountered a protagonist as darkly alienated as I, the misunderstood outsider yearning for entrance into a society which would rather kill than accept him. Thus began my love affair with the vampire and all things dark and Gothic.

Why do I tell you this?

A core objective of First Year Studies is for students to describe what they value and how values can shape their decisions. Knowing who you are and how that impacts your choices is a central element of reflective teaching and learning. Thus, knowing who I am and why helps explain why I chose to teach the vampire narrative as a doorway to understanding race/racism, and why I chose to teach it primarily from the perspective of the outsider. Outsiders see the world differently than those privileged to be on the inside; understanding their perspective allows students to realize that their understanding of the world is not the only reality.

"Being Human: Life Through the Eyes of Outsiders, Monsters, and the Undead," a First Year Inquiry

I began to expand my mind viewing things from a different perspective. Although I am not a huge fan of vampires, I began to find more interest and meaning to them more than ever before— FYS student, Final Reflection, Fall 2011

Curry College, a small private, predominantly white school just outside of Boston, Massachusetts, has, for the last five years, been exploring new ways to encourage retention and academic success.[4] The concept of linking multiple classes by theme is, to my mind, an ingenious way to help students form a collective bond within and without the classroom. This allows for a safe place to express ideas, allowing everyone, the professors included, the freedom to explore and interpret ideas in multidisciplinary and interdisciplinary ways to help foster intellectual inquiry. "Being Human" was linked with a Writing Workshop class to allow students to see how both a literature professor (Brian Duchaney) and an historian approached the myth. Given that the Writing Workshop was intended to look at the broad theme of monsters (both real and imagined) while First Year Seminar focused on vampires, we created a description that would be both general and specific enough to draw in the audience we were hoping for:

> This First Year Studies course, linked with Writing Workshop, explores the ways that outsiders see humanity. What does it take to be a "human being"? What separates us from animals? Can a vampire be a citizen? Can a monster be "good"? By reading and writing about those on the fringes of society, both the real and the imagined, you will attempt to answer those questions. In this way you will reach a richer, deeper understanding of yourself and our world in new and darker ways [Curry College Course Catalog, 2010/11].

The intent was to draw in students interested in the monster narrative including the expected Twihards already familiar with the widest concept of the vampire, and perhaps open to exploring it in different ways.[5] Both courses were split into interlocking modules with common objectives containing core readings (often the same ones from different perspectives) that included music, film, scholarly articles, and graphic novels, all intended to illustrate the connection between the monster narrative and our concepts of fear and alienation.

The vampire narrative follows the same construct as all myths in society. By way of an introduction on the first day of class, we expressed it as follows:

1. Fear: myths (both creatures and vampires) are created by a society to highlight and give voice to our deepest fears.
2. Outsiders and Alienation: we create monsters to help us visualize those fears and illustrate what we are supposed to do with those who refuse to conform.
3. Consumption: in order to tame our fears we consume, commodify, in essence defang them, then spit them back out in new forms that reflect changing values and mores.

As we explained that first day, from a literary standpoint, the vampire exists as a being that parallels humanity but exists outside of it (since, you know, they're mostly dead). They look like us, act like us, drink, drive cars, date, and want to exist. Moreover, the ways that the myth has changed over the years perfectly tracks the rise and fall of different social values, beliefs, commodification of minorities, scientific and technological developments; in short, the progress (both good and bad) of humanity. In this sense, we sought to answer one question repeatedly throughout the semester: What do the undead teach us about our own lives?

Michelle Loris explores the usefulness of using a variety of texts in the classroom in *Using the Novel to Teach Multiculturalism* (2006):

> The novel is both a literary work of art and a representation of human experience, including specific experiences of gender, race, ethnicity, and class. This approach — teaching students to read the novel both as literary art as well as a literary representation of social reality — lends itself to examining the historical, social, and political complexities inherent in any discussion of novels by multicultural writers [54].

I would argue that using art as an expression of the human experience applies to all cultural artifacts used in the classroom from music to film. Therefore the texts the students read ranged from scholarly articles to concept albums such as Nine Inch Nails' *The Downward Spiral* (1994) to film such as *Nosferatu* (1922) and beyond.[6] In this way the students were able to both maximize their own learning style but also experience the vast ways that culture expresses its fears, and how to find meaning in seemingly unlikely places.

Fear or Meet Your Monsters: John W. Polidori's "The Vampyre"

> *Vampires have evolved over the years and we researched the meaning behind [each] theme. This alone had blown my mind. I had no idea that vampires have so many different images and that people had developed meaning behind the vampire. First Year Seminar had changed my views and thoughts about vampires completely*— FYS student, Final Reflection, Fall 2011

The core objective of the first module was for students to *define fear in relation to cultural norms and your own life.* Polidori's "The Vampyre; A Tale" (1819) was an excellent text for exploring the multiple elements that go into our fears and how our fears reflect our indoctrination. The reflective essay students were assigned to write and discuss at the end of the module was, quite simply, "In what ways does Polidori play on the fears/concerns of people of his day and how do those connect to our current fears?" Such a paper required significant scaffolding through lectures, minute papers, and discussion. The Minute Papers were a quick way to wake up the students' brains by allowing them to write for one to three minutes about anything related to a given prompt. The prompts in this module were "Who Do You Fear?" "My Greatest Nightmare"; "The Monsters in My World"; "How We Know What to Fear"; and "In what ways does Ruthven seem familiar?" The lectures most often provided the historical context such as "The Vampire Next Door" and "The One-Drop Rule & Passing."

We approached Polidori from two perspectives: firstly from the perspective of the insider Aubrey, and then from the outsiders Polidori and Lord Ruthven/the Earl of Marsden. This reading came in week three after the students had already explored the monsters in their own lives (real or imagined, i.e., the school bully). In addition, we read Jules Zanger's

Metaphor and Metonymy: The Vampire Next Door (1997)[7] in order to help illustrate the ways in which westerners in Polidori's time shared the same fears about difference that we express today. According to Dunn-Mascetti, "a vampire is a perfectly polished mirror on which we project all our dreams and fancies, sexual and intellectual, and the projection endows this strange creature with an attraction we find impossible to resist" (42). Thus, "The Vampyre" is really a story about repressive social norms, of the importance of maintaining one's social position, the fear of the Other, and the fear of succumbing to one who only *appears* to be like you. Written in a period in which social class was becoming increasingly fluid (by English standards) and people were marrying outside of their narrowly enforced boundaries, a strange outsider with the right clothes and right accent could convince people of his position and therefore overturn expectations about blood and divine rights. The source of the fear in Polidori is not the bloodsucker; instead it is the insidious nature of class and position.

The American students had some difficulty understanding the obsession with class, but they understood the power of appearance and position. This allowed us to explore notions of passing. In a world where there are no passports, no forensics, and no digital photography, how do you know someone is who they say they are? It is one thing to suggest you are a blue blood when you're not. It is quite another to suggest you are human when you are the walking undead. Or indeed to suggest you are white when underneath you are something else entirely. This led us to the American one-drop rule, an idea that was not that far removed from the release of Polidori's work. Both ideas reached their height in the early nineteenth century with challenges to antebellum slavery in America, and pressures from colonials in the British Empire to be treated as citizens. Both reflected the growing fear that the outside might not be an accurate reflection of what lies inside us. This created parallel fears on both sides of the Atlantic, each related to race and class in their own ways. Explicitly connecting the two helped the students understand the socially constructed nature of race and the ability of fiction to reflect deeply embedded social fears. Thus much of the discussion of Polidori centered on the fears we are told to worry about.

The main characters in the story, like Polidori himself, are most concerned with social appearance, something first semester first years can easily relate to. In their Minute Papers about what they feared most, they most often expressed their fear of not being liked, of not making friends, of sitting unwanted in their dorm room. From this point, we were able to look at the Polidori's experiences on the fringes of Romantic author Lord Byron's exclusive social circle, with eyes tailored to understanding what it means to be excluded because of one's birth, something that we have no control over. Polidori's greatest crime, according to Lord Byron, was that he worked at a trade. Today, being a doctor is one of the most reputable occupations, but to the landed gentry in 1816, Polidori was an embarrassing hanger-on, especially since he relied on working for a living to make ends meet. To be disliked because of one's birth is something that the students were able to relate to, which made Lord Ruthven somewhat more accessible and thus sympathetic as a character. The fact that Lord Ruthven is only ever seen through the eyes of the true protagonist, Aubrey, allowed the students to recognize the problems of being denied a voice because you do not fit in with those who control the transmission of image. Conflating that with our fears today, they could make the connection to the view of Mexicans as illegal immigrants and criminals, creatures who wish to invade our nation and undermine the very things that make it great. All presented through a news industry that rarely offers the voices of the group being denigrated, and in this case reduces all brown people to one nationality.

Allowing the students to explore their fears and then connect them to the tale of Lord Ruthven required a step-by-step process involving both lectures and constant discussion. Yet by the end of the module they were all able to successfully write their reflection papers addressing the central question connecting the fears expressed in Polidori's story with those of today. The reflection and minute papers also served as a constantly evolving learning journal letting them see how their opinions and understanding developed or altered with each new piece of the puzzle. The more they explored the multiple elements that go into the construction of values the more they began to question their own beliefs and the artificial divisions they made.[8]

Outsiders/Alienation or Wishing I Was Comfortably Numb: Monica Jackson's "The Ultimate Diet"

From the start of First Year Seminar until now, I have developed as a Curry member in the process of what college is all about. When I started at Curry I never imagined I'd be hanging with a black kid from Mattapan [sic]. I told myself we'd have nothing in common. Now I know those thoughts were given to me by someone else and had nothing to do with what I believed. Now I'm gonna talk to someone before judging them and stop putting people in boxes made by someone else. Boxes are stupid but I'm not"— FYS student, Final Reflection, Fall 2011

This module more specifically explored alienated outsiders from their perspective. The core objective asked students to *explain the ways that specific groups (real and/or imagined) are marginalized and how those attitudes may change over time.* Monica Jackson's "The Ultimate Diet" (2004) served multiple functions for the students and provided both obvious and less obvious evidence of the excluded outsider knocking at the door trying desperately to be seen and welcomed in. In addition, we focused on a parallel reading of Eminem's seminal album, *The Slim Shady LP* (1999), which provided a perfect audio visualization of the impact of exclusion on those born with no access to the American Dream. Both texts thus illustrated the desire of those on the outside to be welcomed in and experience the privileges of whiteness and wealth that they are constantly told by the media are the only avenues to happiness. The ability of students to delve more deeply into music many of them had heard a million times was an important tool for connecting the world to the vampire narrative. One student, a huge fan of the rapper, wrote,

> Before the course had started, when I would listen to music I never really thought of meaning and messages in songs. I would simply listen to them and enjoy them.... First Year Seminar had expanded my viewings on music for I had never viewed music this way before [FYS Student, Final Reflection, Fall 2011].

We began this module by exploring the differences between insiders and outsiders, those elements that make some people coded as "normal" and others "abnormal." By starting with the students' experiences at high school, we examined the key category of insider and considered why certain groups are accepted as "popular." Having already scaffolded this topic through an exploration of fear, the students were primed to recognize the impact of their personal history on their understandings of alienation. We then explored who decided what attributes are valued by society and why, and how those values are particularly American (a nation where brawn is so much more valued than brains). With the beginnings of a thought process about indoctrination, we were able to begin thinking about the ways that groups are stereotyped, excluded, devalued, and how the process of devaluing can be reversed as social norms change. Thus, vampires began as terrors, nightmares, the most terrifying of creatures. Now they are sparkly antiheroes more likely to kill your dog than drink you to death. We then applied the same development model to other nightmare groups–racial minorities, women, homosexuals, Catholics, Jews, the underclass—each of these and more has at one time in history been used as the repository of our darkest fears and treated accordingly.

The purpose of *The Slim Shady LP* was to posit the question *What would an outsider be willing to do to be let in*? The very nature of exclusion is that the Other needs to recognize their own Otherness and desire the elements they are denied. Eminem's album follows a narrative that highlights the glaring gap between rich and poor and the illusion of a level playing field. Poor people are born and remain poor, while rich people are beautiful, exotic, feared, and ultimately despised by the Other forced to exist alongside them. Thus, the students were able to discuss the opposing myths of the American Dream. The vampire, almost always presented as an aristocratic (rich) white male, represents the human obsession with wealth and the lengths people will go to get it. While students had to listen to the entire album, reading it as they would any other text, I focused on two core tracks—"If I Had" and "Rock Bottom."[9] Beyond the general concepts of the album, the students' first piece of homework was to deconstruct "Rock Bottom" by listening and connecting it to the topic of alienation.

The devastating nature of Eminem's experiences provided a stark contrast to their internalized prejudices about the poor and forced them to reconsider the source of those prejudices and the purpose of highlighting differences. The privileges of whiteness and wealth are elements that marry Eminem with the vampire narrative and Monica Jackson's "The Ultimate Diet." After all, as DeBrandt argues in *Angelus Populi*,

> the virtue of physical attractiveness somehow justifies even the worst actions; on some level, we seem to believe people like that are just taking their due. The resentment we feel towards them is balanced by our desire to *be* them, to have what they have and to do what they do. It's that crucial point, the ability to transform a victim into a fellow victimizer, that makes the modern-day vampire so attractive ... and why we turn a blind eye to the cruelty of those we consider our betters [7].

While Eminem's alter ego Slim Shady is willing to fantasize about doing anything to be rich, Jackson's protagonist, Keeshia, is truly willing to kill because the reward (beauty/ popularity) more than outweighs the consequences (the draining of human life). In this context, "The Ultimate Diet" really allowed for dialogue about the Other and fundamentally shifted the ways that the students saw the world. Because of the ways the course had been scaffolded, the students were able to extract those areas of the text that explicitly illustrated the impact of being Othered or being on the outside of society, along with the sense that you are constantly stereotyped, misjudged, and denied the same entrance into the world as those in the majority.[10] Because Jackson is of African descent, her experiences pervade the tale, giving the students a tiny glimpse into the realities of being black in a predominantly white nation. From the start Jackson places Keeshia and her best friend Jelly in a real world in which whites are exotic strange creatures to be constantly feared because of the insurmountable power of white privilege. From the bleeding heart liberals who decide all black children should be tested for aptitudes in science and math and then removed from their communities, to the perception that "white folks don't think much of fat black women" (4) these are women who see whites as the most threatening elements in their world. Moreover, as Americans they are exposed to the same elements of mainstream culture as everyone else, yet seen through their eyes such culture does little more than denigrate, stereotype, and remind them of their unworthiness. Keeshia believes that her weight and her blackness are the greatest barriers to her happiness. If only she were white she would get that promotion; if only she were thin, she would get that man: "If we were back in the projects, we'd be getting fucked" (4). She believes that her identity is fixed and unchangeable but defined by those outside her (she never really diets, just see-saws through various fads). Thus, she figures out how to become a vampire so she can be slender and irresistible, just like her beautiful, promiscuous, serial-killing neighbor. As she says when she first sees the Nubian vampire:

> What if I could get little like that skinny heifer moving in across the way? My life would be perfect. Everything would be easy. Everyone would admire me. I wouldn't have to deal with my goddamn job and my asshole boss.... I'd have the man of my dreams, fuck, I'd have a man, period [6].

The short story takes place today and is therefore able to play on our knowledge of vampires[11] and reflect our obsessions with body image and success without hard work. "The Ultimate Diet" was, however, the greatest surprise for the class. They were intrigued by the idea of a vampire tale written by an African American and concerned about the world she might create. Their privileged status[12] and their internalized assumptions about vampires, race, and gender were really challenged by this funny, erotic (pornographic for them), short tale. Although I had specifically asked them to compare and contrast the short story with "If I Had" ("I'm tired of being white trash, broke and always poor"), they were quick to connect the story to Eminem's "Guilty Conscience," which actually fit better both in tone and content. If the world has decided that you are worthless, if what you are is more important than who you are, how far would you go to cross that divide? Keeshia understands that becoming a vampire means she will become a killer. But that is not nearly as important as the fact that she will finally be someone considered beautiful and therefore successful.

> I'm getting what I've always deserved. For the first time in my life I'm going to be accepted and admired. I'm going to get me a life, even if I die trying [22].

Her superficiality is indicative of the world our students were raised in where appearance is everything, just as it was in Polidori's day. In such a construct, being different is dangerous, fitting in becomes the only cultural norm worth aspiring to, whatever the costs to your humanity. By this point in the semester they were able to connect the expectations and fears they had expressed with the indoctrination they experienced.

Concluding Thoughts or Finding Empathy Through Consumption

First Year Seminar has helped develop my mind into exploring content from a scholarly perspective ... [it] has expanded my mind to view everyday entertainment from a totally different angle— FYS student, Final Reflection, Fall 2011

"Being Human" ... offered students the opportunity to re-evaluate their assumptions about race, gender, and social expectations in order to help create a permanent sense of empathy for those who are different. Through the use of vampire literature the students slowly took a path from judgment based on internalized expectations to moving beyond the surface to see the world in dramatically different ways. The final step in their journey came in the consumption model where the core objective was to *recognize how popular culture is used to promote and express the things we value (and don't)*. Of course they had been tangentially exploring consumption all along, and the ways they had been indoctrinated into a narrow set of values with superficial unattainable goals. The darkly brilliant concept album *Antichrist Superstar* (1996) by Marilyn Manson illustrated these ideas. The opening lines of the album functioned as a doorway to allow students to explore the ways the things we fear are tamed through consuming them, and then spat back out in new forms that reflect that historical moment. Having now understood the process of naming/exposing our fears and creating fictional monsters to contain them, the students were able to express a greater sense of understanding about the contrived lines of difference and how it is fear of the unknown (death, aging, etc.) that drives those fears. Brian Hugh Warner, lead singer of Marilyn Manson, focuses on the fear at home, the vampire next door (i.e., "Man That You Fear").[13] Indeed, Suzy McKee Charnas argues in "Meditations in Red: On Writing the Vampire Tapestry" (1997), "the monstrous is and always has been located primarily not outside us, in mythical creatures, but in our human neighbors on this planet, and sometimes in ourselves" (59). No wonder then that since World War II the monsters have become increasingly sympathetic to the point where they are (in many cases) merely banal. It is hard to create a mythical creature who is more horrifying than a Nazi stormtrooper, a Ted Bundy, or indeed the date rapist.

The graphic novel adaptation of Bram Stoker's *Dracula* by Roy Thomas was an excellent way to close the intellectual loop, allowing them to compare and contrast the three core vampires we encountered (Lord Ruthven, Keeshia, Dracula) and connect them to the values of that society.[14] This adaptation was more closely based on the 1970s Marvel comic than the original novel, making Dracula far more sympathetic and far more central to the plot. He remains the Outsider, but here we empathize with him, and in the words of one of our Twihards "just wished those mean men would let him live happily ever after with Mina who should be happy she gets to be pretty and young forever" (FYS, Final Reflection, Fall 2012). That was quite a different response to Lord Ruthven whom we encountered at the start of the semester and certainly a very different response than would have been expressed in 1897 when the original text was published.[15] At the start of the semester the majority of the students felt no empathy at all for the vampire. By the time we reached Dracula, empathy was their first response.

Their response to Dracula actually mirrored the progress of the vampire narrative, and the overall intent of the course, from fear to alienation to consumption to empathy. By recognizing the purpose of encapsulating fear in the body of the outsider (real or imagined), they were able to take a step back from the indoctrination they have absorbed since birth and become citizens who asked questions about their world rather than merely accepting normality. As one of our more skeptical students wrote:

> My views on stories, music, and images will never be the same after taking this course.... My views about topics such as vampires have completely changed because now I know there are deeper meaning behind just viewing or listening for your entertainment. I will never see the world the same way again, but as Anyiwo kept telling us we probably never even saw the world in the first place we just walked around being comfortably numb. Now I'm awake. You cant unsee [*sic*] what you know.... I believe all students should take this course because it demonstrates what college is all about which is exploring deeper meaning to life [FYS student, Final Reflection, Fall 2011].

Ultimately, the vampire became the image through which students were able to explore their environments and the lens through which they were able to understand many of their concerns. While vampires might not have been their first choice for a first-year seminar, it proved to be the intellectual surprise that inspired them and turned even the most disengaged students into curious actors who could find meaning in things they had previously ignored and merely absorbed. More importantly it proved a truly inclusive model to allow them entrance into discussions of race, gender, and difference helping to create empathetic citizens primed to make a difference in the world.

Notes

1. Students were asked to write a 1,000-word final reflection that answered the question "What I Learned from First Year Studies." I have kept the quotes anonymous to preserve their privacy but the modes of expression are authentically theirs.

2. Curry College has around 2,000 students, predominantly residential, with a 97 percent white population. The school costs the average student $46,000 a year, limiting the pool of students by both class and ethnic background.

3. No, that little boy did not get in trouble. My teacher Mr. Smith told me to calm down and sentenced me to two hours of detention. He informed me that "nigger" was just another name for blacks so I should get used to hearing it.

4. First Year Studies links are capped at 15 students to encourage a manageable cohort.

5. The problems of advising students into this link that met every day proved problematic. But the small class size (12) actually served to foster a much more rewarding experience for both the professors and the students.

6. Concept albums were used in each module. For Fear we used Nine Inch Nails' *The Downward Spiral*. For Consumption we used Marilyn Manson's *AntiChrist Superstar*. In addition, they deconstructed the lyrics to Pink Floyd's "Comfortably Numb" from the 1979 concept album *The Wall* (EMI).

7. Zanger's article was as dense as it got over the semester. Part of our purpose for reading it was to help them learn how to read something they feel like they could not understand and to start to read like a college student rather than a high schooler where they can just get the CliffsNotes and have everything explained to them.

8. The structure of the link, with the students meeting every day, also aided in the deconstruction of typical high school divisions. The class truly became like a little family with each student having their well-defined roles and, like any family, they protected each other like little lions whenever an outsider came into their space. It did result in students who would never have even spoken to each other in other classes becoming close friends like the football player and the slightly odd nerd, aiding in retention and acculturation to college.

9. The reading of this album had been scaffolded by having the students deconstruct the aforementioned Pink Floyd track "Comfortably Numb."

10. The students had two lecture/discussions on Stereotyping and Identity, Tribes, and Peer Pressure.

11. For example, she searches for details about vampires on the Internet and watches reruns of *Buffy the Vampire Slayer*.

12. All but one was white, and all of them came from financially secure backgrounds.

13. Warner looked at serial killers and school shootings like Columbine High.

14. As with reading song lyrics, the reading of the graphic novel had been slowly scaffolded over the course of the semester, beginning with the viewing of the silent movie *Nosferatu* (1922) (which they found surprisingly scary), to an animated version of *The Walking Dead*. For tips on teaching with graphic novels see Stephen E. Tabachnick, *Teaching the Graphic Novel* (New York: The Modern Language Association of America, 2009).

15. Ruthven actually became an adjective that the students used to describe a bad date, i.e., "How was last night?" "It sucked, I was totally Ruthvened." I guess you never know what they will take away from their learning.

Bibliography

Charnas, Suzy McKee. "Meditations in Red: On Writing the Vampire Tapestry." *Blood Read: The Vampire as Metaphor in Contemporary Culture*. Ed. J. Gordon and V. Hollinger. Philadelphia: University of Pennsylvania Press, 1997. Print.

DeBrandt, Don. "Angelus Populi." *Five Seasons of* Angel: *Science Fiction and Fantasy Authors Discuss Their Favorite Vampire.* Ed. Glenn Yeffeth. Dallas: BenBella, 2004. Print.

Loris, Michelle. "Using the Novel to Teach Multiculturalism." *Teaching the Novel Across the Curriculum: A Handbook for Educators.* Ed. Colin C. Irvine. Westport, CT: Greenwood Press, 2008. Print.

Eminem, Marky Bass, and Jeff Bass. *The Slim Shady* LP. Santa Monica: Aftermath Entertainment/Interscope Records, 1999. Sound recording.

Jackson, Monica. "The Ultimate Diet." *Dark Thirst.* Ed. Omar Tyree and Angela Allen. New York: Pocket Books, 2004. Kindle Edition.

Manson, Marilyn. *Antichrist Superstar.* Nothing/Interscope, 1996. Sound recording.

Zanger, Jules. "Metaphor and Metonymy: The Vampire Next Door." *Blood Read: The Vampire as Metaphor in Contemporary Culture.* Ed. J. Gordon and V. Hollinger. Philadelphia: University of Pennsylvania Press, 1997. Print.

"Can you blush?":
Racing the Vampiric Body

Crystal Boson

At first blush, vampire movies are hardly considered to be sites of complex racial commentary. Literary and cinematic versions and recreations of *Dracula* and the *Twilight* movies present vampiric bodies as undead and unraced. White. There are, however, undead bodies that displace this notion. In *Blade II*, a fleeting, interracial interaction between two vampires illustrates the complicated relationship between the undead and whiteness. Rhinehart, who has been trained to kill Blade, asks him, "Can you blush?" This pithy question both addresses Blade's racial and species transgressions, the viewer's eyes are immediately drawn to the racial implications. The curiosity of Blade's body opens a much wider discourse regarding the undead. While vampires are usually known for their pallor, there are darker undead to be explored; cinematic figures like Blade and Blacula are joined by literary bodies, such as soucouyants, Shori from *Fledgling* and the Ghanaian "Firemen." In each of these incarnations, the Undead of Color confront power, race, and privilege that affect both the quick and the not-so-dead.

I first introduced the Undead of Color in my African American literature class. I was met with a great deal of confusion; after all, there is no such thing as Black Vampires, and this class is about African American literature. In the public imagination, the best-known Black vampire, Blade, is a one-off. Vampire bodies are supposed to be the undead forms of normative bodies, and normative bodies are white. When I use the term "Undead of Color," I am not just referencing vampires that happen to be Black; they also lack the same cultural perceptions, socio-cultural positioning within their given texts as "normative" vampires and are not afforded the privileges associated with neither whiteness nor vampirism.

The goal of the course was to address issues of racism, colorism, sexism, and class struggles that are written about and by African Americans. While the students engaged the canonical texts, the introduction of the Undead of Color brought about a sense of newness and tangibility to the topics. The inclusion of Afro-futurism, Black sci-fi and other pop-cultural genres served as a starting platform to introduce new ways of conceptualizing the Black body, living or undead.

The introduction of the Undead of Color always hinges on the idea of the subaltern. If the subaltern is never truly allowed to speak, are Black Vampires subaltern bodies? In most cases, they are able to successfully fight against the various colonialist systems that seek to oppress them; are these bodies marked as subaltern solely because of race, or do their various forms of empowerment[1] mark them as something else? When teaching about bodies of color, living or undead, it is vital to emphasize the difference between colonialism and empire. In cases of semi-vocal subalterns like Blade or Shori, it is possible for empire to represent "the control of physical and human resources of given territories by external forces, while 'colony' stresses the settlement of such territories by outsiders on lands held by the 'empire'" (Leistyna 3). It is both possible for the colonizing sites to be the actual physical and cultural landscapes, which is the case for Blade or the soucouyants and for the bodies of the Undead of Color to be actual contested sites, as is largely the case for Shori and the Firemen.

All of the above-mentioned Undead of Color not only add a layer of richness to the canon of vampiric lore, but they are evident ways to talk about post-colonial theory and racialized conceptions of the body. When addressing the idea of the vampiric undead to a classroom, the ideas of power, seductiveness, control and sexuality are instinctively written onto their presumed White/de-racialized bodies. Most often, when Black Vampires are introduced in films, such as *Blacula* or *Blade*, they are desexualized, hyper violent, or highly animalistic. Introducing into the classroom the vast literary body of racialized, undead bodies allows students to clearly address issues of race, sexuality, power, and the idea of subaltern bodies with multiple subject positions.[2]

Before engaging with Black Vampires, the students had read Kathy Wilson's *Your Negro Tour Guide*. In this text, Wilson speaks directly to situations where she feels disenfranchised. The students were then asked to compare Wilson's reactions to racist situations to Blade's reaction to heavily raced situations. The students observed that both Blade and Wilson utilized sarcasm and rhetorical confrontation to counteract instances of rhetorical violence. In class I posed the question, "Is language a suitable weapon for Black Vampires to counteract racism and physical violence?" The students formed groups and compared the reactions of Blade[3] and Shori to instances of physical violence and racism enacted against them by the white vampires that meant them harm. The Black Vampires speaking verbally against the racism and intended violence exhibited by the White Vampires established their role as vocal subalterns; they are literally speaking against the violence that is directed towards them. They are aware that the White Vampires wish them harm, and see them as lesser beings, yet assert their agency, cultural positionality, and personal power through both speech and physical action.

Undead of Color bodies can also serve as theoretical frameworks to introduce the concepts of the subaltern and vocal subalterns. They are marginalized within already disenfranchised communities, and are expected to die out, or though their own agency address the problems and dangers that various other groups present them with. When they engage in actions that are self-libratory, they are misinterpreted or ignored by outside discourses. For example, in class we examined the NRA's rhetoric calling for gun control when the Black Panthers issued a call to arm Black communities. The rhetoric of weaponized Black bodies as dangerous was juxtaposed with Blade's necessity to self-arm to defend himself both against the dominant, Undead community and from living police officers. The students discussed the ways that the in-movie media coverage of Blade as a dangerous psychopath was similar to the rhetoric used against the Black Panthers; both were deemed as deviant threats to the larger society. Using Blade as a fictional, subaltern example, I encouraged my students to find more literary and historic examples of rhetoric surrounding Black bodies and their positionality as community dangers. The students noted that when the bodies they researched engaged in actions that were self-liberating, they were misinterpreted or ignored by multiple communities and embodiments.

Before we could reach that point of discussion, we had to figure out who the "Undead of Color" are. I first taught this course in 2009; my students had no access to *Blacula*, and considered Blade to be a one-off. Popular conception holds that undead bodies are normative bodies, just not living ones. Normative bodies are not historically or culturally Black bodies. The vampires I taught about were not constructed as Undead bodies that happened to have dark skin. These bodies lacked the same cultural perceptions, socio-cultural positioning within their respective texts, and the privileges associated with whiteness or vampirism. While normal vampires are rich, sexy, and powerful, Black vampires are dangerous, societal deviants, and lone destroyers. They just don't look the part. My students told me that vampires have blonde hair, piercing blue eyes, and ghostly white skin. By having my students confront this idea of normalized whiteness, they were able to access how whiteness has been rendered both normal and invisible.

The idea of an Undead of Color body decenters the idea of racial invisibility and calls attention to ideas of colonialism, power, and the subaltern that are often overlooked in larger conversations about vampires. These vampiric bodies are markedly different than the unraced, normative undead, whose power and sexual prowess is never questioned.[4] By expanding the conversations of both Undead and "normal" bodies past the idea of invisible whiteness, students are encouraged to re-evaluate their conception of fantastical and realistic bodies, their relationships with power and representation, and the role they play in the cultural imagination. Here, the idea of the "Undead" can be expanded from just vampires to a much wider range of possibilities. These bodies are not just the black-caped monsters of old, or the more recent, sparkly pretty boy; the new Undead are non-normative bodies.

The term "of Color" does as much rhetorical heavy lifting as "Undead." Rather than existing within the constructed racial binary of either Blackness or whiteness, the idea of being "of Color" grounds the representation in a bi-directional, transnational discourse. The bodies explored here are not just "Black" in the conception most widely held within the United States. They are also diasporic bodies, classed bodies, gendered bodies, and bodies that flow across and beyond racial lines. They are situated within their own cultures and fight to exist in such. The term Undead of Color is not chosen lightly; its heavily weighted rhetorical positionality allows the student to situate each body within its own cultural context, and step away from the conception of these bodies examined being "normal" vampires, only blacker.

The vampiric bodies here explored cross various genre boundaries. They exist in film, folklore, and literature, yet all within a similar plane of difference. Each of these Undead bodies: Blade and Blacula from their self-entitled films, Shori from Octavia Butler's *Fledgling*, and the mythical soucouyants exists within various forms of colonial landscapes where they are forced to recognize their own marginal positionality and carve out for themselves a space that is both functional and libratory. An exception to this idea is the Ghanaian Firemen. They are humans who are forced by the colonial system to steal blood and life from their communities to feed the colonizer. They live within a direct colonial construct and are forced to internalize the system to ensure their own survival. Their violence and cultural cannibalism has forced these living bodies into the realm of the horrible and mythical, and they serve as racialized cautionary tales against the internalization of colonialism.[5]

In each of the cases, some degree of violence, whether it is racial, sexual, communal, or culturally-based, is enacted upon these bodies. Their positionality on the outskirts of multiple cultures marks them as subalterns; they are isolated from all communities, hated, hunted, and feared. At varying points they are forced to work within the colonial system to assure their own survival. In all cases but the Ghanaian Firemen, these Undead of Color are able to successfully, if at times violently, navigate the multiple oppressive and colonial systems that seek to control or destroy them. This navigation functions as a clear template for introducing the ideas of subalterns and their varying degree of vocality to interdisciplinary classrooms. Their bodies are perfect literary representations of the crash sites of race, sexuality, agency and power. While normative vampire myths have always been used to discuss power, sexuality, and agency, the stripping away of the unraced, and presumptively White skin of the undead, and making race an issue of both human and vampiric terms, allows for a wider conversation regarding those themes and their relationship to various forms of colonialism.

The two most iconic Undead of Color bodies are Blacula and Blade, his postmodern incarnation. Both figures are undeniably hyper-masculine, powerful, and exhibit racialized pride; both Blade and Blacula are created through acts of miscegenation on multiple scales. Human and vampiric racial lines are violated through acts of forcible violence against both them and the women they loved at the hands of colonial and raced aggression.

Both Blade and Blacula began with an overt act of racial miscegenation. Blacula was a victim of Dracula as a colonial power that attempted to subdue both him and his wife.[6] In a similar act of sexual and colonial predation, Blade was "born" a vampire; a white vampire attacked his mother while she was pregnant. Her baby (Blade) is thereby doubly biracial; his newly created father is White, a fact that is later brought up mockingly throughout the movie, and he is now racially a vampire as well. Blade, a tragic mulatto, is torn between both worlds, and is constantly overtaken by the hideous, historical, one-drop rule.[7]

Moving from the cinematic to the literary, Shori, from Octavia Butler's *Fledgling*, is an experiment of miscegenation, born out of Ina and human DNA. There is a special emphasis for the blackness in her DNA, which, much like Blade, the drops of black blood give her strengths and access that other vampires are denied. It also opens her body up to two-fold racism on both the human and vampiric level. She is a constant outsider, and with few cultural markers, is forced to navigate through the human system of racism, and the Ina colonial ideas of blood purity, mongrel races, and racial servitude.

Straddling between the boundaries of fiction and folklore sits the soucouyant. In Trinidadian and Dominican folklore, she is a vampiric figure that wears the skin of an old woman by day, but drains the blood of her community by night in the form of a giant ball of fire. She is shape shifting, consumptive, isolated, and a figure that needs be feared, silenced, and destroyed. She is the subaltern. The myths spun about her name are filled with seemingly helpful instructions detailing her identification, detainment, torture and eventual murder. She is also a figure that appears often in the works of Nalo Hopkinson, who presents her body as vocal subaltern that is aware of its positionality on the outskirts of multiple cultures but works to find ways to empower itself within these destructive discourses. The soucouyants referenced most in this text are the ones produced by Nalo Hopkinson, in her works *Greedy Choke Puppy* and "Brown Girl in the Ring." In each case, the soucouyant is given a literal voice, a fleshed and fired body, and her own access to agency.

Situated within both myth and reality are the Ghanaian firemen: these are men born directly out of colonial violence. While still living within their cultural and colonized communities, they are given official uniforms, distinction, and power by the ruling, colonial bodies. In return for this status, they are rumored to waylay travelers, kill them, take their blood, and deliver this life force to the colonizers.[8]

All of the Undead of Color function as subaltern bodies and can be used as examples to introduce students to Spivak's conception of this theory. The subaltern here is presented as a person or group who falls outside of the hegemonic power structure. Spivak asserts, that, "if, in the context of colonial production, the subaltern has no history and cannot speak, the subaltern as female is even more deeply in shadow" (Spivak 82–3). This is very much the case for the soucouyant, a figure that dwells within multiple rhetorical and cultural badlands. She is without the dominant discourse, as her body is definitely a racialized one. By definition, she is an elderly, Black body, and is viewed as different both by the dominant discourse of whiteness, and the community that she is simultaneously part of and separate from.[9]

Each of the Undead of Color function in a subaltern space: Blade and Shori are racialized experiments, and represent the result of two racialized mixtures. As a result, they are neither accepted by their vampiric race, nor the human race, as they exhibit traits of both, and are clearly marked by their black skins. There is also, in the case of both, a marked attention on their being products of miscegenation, and violence is constantly brought against them. Each of these bodies can facilitate discussion regarding the idea of subaltern bodies being both raced and gendered.

To provide a concrete example, a soucouyant is constructed as "the old woman who lives alone at the end of the village road, seldom seen, her house always closed up and she sleeps the day away" (Besson 31). Even situated within a landscape surrounded by people she has grown up with her entire life, she is denied both name and voice.[10] Regarding soucouyants, my students noted that her position on the very edges of the community allowed the villages to demonize her, and have little problem escalating from metaphoric violence to actual, physical violence. They asserted that because she is not part of the community, they had no problem tarring, feathering, and having the outside church come and finally kill her.[11]

Much like Spivak's conversation regarding the practice of sati in India, the ideas of ritual and superstition were conflated with criminality[12] and thus necessitate official punishment. The village has determined her guilty through the lenses of superstition and rumor, and called upon the authorities of the dominant discourse to not only agree with their supposition, but to help administer punishment. Her body is considered to be guilty by both discourses, and soon, according to the tales collected by Besson,

> the village boys and men have filled her skin with coarse salt and pepper and will soon come and get her, with a drum of boiling tar, the Priest and his silver cross, the church bells—and then, the end [Besson 31–2].[13]

The colonial-sanctioned death of the soucouyant elicited class conversations about power, control, and internal/external violence in colonial systems. The students broke into groups, which each group discussing a hierarchical group's role in the murder. This exercise was not to place blame on specific groups, or to specifically decry the role of violent outsiders on indigenous populations. The students were instructed to list the power relationships between the soucouyant and their group, and the group's relationship to the colonial discourse. For this exercise, the body of the soucouyant was included as a group under scrutiny. The students were asked to gage the soucouyant's participation in colonial and indigenous expectations for her raced and gendered body. Later, the class came together to discuss their selected positionalities and how they related with the other group positions. The inclusion of the soucouyant, and a conversation about participation in expected cultural roles lead the class to talk about problems of internal colonialization, body policing, and the gaze.

Normally, the subaltern body in both of its forms is controlled and demonized by the perceptions of the dominant and communal discourse that views it. Hopkinson is aware of this gaze and its impact on what can be considered the soucouyant's social skin.[14] Sarah Ahmed discusses the problematic nature of the gaze on the body, and how that gaze attempts to police and enforce normativity.[15] Ahmed speaks of this movement by transgressive bodies when referencing queerness, but the same concepts holds for the soucouyant. The soucouyant body is demonized because it is not properly oriented within the cultural discourse. Sarah Ahmed asserts, "If orientation is about making the strange familiar through the extension of bodies into space, then disorientation occurs when that extension fails" (Ahmed 175–80). Because her body is one that causes and reflects social disorientation, the soucouyant is forced into a negated space by the dominant discourse that is in search of cultural and spatial comfort. The discourses that disenfranchise her are extremely invested in constructing her as dangerous and demarcating their cultural boundaries and ones that exclude and silence her. To access this idea, the students read Spivak's "Can the Subaltern Speak?" and have in class round tables to decide what "speaking" means in regards to disenfranchised bodies.

For one especially fruitful roundtable, the class broke into groups and each selected an Undead of Color body. Using the previously mentioned group exercise as an example, they examined the positionality of their fictional body, and its relationship with the hierarchical discourses surrounding it. They then came together to talk to each other about those positionalities, and how they affected their fictional body. This speaking to each other in the classroom helped solidify the idea that subaltern bodies can exist both in diasporic and "home" i.e., American landscapes. They also, through their internal conversation, realized that these colonial ideas are connected, and that subaltern bodies have shared struggles and means of communication, regardless of location or landscape. They were able to link the soucouyant's struggle for livelihood and cultural positionality with Blade's struggle against racial and physical violence; they were able to link those conversations with Shori's push for self-actualization in the face of racial violence from various sources, both indigenous and colonial.

Returning to the cinematic Undead, both Blade and Blacula are presented to the student as bodies of Color that are forced to violently confront the colonial system that polices their cultural embodiment, sexual agency, and physical bodies. They are both fighting against a monolithic colonial structure (in Blacula's case, the White police force, in Blade's case, the vampiric community which is overwhelmingly White) and are forced to craft a self-sustaining space for themselves through their own agency. Both men work outside of the expected racialized discourse that views them as Black men, and therefore threatening, to protect themselves and those they deem worthy.[16]

The inclusion of the Undead of Color in the classroom provides concrete examples of many concepts of post-colonial, feminist, and gender theory and serves as ground for both historical and contemporary deconstruction. A key conversation inclusion of the Undead of Color lends itself to in the classroom setting is one of racial and cultural hybridity. The Undead of Color represent a deliberate mixing of culture, race, and blood; they are placed far outside of the normative construction of all cultural possibilities, and thus occupy a third space while conceptions of racialized and social purity do, but simultaneously, do not apply. In the case of all of these undead bodies, their cultural purity is at the heart of the conflict regarding their existence. Their overtly raced lives conflict with the idea of vampiric White purity, while their Undead blood puts them outside of the possibilities of humanity.

Jennifer Brody's examination of "purity, whiteness, and hybridity continues to be relevant" (Brox 398) when exploring the positionality of the Undead of Color in their various texts. In the case of Shori, Blade, and Blacula, the emphasis on their human race is biological, and the main marker of their difference. Shori and Blade are both labeled as "half-breeds," lending themselves greatly to discussions regarding cultural miscegenation and the spaces that subalterns are forced to occupy when they are largely rejected by all of the cultures that surround them.

They are also sites that foster discussions regarding colonialism, anti-colonialism, and neo-colonialism. Blade, in particular, is extremely helpful in introducing the idea of anti-colonialism within the classroom. Within this text, anti-colonialism "signifies the point at which the various forms of opposition become articulated as resistance to the operations of colonialism in political, economic, and actual institutions. It emphasizes the need to reject colonial power and restore local control" (Ashcroft 14). The vampires in Blade's universe very much function as a colonial power. Within their ranks is a marked distinction between pure bloods and vampires who were formally human. Blade is at the bottom of this vampiric hierarchy, as he is racially and genetically mixed, relegating him to a status that is neither human nor vampire. The vampires in this world control the police, the economy, the night-life, and very large parts of the culture that both humans and vampires interact with, representing total colonial power. Blade works against their system, stealing from both humans and vampires to finance his hunting operation and base of operation. He also is fluent in the vampiric language and quickly learns their folklore in order to defeat their ranks. Blade is an evident case of the colonized knowing the colonizer better than they know themselves. He is able, with the help of Karen, to defeat their religious, economic, and cultural systems, all the while, being largely rejected by both the human and the vampiric world.

Blade, and his violent militancy, is a helpful tool to exploring revolt by the subaltern in the classroom setting. Blade is presented in the film series as a hero, even though he is violent, destructive of the normative and colonial system of control, and a racialized outlier. His body serves as a site that calls students to become introspective: why are they rooting for the character that seeks to upend the colonial system that everyone else in the movie relied upon? Through Blade's body, viewers are forced to confront the idea of the colonized body striking back, armed with the weapons of the colonizer and acknowledge of them deeper than that held of the colonizer themselves. Students often easily identify themselves with Blade, as lone antiheroes destabilizing the system of "The Man." My students of Color especially identified with Blade, they felt that they were in a landscape that can be considered hostile and isolating. While they are doing this, however, they are forced to interrogate the racialized system of miscegenation, blood and violence that he embodies.

Blade combats racism against his body with violence and uses it to extract vengeance for White on Black sexual violence. While the image of a White male sexually violating Black women is nothing historically new, it is something that pop culture is reluctant to explore. The direct conversations about miscegenation, mixed blood, and racialized power force the reader to come to terms with the reality of one-directional forced miscegenation, the cultural outcasts it creates, and the potential for those outcasts to respond with violence.

This idea of subaltern victims responding with violence then opens the classroom to larger historical discussions of race, power, and revolution against colonial power. In my past experience of posing this question to a classroom, an overwhelming majority of students state that it is justified for Blade to respond with violence to a cultural system that views him as a racial inferior, forcibly violates and enslaves his mother, forces him to societal margins, and uses organized and constant violence against him. However, these same students voice direct discomfort when taking these ideas from the realm of fictions to historical reality, grounding them in the Vesey revolt, or the Haitian revolution. Blade functions as a medium that allows students to conceptualize the idea of subalterns using violence as a method of working within an anti-colonial construct. Their rationale for Blade's justification for violence and revenge opens a doorway to larger conversations about the positionality of subaltern bodies in America that systematically and historically have had violence used against them and been forced to the margins of society.

The vampiric (un)race in the film, represented most clearly by Deacon Frost, serves as another mode of discussing class, and racialized repression. It is evident within the film that Deacon Frost is not "pure" and has ascended the cultural ranks of vampirism through uncouth means. He is the vampiric form of "new money" and is willing to kill, torture, and isolate enemies in order to obtain his desired social status. His mixed blood, and his personal role in Blade's forced creation, speaks to historical ideas of class, sexual violence, and racism. Students can easily identify Frost as the villain in the narrative; he is selfish, hypocritical, violent, and extremely racist, despite his own liminal racialized status. A larger conversation around his role as a violent participant in miscegenation, violence maker, and enforcer of colonial ideas help students link his fictional body to historical narratives of American race relations.

For example, Frost's role as enforcer of colonial ideas was extremely helpful in our class discussion on the Tulsa Race Riot of 1921 and the destruction of Black Wall Street. The students were able to connect the Black community's prosperity, self determination, and self arming with the self arming and self protect that Blade engages in. They were also able to link Frost's determination to destroy the Blade, the "monster" he created, with the surrounding white community's desire to destroy a prosperous community that was created as a result of Jim Crow laws, redlining, and threats of violence. The students noted the community that destroyed Black Wall Street was made up of people who were marginalized along the lines of class. They, much like Deacon Frost, were on the margins of the dominant community, and used what power they had to harm those lower on the hierarchical scale.

While Blade and Blacula both represent colonialism and anti-colonialism on the landscape of the United States, the idea of the Undead of Color allows for a transnational scope. The Ghanaian Firemen are tangible, living bodies that have been forced to the cultural outskirts of myth by direct dealings with colonialism. Unlike Shori, or Blade, the Firemen have no libratory actions, either for themselves or the communities that they live in; they are the face of colonialism when it is internalized. Discussing the fear the local people have of the firemen, which is deeper than the fear they hold for the banyama, leads to classroom discussion about the horrors of colonialism, and its more damaging effect of internalization.

Rather than serving anti-colonial or post-colonial functions, the Firemen serve as cultural examples of colonial attitudes still held, and the false and dangerous cultural hierarchies and divisions they create. Using their bodies as a backdrop, I question whether it would be acceptable for the community to rise up against the firemen with violence? This discussion is linked then to the anti-colonial activities of Blade, and Shori's utilization of post-colonial cultural recognition in using the colonizer's legal system against themselves. The Firemen sit at the crossroads of these ideas, leading to discussions about the viability of violence in the face of colonization, even if the violence is enacted against members of ones own community.

A close examination of the positionality of the Undead of Color forces the reader to combat the colonizer imaginary, and deconstruct the way that we "read, interpret and debate- can itself come under scrutiny, exposing the brute imperial privileges that are routinely masked by the ideology we inhabit" (Leistyna 3). Deconstructing the colonial imaginary is often a painful process, which causes students to rub against the idea that they are often living and functioning within and underneath a colonial mindset and that their perceptions towards bodies of color are shaped by this system. The students are asked to examine the way that bodies of Color are treated and represented through literature. In one case, I had a student say, "This is too messed up to even talk about." In an attempt to tease out this statement, the student claimed that it was extremely painful to openly address the way that Black bodies are represented and presented as evil, or deviant. This realization is often met with silence, one in which it is impossible to tell whether the student has withdrawn because they are feeling "shut down and marginalized by a topic that is either too personal or too political, or both" (Marsh 67). To counteract this silence, I often offered up personal stories, and told the students my attachment to characters like Shori and Blade. I was able to relate my own experiences counteracting racism and rhetorical violence through sarcasm and use my experience to make the text tangible and easy to talk about for the class.

While this silence may seem initially problematic, it is an important moment to teach, through. It is important for students to recognize and understand, especially within interdisciplinary classrooms, their own cultural positioning within colonial systems and the perceptions that colonial system forces upon subaltern bodies. By openly discussing these unequal systems, educators call attention to the conception of the post racial, and how that idea does not take colonialism, neo-colonialism, or anti-colonialism into consideration. It also helps them recognize that neither culture nor myths are monolithic and perpetually "unraced." By acknowledging these cultural crash sites, and their literary interpretations, educators and students are more able to recognize and destabilize their own privilege, in addition to introducing them to literary, historical and cultural diversity that is often lacking in interdisciplinary classroom settings.

Teaching the Undead of Color opens the classroom for various discussions on race, power, and colonialism. By their very existence, they force students to interact with and deconstruct their ideas of whiteness being normative for either the living or the Undead and expose them to different cultural conceptions of race, power, and anti-colonialism. They do not exist just as raced offshoots of current popular culture; each of these embodiments is grounded in cultural and historical representations that are largely missing from classroom conversations. The introduction of overt race into discussions about vampires does more than just highlight racial differences, it exposes students to conversations about the perceptions of blood, the fear at its mixing, and the subaltern possibilities that inhabit those bodies.

Notes

1. The character Blade is independent both culturally and financially of any external, sanctioned sources. Shori, from Octavia Butler's *Fledgling*, is culturally powerful. She possesses powers that the other, White Ina, do not, and she is the body that is viewed as the future of the Ina race.
2. Undead of Color bodies can also serve as theoretical frameworks to introduce the concepts of the subaltern and vocal subalterns, as they are very much constructed as subaltern bodies. They are marginalized within already disenfranchised communities, and are expected to either die out, or through their own agency

address the problems and dangers that various other groups present them with. When they engage in actions that are self-liberating, they are misinterpreted, or ignored by multiple communities and embodiments. Undead of Color bodies can serve as a theoretical framework to introduce the idea of subaltern bodies and the methods they use to address their own disenfranchisements and other destructive discourses.

3. The students specifically referenced a scene in *Blade II* that is mentioned at the opening of this essay, and Shori's defense at the Ina council.

4. When addressing the Undead of Color, the student is encouraged to realize that Whiteness maintains its power in our racist cultural symbolic through its invisibility: to be white is not to be of a race, it is just to be "human," "a person," "an individual." This is also how maleness and heterosexuality operate: in erasing themselves as anything particular, they parade (silently, invisibly) as the universal, as the norm, as "natural" (Winnubst 6).

5. This can be seen in *Speaking with Vampires* by Luise White.

6. In his short onscreen role as a living man, Prince Mamuwalde was an African diplomat, traveling with his wife to "put the best foot forward" for the race. His host, who the viewer later discovers is Dracula, desires the Prince's wife, in spite of her dark skin, which he claims marks her as savage. As he attempts to make her a sexual and colonial conquest, Mamuwalde fights back, first verbally, and then with actual physical violence. His attempt to free his wife ends in failure, and Dracula feeds upon and kills his wife in an act of colonial and sexual conquest. He then feeds upon and turns Mamuwalde into a vampire and locks him away in a coffin. In a final agency-robbing act, Dracula spitefully christens him Blacula. His race becomes his primary marker, and is a title created as a diminutive. This naming marked him as permanently racialized, and constantly Othered.

7. His dark skin and human blood account for his ability to walk in the sun and not burn, but he is described as having human and vampiric weaknesses. He has his feet rooted in both worlds, but is denied and in turn rejects both. Blade, with the help of his adopted, white father figure, is left to craft for himself an anti-colonial existence where he fights against the vampiric system that oppresses him while in turn trying to redeem for himself some aspect of humanity.

8. They are deemed especially terrifying because they still live within and can easily pass for the community. They represent the immediate and tangible dangers of internalizing colonialism: they may not be the undead, but they aid them in their consumption of colonized bodies, which is just as bad if not worse.

9. The body of the soucouyant is marginalized along several lines. In Spivak's "Can the Subaltern Speak?" she references Guha's hierarchy of bodies in regards to their subaltern status. My students noted that the body of the soucouyant is deemed both foreign and dangerous to the first three tiers of the hierarchy. The students identified the dominant foreign groups as the Christians with their church bells and bubbling tar, the dominant indigenous group at a larger level as a masculine value that allowed the bodies of old women to be pushed to the margins, and the dominant indigenous group at a local level as the men and boys who came to kill the soucouyant. The students noted that there were multiple levels of power and control going in one direction in the narrative. They observed that even though the soucouyant was attacked and harmed on a local level by those with more power than her, the judgment on her body was ultimately rendered by the outside colonial power. Without the sanction of the colonial power, the ultimate murder of the soucouyant would not have been able to be enacted. The conversation surrounding the directionality of power allowed the students to be more mindful of the damage that colonial power enacts on indigenous systems, and how that damage allows harm to be internally perpetuated.

10. The enclosed nature of her house serves both to keep her in, and the gaze of the populous out; they are free to conceptualize whatever image they please of her, and she is able to do anything to refute that image. She dwells on both the physical and cultural outliers. Her age and isolation imply that she is far past any form of reproductive sexual legitimacy in the eyes of the community, which makes her extremely troublesome. Her neighbors enact metaphorical violence against her by denying her food, cultural support, and communal comfort; her positionality on the outskirts means she does not receive any aid from the community.

11. The folklore surrounding her claims that she sheds her skin and emerges as a ball of fire that feeds on the life blood of her community members. To counteract her alleged acts of vampiric terrorism, the villagers hunt for her discarded skin, fill it with salt, and then have the local, colonial authorities come to destroy her with religious and earthly authority. Colonial priests are called in to bring church bells, holy water, and boiling tar to exorcise her evil from the community. The communal need to bring in colonial powers to rid themselves of internal evil again invokes Spivak for classroom discussions regarding colonialism and patriarchy. The soucouyant, becomes the victim of internal, and colonial patriarchy. It is the men and boys of the village that have spoken against her and seek to destroy her. In the folkloric construction, there is no mention of women or girls enacting this violence; it is a specific tactic utilized for policing those of perceived deviant gendered performance.

12. "I am suggesting that, within the two contending versions of freedom, the constitution of the female subject in *life* is the place of the *différend*. In the case of widow self-immolation, ritual is not being redefined as superstition but as *crime*" (Spivak 297).

13. She is here silenced and killed through the community action: first the salting of her skin, and then through the boiling tar. The communal punishment is then made more official by the reification of the act by the dominant discourse, who will bring their religious and political authority (the Priest and the official ringing of the church bells). The ringing of the church bells is extremely symbolic; first it serves to silence her screams. The text conveniently is silent on her screams, but they obviously must be present. By the text not mentioning her protest in any form, it serves as another layer of silencing and relegating her to the layer of the subaltern. She is not even humanized through vocalizing her suffering. The bells also serve as a signifier to the larger dominant discourse that the official governing bodies have decided to take part in the actions of the modal subaltern and legitimize their demonization of a gendered and more disenfranchised body. This enaction of double punishment serves to double silence the soucouyant and render her as subaltern through multiple lenses.

14. Focusing here on literary vampires, Hopkinson's soucouyants are highly effective examples of vocal subalterns. Not only are they given a direct, literal voice, but they are presented as agents who can assume their fire-formed mantle as one that is both performed and performative. This focus on agency allows a clear portrayal of the constructed familial and communal ties that the original folk narratives lack. Hopkinson allows these subaltern, gendered forms to speak through multiple mediums on the modally enforced silence, their self created cultural ties, and the performative aspect of their nature. Essentially, Hopkinson rhetorically moves the figure of the soucouyant from the forced outskirts of literal and rhetorical landscapes to a self-chosen space that allows for multiple modes of interpretation.

15. When anybody, mainly here the Soucouyant body, does not ascribe to the normative ways of performing, there is a great deal of potential for violence, whether it be physically tangible or metaphoric. The transgressive body is forced to move to the outskirts of acceptable space, and there more violence in this migration. The subaltern's constant state of repositioning often rubs up against the ideals and concepts that are considered normative, and is very often damaged by this contact.

16. There is also a clear occasion to discuss sexual control and the Black male body with these two texts. Students will note that both Blade and Blacula are denied romantic attachments in their films. Blade is presented as asexual, taking no sexual or romantic interest in Karen. Blacula twice loses his romantic attachments, as they were both killed by the colonial system that attacked him. In the case of Blade, it is notable that he is only allowed the metaphoric act of vampiric sexual penetration on a member of his own (human) race, and only after she has been bitten by another, unraced, vampire. The exclusion of both Blacula and Blade from the sexuality inherent within traditional vampirism leads to conversations regarding racial miscegenation, the historical control of Black male sexuality, and the sexual availability of the bodies of Black women. In the cases of both films, Black female bodies are viable sites for multiple vampiric penetrations. This observation can be offered in a classroom setting along with historical narratives regarding respectability and sexual control of the body. As these bodies of Black women are viable sites for penetration, by both the colonial vampiric community and the Undead of Color, it is important to note, that both Blacula, and in the first Blade film, these are the bodies the film revolves around protecting.

Bibliography

Ahmed, Sara. *Queer Phenomenology: Orientations, Objects, Others*. Durham: Duke University Press, 2006. Print.

Alexander, M Jacqui. "Erotic Autonomy as a Politics of Decolonization: An Anatomy of Feminist and State Practices in the Bahamas Tourist Economy." *Feminist Genealogies, Colonial Legacies, Democratic Futures*. New York: Routledge, 1997. Print.

Ashcroft, Bill, Gareth Griffiths, Helen Tiffin, ed. *The Post-Colonial Studies Reader*, 2d ed. New York: Routledge, 2006. Print.

Besson, Gerard, ed. *Folklore and Legends of Trinidad and Tobago*. Port of Spain, Trinidad and Tobago: Paria, 1989. Print.

Brox, Ali. "'Every Age Has the Vampire It Needs': Octavia Butler's Vampiric Vision in *Fledgling*." *Utopian Studies* 19.3 (2008): 391–409. Print.

Dittmar, Linda, and Pepi Leistyna. "Teaching Post-Colonial Literatures in the Age of Empire." *The Radical Teacher* 82 (2008): 2–7. Print.

Marsh, Kristin. "Taking Our Bodies Back: Empowering Students to Take the Classroom Back." *Radical Teacher* 92 (2011): 67. Print.

Spivak, Gayatri Chakravorty. "Can the Subaltern Speak?" *Marxism and the Interpretation of Culture*. Ed. C. Grossberg and L. Nelson Basingstroke: Macmillan Education, 1983. 271–313. Print.

Winnubst, Shannon. "Vampires, Anxieties, and Dreams: Race and Sex in the Contemporary United States." *Hypatia* 18.3 (2003): 1–21. Print.

Unknowable and Immeasurable: Queer Studies, Assessment and the Ever Resistant Vampire

Seri I. Luangphinith

He can do all of these things, yet he is not free. Nay; he is even more prisoner than the slave of the galley, than the madman in his cell. He cannot go where he lists; he who is not of nature has yet to obey some of nature's laws–why we know not.... His power ceases, as does that of all evil things, at the coming of day. Only at certain times can he have limited freedom. If he be not at the place whither he is bound, he can only change himself... — Bram Stoker, *Dracula* (1897)

"Free" and yet "more prisoner than the slave of a galley," the vampire represents not only a liminal space of sexuality and mortality, but its signification of the places in-between and beyond boundaries offers educators an opportunity to rethink the way we teach issues of diversity and why. Many in the academy recognize that "diversity" itself is not limited to race and gender (what we would assume as physical manifestations of difference), but extends outwards to encompass such "closeted" concepts as gendered and sexual identity. It is this crux, between that which is thought to be made manifest versus that which can be cloistered, is what makes Nosferatu a perfect symbol of the immeasurable potential and frustrating obstacle queer studies poses in terms of the teaching and learning of alterity. Specifically, the vampire offers an engaging entry into a world of "men feasting on other men," a tangible symbol of *monstrosity* and the accompanying homophobic reaction to the "unspeakable" as a means to "divide and manipulate the male-homosocial spectrum" (Sedgwick, *Between Men* 90). But conversely, courses solely devoted to such material often replicate the very boundaries of inclusion and exclusion, such as the Victorian "molly houses" Eve Sedgwick speaks of, institutions that amplify the "structure ... of discriminations for defining, controlling, and manipulating these male bonds" (86). Thus the vampire, in his often singular pursuit of self-destruction and that of his own partners (that have also included children and women), also resists what Jacinth Samuels calls "queer theory's remarkable capacity for inclusivity and its relation to a liberal humanist discourse ... [and] purported universality" (93). Therein lies the conundrum the vampire and its study presents for assessment, in trying to "know" how well we develop empathy and deconstruct social biases when the vampire and other monsters like him/her symbolically reject these very notions that underpin our conventional understanding of "diversity."

Let us begin by first exploring how this course utilized the trope of the vampire in the much larger context of queer studies. English 475 at the University of Hawai'i at Hilo is a rotating elective course in literary theory for the English Department. In the fall of 2010, it was devoted to queer literature and film and simultaneously certified for credit under the Women's Studies Program. The course was conceived and defined in the following manner:

Course Description

Sexuality and taboos regarding sexual behavior serve as guideposts for any society or civilization. Our views on sex, or rather the way we judge sexual behavior, inform social beliefs, which in turn enforce gendered roles and differences, such as found in the terms of "man" and "woman." Yet, it is the socio-political function of sexuality that calls into question certain assumptions, such as heterosexuality being "natural" or "dominant," or that by "nature," women are mothers (implying that they mate with men, or that biological sex is always heterosexual). A reading of literature from many time periods, across multiple cultures reveals that such judgments are often challenged by a more subversive view of sexual identity. This is the realm of Queer Theory, which undertakes an immense re-reading of literature and film and addresses how homosexuality and homo-social interests are deeply coded within both. Understanding the "epistemology of the closet" is the key in understanding how defining "proper" genders and gendered conduct is a matter of power and privilege and how such definitions are always on the verge of being undermined.

Learning Outcomes

Upon completion of this course, students will be able to:

1. Recognize and utilize terms (i.e., "epistemology of the closet") and theories associated with Queer Studies in their discussions and writing.
2. Interpret theoretical primary and secondary sources into plain language.
3. Demonstrate the importance of "Diversity" Learning in their own education/lives. (Answer the question: What can this body of knowledge do for me?)
4. Demonstrate the importance of "Writing-Intensive" in their own education/lives. (Answer the questions: What does writing in this subject teach me? How can this subject matter help me to become a better writer?)
5. Demonstrate self-directed work that meets external expectations of excellence.

From the very beginning, the concept of diversity was explicitly imbedded in the curricular expectations of the course — apart from introducing students to a generally non-traditional theoretical approach to identify formation and literary analysis, the course tried to simultaneously address the non-traditional (in this case "Queer") from the vantage point of social difference that could be linked to the discussions of representative populations on campuses, surveys, and data on retention and recruitment; and instead, in the manner that James A. Anderson argues in that what teachers should be aiming: "offer[ing] the opportunity for far greater impact: (1) intellectual diversity and (2) the diversity of skill levels, learning styles, and cognitive frameworks in any given student body and between one or more student groups" (33). More important, Anderson goes on to argue that students "must exhibit a parallel appreciation for intellectual diversity — new knowledge, different perspectives, competing ideas, and alternative claims of truth" (33). Such ideas, in turn, led to my assumption that such complex analyses could thus engender critical thinking and academic writing (which is why the course was also designated as writing-intensive but which is beyond the scope of this protracted essay to address). Nevertheless, looking at issues of sexuality from the vantage point of literary theory (as opposed to the anthropologic study of a sub-culture) was intended to encourage what Anderson calls "intellectual diversity."

Being from Hawai'i, I also realized that these idealistic goals needed tempering by an understanding that culturally, many local students may not have been exposed to the kinds of conversations that underpin the established academic discourse of queer studies. I could not assume that "Stonewall" and "Proposition 8" would register with my students given Hawai'i's colonization and its adverse impact upon gendered and sexual identity. It is because of this unique context that I began the class (which included a mix of both resident and mainland upper-division students, half of whom were not English majors) with an introduction to the indigenous history surrounding the *aikāne* (crudely translated to same-sex "friendships") and some of the forgotten research of Robert J. Morris on the stories and *hula* (dance) traditions that "belong[ed] to a world where homosexual relationships were not even an issue" (76). We then moved to problematic early white writers such as Charles Warren Stoddard and his "Chumming with a Savage: Kána-Aná" (from the 1895 *South Sea Idylls*), which depicted images of feminized and sexualized Native boys, reprinted for a modern audience and celebrated by outlets such as Gay Sunshine Press. Understanding the "mainland" penchant for such stereotypes, which chronologically paralleled the transformation of the Islands into a tourist landscape of exploitative capitalism and runaway urban development, allowed us to address our own "monsters" and the homophobia specific to these Islands. For this discussion, we turned to Gary Pak's "A Toast to Rosita," which offers up a problematic characterization of Native queerness. On the one hand, the Native Hawaiian Rosita Kamali'i serves as a symbol of resistance for her singular protest at the State Capitol which leads to her arrest and her battle cry, "The 'aina [land] belong to the people. Stop the freeway!" (123); but, on the other, Rosita serves as a target of scorn for the very people she seeks to protect:

> One Sunday afternoon, some of the fathers gathered in our garage to talk story and get drunk. We hung around, outside of their circle, listening to them talk.
> "Dose fricken mahus!" our father said. "Dey bettah get deah act together and get outta dis place."
> "No joke," another father said. "I no like 'em around my kids."
> "Dey bettah bag or I going break deah asses."
> "Eh Mo," one of the other fathers said playfully in a strained feminine voice. "Maybe dey like you do dat."
> The fathers broke out laughing. One of them dropped his can and beer spilled out, making a thick foaming circle [119].

Pak's story provided a convenient introduction to the concept of "otherness" as an intersection between disenfranchised indigeneity and the hypermasculinity that informs local male identity. Rosita, the "māhū" (loosely translated as "homosexual," "trans-sexual," or an effeminate man) is continually threatened with bodily harm and is eventually killed off by the writer in a suicide but comes back at the end as a "cold hand of the unknown ready to snatch us from behind" (126). The symbolic role of the Queer in local literature served as the perfect transition into the concept of "monstrosity" or that which forms the boundaries of acceptance and exclusion, leading us to the ultimate figure of liminality — the vampire.

Leaving Rosita behind, we swept into the core part of the course that dealt with more specific monsters and the larger, theoretical approaches to sexuality they symbolized:

Week 4   Sept. 13*   **Monsters R US: Homosexual Panic**
- Mary Shelley, *Frankenstein* (1818)
- Selections from Bram Stoker's *Dracula* (1897)
- Selections from www.glbtq.com's entry on English Romanticism

Week 4	Sept. 13*	**Monsters R US: Homosexual Panic**

- Eve Sedgwick, *Between Men: English Literature and Male Homosocial Desire* (1985), Introduction and "Toward the Gothic: Terrorism and Homosexual Panic" (Chapter 5)
- Start discussion on criteria for proposals (Review LEAP and AACU's *Making a Real Difference with Diversity: A Guide to Institutional Change*)

Week 5	Sept. 20*	**Monsters R US: Homosexual Panic** (cont)

- *Gods and Monsters* (1998)
- Selections from Eve Sedgwick's *Epistemology of the Closet* (1990)

Week 6	Sept. 27*	**Gothic as Queer**

- Anne Rice, *Interview with a Vampire* (1976)
- George E. Haggerty, "Anne Rice and the Queering of Culture" (1998)
- Judith Butler, *Gender Trouble* (1999), Preface and "Prohibition, Psychoanalysis, and the Production of the Heterosexual matrix" (Chapter 2)

Week 7	Oct. 4*	**What a Love Triangle Really Means...**

- *Y tu Mamá También* (2001)
- Eve Sedgwick, *Between Men: English Literature and Male Homosocial Desire*, "Gender Asymmetry and Erotic Triangles" (Chapter 1)

By this time, the concept of monstrosity was intended to facilitate understanding of how "obligatory heterosexuality" is enforced through homophobia and is a "*necessary* component of ... patriarchal institutions" (Sedgwick, *Between Men* 3) and to understand why a writer like Bram Stoker, who had direct connections to Oscar Wilde (including marrying a woman who had been "courted" by the latter), would change the Count's line from "To-morrow night, to-morrow night is yours" in British editions to "To-night is mine" in the 1899 American version (Stoker 52). According to the editors of the Norton Critical Edition of *Dracula*, "Stoker's deletion of this sentence was understandable, for it leads to a different novel, one probably unpublishable in 1897 England. Stoker may have imagined that the America that produced his hero Walt Whitman would be more tolerant of men feeding on men" (Stoker 52).

In light of western society's heterosexual mandate, the class also undertook discussions of key passages from readings, such as how "the image of coming out regularly interfaces the image of the closet, and its seemingly unambivalent public siting can be counterposed as a salvational epistemologic certainty against the very equivocal privacy afforded by the closet" (Sedgwick, *Epistemology of the Closet* 71). In other words, analyzing the discourse of LGBT via the "closet" and the monsters it hides versus a public space which need not nor should remain hidden helped us to enter analyses of Gothic stories that could be read as reflective of "coding," that is, how narratives of homoeroticism could be publicly expressed for multiple audiences. In particular, re-reading Victor Frankenstein's relationship with Henry Clerval and the nameless monster led us to an unconventional discussion on Sedgwick's concept of triangulation, usually an erotic configuration between two men with the sought after woman facilitating the relationship. A similar male-male-male pattern binds Lestat, Louis, and Armand in Anne Rice's novel. These were homoerotic relationships that went unspoken yet frustrated other characters, like Rice's Claudia who proclaims in an outburst: "If you were a mortal man; man and *monster*! ... If I could show you my power ... I could make you want me, desire me! But you're unnatural!" (266). From this perspective, the un-dead signifies an empowering space of what can never be fully understood as it can never be fully extricated from the shadows. What exactly "is" unnatural is what Claudia can't name, a condition of refusal and deferral beyond her feminine reach.

Nevertheless, the vampire is not totally unaware of women. For example, in Stoker's novel, the Count's attentions turn towards Lucy Westenra and Mina Harker, and in Anne Rice's version, Louis's very unconventional relationship with his young child protégé, Claudia, even urges him to admit, "Desire her, I did, more than she knew" (266). The vampire's escape from being pigeon-holed into a specific sexual space was also discussed by the class. Specifically, "'identity' is assured through the stabilizing concepts of sex, gender, and sexuality, the very notion of 'the person' is called into question by the cultural emergence of those 'incoherent' or 'discontinuous' gendered beings who appear to be persons but who fail to conform to gendered norms of cultural intelligibility by which persons are defined" (Butler 23). From this secondary perspective and given the examples from Stoker and Rice, the vampire is less than a signifier of an absolute binary between heterosexuality and homosexuality/homosociality, but a source of "incoherence." Furthermore, as Butler's arguments pointed us in the direction of deconstructing otherness, we could not help but also engage in the problem of how women in such Gothic novels are always subject to destruction if not violent annihilation: from Frankenstein's visceral shredding of the monster's female companion to the beheading of Lucy Westenra to the rendering of Claudia into a "blackened, burnt, and drawn thing" (Rice 301). In any event, the feminine erasure that often happens in stories of monsters (and even in more "mundane" films such as *Y Tu Mamá También*) was discussed as one aspect of Queerness by which homosociality and misogyny can be expressed as complementary narratives in the same story.

By the time we entered into reading George E. Haggerty's "Anne Rice and the Queering of Culture" in the fourth week, students in the class were experiencing the need to self-identify their positions within their weekly journals as had been planned at the outset of the class. These 2–3 page "free-writes" were intended to keep students engaged with the readings (which they were asked to "respond to" in their weekly reflections), and to also develop an artifact that could be assessed with our new Cultural Diversity Rubric, which was developed at a WASC workshop the previous spring by the Assessment Support Committee that I was chairing at the time (Fig. 1). Students' perceptions and their responses to readings were thus encouraged to be couched in the personal and engaged in diversity-centered pedagogical approaches that promote the "challenging [of] an individual's worldviews about self and others" (Diaz-Lazaro et al. 192). Furthermore, diversity studies is traditionally cognizant of how others have been treated and is "concerned principally with the inclusion and success of historically underrepresented groups. It focuses on both social justice and education, in that it seeks to redress the historical disadvantage suffered by these groups and also positions them to enhance diversity as an educational resource for all students" (García et al. 7). Such were the principles embedded in our draft rubric, which was aligned with our emerging, widely discussed Strategic Plan that the campus felt had to be more indigenous-centered. The Committee attempted to utilize Native Hawaiian values as the basis for delving into multiculturalism, and thus generated a rubric promoting the segregation of that very understanding into discrete areas of reference — the "I" (*Au* or *Mākou*), "others" (*'Oukou* and *Lākou*), and a separate place where inclusion is possible (*Kākou*). These areas make perfect sense in *that* context — while native Hawaiians are part of a hybrid cultural and social arena, there are accepted protocols when an indigenous (as opposed to a multicultural) perspective or practice is required if not preferred.

FIG. 1. RUBRIC FOR CULTURAL DIVERSITY

	Sense of Place (Engagement) *Homa Hawai'i*	Sense of Humanity (Respect) *Kākou*	Sense of Others (Empathy) *'Oukou/Lākou*	Sense of Self (Humility) *Au/Mākou*
4 **Hua** (Advanced—the ripening of the full fruit)	• Demonstrates *kuleana* (responsibility) for and *'ike kū hohonu* (sophisticated understanding) of Hawai'i's uniqueness as the home of indigenous people, immigrants and immigrant descendants. EX: *"The Pāpa'ikou Mill Beach represents an opportunity for dialogue over the complex convergence of private property rights and public access"* or *"The telescopes on Mauna Kea present a quandary for various stakeholders, including scientists and indigenous activists."*	• Expresses a multicultural approach to describing or interacting with others. EX: *"I am not a Muslim but I respect a culture's choice in limiting certain types of garments."*	• Demonstrates sophisticated understanding of social and cultural complexities in and/or among different groups. EX: *"I am straight and I see marriage as a union between man and woman, but I can respect the gay community to undertake such a commitment."*	• Critically analyzes how s/he is shaped by diverse cultural and social experiences. EX: *"I may be white, but I am a mixture of different backgrounds (my mother was Irish, my father was English)—and these heritages were often at odds with one another over who could rightfully immigrate to America"* or *"I am a Native Hawaiian who recognizes multiple heritages within my own family, and for this reason, issues of sovereignty are very complicated."*
3 **Kumu** (Competent—the forming of the tree)	• Demonstrates *mahalo* (appreciation) for and *'ike pono* (clear understanding) of Hawai'i's uniqueness as the home of indigenous people, immigrants and immigrant descendants. EX: *"Hawai'i's beaches need to be protected from greedy foreign developers"* or *"Given the ancient laws, anyone should have access to any beach at any time they want."*	• Acknowledges diversity but still exhibits some bias. EX: *"Muslims have a right to follow their religious principles, but they need to respect women's rights."*	• Meaningfully expresses social and cultural complexities in and/or among different groups. EX: *"Gays and lesbians have recently indicated a desire to engage in straight practices such as marriage."*	• Meaningfully expresses how s/he is shaped by diverse cultural and social experiences. EX: *"I may be white, but I really am a mixture of different backgrounds (my mother was Irish, my father was English)"* or *"Being Native Hawaiian means recognizing all of my kupuna, some of whom are Japanese and Anglo-American."*
2 **Mole** (Emerging—roots emerge)	• Exhibits *hoihoi* (interest) in and *'ike kumu* (basic understanding) of Hawai'i's uniqueness. EX: *"Hawai'i's beaches are among the finest in the world but owning one is hard."*	• Limited recognition of one's own biases when describing or interacting with others. EX: *"I think women need to be liberated from the veil in Iran."*	• Identifies (without judgment) differences in and/or among cultures and social groups. EX: *"Why New York would allow gays to marry is beyond me."*	• Identifies differing views on his/her own cultural and social backgrounds. EX: *"Being white in Hawai'i has its challenges because many people see me as just that—a white person."*
1 **Kupu** (Beginning—the budding of the plant)	• Exhibits *manakā* (disinterest), *'ike ihi* (superficial understanding) or *'ike hemahema* (faulty understanding) of Hawai'i's people, history and/or landscape. EX: *"If I owned a beach in Hawai'i, I should be able to kick everyone off. It's my private property."*	• Expresses a cultural self-centered approach to describing or interacting with others. EX: *"Muslims obviously hate women for making them wear veils."*	• Descriptions of different cultures and/or social behaviors may reflect some judgmental bias or stereotyping. EX: *"Allowing gays to marry would be a disaster for this nation."*	• Has a limited understanding oh his/her own cultural and social background. EX: *"I am just an American, why can't we all just get along?"* or other uncritiqued expressions of self.

This brings me back to my choice of words at the beginning of this exposition of my class lecture notes: "idealistic." Because the problem from a "Queer" perspective, for Haggerty and for some of the students in the class, is in answering issues of "inclusion" which is inevitably tied to the problematic corollary: "for whose purpose" do we serve in laying open discussions of the "closet?" In hindsight, my attempt to so closely align the personal to the debate on the vampire's "Queerness" may have overemphasized the divide between Self and "Other," and underestimated the symbolic quandary posed by studying Queer. In particular, study generates "spectacle," and part of what makes Haggerty uncomfortable is the intimate gaze books like *Interview with the Vampire* (and by extension, one might argue, classes like English 475, "Queer Literature and Film") afford the larger mainstream. Opening the LGBT community and its culture to a wider audience feeds Orientalist curiosity about "the Other":

> For those of us who are gay, it may seem almost too good to be true that these queer figures go down so well, that they leap out of their darkened hiding places into the hearts of millions. I argue that it *is* too good to be true. I think Rice's vampires express our culture's secret desire for and the secret fear of the gay man; the need to fly with him beyond the confines of heterosexual convention and bourgeois family life to an exploration of unauthorized desires, and at the same time to taste his body and blood; to see him bleed and watch him succumb to death-in-life [6].

And this is perhaps the gray area that diversity studies (at least from an assessment standpoint) has not been prudent in addressing. Loreto R. Prieto suggests that "awareness of self and others remains a key component of identity development throughout the early and middle stages of growth. Scholars also stress the importance of forestalling the tendency of this process to turn toward White, male, or heterosexual guilt — a typical majority culture reaction to realizing the cultural privilege one possesses personally or institutionally" (36). But Prieto's approach overlooks how for some communities, displays of difference are not always desired. To comprehend Queerness is to recognize what "awareness" accomplishes, and why in a queer studies class such scrutiny opens up an ontological can of worms for many students. Speaking "*of* gays" renders the community to the object position, essentially engaging in an Orientalist move and possibly falling into the guilt Prieto speaks of. Worse yet, speaking "*as* a gay person" renders the individual student open to the full gaze, a negation of the safety of the closet when choice is removed. What becomes clear is that the negotiation of the "closet" and the dual empowerment/disempowerment posed by surveillance and identification imbedded in the binary of self and other is a fundamental problem in addressing Queer topics, a problem that does not necessarily inform nor impede studies of diverse cultures or races. After all, "outing" oneself as "Native" is not politically charged as "outing" oneself as "gay." In fact, contemporary ethnic and racial identities are currently predicated on public (and authenticated) spaces of authority — whereas even in this contemporary age, there are openly gay voices who urge caution: "It's not advisable to be honest. It's not very easy. And honesty, I would not advise any actor necessarily, if he was really thinking of his career, to come out" ("I wouldn't advise" para. 13).

More precisely, these words were uttered by Rupert Everett, whose latter comments on the unfairness of straights being able to play gays whereas a "gay man can't play straight," elucidate the oppositional rendering of identity that lies imbedded at the heart of queer studies, that had by week six emerged in students' weekly journal entries:

- So, how is it that monsters work as a metaphor for homosexuals today and are they among us? Yes, they are among us, but only in our metaphorical closet. They are there because that is where all things scary are cast. They become the dark, ill-defined entity that we really don't know or understand, but are certain arrives with doom. Subsequently, they are persecuted as such, and hide in the closet, or they are feared, and we lock them up [Callos 2].

• People are vastly different in the desires of their hearts. People, in general, do not speak of their most secret ambitions, wants, needs, and fetishes. It is not proper. Rice, in her scantily veiled look at queer life, is supplying a conduit that the main stream most desperately needs to understand the world that so many of us find ourselves living in. Haggerty said that she has done a "disservice" to the LGB [sic] community.... I would say that she has not only done a service to us, but also to those in the straight community that secretly desire to be part of our world [Fuhriman 2].

What is fascinating and perhaps a bit disconcerting is the use of pronouns. The first repetitiously uses the third person plural "they" in reference to what "we really don't understand"; the second ties "I" and "us" together in agreement with Haggerty's scathing review of Rice and the straight community's "secret desire to be a part of our world." What may seem like a simple exercise in grammar actually mirrors the greater problem posed by the binary distinction between hetero- and homosexuality — such was the case in many of the journals and papers submitted at this time. And so while *Dracula* helped us to discuss the problem of binary definitions, they came back to haunt many in their own writings as they struggled with how to evade what is essentially so embedded in the very language we use.

Ironically, all the while, students remained cognizant of the vampire's own evasion of simplistic duality. Another student weighed in on the symbolic refutation embodied by this creature:

These character's power dynamics are recognizable and seen in everyday society, but the origin of the relations emerge more from personalities, rather than their sex, or gender. The taboo relations—homosexuality, incest, pedophilia all present themselves in the context of this vampire story, in a manner subtle enough not to engage outrage and protest, but insight intrigue and popularity. The vampire, sexless and genderless, lies outside/our framework — they are the "other," not subject to the rules we adhere by. They therefore live beyond the power of cultural restraint, which symbolizes itself in their physical strength and immortality, which break the rules of the natural world. But within this vampire life — in which rules of society don't apply, they live as outcasts—forced to keep in the shadows [Cornelius 3].

This brings us to the problem of assessment. How is such writing and thinking even measured? Given the experimental development of the rubric, the students and I tried to use it in conjunction with our work since feedback from the class was meant to gauge whether the draft could even work. When asked to engage in a 20-minute anonymous free-write evaluation of the new Cultural Diversity Rubric during week seven, all twenty-three students within the course expressed extreme displeasure with its limitations. The section on "Sense of Place" did not relate to what we were doing (after all, vampires are not a known character in Hawaiian myths and legends), and the other categories — the separating of "Self" from "Others" — was immediately castigated along the same lines as our discussion underpinning the Gothic. One student wrote: "It is difficult to implement new and more fair and accurate language for role-gender complexities that disservice many through limitations of gender issues." Another argued: "Cultural diversity is an abstract concept. It is not like measuring the temperature of a room or the amount of rain that has fallen on a given afternoon."

Overall, the students of English 475 felt the "diversity" being assessed in the rubric vague, inappropriate, and too heavily reliant on racial/cultural differences as best expressed in the following critique: "This rubric would have a hard time assessing the sexual relationship [of the stories] and how well the reader is comprehending this information." This brings me back to Anderson's arguments previously cited — perhaps when we address issues of diversity, we should not be looking for "appreciation" or even "understanding," conditions of the mind that replicate what Edward Said unraveled for us in Western approaches to the "East." Rather, we should be engaging the realms of critical understanding that take us into a place where one "throws no shadow; ... make[s] in the mirror no reflect" (Stoker 211). In other words, a good enough goal may be to simply grasp the concept of that space of immeasurableness and incomprehensibility — being comfortable with the fact that (the) Queerness (of the Vampire) is not a celebrated or idealized state of mind, but a wretched condition "impossible from the beginning because ... [of] what you know to be wrong. You can only have the desperate confusion and longing and the chasing of phantom goodness" (Rice 334). Perhaps the ultimate power of the vampire is in the refutation of the celebratory. As Joseba Gabilondo points out in his analysis of Hispanic blood-thirsty demons (as in films like *From Dusk Till Dawn*): "when the Other cannot be consumed, its sexuality comes to the fore and is represented in its irreducible excessiveness: the Other is Queer" (249). In other words, even if the vampiric discourse provides a "hybrid excess of both agency and sexuality" (251), in more practical terms, the crossing of binaries and borders offers no permanent nor idealistic alternative to the tortured Queerness that makes such crossings possible.

As a side note, I should add that the rubric was a bigger success in a separate class devoted to more multiethnic perspectives— Education 473 Elementary Literacy, Language Arts and Social Studies Methods. The results from this course, which was offered at the same time as English 475, were generally affirmative. Students were asked to draw diagrams and images that they felt reflected their level of competency in these four areas and were then prompted to evaluate the rubric and their experience using it. These diagrams were submitted by the Education 473 cohort, and were accompanied by such comments as "The rubric itself is accurate and precise. Although [*sic*] the use of the word 'meaningfully' is vague" and "This rubric would help a person's understanding because it is very detailed and descriptive about what a student needs to know." But as successful as these drawings may have seemed to the students, it should be noted that they all stuck to more visual and tangible markers of difference — be it languages or nationality. None of them touched upon the issue of sexual or gendered identity; it simply does not appear at all.

If Queer "make(s) in the mirror no reflect," if the vampire cannot be pegged as either straight or gay, and if our understanding of those concepts are hampered by the instability of such binaries to begin with, we should therefore not expect that understanding what the monster and all s/he/it represents can be easily measured on an analytic rubric. I will admit I have no numerical data to share with my readers. All I have are reflections on the difficulty posed in trying to scrutinize the symbolic complexity of monstrosity, insights that led me to a greater appreciation for problems posed by assessing goals in diversity studies. Such insights lead me to suggest that we should accept students *not* feeling comfortable in being scrutinized themselves. When asked, all twenty-three students declined to have their journals made available for public assessment by the committee and they also declined sharing these amongst themselves. One student went so far as to say, "I don't want to have to share what are my innermost thoughts. Such writing is an intimate intellectual relationship between me, the student, and my teacher— those who may not understand the complexity of queer studies should have no right to see my work out of context." Three writing samples from English 475 only appear here with those students' permission. So from the viewpoint of the Policy Institute of the National Gay and Lesbian Task Force, this particular class probably failed to "create [a] welcoming and inclusive climate that [is] grounded in respect, nurtured by dialogue and evidenced by a pattern of civil interaction" (Rankin 3). But such idealistic goals of fraternity, empathy, and openness are themselves refuted by "monsters" like Victor Frankenstein, who rejects Captain Walton's desire "of finding a friend who might sympathize with me" (Shelley 16). Dracula also admits being "a stranger in a strange land, he is no one; men know him not–and to know not is to care not" (Stoker 26). And even in turning back to Rosita Kamaliʻi — the narrator's fascination with the *mahu* only succeeds in building the compassionate gaze towards but never an actual emotional exchange or friendship with the Queer in question. So even as we, the teacher and students of English 475, moved on to Gloria Anzaldúa, Langston Hughes, and Klaus Theweleit, the existential narcissisms of the Nosferatu and his kindred monsters would return, time and time again, to our thoughts, ever urging us to "accept the most fantastical truth of all: that there is no [absolute] meaning to any of this!" (Rice 237). Such "wisdom" is, by any standard, immeasurable.

Acknowledgments

Many thanks to Dr. Michele Ebersole and Dr. Keola Donoaghy for their work in helping to draft the first iteration of the Diversity Rubric. Further thanks is extended to Dr. Ebersole and her students from Education 475 (Fall 2010) and to my three students who bravely share their work herein–Ms. Kathleen Callos, Ms. Chloe Cornelius, and Mr. Kyle Fuhriman. Lastly, *mahalo nui iā Dr. Kalena Silva, he Polopeka o Ka Haka ʻUla o Keʻelikōlani, no kona mau manaʻo waiwai i nā hua ʻōlelo — "aikāne" a me "māhū."*

Bibliography

Anderson, James A. *Driving Change Through Diversity and Globalization: Transformative Leadership in the Academy.* Sterling, VA: Stylus, 2008. Print.

Callos, Kathleen A. "Monsters: Do you see any monsters around you?" 1 Oct. 2010. University of Hawaiʻi at Hilo.

Cornelius, Chloe M. "Journal — Anne Rice." 28 Sept. 2010. University of Hawaiʻi at Hilo.

Diaz-Lazaro, Carlos M., Sandra Cordova, and Rosslyn Franklyn. "Experiential Activities for Teaching About Diversity." *Getting Culture: Incorporating Diversity Across the Curriculum.* Ed. Regan A. R. Gurung and Loreto R. Prieto. Sterling, VA: Stylus, 2009. 191–99. Print.

Fuhriman, Kyle S. "Journal 6." 28 Sept. 2010. University of Hawaiʻi at Hilo.

Gabilondo, Joseba. "Like Blood for Chocolate, Like Queer for Vampires: Border and Global Consumption in Rodríguez, Tarantino, Arau, Esquival, and Troyano (Notes on Baroque, Camp, Kitsch, and Hybridization." *Queer Globalizations: Citizenship.* Ed. Arnaldo Cruz-Malavé and Martin F. Manalansan IV. New York: New York University Press, 2002. 236–63. Print.

García, Mildred, Cynthia A. Hudgins, Caryn McTighe Musil, Michael T. Nettles, William E. Sedlacek, and Daryl G. Smith. *Assessing Campus Diversity Initiatives: A Guide for Campus Practitioners.* Washington, DC: Association of American Colleges & Universities, 2001. Print.

Haggerty, George E. "Anne Rice and the Queering of Culture." *NOVEL: A Forum on Fiction.* 32.1 (1998): 5–18. Print.

"I wouldn't advise any actor thinking of his career to come out." *The Guardian.* 28 Nov. 2009. 16 Nov. 2012. Web. http://www.guardian.co.uk/film/2009/nov/29/rupert-everett-madonna-carole-Cadwalladr.

Morris, Robert J. "Same-Sex Friendships in Hawaiian Lore: Constructing the Canon." *Oceanic Homosexualities.* Ed. Stephen O. Murray. New York: Garland, 1992. 71–102. Print.

Pak, Gary. "A Toast to Rosita." *The Watcher of Waipuna and Other Stories.* Honolulu: Bamboo Ridge Press, 1992. 113–26. Print.

Prieto, Lorenzo R. "Teaching About Diversity: Reflections and Future Directions." *Getting Culture: Incorporating Diversity Across the Curriculum.* Ed. Regan A. R. Gurung and Loreto R. Prieto. Sterling, VA: Stylus, 2009. 23–39. Print.

Rankin, Susan R. *Campus Climate for Gay, Lesbian, Bisexual, and Transgendered People: A National Perspective.* Cambridge: National Gay and Lesbian Task Force, 2003. Web.

Rice, Anne. *Interview with the Vampire.* New York: Ballantine, 1976. Print.

Samuels, Jacinth. "Dangerous Liaisons: Queer Subjectivity, Liberalism, and Race." *Cultural Studies* 13.1 (1999): 91–109. Print.

Sedgwick, Eve Kosofsky. *Between Men: English Literature and Male Homosocial Desire.* New York: Columbia University Press, 1985. Print.

_____. *Epistemology of the Closet.* Berkeley: University of California Press, 1990. Print.

Shelley, Mary. *Frankenstein.* Ed. J. Paul Hunter. Norton Critical Editions. New York: Norton, 1996. Print.

Stoker, Bram. *Dracula.* Ed. Nina Auerbach and David J. Skal. Norton Critical Editions. New York: Norton, 1997. Print.

The Vampire Cult of Eternal Youth
Jean R. Hillabold

Young adult readers and vampire characters seem like a natural fit. As a friend of my stepson once said in the 1990s, teenagers (apparently including himself at the time) believe they will either live forever or die tomorrow. Vampires in fiction do both of those things: they "die" to the mortal life of change, growth and decay, and they "live" in immortal bodies until or unless they are destroyed by violence. Young adult readers (including those in the typical university age range, approximately 18–22) seem drawn to vampire literature because vampires can be seen to represent typical young adult concerns, such as a need to adjust to recent changes in one's own body, a desire to find and fit into the "right crowd," the need to understand one's own sexuality and find a date, a curiosity about conscious-ness-changing substances, and a desire to be strong enough (physically and psychologically) to survive anything.

I have taught a generation of young adults as an instructor of English 100 and English 110 (first- and second-semester English classes which are mandatory for most students) in a Canadian prairie university since 1991. In 1999, I was "turned" from a marginal, casually-employed member of the teaching staff into a tenured instructor when a new employment position was created to ensure permanence and reliability in the delivery of first-year "ser-vice" courses.

My role is to introduce a captive audience of students to the importance of understand-ing written material, and to the art of writing academic essays. My students have become increasingly diverse as the percentage of the general student body from non–English-speak-ing countries has expanded in response to the university's international recruitment strategy. At the same time, my Canadian-born students have become less familiar with printed books than with television, movies and video games.

Teaching vampire literature is a way to bridge the gap between the stories that most young adult students read or watch for pleasure and an analysis of printed reading-matter. A course or a unit in vampire literature can thus lure students into academic culture, and specifically introduce them to literary criticism. If discussing the activities of vampire char-acters and writing essays about them gives students some insight into their actual lives, stu-dents are more likely to see the relevance of an academic (theoretical rather than practical) education to their real concerns.

Vampire characters usually have a supernatural ability to attract mortals despite the danger that vampires represent. Although vampires are understandably hated and feared by humans on a conscious level, their superior powers enable vampires to pass for "normal" (but superior) humans. In that sense, vampires represent a young-adult dream of being powerful, popular, and sexually attractive. Like the "ugly duckling" in the story by Hans Christian Andersen, the wallflower or loner who has been bullied or excluded by his or her peers because of some perceived difference from the "norm" can identify with a vampire character who survives outside the social "mainstream." In some modern vampire novels, vampires are clearly associated with non-heterosexual (and otherwise unconventional) sexuality. Their association with Goth culture seems obvious.

Vampires, as beings who feed exclusively on human blood, can be seen as members of a secretive club who thrive on a forbidden substance. In a time when young adults are flooded with warnings about the dangers of experimenting with "drugs" (including tobacco and alcohol, especially when one is under the legal drinking age) and the horrible, irreversible effects of intoxicating substances and even "junk food" on body and mind, vampires seem remarkably invulnerable to what they ingest. Unless it is deliberately poisoned, human blood enables vampires to remain physically attractive and mentally sharp. Vampires thus embody an ability to indulge in dangerous pleasure and get away with it, potentially forever. Characters whose bodies never change clearly have no need of regulatory warning labels.

Vampires represent contradictory fears and desires. As the villains of horror fiction, they can be seen as dangerous strangers with repulsive habits, or as carriers of "vice." Vampire characters in novels written since the 1970s (such as Anne Rice's vampire novels, *Sabella, or The Blood Stone* by Tanith Lee, *I, Vampire* by Jody Scott, and a spate of more recent vampire novels such as the "Sookie Stackhouse" and *Twilight* series), however, seem to represent a desire for eternal life in a physical body which is impervious to disease — particularly to AIDS and to every other pandemic that seems to arise suddenly from unclear origins — and to the "normal" human aging process.

While young adults generally seem unable to imagine themselves looking as old as their parents or grandparents, those who resent adult authority and the conservative value system which seems to go with it are afraid of being transformed over time, despite their best intentions, into "the enemy." The radical student slogan "Never trust anyone over thirty" was a rallying-cry for the youth of the 1960s which set a clear age-boundary between "us" (the post-war "Baby Boom" generation that valued freedom and pleasure) and "them" (the war-mongering, materialistic rulers of society in general). Although this slogan now seems quaintly retro, conflict between generations persists, and young adults still dread becoming like their parents.

Vampire characters, who are usually "turned" in young adulthood, become so different from their mortal relatives that they have to choose between revealing their true but unbelievable condition, or sensibly leaving home and seeking out others like themselves. A vampire who never ages on the outside can acquire valuable adult knowledge without settling for a life of social conformity. Vampires never decline into middle age, let alone into the social irrelevance associated with age-related retirement from the work force. Becoming a vampire apparently means never losing touch with the current zeitgeist.

Interview with the Vampire

Vampire literature entered a kind of "second wave" when Anne Rice's groundbreaking first novel, *Interview with the Vampire*, was published in 1976. Earlier vampire stories consisted of ancient folklore which inspired John Polidori's "The Vampyre" in 1819, the first vampire tale in English, and several later horror novels: the mid–Victorian *Varney the Vam-*

pire; or, The Feast of Blood (originally a series of pamphlets with contested authorship, 1845–47), *Carmilla* by J. Sheridan LeFanu (1872), and *Dracula* by Bram Stoker (1897).

Anne Rice's debut novel made the consciousness of a vampire character accessible to readers in general because the narrator, Louis, is much more than a predatory villain like the vampires of nineteenth-century horror fiction. Just as typical young adult readers experience a series of transitions in their actual lives, this novel fully describes a transition between mortal life and the "life" of a kind of living statue while the novel itself represents a transition in vampire literature.

Fans of the *Twilight* and *True Blood* series of novels may not know that sympathetic vampires who wrestle with moral dilemmas are all, in some sense, descendants of Louis. Therefore *Interview with the Vampire* would be a good choice of novel to teach in an upper-level English class in secondary school, or a literature-and-composition class in university. This novel is now old enough, and influential enough, to be considered a classic in its genre, but not so distant from present-day culture that students are likely to consider it "boring" or "irrelevant."

The entire "interview" is intended by Louis, the interviewee, to be a warning to mortals about the danger that lurks among them. Louis is a formerly devout Catholic who slid into a life of murderous depravity, had an epiphany, and is now an informer who tries to scare his audience "straight" by revealing the horrors he has seen and experienced. Yet at the end of the novel, Daniel the mortal interviewer (the immediate audience for Louis' tale) begs to be transformed into a vampire. The question for the reader which arises from this plot is: What would you do in Daniel's place? Would Louis' moral anguish inspire you to appreciate the innocent pleasures of mortal life, despite its vulnerability to change, suffering, and inevitable death? Or would you prefer to make the traditional pact with the Devil by giving up sunlight (a place in the natural world) and a sense of kinship with everything living in exchange for "damning" power, beauty and pleasure without limits?

This extreme dilemma is parallel to many choices that young adults must make in the real world. *Interview with the Vampire* is a kind of supernatural *bildungsroman*, or novel of development, in which a young person is educated by experience while trying to find a personal value system, true friends, a satisfying vocation, a place to live (both a cultural and a physical milieu), and true love with a soul-mate.

After students have read each chapter, I write discussion questions on the blackboard or hand out a photocopied list, then divide the class into groups of between three and five students each. As each group discusses possible answers to the questions, at least one recorder in each group must write notes, including notes on any disagreements (or diverse opinions) that arise. After a limited period (usually thirty minutes), the class is reunited so that answers can be discussed and compared.

If a particular class includes a majority of students who are very reluctant to express opinions in public, even in small groups, or if it includes cliques of friends whose discussions tend to digress into personal conversations, I hand out a list of questions and give students time to write down answers which (in some cases) I collect and write comments on without assigning grades.

SAMPLE DISCUSSION QUESTIONS

Set 1. Louis feels responsible for his brother Paul's death, but is he really? Louis himself is confused about whether Paul was a prophet of spiritual truth, or a mentally ill religious fanatic. Which label seems more fitting? Are both labels culturally specific?

Set 2. Does Louis accept the fact of slavery because he accepts racism, colonialism and exploitation in general? Is he simply a man of his time who can't be expected to see his own culture from a modern perspective? What is Louis' opinion of the French Revolution and the Louisiana Purchase?

Set 3. Why does Louis refuse to feed on human blood after passively consenting to be made into a vampire? Why does he finally give in to temptation and kill a mortal man by draining his blood?

Set 4. Does a moral code based on compassion for others require a religious framework? Is physical pleasure inherently immoral, or is it an essential component of human nature? (If the answer to both these questions is "yes," then, as the saying goes, "we're all screwed.") Does the novel indicate whether traditional Catholic theology has any basis in reality? Is there a God in the world of this novel?

Set 5. Does Louis express a feminist value system when he counsels Babette Freniere to retain control of the family plantation after the death of her only brother? Is he unnecessarily reckless when he reveals himself to her?

Set 6. Lestat prevents Louis from leaving him by giving him a "daughter," the five-year-old Claudia, who is turned into a vampire. Is this a better choice than leaving her alone with the corpse of her dead mother? Does the resulting unholy "family" of Louis, Lestat and Claudia have any good qualities?

Set 7. Claudia is explicitly compared to "the Nightmare Life-in-Death" in *The Rime of the Ancient Mariner* by Samuel Taylor Coleridge. (Copies of this long narrative poem can be handed out.) Is she more innocent than her two vampire "fathers," or less human, or both? Why is Claudia bitter when she comes to realize what was done to her, and what she missed by never having the chance to grow into an adult woman?

Set 8. Who is responsible for the murder of Lestat? Is the murder of a vampire as evil as the murder of a mortal? Are provocateurs, perpetrators and accomplices all equally guilty?

Set 9. Why does Claudia seek her "roots" as a vampire in Eastern Europe, while Louis is more interested in seeking his in France? What do they each discover? What causes a rift between Louis and Claudia in nineteenth-century Paris?

Set 10. Louis, Lestat and Armand represent three distinct philosophies of life, expressed in dialogue. Which philosophy is more appealing? Which of these vampire characters (if any) seems to be the author's mouthpiece? (See Appendix A.)

Set 11. The Théâtre des Vampires in Paris is parallel to a community that practices BDSM as well as nonconsensual violence. Why do some mortals choose to offer themselves to vampires? (See Appendix B.) Do the vampires take care of their willing "slaves?" Are the mortals who pay to see the vampires "perform" simply too naive to understand what they are watching?

Set 12. The vampires of the Théâtre des Vampires deliberately destroy Claudia and her new "mother," Madeleine. Why? Is their murder of Claudia as immoral as the murder of Madeleine? Why do the vampires have laws against "turning" a child or killing one's own maker?

Set 13. Louis regards his destruction of all the vampires of the theatre as a moral act, and he regrets his former passivity. Do you agree with him? Why does Louis become disillusioned with Armand, and why does Armand leave him?

TOPICS FOR DEBATE

If a particular class handles group discussions well, I tell them to form teams to defend one of the two positions in one of the following debate topics. After some preparation,

Team 1 and Team 2 can each try to prove that their own position is the most logical by stating their case and questioning the other team. If a particular class seems better suited to individual in-class writing assignments, I tell each student to choose a topic and brainstorm as much evidence as possible to defend their chosen thesis, as though they were writing the outline for an argumentative essay.

Whether students choose the more conventionally ethical position (#2 in each case) or the "devil's advocate" position (#1), this exercise forces more conservative students to analyze what they have been taught is "right" instead of blindly accepting it, while it also forces knee-jerk rebels to find the logic in a hedonistic value system.

A

1. Louis' desire to protect the Freniere family is a sign that he is self-destructive and out of touch with reality, since he still seems to think of himself as "human."
2. Louis' concern for human beings shows that he is still more "alive" in some sense than is Lestat. It would be self-destructive for him to give up his Christian love for his neighbors.

B

1. What the vampires do to human beings is no worse than the exploitation of:
   • women as a group by men as a group, or
   • "people of color" by white racist institutions, or
   • nations conquered in war, or
   • animals who are hunted or raised in captivity as food for humans.

   Anyone who considers the vampires more evil than human beings is ignoring a lot of human history.
2. Evil is not a relative concept. The blood-hunger of the vampires is not morally acceptable, and therefore they have a moral obligation to avoid killing humans even if that means they have to starve themselves.

Vampire Eroticism

Sexual feelings, and sexual behavior, are major concerns for young adults, who typically are engaged in dating relationships rather than long-term commitments. Some first-year university students react with embarrassment to any reference to sex in literature, or they object to it as "inappropriate." Their embarrassment seems compounded if they feel undecided about their own sexual orientation, as many young adults do. The blood-hunger of vampires in horror fiction (as distinct from sexually explicit genres) is both suggestive of sexual desire and an acceptable metaphor which enables young adults to discuss volatile desire in general terms without having to express their own sexual confusion directly.

The eroticism of Anne Rice's vampires is non-genital, since their unchanging bodies, which become denser (more like statues) over time, seem unable to perform sexually like those of mortals. The lack of genital focus among these characters seems to be a contributing factor in the ecstasy they experience when drinking the blood (energy) of mortals, and in their passionate, unorthodox attachments to each other.

The homoeroticism of the male vampires in *Interview with the Vampire*, especially that between Louis and Lestat, is by now well-documented; Anne Rice has openly acknowledged the erotic (not explicitly sexual) subtext in the "couple" relationship between these two characters.[1] In discussions about this relationship, which causes considerable distress for Louis, I ask students whether his feeling of being trapped in an unbreakable bond with the "crude," ungentlemanly Lestat is a sign that these two characters are incompatible, or that Louis, as a gay man who was raised Catholic, is uncomfortable with his own sexuality. In discussions about vampirism as a metaphor for male-on-male sexual attraction, involving guilt, fear and secrecy, some students claim that this metaphor has become outdated since 1976.

My students have generally sympathized with Louis and despised Lestat, so it seems worthwhile to ask them to identify the motivations of the two characters: does Lestat simply "turn" the suicidal Louis because Lestat wants to take over Louis' plantation, as Louis suspects? Or is Lestat more loving from the beginning of the relationship than Louis is able to see? Is Louis' guilt-ridden passivity actually worse, in some sense, than Lestat's apparent brutality? I sometimes remind Lestat-blaming students that by the conclusion of the novel, Louis admits that he has been unfair to Lestat, who forgives Louis for protecting Claudia after she has tried to kill him. Students who are aware that Anne Rice chose to write her next vampire novel, *The Vampire Lestat* (1985), from Lestat's point of view usually admire him more than do students who are unfamiliar with the novel series, and some of them suggest reasons why the author left Louis behind as a viewpoint character after one novel.

When Claudia enters the "family" as a child vampire, she and Louis form a bond which suggests an incestuous father-daughter relationship, and they consider themselves "lovers." After Claudia has acquired adult knowledge, Louis describes her as "an eerie and powerful seductress" (102). When asked to explain what this means, students often avoid referring to seduction in a narrowly sexual sense. I explain that Claudia's frustration as a sensual woman trapped in a child's body can be seen as representative of the suppression of women's sexuality in nineteenth-century society, and some students, especially young women, seem sufficiently aware of a sexual double standard even in their own time to understand Claudia's dilemma. Some students seem to believe that Louis' sense of parental responsibility for Claudia as his eternal "child" is logical, although Armand suggests that it isn't.

When the Dominant/submissive implications of the vampires' desire for human blood, and the willingness of some humans to provide it, or to "invite" death, as does Louis in the beginning of the novel, are explained to first-year students, they generally recognize the reference to a sexual "scene" that exists in the present. Most students are willing to discuss the question of whether there is such a thing as a non-verbal sexual invitation, and if so, how it can be accurately perceived.

Ars Longa, Vita Brevis *(Art Is Long-Lasting, Life Is Short)*

Mutability, the constantly-changing nature of everything living, is an important concept in literature, and in the history of human thought. It could be argued that general disappointment with the unpredictability of life — and its predictable ending in death — has been the motivation for various beliefs in a realm of static perfection, such as a Christian heaven. In *Interview with the Vampire*, the vampires are associated with works of art, and the world of artistic imagination is favorably compared to the real world, which is often ugly and discordant as well as mutable. In this novel and elsewhere, the essential impulse to create art (or to leave the messy world of living flesh and become a vampire) seems to come from an intense desire to preserve a moment of beauty and joy forever.

Static images in this novel—dolls, paintings, statues—are contrasted with flowers, which bloom for a season, with candles, which are inevitably snuffed out, and with ephemeral mortals. Several of the vampire characters are specifically associated with certain art forms. Armand (originally Amadeo, meaning beloved) was a painter's model in Renaissance Italy and was "turned" by the artist, a vampire himself who wanted to preserve the beauty of his seventeen-year-old lover. In some sense, Armand serves first to inspire art, and then becomes an art-form. Madeleine, who becomes Claudia's vampire "mother," compulsively makes dolls that resemble her deceased daughter; her aim is not to please children but to preserve the image of the child she could not bear to lose. Claudia herself is repeatedly described as doll-like.

The Picture of Dorian Gray

Plots about mortals who find ways to leave the heartbreaking, mutable world through art are not confined to vampire stories. The themes and visual imagery of Oscar Wilde's novel of the 1890s, *The Picture of Dorian Gray*, are surprisingly parallel to those of *Interview with the Vampire*, and therefore Wilde's novel could be taught in the same course as a kind of forerunner of the "second wave" of vampire literature.

Dracula, probably the best-known novel of the "first wave," appeared several years after *The Picture of Dorian Gray* was first published in *Lippincott's Monthly Magazine* (1890) and then as a book (1891). Controversy over this novel, even after it had been edited to avoid offending a "mainstream" audience, was so widespread that Bram Stoker, author of *Dracula*, was likely to be aware of Oscar Wilde's novel and his public persona. Stoker might well have been influenced by Wilde.

I have taught both *Interview with the Vampire* and *The Picture of Dorian Gray* in first-year courses, but never in the same course. If and when I teach them together, I will introduce them as expressions of a universal human desire for more permanent access to pleasure and beauty than human life can offer. The movie version of *The Picture of Dorian Gray*[2] interprets the novel as a didactic tale about the consequences of specifically heterosexual self-indulgence, but the novel could more fruitfully be taught in a context of horror fiction, including the nineteenth-century vampire stories which clearly influenced Anne Rice.

In Oscar Wilde's novel, as in Anne Rice's, there is a price to pay for becoming an "immortal." Dorian Gray is a kind of male debutant who "comes out" into adult (male) society by becoming the model for painter Basil Hallward, an idealist who sees the beauty of an ancient Greek statue in Dorian, as his first name suggests. Basil is clearly infatuated with Dorian, who seems at first to be oblivious to his own attractiveness. In this phase, Dorian seems as innocent as each of the vampires in *Interview with the Vampire* before each one is "turned."

Basil reluctantly introduces Dorian to his friend or acquaintance (who refuses to define their relationship), Lord Henry Wotton. Lord Henry tells Dorian he is marvelously young, and that youth is the best period of life, but that it doesn't last long. Dorian thus becomes aware of his effect on others, and that he is guaranteed to lose something of great value over time. Dorian wishes aloud that he could always look the way he does at that moment. The strength and desperation of his wish seems to create a magical exchange, so that he becomes his own static image, and the portrait ages for him.

After he has been corrupted by Lord Henry, who delights in *épater le bourgeoisie* by making aphorisms that reverse conventional morality, Dorian becomes a kind of emotional vampire who corrupts others. Dorian finds that he can inspire love without feeling it himself, and without showing the outward signs of corruption which Basil, his visually-oriented admirer, insists must always appear on the faces and bodies of immoral people. As a portrait painter, Basil aims to reveal personality in his art, and thus Dorian's true personality is captured in Basil's portrait of him.

The triangle of Lord Henry (an apparently cynical guide and mentor), Basil (a serious, emotional seeker of moral "truth") and Dorian (their "child," the product of their combined influence) is parallel to the unholy "family" of Lestat, Louis and Claudia. Each of the major characters in *The Picture of Dorian Gray*, like the major characters in *Interview with the Vampire*, represents a philosophical position.

Basil is often appalled by Lord Henry's words, as Louis is appalled by the "insensitivity" of Lestat. However, Basil admits that Lord Henry only *says* bad things without doing them, and Louis eventually admits that he misjudged Lestat. Dorian, apparently under the influence of Lord Henry (whose social insights Dorian seems unable to understand fully), becomes dangerous to everyone around him. It seems noteworthy that when Basil sees Dorian for the first time, Basil tries to leave the premises because he is afraid of being "absorbed" by a stronger personality. In *Interview with the Vampire*, Claudia at first kills impulsively because she is a child; as she ages within, she shows the ruthlessness of a vampire who can barely remember being human. Addictions to intoxicating substances are part of a slide into "vice" in both novels. The blood-addiction of Anne Rice's vampires could be seen as a metaphorical version of Dorian Gray's addiction to opium.

Lord Henry states his philosophy of life more articulately than the other characters. Here is Lord Henry's speech to Dorian, divided into sections.

> I believe that if one man were to live out his life fully and completely, were to give form to every feeling, expression to every thought, reality to every dream — I believe that the world would gain such a fresh impulse of joy that we would forget all the maladies of medievalism, and return to the Hellenic ideal — to something finer, richer, than the Hellenic ideal, it may be.
>
> But the bravest man amongst us is afraid of himself. The mutilation of the savage has its tragic survival in the self-denial that mars our lives. We are punished for our refusals. Every impulse that we strive to strangle broods in the mind, and poisons us. The body sins once, and has done with its sin, for action is a mode of purification. Nothing remains then but the recollection of a pleasure, or the luxury of a regret. The only way to get rid of a temptation is to yield to it. Resist it, and your soul grows sick with longing for the things it has forbidden to itself, with desire for what its monstrous laws have made monstrous and unlawful.
>
> It has been said that the great events of the world take place in the brain. It is in the brain, and the brain only, that the great sins of the world take place also. You, Mr. Gray, you yourself, with your rose-red youth and your rose-white boyhood, you have had passions that have made you afraid, thoughts that have filled you with terror, daydreams and sleeping dreams whose mere memory might stain your cheek with shame — [Wilde 19].

Dorian begs Lord Henry, "Stop!" and says, "There is some answer to you, but I cannot find it" (19).

Lord Henry's provocative speech and Dorian's shocked, inarticulate protest suggest opposing sides in a debate: Lord Henry's advocates on one side, protectors of Dorian's innocence on the other. When asked to speculate on the "passions" which Dorian might be ashamed of — a desire for intimacy with another man in an era when homosexuality is illegal, a desire to prey on others with impunity, or a desire to be possessed — students usually find all those possibilities to be plausible.

I haven't organized such a debate before, but I would like to divide students into teams to (1) defend any or all of the parts of Lord Henry's speech (that society would be vastly improved if everyone followed their impulses, that self-denial is more harmful than self-indulgence, or that thoughts, passions and dreams are "great events") or (2) compose the "answer" that Dorian Gray can't put into words. Since Dorian himself is unable to explain why he feels threatened by Lord Henry's argument, composing a rebuttal for Dorian would help students learn how to write logical, coherent essays.

Mixed Messages

The Picture of Dorian Gray is a short, experimental novel by a writer who was not primarily a novelist. The actual plot, which could be called "Dorian's Downfall," is a kind of Victorian morality tale about the effects of uncontrolled narcissistic hedonism and a life of deception. This part of the novel could be considered a predecessor of Louis' long interview, written several generations later, which is intended as a warning to mortals about an eternal "life" of damnation on earth.

However, both the omniscient narrator of *The Picture of Dorian Gray* and Louis the vampire undercut conventional morality by showing, in lush detail, the temptations that lead to a fall from innocence or ordinary mortality. Much of Oscar Wilde's novel consists of dialogue (as in one of Wilde's plays); in witty repartee, Lord Henry consistently defeats both the earnest Basil and the impressionable Dorian. Neither Basil nor Dorian ever finds a satisfying rebuttal to the doctrine of estheticism, as expressed in the preface to the novel (see Appendix C), or to Lord Henry's satirical approach to Victorian decorum.

Wilde, or the omniscient narrator, seems ambivalent about the erotic implications of the triangular relationship of Lord Henry, Basil and Dorian, which are only hinted at in the novel. There are persistent references in the novel to a tradition of upper-class British hypocrisy, in which marriages formed for practical reasons often served as covers for all sorts of "unsuitable" liaisons ranging from same-sex to cross-class, cross-generation, cross-religion, commercial (involving the sex trade) or sadomasochistic. Dorian, an orphan, is described as the alluring fruit of an ill-fated love match between members of different social classes.

Much of Wilde's novel consists of historical allusions and descriptions of beautiful objects, many of which are described as more appealing than human companions. This part of the novel could be called "A Catalogue of Art Through the Ages." Although Dorian never seems to have any religious convictions, he becomes a collector of ecclesiastical garments, and he relishes his "idolatrous" appreciation of them. A life of esthetic pleasure is shown to be as seductive in this novel as it is in *Interview with the Vampire*. (Much of the information in the "catalogue" is likely to be foreign to modern students, so a vocabulary list is provided. See Appendix D.)

Dorian is greatly influenced by an unnamed book that Lord Henry lends him:

> It was a novel without a plot, and with only one character, being, indeed, simply a psychological study of a certain young Parisian, who spent his life trying to realize in the nineteenth century all the passions and modes of thought that belonged to every century except his own, and to sum up, as it were, in himself the various moods through which the world-spirit had ever passed, loving for their mere artificiality those renunciations that men have unwisely called virtue, as much as those natural rebellions that wise men still call sin [Wilde 109].

This book seems to be *À Rebours* (see "Huysmans, Joris Karl" in Appendix D), which Oscar Wilde had read in the original French. Like the central character of the book he reads,

Dorian craves direct experience beyond the limits of a normal lifespan. In this sense, he resembles a vampire who preys as much on the general spirit of various eras as he does on the blood of individual mortals.

Gender Issues

Dorian seduces a seventeen-year-old Shakespearean actress, Sibyl Vane, who appears both androgynous onstage (much like young male actors of Shakespeare's time who played female roles) and pleasingly artificial, since she has a gift for appearing to be someone she is not. Like Claudia in *Interview with the Vampire*, Sibyl is described as a doll-like child-woman. Like a vampire being destroyed by the light of day, Sibyl is destroyed by honest emotion. When she falls in love with Dorian, she is unable to express emotions she doesn't actually feel, and therefore she is unable to perform as an actress. She is ridiculed by her audience and abandoned by Dorian, to her bewilderment. She loses her will to go on living.

If Dorian is interpreted as a "closeted" gay man, his interest in Sibyl can be ascribed to her ability to appear boyish or at least gender-neutral. When she expresses herself as a woman, he is disillusioned. However, he has already shown a tendency to use and discard other human beings, treating them worse than he treats the objects he values. His treatment of Sibyl resembles a child's temporary interest in a doll that is then outgrown and ignored.

Adult women are noticeably absent as central characters in both *The Picture of Dorian Gray* and *Interview with the Vampire*. Most first-year university students seem unaware that gender issues within literature and in literary history are explored in feminist literary criticism, although students are generally aware of "women's studies" based on analyses of culture. Discussions about the two novels serve to raise students' consciousness of gender-related concepts in literature and encourage students to investigate further.

Open-ended questions which have led to lively answers include:

1. Why do you think there are no adult women in the forefront of these novels?
2. Do you think that Oscar Wilde write a novel about men because these were the people who interested him most in the real world?
3. Do you think that Anne Rice wrote a novel about men because she was influenced by novels like Oscar Wilde's, or because male characters provided a vehicle for her thoughts and feelings which wouldn't appear to be "confessional," or because novels about men were still taken more seriously than novels about women in the 1970s?

Dorian's vanity, his identification with his physical beauty and his use of it to manipulate others, can be seen as traditionally feminine qualities. His vanity is ultimately self-destructive, since it prompts him to destroy the ugliness of his inner self, as revealed in his portrait. Dorian unintentionally kills himself when he slashes his image with a knife, and this action can be compared to botched amateur cosmetic surgery which causes disfigurement and even death.

Small-group discussions of "looksism" and the beauty industry in our own society can illuminate the willingness of Dorian Gray, the vampires in Anne Rice's novel, and an alarming number of actual people to harm themselves and others in order to keep or acquire a currently fashionable type of beauty. Students who have taken women's studies, journalism or media courses are likely to lead these discussions, which should ideally be kept within a time limit so that students' real world concerns don't completely distract them from the novels.

ART IMITATES LIFE

Both novels should be discussed as fiction, and students should be encouraged to evaluate the plots and characters in each on their own terms. However, there are good reasons for introducing students to the real-life circumstances in which literature is written. Too many students enter university with a belief that the literature of the past has no relevance to the concerns of actual people, past or present. When information about authors' lives is presented to students as supplementary material which can enhance their reading experience, students often become more engaged with the reading-matter they are assigned to analyze. I have found that my students usually give me more of their attention when I tell a personal anecdote about myself as a writer or about an author under discussion. I hope that such tidbits trigger epiphanies about the necessary relationship between life and art. When teaching the two novels under discussion, I always discuss events in the authors' lives which correlate with events in their books.

In *The Picture of Dorian Gray*, Dorian is an attractive young man who ruins lives. In the real world, Oscar Wilde's literary career and his social status were destroyed when he sued the Marquis of Queensbury, at the instigation of the Marquis' son, for calling Wilde a "posing sodomite." (Whatever this actually meant, it does not sound like a compliment.) The following exposure of Wilde's private life in a courtroom resulted in a prison sentence, after which Wilde changed his name and moved to France, where he died before the end of the nineteenth century. Wilde's relationship with Lord Alfred Douglas, the "beautiful boy" in his life, had as eerily destructive an effect on Wilde as Dorian Gray, the character, has on Basil the artist who paints his portrait, and whom Dorian murders to eliminate him as a witness. The story of Oscar Wilde's downfall, and the esthetic persona he created at the height of his popularity, became as well-known as his literary work. Students are usually interested to learn about Oscar Wilde as a fin-de-siècle esthete, a scandalous celebrity in his time and a forerunner of today's openly-queer (gay, lesbian, bisexual and transgendered) writers.

Interview with the Vampire is a kind of meditation on death and the desire to transcend it. Anne Rice has acknowledged that the novel was her attempt to cope with her grief after the death of her only child at the age of five, and she has identified the vampire Claudia as a representation of her daughter Michelle, or of Rice's own intense desire to preserve her forever, regardless of the cost. Most students agree that the vampire characters in the novel can be read as "ghosts" who each have unfinished business from their mortal lives to resolve, and who "haunt" and thereby weaken the living.

Conclusion

Vampire literature can be introduced and contextualized in various ways. Just as vampire characters from the nineteenth century to the twenty-first (unlike their horrifying predecessors in folklore) fascinate willing mortal victims, vampire stories can seduce students into an interest in literature in general, and in its philosophical underpinnings. Like vampires themselves, literature about immortal characters is protean and strangely relevant to the issues of the time in which it is read, long after its beginnings.

Fantasy fiction in general, and vampire stories in particular, appeal to diverse groups of students. If it is important (as I think it is) to preserve literate culture and pass it on to younger generations, books that appeal to young adults make this mission relatively easy. Those of us who are well aware that we won't live forever can infect our students with a love of reading and writing which can last a lifetime, and be passed on by those who inherit our teaching jobs. It's a great consolation for being mortal.

Note: the following appendices can be photocopied and given to students as supplementary material.

Appendix A: Belief Systems

Louis' Moral Belief System (Conventional Catholic Morality)
- If some actions are good/morally desirable, some others must be bad/evil.
- If good acts/good souls deserve to be rewarded, bad acts/bad souls deserve to be punished.
- If God is just and all-powerful, He can make sure the guilty get punished and the good rewarded.
- Punishment can be seen as a sign that one has done wrong.
- Contrition, penance and punishment purify the soul so that one can eventually deserve peace and happiness.

Lestat's Esthetic/Practical Belief System
- If it feels good, it's worth doing. Sensory pleasure (good sights, sounds, tastes, smells, feelings) is its own reward.
- There is no logical reason to care about the welfare of any being you can use with impunity, especially if that being's interests clash with yours.
- Guilt and fear are irrational and self-destructive.
- Pleasure is everyone's goal. Anything that prevents you from obtaining it should be removed or overcome.

Armand's Agnostic Belief System
- Good and evil exist as intellectual concepts, and are projected by conscious beings onto an amoral universe.
- Good and evil are not absolute. There are different degrees and types of both. Just as theft is less evil than murder, ordinary politeness and the innocence of children are both less virtuous than extreme altruism.
- There is no evidence that the universe was created by a just God, or that any beings are inherently good or evil by nature.

Appendix B: Fear and Desire as Two Sides of the Same Coin

Why are some mortals willing to surrender to vampires?
- Death (rest) can seem more attractive than life (full of change and conflict).
- Loss of blood results in giddiness, heightened senses similar to a drug "high."
- Surrendering to a stronger will offers relief from responsibility and guilt.

Fear and desire are closely connected:
- What we want isn't always good for us.
- What we fear is sometimes what we secretly want.

- The blood-hunger of vampires represents fear of being "swallowed up" by a human lover and desire for this intimacy.
- Desire to become a vampire can represent a desire to keep emotions, a relationship or one's own body frozen in time.

Appendix C: The Doctrine of Estheticism

According to Lord Henry: "To be Greek, one must have no clothes; to be medieval, one must have no body; to be modern, one must have no soul."

- Pleasure and love are more valuable than goal-oriented activities.
- Beauty ("Hellenism") is more valuable than moral goodness ("Hebraism").
- Ancient Greek culture and standards of beauty should be revived.
- "Medieval" spirituality is perverse in the worst sense.
- The body and the soul need to be reunited after centuries of being divided.

Appendix D: Glossary for The Picture of Dorian Gray

Ambergris: ash-colored substance produced by the sperm whale, traditionally used in making perfume.

Aragon: name of a family of Spanish origin that ruled Sicily and much of southern Italy from the 1200s to the 1400s. King Alfonso of Aragon (1385–1458) was known as a patron of the arts.

Baglioni: name of family in Renaissance Italy, notorious as condottieri.

Blue Book: (1) directory of socially prominent persons, (2) British parliamentary or other official publication.

Borgia: name of a powerful family in Renaissance Italy: Roderigo, Pope Alexander VI (1431–1503), his son Cesare (1476–1507), daughter Lucrezia (1480–1519).

Bride of Christ: a nun.

Caligula: Roman emperor, A.D. 37–41.

Calumny: slander, malicious gossip.

Caryatides (plural): stone columns in the form of women which support the roof of a Greek temple.

Censers: containers in which incense is burned.

Champak: an East Indian tree of the magnolia family with fragrant golden flowers and wood used for furniture and carvings.

Charles VI: Holy Roman Emperor (1685–1740), ruler of Habsburg Empire (Germany). He left no male heirs, so his reign was followed by several wars of succession.

Chasuble: A sleeveless outer vestment worn by the celebrant at mass.

Cibo, Giambattista: birth-name of Pope Innocent VIII (1432–1492, pope from 1484 until his death), known for launching the Christian Inquisition against witchcraft with papal bull, *Summis Desiderantes*, 1484, addressed to inquisitors.

Condottieri (plural): professional soldiers of fortune, mercenaries of the Italian Renaissance, known for their cruelty.

Cope: (1) A long cloak worn by clergymen over an alb or surplice, (2) any cloaklike or canopylike covering.

Dalmatic: An ecclesiastical vestment worn over the alb by the deacon and by bishops on certain occasions.

Debrett (shortened form of Debrett's Peerage and Baronetage): reference work on the peerage of England, Scotland and Ireland, originally published in 1769, taken over by John Debrett, who added his name to the fifth edition in 1802.

Décolletée (French): showing cleavage (literally, without a collar).

Domition: Roman emperor, A.D. 81–96.

Ebony: a hard, heavy, durable wood, usually black, from various tropical trees grown in India and Ceylon.

Edward II: English king, 1307–1327, defeated by Robert Bruce (King of Scotland) at Bannockburn in 1314. Edward had a favorite, Peter of Gaveston, who is believed to have been his lover. See Christopher Marlowe's tragedy.

Elegabalus: Roman emperor, A.D. 218–222.

Ezzelini: name of three generations of Italian Renaissance rulers named Ezzelino da Romano. One, known for his ferocity, is said to have been converted by St. Anthony of Padua (1195–1231).

Fitzherbert, Mrs. (Maria): Catholic widow, morganatic wife of the Prince Regent, later George IV. She refused to be the prince's mistress, but could not become his official consort.

Frankincense: gum resin from various Asian and African trees, burned as incense.

Ganymede: cupbearer of Zeus in Greek mythology, originally a prince of Troy who was carried off because of his beauty.

Gautier, Théophile: French Romantic writer, author of *Mademoiselle de Maupin*, about a cross-dressing, bisexual heroine. In preface, author states: "Nothing is beautiful unless it is useless."

Gladstone bag: hinged traveling bag that opens into two compartments, named after William Gladstone, Prime Minister of Great Britain four times in succession, 1868–1894.

Hock: German white wine.

Huysmans, Joris Karl: French novelist of Dutch ancestry (1848–1907), author of *À Rebours*, 1884 (*Against the Grain* or *Against Nature*), about a decadent hero, bored with life, who seeks excitement in the arts. This novel influenced Oscar Wilde, who read prolifically in French.

Hylas: Greek name meaning "matter," a character in George Berkeley's *Three Dialogues Between Hylas and Philonous* (1713) in which Hylas argues for the existence of "material substance." Hylas is said to be based on the English philosopher John Locke.

Lapis lazuli: (1) a deep-blue stone consisting of a mixture of different minerals, (2) sky-blue, azure.

Macerated: thin, starved.

Malatesta, Sigismondo: Italian condottiero (1417–1468), effective military commander, known as the "Wolf of Rimini."

Mentone: winter resort in southeastern France, on the Mediterranean.

Michel Angelo (Michelangelo): scientist and artist in Renaissance Italy (1475–1564).

Montaigne: French writer (1533–1592), creator of the personal essay.

Narcissus: Character in Greek mythology who falls in love with his own reflection in a pool.

Orphrey: an ornamental border on an ecclesiastical garment/rich embroidery.

Palmate: shaped like a palm, or a hand with fingers extended.

Patti, Adelina: opera singer (1843–1919), born in Spain to Italian parents, known for the purity of her soprano voice.

Profligate: extravagant or immoral.

Spinel: Any one of a group of minerals, characterized by hardness and eight-sided crystals, used as gemstones.

Sudaria (plural): (1) cloth for wiping the face, (2) cloth of St. Veronica, (3) any cloth venerated as a relic.

Tannhauser: A Wagner opera, circa 1845, about a German poet of the 1200s who is associated with the knight Tannhauser, who dallies with Venus, Greco-Roman goddess of love and beauty.

Tiberius: Roman emperor, A.D. 14–37.

Trouville: resort town in northwestern France, on the English Channel.

Ulster: a long, heavy overcoat.

Whitechapel: lower-class district in east London, England, where Jack the Ripper murdered his victims in 1888.

Winckelman: German classical scholar (1717–1768) who originated the concept of ancient Greece as the home of "noble simplicity and silent greatness."

Notes

1. See, for instance, two online sources, www.examiner.com/article/sexuality-and-anne-rice-s-vampires and www.fanpop.com/.../26466/title/anne-rices-vampires-love-sexuality, for discussions of homoeroticism and sexuality in the novel. Retrieved Dec. 1, 2012.

2. Metro-Goldwyn-Mayer, *The Picture of Dorian Gray* (1945), starring George Sanders as Lord Henry Wootton, Hurd Hatfield as Dorian Gray, and Lowell Gilmore as Basil Hallward.

Bibliography

Rice, Anne. *Interview with the Vampire*. New York: Ballantine, 1976. Print.
Wilde, Oscar. *The Picture of Dorian Gray*. New York: Bantam, 1988. Print.

Stories That Sparkle in Sunlight: Using *Twilight* to Teach Writing

Amy Hodges

"Are there any vampires in *Northanger Abbey*?" asked one of my students when I stopped to talk with her group about an in-class assignment. "I am feeling an Edward vibe from this Tilney guy," she added thoughtfully. Although Stephenie Meyer's immensely popular *Twilight* series is perhaps justifiably condemned for its questionable writing style, plot development, and literary value, for this student it was an important point of access to other types of literature. For the uninitiated, Edward is one of the major characters in the series, a youthful vampire who falls passionately in love with everyday teenager Bella Swan, and the student's experience of reading the four novels in the series (*Twilight*, *New Moon*, *Eclipse*, and *Breaking Dawn*) enabled her to classify Jane Austen's character Henry Tilney as a type of romantic hero. I teach Meyer's novels as a way to help students reflect on how cultures shape "highbrow" and "lowbrow" texts, as well as perceptions of "highbrow" and "lowbrow" readers. Moreover, I use *Twilight* as a theme for a first-year composition course, not only because many students look forward to coming to class and talking about their favorite book, but because a course connecting *Twilight* to vampire literature and other relevant texts (in my case, *Northanger Abbey*, "The Vampyre," "The Giaour," *Carmilla*, and *Dracula*) can help students respond to different audiences, examine a wide variety of rhetorical devices, apply their writing skills to new contexts, and write about their world critically and innovatively. In this essay, I provide strategies for setting up such a course, as well as writing prompts that instructors may adapt for their students. This essay is informed by a first-year composition course I taught in the spring of 2012 at the University of Arkansas titled "Monstrous Desire: The 19th-Century Origins of the *Twilight* Series."

Twilight can be a particularly fruitful text to teach not only because many students are interested in the series and the issues it raises, but because it is easy for a writing instructor to situate the series within many animated, fascinating, and, at times, heated cultural conversations about reading and writing. When asked what their goals were for this course at the beginning of the semester, a number of my students reported that they wanted to be better readers, often phrasing their objectives in terms of reading "more deeply." Like many students across the nation, the first-year students at my public university tended to trust that a gap exists between high school and college expectations for reading. At least in part, the cultural forces of No Child Left Behind and the Common Core Standards contributed to their sense that their previous education left them underprepared for the challenging demands of post-secondary and adult life. Indeed, the standards for English Language Arts & Literacy in History/Social Studies, Science, and Technical Subjects present a compelling picture of the type of young adult reader schools should be producing. Their readers "readily undertake the close, attentive reading that is at the heart of understanding and enjoying complex works of literature," "habitually perform the critical reading necessary to pick carefully through the staggering amount of information available today in print and digitally," and "actively seek the wide, deep, and thoughtful engagement with high-quality literary and informational texts that builds knowledge, enlarges experience, and broadens worldviews" (3). While becoming this kind of reader is no doubt a noble aspiration, not every student who enters a public university feels capable of performing these tasks. Compounding this problem, these students also tended to perceive that the reading they did for pleasure, such as the *Twilight* series, had little to no application to the reading they did to fulfill academic requirements, a perception that probably applies to many students at different institutions.

Moreover, despite reports that today's students read more literature than previous generations (National Endowment for the Arts 1), popular opinion still seems to cast young adults as unintelligent, degenerate readers who wouldn't know a good book if it hit them in the face. The *Twilight* series is a particular lightning rod for this perception, as it has many critics who disparage the machinations of the plot and the development of the characters. Several reviews also present fans of the series as unintelligent and ill-informed, such as writer Brian McGreevy's claim that Edward, as an unmasculine "Castrati vampire," limits the creativity of young readers:

> Just as the Frito-Lay Company has created virtually nutrient-free vehicles of corn syrup and salt that make our youth fat, slow, and indiscriminate, the Castrati vampire is a confection that has the same impact on the psycho-dramatic imagination of today's youth.

McGreevy is not alone in suggesting that the perceived degeneracy of *Twilight* and other mainstays of young adult vampire literature contribute to the degeneracy of youth culture in general. My students often spoke of friends and family who derided their choice of reading material, an attack — sometimes direct and sometimes indirect — on their generation as a whole.

Generally, popular opinion on and academic reception of Meyer's novels tends toward disgust and disbelief, a stance that a number of my students shared. Particularly in reference to the cringe-inducing sequence of events in the final book in which the werewolf Jacob Black "imprints on" (falls in everlasting love with) Bella and Edward's half-vampire newborn daughter Renesmee, many professional critics express their distaste for students' beloved reading material. In her review of the first *Breaking Dawn* movie, fantasy author Elizabeth Hand responded to Jacob and Renesmee's relationship by writing, "Reader, I hurled." When discussing the many romantic relationships in the books, students may also respond strongly to many feminist critics, who point out problems in the gender roles the series seems to encourage. For example, Christine Seifert's response to avid readers of *Twilight* argues that "Edward is a controlling dick" and Bella "a throwback to a 1950s housewife." Other popular responses posit that Edward fails to live up to the standard of his dangerous vampire predecessors; writer Brian McGreevy describes him as a "pallid emo pansy with the gaseous pretentiousness of a perfume commercial." Overall, instructors who choose to teach *Twilight* will have very little trouble finding critical responses to the series online.

Additionally, academic reception of the series may challenge or compound students' perception that the texts they read for pleasure in high school are not suitable for college-level analysis. Academic sources like Maggie Parke and Natalie Wilson's *Theorizing* Twilight: *Critical Essays on What's at Stake in a Post-Vampire World*; Melissa A. Click, Jennifer Stevens Aubrey, and Elizabeth Behm-Morawitz's *Bitten by* Twilight: *Youth Culture, Media, and the Vampire Franchise*; and Giselle Liza Anatol's *Bringing Light to* Twilight: *Perspectives on a Pop Culture Phenomenon* tend to be read by fans as unfairly judging a set of books that, in many cases, was intricately intertwined with the students' sense of self. Anne Torkelson's essay "Violence, Agency, and the Women of *Twilight*" was a particularly challenging read for my students. While some appreciated the truth of her claim that "the *Twilight* saga perpetuates myths of rape culture, normalizes and romanticizes violence against women, and reinforces a power structure that denies female agency and positions male dominance as the natural social hierarchy," others strongly rejected her essay as failing to appreciate the fantasy elements of the story (210). These discussions revealed some important guidelines for selecting additional readings for the course: on one hand, students who love *Twilight* can be very willing to question public discourse and academic research on the series, and therefore develop skills in critical reading and responding to sources. On the other, if I supply critical, sometimes scathing, reactions to the series, I may inadvertently support the perception that *Twilight* readers do not truly understand (in the same ways that academics understand) their favorite reading material. Ultimately, in class discussions of academic and public responses to the series, I try to help students negotiate this complicated power structure and find middle ground between their love of pleasurable reading and the types of critical reading skills valued in the academic world. Although finding thoughtful and provocative responses to the series is easy, students may find it difficult to reconcile the public representation of readers of *Twilight* with their own experiences.

I discuss student perceptions of reading here because the question of what, how, and why our students read is crucial to the success they experience (or don't experience) in our classrooms. Local research on students entering college in Arkansas suggests that reading for pleasure matters to young adults in ways that their assigned reading does not, a trend that probably applies to institutions across the country. For example, according to a 2009 study by Stotsky, Goering, and Jolliffe, most Arkansas teenagers' school-related and non-school related reading material did not come from the traditional high school curriculum. Instead of *To Kill a Mockingbird*, *The Great Gatsby*, *Romeo and Juliet*, or *Lord of the Flies*, the four most-read books by an overwhelming margin were the *Twilight* series: *Twilight*, *Eclipse*, *New Moon*, and *Breaking Dawn* (3). Thus, the authors conclude,

> students going on to college from an American high school have had few common reading experiences aside from a large number of relatively easy-to-read contemporary young adult fantasies, and that their tastes for mature fiction and nonfiction have clearly not been developed [2].

If Arkansas students (and probably many others) enter college sharing their experiences reading *Twilight* and other young adult books, Jolliffe and Harl's 2008 study of first-year students at the University of Arkansas suggests that these reading patterns continue through the first year of college:

> We found students who were actively involved in their own programs of reading aimed at values clarification, personal enrichment, and career preparation. In short, we discovered students who were extremely engaged with their reading, but not with the reading that their classes required [600].

Undoubtedly, students like these exist at many institutions, and some departments may believe that young adult fiction — particularly paranormal romance — does not have a place in an academically rigorous curriculum. Regardless, I feel that if we teach courses that draw upon students' previous reading experiences, particularly those of *Twilight* and similar young adult fantasies, we do more than teach important literacy skills. We encourage the development of intangible measures of potential college success: self-efficacy, a sense of belonging, and acceptance of students' literacy identities.

However, I also think it is important to use *Twilight* as a means of introducing students to new reading experiences. Although a number of texts could work in conjunction with the series, I use nineteenth-century British literature. John Polidori's short story "The Vampyre," J. Sheridan LeFanu's novella *Carmilla*, and Bram Stoker's novel *Dracula* provide access to canonical texts of vampire literature. In order to introduce students to the origins of the Byronic hero, they read Lord Byron's poem "The Giaour." At the beginning of the semester, students reflect on the relationship between reading, identity, and forbidden or criticized texts by analyzing Jane Austen's *Northanger Abbey*. Few, if any, *Twilight* readers will have read these texts, although mine have some knowledge of what they perceive to be Austen's sedate, courtly, and Colin-Firth–infested world through movie adaptations of *Pride and Prejudice*. Also, most have some knowledge of *Dracula* as a foundational text of vampire literature, but their understanding of the book is more influenced by movie adaptations and secondhand accounts than anything else. Thus, I provide historical and cultural background for many of these works in class.

However, class sessions that focus on *Twilight* itself may place instructors in an unfamiliar position: the position of a student. Particularly for students who self-select into a course on *Twilight*, fans of the series tend to have an extensive individual and collective knowledge of each book. Instructors may be pleasantly surprised by the enthusiasm shown by their students about their reading assignments. In my classes, if I have a question about particular details of the plotline or characters, a student often provides very specific information as an answer — sometimes, with a chapter or even page number reference off the top of that person's head. Yet fans' knowledge of the text does not correlate with blind affection for the series; the majority of my students say that they would classify themselves as a fan of the series, but many qualify this statement by making a distinction between themselves and "superfans" of the series (known in *Twilight* circles as "Twihards") or adding that they did not like certain aspects of the series even as they enjoyed the overall effect.

I only assign readings from *Breaking Dawn*, not any of the other books in the series, during the semester, because I email students before the semester begins and ask them to read the first three books or watch the first three movies. If students self-select into a course, the chances are high that they already know (or think they know) a great deal about the series, and I want to support that knowledge and apply it towards developing new writing skills. Moreover, the semester is only so long, and I would rather spend time on texts that students require more structured guidance on. If advance reading is not possible, instructors could schedule movie screenings of *Twilight*, *Eclipse*, and *New Moon* or provide one of the many summaries available online. I divide *Breaking Dawn* along the lines of the three sections of the novel: the first section narrated by Bella, describing her wedding, honeymoon, and discovery of her pregnancy; the second section narrated by Jacob, who faces tensions within his group of werewolves over Bella's child and tensions within himself as he struggles with Bella's worsening condition; and the final section narrated by Bella, describing her new vampire abilities, her relationship with Edward and Renesmee, and the final confrontation with a vampire ruling group called the Volturi. The first section of *Breaking Dawn* is paired with *Northanger Abbey*, the second section is paired with "The Giaour," "The Vampyre," and the first part of *Carmilla,* and *Dracula*, along with the last half of *Carmilla*, complements the final and longest section of *Breaking Dawn*. I divide the primary text in this way so as to encourage intertextual analysis between vampire literary works of the past and present. Both fans and non-fans are pleased by this structure, as fans have something to look forward to and non-fans have some other interesting reading before they must return to *Twilight*.

Overall, students' love, hate, or other reactions to the series means that they very clearly understand the complicated effects that texts can have on readers. Even students who have not read the series before can see its profound impact on popular culture. Thus, students' positive or negative experiences with *Twilight* work well with writing pedagogy that emphasizes the social aspects of reading and writing. My writing assignments all begin with a narrative that situates the student in a conversation with an audience, such as fellow readers of *Twilight* online, their literature professor and the academic literary community, their peers at the university, and other university faculty. These situations asked the students to present their reading of the series in a way that interacted with others' readings of *Twilight* and related books. In the following sections, I share specific portions of writing assignments I developed in order to show students how their reading experiences with *Twilight* had some relevance to the types of work done in academic and professional writing.

The first project presents the following scenario:

> You are a respected writer for an online popular culture magazine, and your editor slides a printout of an article on *Breaking Dawn* across your desk. She asks you to write an opinion column evaluating and responding to the article. Your officemate reminds you that the online magazine's audience will probably be familiar with the book and the movie, and they'll be most interested in hearing what you think about the issues raised by the series.

Students must choose the source they want to respond to and write an opinion column aimed at an online audience. They learn how to anticipate others' readings of *Twilight*— as noted above, popular reception of the series tends toward the inflammatory — and how to situate themselves in relationship to those readings and their chosen critic. This writing assignment draws upon experiences that are familiar to *Twilight* readers, such as reading online reviews and telling others what they think about the books, but the experience of writing to an online audience and reflecting on that task challenges them to think more deeply about the form and style of their communication.

To lead up to this project, I focus on the elements of the rhetorical situation (audience, purpose, exigence) and how these elements are reflected in the texts we read and write. After reading couple of chapters from the beginning of *Breaking Dawn*, I ask, "What assumptions did Stephenie Meyer make about the information her readers recalled from earlier books in the series? Why do you think people write texts responding to *Twilight*— fanfiction, reviews, social media updates, forum posts, and the like? Why do audiences read these texts?" If I ask, "What are some possible unintentional messages that readers take from the text?" I am likely to hear many stories about friends who "just didn't get it," and students are often quite willing to analyze the contexts of the reading and writing situations of those friends. Additionally, writing classes can explore the concept of genre through the various ways that readers respond to *Twilight*. I help students analyze online opinion columns (like the ones they have to write for their project) in order to determine textual and visual features of the genre. My students enjoyed Christine Seifert's "Bite Me! (Or

Don't)" article in *Bitch Magazine* (available online), Laura Miller's "Touched by a Vampire" on Salon.com, Jo Keroes's "Oh No. Not Twi-Moms" on MommyTracked.com, and Erika Christakis's "The Harsh Bigotry of Twilight-Haters" on Time.com, just to name a few. Overall, through the lens of *Twilight*, first-year students can engage with important terminology in composition while applying that terminology to reading and writing situations they are familiar with.

Pairing sections of *Breaking Dawn* with *Northanger Abbey* sparks many interesting conversations on genre, an important aspect of the rhetorical situation. In particular, most of my students are not aware of the novel's scandalous past; for the most part, they have viewed novels as the authoritative narrative of culture, not knowing that debates like the ones over *Twilight* have occurred in the past. I often provide contemporary reviews of Austen and the Gothic novels she alludes to in *Northanger Abbey* for historical and cultural context. Thus, they see that genres have been shaped over time, as new readers and writers live through different rhetorical situations than their forebearers. Writing instructors can help students compare and contrast many different genres in order to help them see distinguishing features of those genres. For example, I have my students create a movie adaptation of *Northanger Abbey* for today's audiences, and I ask them questions like "How will you change the original characters (Catherine Morland, Henry Tilney, Isabella Thorpe, John Thorpe, etc.) to meet the genre's form and the expectations of your audience?" For students unfamiliar to online opinion columns and reviews or for those with less access to such forms, seeing new genres as products of rhetorical situations can help them produce successful writing projects.

For the second project, students read *Twilight* and their own choice of one nineteenth-century text on the syllabus, and then they analyzed those works in terms of the social practices and issues the texts addressed:

> On a visit to your favorite professor's office, you start talking about the other courses you're taking. Your favorite professor says, "I've heard about the *Twilight* series. But I think it's silly to study something so simple at the college level. College students should be writing about great works of literature that address complex social problems." To prove to your favorite professor that you are capable of college-level depth of thought, you decide to write an academic essay that compares and contrasts the perspectives on a particular social issue or problem in *Twilight* and another literary work.

Many teachers of literature would be familiar with the idea of teaching students how to write a literary analysis, and, indeed, additional instructions could make it clear to students that more traditional academic papers are expected for this project. This project teaches academic literacy by showing students how academics justify their responses to texts and contextualize those responses with other texts that have been accepted by the academic community — in short, by using reasonable argumentation and reliable sources.

Thus, the weeks leading up to this project are focused on academic conventions of argumentation and source-based writing. Although some students disagree with how academics have analyzed the *Twilight* series, not all are immediately capable of constructing a formal argument that supports their impressions. When in a heated debate over the significance of *Twilight*, someone inevitably remarks, "It's just a story," suggesting, perhaps, a resistance to further academic analysis of the text. However, the vast majority of their comments on the series belie that statement. When they talk about their experiences reading the series (for traditional first-year students in 2012, often in their early teens), *Twilight* is rarely "just a story." Students report losing themselves in the books, deeply identifying with characters, and talking (and speculating) incessantly with their friends about the events in Bella's life. Even the readers who dislike the series can mine the text for hidden or missing salacious aspects of the characters, such as evidence that supports their stance that no 17-year-old should be dating anyone, vampire or not, over 100 years old. Essentially, many of my students tend to see themselves as subjects capable of making more meaning out of their reading than was on the surface of the text; they may position themselves as authoritative readers without perceiving themselves to be *academic* readers.

Thus, discovering thematic similarities between *Twilight* and other works of vampire literature may help first-year students articulate their growing or emerging sense of what it means to read a text as an academic as well as a reader who enjoys what he or she reads. These works of literature provide ways for students to contextualize popular culture's criticisms of the young adult reader and to validate their own reading experiences as conducive to the type of work done in the college literature classroom. In particular, other works of vampire literature help students see their own reading experiences as potentially useful, or at the very least, not antithetical to the work of academic readers. Because my first-year students tend to have a difficult time reading older works of literature, we spent much of our time working with the building blocks of an academic argument in the field of literature: a sound close reading. Instructors can focus on other elements of academic writing that they see as most important to a successful argument, such as structure, providing adequate evidence, or rhetorical modes.

For the third project, students form groups and present their research to an audience of their peers:

> When chatting with some of your friends in your student organization, they ask you a lot of questions about your continuing study of the *Twilight* series in your FYC class and your growing knowledge of vampires, literature, and culture. "All of this sounds really interesting," one of your friends says to you. "Our organization has to put on a spring event for the student body, but we haven't decided on what exactly it should be. I bet the other students on this campus would be interested in learning about something fun like vampires." With the other members of your student organization, you decide to put together a vampire symposium for the students at the University of Arkansas, and you volunteer to lead a small group that will present at this symposium.

Whereas the first two writing projects were hypothetical situations, I encourage my students to actually put on a campus-wide vampire symposium, giving them a wider audience to write for. Students choose their own groups and a topic from a list I provide, and other instructors might choose to provide additional guidelines for presentation content or format. Each group has a time limit and a requirement that all students participate in the development and presentation of their material. I put together a program, arrange for a larger classroom space, and write publicity materials for the event. Some students worry about how their peers will respond to the content of the presentations, others (particularly first-year students) are uncomfortable speaking in front of crowds, but instructors can modify the publicity of the event as they see fit. Other students relish the opportunity to share their knowledge, and they can help out with flyers, presentation technology, and social media for the event. After the symposium, my students, even those who were anxious about speaking in front of their classmates and peers, unanimously praised everyone's presentations, and they frequently state that they enjoyed this project on their student evaluations.

In my assignment instructions, I indicate that students should include academic and popular research in their presentations, and the most successful presentations adapt that research for their audience of fellow college students. With the help of university librarians, we explore the library's resources and complete annotated bibliographies. I devote much of my class time to working with individual groups, helping them set goals, delegate responsibilities, and resolve conflicts. We also look at presentations on YouTube that students deem successful, and analyze the rhetorical strategies those writers used. One or two class days are set aside for students to practice their talks before the symposium. This project requires students to put their literacy skills into action and to consider how to write texts for public discourse; additionally, by writing to someone other than their instructor, first-year students develop an awareness of the local university community and their needs as an audience.

For the final project, I assign a reflective essay, although multimodal compositions are also encouraged. Students are asked to draw connections between their everyday modes of writing, academic modes of writing, and new discourses that they want to enter:

> "At this point in the semester," your Composition instructor says, "you've written for three different audiences: an online pop culture magazine audience, an academic audience, and your peers. You've also completed two semesters of college-level writing courses. At this point in your academic career, the university community, and particularly university writing faculty, would like to know what you have learned and how you plan to use this knowledge in the future. As your writing instructor, I would like to know what you have learned about writing and reading from our exploration of issues in the *Twilight* series and other works of vampire literature."

The assignment specifies that the reflective essay or multimodal composition should have three parts. Students write about a type of writing that they do every day or very often, and I provide examples of such writing, like updates to social media sites, text messages to friends, forum posts, and comments on websites. They also tell their audience about their experiences with academic writing in university courses, both composition and non-composition, although some students can find it difficult to connect their writing experiences in English class with other classes. Finally, students reflect upon a type of writing that they want to learn how to do, perhaps a type of writing they will need to perform in their future chosen profession.

By the end of the semester, I want my students to see themselves as readers who are capable of reading and writing in intelligent ways about *Twilight*, but, more importantly for the purposes of first-year composition, to see themselves as readers and writers who can connect their profound, critical, or ambivalent experiences with popular young adult vampire literature to the kinds of important reading and writing conversations that occur inside and outside of the academy. Paul Armstrong comments that "[r]eading is the elephant in the room, an unavoidable presence, no matter how we behave" (89). For many of us teaching vampire literature, another elephant in the room, our students' love (or hate) of the popular *Twilight* series, challenges us to reconcile our learning goals with their previous reading experiences. *Twilight* and young adult books like it do not have to be anathema to academic learning, reading, and writing. Regardless of different opinions about the quality of writing or the questionable messages about women contained in the series, I believe that students can see that *Twilight* means something to many people in their culture. Instead, supporting and developing students' sense of what texts can do to readers and using the social aspects of reading and writing can strengthen their understanding of academic writing. Perhaps my students and I may differ on whether or not vampires should sparkle in sunlight, but we certainly agree that the *Twilight* series helps us see new facets of literacy.

Bibliography

Anatol, Giselle Liza, ed. *Bringing Light to* Twilight: *Perspectives on a Pop Culture Phenomenon.* New York: Palgrave Macmillan, 2011. Print.

Armstrong, Paul B. "In Defense of Reading: Or, Why Reading Still Matters in a Contextualist Age." *New Literary History* 42 (2011): 87–113. *MLA Bibliography.* Web. 12 Dec. 2012.

Christakis, Erika. "The Harsh Bigotry of *Twilight*-Haters." Time.com. Time Inc., 21 Nov. 2011. Web. 12 Dec. 2012.

Click, Melissa A., Jennifer Stevens Aubrey, and Elizabeth Behm-Morawitz, eds. *Bitten by* Twilight: *Youth Culture, Media, and the Vampire Franchise.* New York: Peter Lang, 2010. Print.

"Common Core State Standards for English Language Arts and Literacy in History/Social Studies, Science, and Technical Subjects." *Common Core State Standards Initiative.* National Governors Association Center for Best Practices and the Council of Chief State School Officers, 2 June 2010. Web. 12 Dec. 2012.

Hand, Elizabeth. "Love Bites." Washingtonpost.com. *The Washington Post,* 10 Aug. 2008. Web. 12 Dec. 2012.

Jolliffe, David, and Allison Harl. "Studying the 'Reading Transition' from High School to College: What Are Our Students Reading and Why?" *College English* 70.6 (2008): 599–617. *JSTOR.* Web. 12 Dec. 2012.

Keroes, Jo. "Oh No. Not Twi-Moms." MommyTracked.com. Mom Inc., 22 Jan. 2009. Web. 12 Dec. 2012.

McGreevy, Brian. "Why Don Draper Is a Far Better Vampire Than Any of *Twilight's* or *True Blood's.*" Vulture.com. New York Media, 29 July 2011. Web. 12 Dec. 2012.

Miller, Laura. "Touched by a Vampire." Salon.com. Salon Media Group, 30 July 2008. Web. 12 Dec. 2012.

National Endowment for the Arts. *Reading on the Rise: A New Chapter in American Literacy.* NEA, January 2009. Web. 12 Dec. 2012.

Parke, Maggie, and Natalie Wilson, eds. *Theorizing* Twilight: *Critical Essays on What's at Stake in a Post-Vampire World.* Jefferson, NC: McFarland, 2011. Print.

Seifert, Christine. "Bite Me! (Or Don't)." *Bitch Magazine.* Bitch Media, 2008. Web. 12 Dec. 2012.

Stotsky, Sandra, Christian Goering, and David Jolliffe. "Literary Study in Grades 9, 10, and 11 in Arkansas." University of Arkansas Department of Education Reform, n.d. Web. 12 Dec. 2012.

Torkelson, Anne. "Violence, Agency, and the Women of *Twilight.*" *Theorizing* Twilight: *Critical Essays on What's at Stake in a Post-Vampire World.* Eds. Maggie Parke and Natalie Wilson. Jefferson, NC: McFarland, 2011. 209–233. Print.

Vampire Literature:
The Missing Component
in Writing for the Sciences

Neena Cinquino

Students Comprehend in Terms of Bella and Edward

Vampire speak invades today's society — the heartthrobs of Stephenie Meyer's *Twilight* series possess teens, adults, even children — and inevitably reaches the classroom, too. However, this should be considered a welcome intrusion. The Gothic tradition excites participants on all fronts, both readers and viewers alike, and can be used to diversify different departments' syllabi. In a collegiate level writing course geared toward science students, vampire literature is both complementary to scientific writing assignments and enjoyable to aspiring scientists, doctors, and researchers. In a writing-based course with required assignments like abstracts, memos, proposals, lab reports, and argumentative and process-description essays, vampire literature is a catalyst for discussion and engagement for the scientifically savvy mind. Science is not far from science fiction, and the inhuman surely resounds with those interested in scientific discovery and research.

Literature focused on this inhuman being proves the strongest link to a course based in writing for the sciences not only because of its roots within the field, but also due to society's timely interest in vampires like Edward Cullen and Bill Compton. Whether via the outlet of books, movies, or television shows, vampire literature is current and relatable to a student audience. However, at the core of *Dracula* and even *Carmilla* are figures of scientific question: What is a vampire? Early on, it is interesting to ask students to diagnose these undead characters. (For the aspiring doctors in the room, it is an agreeable task.) Despite the outward differences between traditional writing texts and vampire literature, the latter serves as an avenue to introduce all the aspects of science-based writing that are important: the use of literary devices, description, and suspense. Though devices and description differ in fiction from expository writing, students first recognize their successful use in vampire literature and then apply these techniques to their own writing. In turn, vampire literature helps scientists of tomorrow understand the importance of maintaining the interest of the readers of their lab reports, keeping them in suspense. They learn to entice in an abstract on environmental concerns and pace description in a paper on the process of water purification. The inclusion of vampire literature creates stronger writers in the scientific community. Composition courses geared toward students' future endeavors are practical, but with the incorporation of the right outside literature students are pushed to reach new bounds and stretch the capacity of their own writing. In past semesters students have commented, "You find the funniest passages." I consider this an acknowledgement that students' brains are turned on and tuned in.

Mark Richardson discusses the resistance to incorporating literature within a writing course; however, he pulls focus from *if* instructors should include to *how* this can be done successfully (279). He remarks: "The debate is not easily resolved. It will persist as long as teachers of writing continue to reflect, as we inevitably must, the central dichotomy of post-secondary education of our time — perhaps of all time: is college to be an education in humane knowledge and the values of examined life, or is it to be training for a successful career?" (Richardson 279). The incorporation of vampire literature within Writing for the Sciences respects each end of this conflict.

Mina Records as Dr. Van Helsing Questions to Create a Case

In initially reviewing the syllabus, students verbalize, "Why are we reading this?" The first work of literature that is both practical, while also inspiring in the classroom, is Bram Stoker's *Dracula*. This work is the basis of this essay's discussion. *Dracula* sets out to proclaim honesty: "All needless matters have been eliminated, so that a history almost at variance with the possibilities of later-day belief may stand forth as simple fact" (Stoker 5). Facts are the answers that scientists seek, and the search for truth propels the field of science. Quickly students recognize the pursuit for answers in this and other works of vampire literature.

Editors of the Norton edition of *Dracula*, Nina Auerbach and David Skal, note that the aforementioned introduction is meant to resound with those following the empirically based, Victorian scientific method of the time. And so it begins. Science is at the heart of Stoker's tale. The work consists of the journal entries and personal accounts of its players. The reports are specific, leaving no room for error in replication — an important component of a student's lab report. The work opens with Jonathan Harker's musings and suspicions as he ventures to Count Dracula's lair. He is filling in for another. He quickly notices that things in the home are not normal by his standards, and his life hereafter will never be the same. Student scholars exist to ask questions; they are the next generation of inquisitive minds. After reading Harker's introductory journal entries, students can react to his uncertainty. After reading each entry, students can generate a hypothesis: Jonathan Harker has entered the home of a monster and will not exit alive. Or Jonathan Harker will become the monster. Students should not only create a hypothesis in this assignment, but also should find evidence for their claim. Early on students push, "Count Dracula *is* a vampire." I respond with, "Where is the proof?" Evidence is found only through a close analysis of the text.

In addition to Harker's entries, students have much to learn from other characters of the work, as they base their findings in science and medicine. Doctors and consultation, diagnoses and attempted remedy flood the pages of *Dracula*. The language of the work helps students of a Writing for the Sciences course to immediately feel at ease. In fact, the doctor-speak inspires hopeful doctors, researchers, and diagnosticians. Seemingly departed from the case of the Count, Dr. Seward deals with a patient, Renfield. The two horrors are at first separate, and subsequently, students are presented with another medical mystery. In a critical thinking assignment, students recall Renfield's symptoms and demonstrations of his psychotic behavior. Students then think analytically about the man's case, and after, in their own words, they diagnose the man's neuroses: "It seems to me that Renfield suffers from X, because of his exhibition of Y." At this point in an assignment, student can create another hypothesis that is based on evidence. The two hypotheses evolve throughout the semester, and some students find their connection sooner than others. Richardson observes: "Writing teachers must always achieve a tricky balance: they want students both to acquire/create knowledge and also to communicate that knowledge in specific ways to specific readers. The real question, then, is how do reading and writing about literature play out in the acquiring and creating of knowledge? And this is where the deeper problem sets in" (280). The creation of multiple hypotheses throughout the semester answers to this concern.

Through this second hypothesis, instructors direct students to notice Dr. Seward's continuous allusion to mania in his patient. This term is important for it enables students to understand the changing of both medical practice and its terminology over time. This makes for a good transition to the Oxford English Dictionary and an assignment where students can utilize this text. In an assignment, students choose vocabulary from their reading and trace their origins to the twenty-first century. Etymology and its subsequent development are important for students to understand in any writing course, no matter the discipline. The term "mania" and its subsequent evolution over time introduce this assignment. The discussion this elicits then causes students to question the field of science's evolution. I ask, "how has the medical field altered its practices, and is it integral to study the origin of practice?" Certainly the OED signals the importance of a word's lineage, but can the same be said of science? Again, the text is used as a catalyst for discussion and discovery in Writing for the Sciences. The conversation in the classroom is unparalleled and representative of the scientific mind.

Students may ask, "But why does my paper need an outline? Do I need to revise?" At the heart of discovery in Dracula is the importance of writing. One uncovers the mystery of Dracula by following the meticulous documentation of events. Without the players' reproduction of events in writing, nothing would be remembered. Especially celebrated is Mina Harker, as she single-handedly collects and transcribes a unified account. The others are tremendously grateful; she is continually applauded throughout the work. Lucy relates, "I must imitate Mina, and keep writing things down. Then we can have long talks when we do meet" (Stoker 103). The importance of writing is stressed throughout the semester in a Writing for the Sciences course. Mina's diligent note taking can be applied to the copious notes that students must take during and after an experiment. Students must also carefully reproduce steps of a laboratory report with precision. Along with precise reproduction, considerate elimination is needed. The others relied on Mina's portrayal, just as scientists rely on one another; reproduction is the currency of science. In an assignment, students outline Harker's journal entries and Lucy's letters, consciously omitting minor details. This assignment can take students to a secondary assignment: the composition of abstracts for the different chapters of Dracula. A final abstract assignment could be the creation of an abstract for the entire novel: a difficult task, but later in the semester it is achievable for students. These assignments exhibit the effective scaffolding method. The abstract is an important component to a Writing in the Sciences course. Like Mina, students need to choose what is important to record in an abstract.

Mina's dedication and students' conscientiousness displayed in an abstract illustrates Dr. Van Helsing's drive throughout the work. Van Helsing's commitment to proof belongs in every introductory composition handbook, as a thesis-driven paper is only successful with the proper support, and in some way, every paper is thesis-driven. In the face of skeptics Dr. Van Helsing continues, "It is so hard to accept at once any abstract truth, that we may doubt such to be possible when we have always believed the 'no' of it; it is more hard still to accept so sad a concrete truth, and of such a one as Miss Lucy. Tonight I go to prove it. Dare you come with me?" (Stoker 173). This is a dare to present the truth, which quite closely resembles an essay's introduction: attractive through the thesis it maintains. Dr. Van Helsing is determined to demonstrate the proof behind his theory.

Every student of composition, whether or not of a field-driven nature, should maintain the same commitment. Dr. Seward notes that Dr. Van Helsing "went about his work systematically," just as a student would conduct himself in drawing connections between their evidence and thesis (Stoker 175). When the group still stands in disbelief, Dr. Van Helsing himself calls for more proof. Dr. Van Helsing is strong in his conviction, but considers the opposition in order to strengthen his argument. This is a strong tactic in thesis-driven writing: the acknowledgement of the argument's most critical opponent. Whether a student is producing a laboratory report or essay of scientific discovery, one can apply this strategy. The result provides not only success, but also audience encouragement. Students can gain the same dedication and practice acknowledging the opposition in an assignment where students argue for two different sides of one issue. Genetically modified food, herbal supplements, and anti-seizure medications are just some of the issues that students can dissect. Half the class defends one side, while the remaining half finds the most convincing claims for their pro vitamin D supplement argument. This assignment can be done while reading or at the end of *Dracula*, and it translates to real life, on the job scenarios. In constructing a grant proposal, writers need to consider their opposition in order to obtain the desired funding.

In the novel's culmination, Dr. Van Helsing pronounces, "We want no proofs; we ask none to belief us! This boy will someday know what a brave and gallant woman his mother is. Already he knows her sweetness and loving care; later on he will understand how some men so loved her, that they did dare much for her sake" (Stoker 327). On the surface Dr. Van Helsing poses a contradiction, but one can assume that the doctor's dismissal of others' approval rests in already having proven the truth. Dr. Van Helsing says that someday Mina's son will *know* of his mother's heroism; he will neither speculate nor suppose, but know. Like Dr. Van Helsing, students defend their argument with confidence in a mock debate. This debate stems from prior careful consideration of the opposition, and most importantly, this assignment can give rise to one's passion. One student expressed her newfound passion for the care and prevention of heart disease in young women, and she was the argument's opposition.

Similarly, please consider a memorandum by Mina that begins: "*Ground of inquiry.—* Count Dracula's problem is to get back to his own place" (Stoker 304). What follows is Mina's assessment of the situation and an outline of possible modes of the Count's travel. This is an exercise of the critical thinking that students need in assessing the opposition. This also resembles the prewriting stage of any composition piece. First, there is always a question, and then a student must think critically to determine which avenue or avenues would be best to approach it. Again, Stoker's work resembles the process by which one should compose an essay or laboratory report. Mina's memorandum initiates an assignment. As a first step to prewriting, students of Writing for the Sciences are asked to settle the ground of inquiry. Before assessing the assignment, students must determine why the subject is even essay-worthy. They should answer the "So-what" question that makes an argument important: What makes the argument compelling, and how does the argument fit into a preexisting framework? After understanding "So-what" from a class lesson, this step becomes instinctive and begins the process of prewriting for students.

Considering the text as a whole, the chapters within the larger framework of the text *Dracula* are a catalyst for discussion not only relating to literature and theory, but also as a starting point for composition construction, with scientific content. The nature of this work draws in a scientifically-attuned mind and the result can be masterful. Students learn to read analytically and to find the evidence from the text before racing to preconceived conclusions. The detailed plot of *Dracula* resembles to the recipe for the methods section of a laboratory report. Students see what detail is necessary for replication. *Dracula* could either be used as a master text throughout the semester, reading a few sections each week until reaching the conclusion, or as a taste over the course of several classes. In the first option students read from the text each week, slowly gaining an understanding of the elements of composition from *Dracula* and apply these elements to their scientific writing. In the latter, students read the first four chapters of the text, which are Jonathan Harker's first journal entries. (The hope is for students to find the text so appealing that they continue reading on their own.) In these four chapters, the elements discussed thus far are magnified from the initial entries. Other vampire texts, like *Carmilla*, can be used to supplement what is found in the conclusion of *Dracula*. However, either approach can work for a Writing for the Sciences class. Dr. Seward concludes, "It is really wonderful how much resilience there is in human nature" (Stoker 279). But one must note that the same is true of composition, especially its teaching in the most introductory stages.

Continuing to Question: Carmilla

Composition can also be introduced through an examination of *Carmilla*. A student asked, "What is *Carmilla*?" Again — another "funny" assignment. Similar assignments can be used to analyze J. Sheridan LeFanu's text, and the text can either be read in its entirety throughout the semester or analyzed in sections. Like *Dracula*, LeFanu's work asks questions that should be considered in composition courses, but it is a text that undergraduates may have less knowledge of. *Carmilla*, as a piece of vampire literature, is especially advantageous to a Writing for the Sciences course since, like Stoker's *Dracula*, *Carmilla* is set up as scientific documentation. Readers experience not fantasy in *Carmilla*, but encounter a truthful account, as told by several trusting narrators. Similarly, LeFanu's nineteenth-century audience was less attuned to vampirism, yet this now commonplace knowledge of vampires can be used as a tool for today's students. As in Stoker's novel, students need to essentially work harder and fight assumptions; students should create a hypothesis based on physical evidence from the text.

Similar to *Dracula*, in *Carmilla* there are also a multitude of narrators. There is the author of the prologue, Doctor Hesselius, as it is his paperwork, and Laura, who is composing her story for a girl in town. One may even consider the General a narrator as he relays the story of Millarca. In an assignment students analyze the effect of each narration. This presents an opportunity to understand subtle difference in tone and voice and alteration in point of view. The result of *Carmilla*'s narration is a case study, which is relatable to even those science majors that may resist literature at all costs. (The length of the short work also enables students to read the work as a whole, without feeling as though they are neglecting subjects that they deem more important to their major.)

The opening chapter of *Carmilla* introduces a new narrative voice. It begins with a catalog of sorts. This set-up frames the work as a historical text, causing readers to trust its narrator. Despite the obvious fantasy of the work, one has reason to be entirely invested in its truth. The narrator even reveals that she is someone who was "studiously kept in ignorance of ghost stories, of fairy tales, and of all such lore as makes us cover up our heads when the door cracks suddenly, or the flicker of an expiring candle makes the shadow of a bedpost dance upon the wall, nearer to our faces" (LeFanu 8). The second chapter begins: "I am now going to tell you something so strange that it will require all your faith in my veracity to believe my story. It is not only true, nevertheless, but truth of which I have been an eyewitness" (LeFanu 12). There seems no reason to question the narrator, and thus LeFanu has already deceived his readers. In a preliminary free writing assignment, students should examine this voice and the "truthful" account that prevails.

This same narrator tells of the first most noteworthy occurrence in her life. At this point in the narration, there is no proof of a girl's entrance into her room; however, students wonder what viable evidence exists. This is precisely what an instructor should target in the classroom. Students trace the details given and conclude whether or not there is truth in the account, despite a seemingly reliable narrator. Then students are in a place to make predictions, which lead to hypotheses. This step is important to students of science and can be shown though Gothic literature. Vampire literature, like *Dracula* and *Carmilla*, serves this purpose and enables analytical minds to flourish. In essence, in reading this Gothic tale, students gain a skill set applicable to their future endeavors as researchers and scientists. Typically, the composition assignments for Writing the Sciences are meant to lend the most valuable knowledge; thus, vampire literature readies the mind and puts important lessons of composition into practice.

Audience is a difficult concept for beginner writers to grasp. Through reading vampire literature students view the tactics used to entice readers, without bogging them down with too much fiction. Of course *Carmilla* is a fictional work, but it is composed like a scientific case study. This tone creates one that is similar to the text that an aspiring scientific writer will be exposed to in his career. Even in a laboratory report or professional memo, the writing should consist of something more, something that is hard to explain through traditional writing texts. It can be difficult to illustrate to students of Writing for the Sciences the correct balance between brevity and spice. Vampire literature and other Gothic works make this easy, specifically *Carmilla*. They are relatable for science students and covered in esoteric language that they understand, thus creating a perfect example of what is expected at the highest level of scientific writing. The introduction of vampire literature like *Carmilla* and *Dracula* into science courses enables instructors to educate, while still eliciting interest.

One could expect students of science to exhibit a lack of interest in an English course. Students of Writing for Sciences may know what their futures hold in terms of coursework and schooling. Of course, there are setbacks, as well as surprises, but generally students have already recognized their strengths and have applied them to a related scientific field. The downside of this is a possible lack of self-motivated application to unrelated areas, such as creative writing. Another advantage of the incorporation of vampire literature in Writing for the Sciences is the inspiration that may follow. It is an instructor's task to help students get there. This is accomplished through free writing exercises. Students find that they uncover skills they never knew existed, and this in turn benefits their overall composition.

For example, professors can assign creative writing prompts to students after reading *Carmilla*: Describe a disturbance that you experienced in the night. The inclusion of vampire literature to Writing for the Sciences is beneficial on multiple fronts.

Unfortunately, students of science may not factor in enough time to access their own creativity. Free writing in Writing for the Sciences proves advantageous to students' future endeavors; students less often find themselves stumped, and instead, use one of the experimenting writing tactics (free writing, clustering, bubbling, listing) to form ideas. Richardson stresses writing's role in teaching students to generate their own designs and to not merely rely on the academy. External outlets assist this thinking: "Comparing works of literature to television shows, explicitly or implicitly, for example, mediates between the world of knowledge the academy has to offer and the kinds of knowledge students bring with them already" (Richardson 292). This sparks another assignment in Writing for the Sciences. Instructors can ask students to compare *Dracula* or *Carmilla* to events in their daily lives or articles read from scientific journals. Prompted free writing leads students toward imaginative thinking, and this travels via vampire literature.

Dissection of Writing for the Sciences' Syllabus

Depending on a class's pace, an instructor may want to incorporate one of these Gothic works in its entirety within a syllabus or in bits and pieces. Either way the important composition components entangled within vampire literature will be revealed. If one work, possibly *Dracula*, is used as a master text then students are able to really delve into the piece and locate all the elements necessary for expository writing found within this work of vampire literature. Conversely, if all the works are used, an instructor is able to choose the best examples from each piece. To demonstrate, *Dracula* could be used to show how the evidence must add up to one's thesis, while *Carmilla* displays different perspectives. This choice is entirely up to each individual instructor, but nonetheless vampire literature is the ideal supplement to traditional composition texts and writing handbooks, whether once per week or during each class meeting. In either approach, a piecemeal structure initiates scientific thought.

To explain further, Stoker unmistakably does not include proof of the Count's vampirism. Indeed, the bulk of vampiric acts are left out of readers' vision, leaving the images to sheer imagination. This keeps readers in a blind spot of Stoker's *Dracula*, yet the result of the obscuration enhances students' analysis of the text. It perpetuates their search for answers. Throughout their assignments to generate hypotheses, students cannot assume that Dracula is a vampire, but instead they must find the evidence. This skill is heightened through a serialized reading structure. The structure of *Dracula* enables students to fill in the blanks. On a syllabus with twice-weekly class meetings, students are assigned only one section of *Dracula* each week. In Week One students would read Chapter 1: Jonathan Harker's Journal. Weeks Two through Four would include another journal entry by Harker. With each entry, students collect more evidence. Then students constructively put the pieces of the puzzle together. Though many undergraduates may not have read Stoker's famed work in full prior to the course, students may still be familiar with the story of *Dracula*. The role of Wikipedia and YouTube and movie adaptations should not be considered an enemy; even if one knows that Dracula is in fact a vampire prior to reading, the story is not ruined and the mystery is not lost. As Lucy's illness spirals, students, as mindful scientists, are asked not to jump to conclusions, but to read and ask questions. The "two little red points" upon Lucy's neck should not be taken for certain as the implication of vampiricism (Stoker 89). Instead, students need to find the evidence in the text. If a student is attentive to the implicit indications, then there is much more to gain.

Other Gothic Literature to Consult

Though Mary Wollstonecraft Shelley's *Frankenstein* and Robert Louis Stevenson's *The Strange Case of Dr. Jekyll and Mr. Hyde* do not fall into the category of vampire literature, there is room for them in this discussion as they are both Gothic works that can be used in a scientific composition course. Additionally, like vampire literature, they center on a "monster." This monster is gradually revealed in each work. One lesson that stems from all the before mentioned works, both vampire literature and Gothic, is centered on description and detail. Consider the following passage:

> Such were the professor's words—rather let me say such the words of the fate—enounced to destroy me. As he went on I felt as if my soul were grappling with a palpable enemy; one by one the various keys were touched which formed the mechanism of my being: chord after chord was sounded, and soon my mind was filled with one thought, one conception, one purpose. So much has been done, exclaimed the soul of Frankenstein,—more, far more, will I achieve: treading in the steps already marked, I will pioneer a new way, explore unknown powers, and unfold to the world the deepest mysteries of creation [Shelley 49].

In class, students reexamine the use of description and detail in this passage and respond. They notice that what could be said in a few words is made more stunning by Shelley. This leads to: How can detail function successfully in scientific writing? A follow-up lesson examines cause and effect analysis, specifically its successful use of detail. Almost all aspects of expository writing can be drawn from Gothic literature.

Similarly, an instructor may choose to examine *The Strange Case of Dr. Jekyll and Mr. Hyde* to highlight the art of revelation and pace through the use of description to students. The components of description, detail, and pace can be taught through a variety of lenses, but Gothic literature heightens students' interest and masks any potential discomfort of learning composition. It is a lesson in disguise.

Research is an important component of Writing for the Sciences, and is one that could be taught through disguise. In any introductory course students struggle with the incorporation of sources: specifically, what is relevant, how much is relevant, and where to then place this information in one's own work. Thereafter, citation is conquered. An allusion to Samuel Taylor Coleridge's "The Rime of the Ancient Mariner" marks the introductory pages of *Frankenstein*. This reference generates an opportunity for students to see research at work. An instructor should bring to class an excerpt of Coleridge's piece and then ask students: Why did Shelley choose to include this? What is the purpose of incorporating another's work within the novel? Of course students at this point have seen examples of research-driven essays, but the discussion of Shelley and Coleridge is likely to stick.

Vampire literature, characterized as part of the Gothic genre, it relatable to students by the five characteristics that both the genre and young adulthood share. Wendy Rodabough, though specifically examining adolescent years, considers the similarities as key to their inclusion in the classroom: "The first one may be described as extremes of emotion;

the second as the journey of self-revelation; third, the individual against the unknown; fourth, rebellion against authority; and, finally, sympathy with the outcast" (69). An under-graduate student may be filled with uncertainty. An introverted student may find solace in Frankenstein's depiction; both are outcasts in their disparate settings. These parallels invite an assignment as personal reflection. This is a good way to end a successful semester. Students can answer: What has vampire literature taught me about myself and my writing?

Vampire Literature Is the Missing Element

In any collegiate-level course, whether in the engineering or English department, it is important to keep students reading. Just as writing produces critical readers, continued reading enhances writing skills. This must be enforced within Writing for the Sciences. Along with vampire literature, Writing for the Sciences students should read newsworthy articles published on scientific subjects. A weekly reading of a city's periodical may prove beneficial for these students. This reading works with the assigned vampire literature. It functions as a wonderful point of comparison. The differing style of a front-page article and Jonathan Harker's journal entries may cause a student to ask why this contrast exists. This then leads to discussion of purpose and audience, specifically how an author utilizes tone. There is no need to classify Writing for Sciences as solely a composition course. Similarly, it is detrimental to consider it as a class only within the range of science. It is important to recognize its all-encompassing qualities, which are brought out through the use of vampire literature.

In *Dracula* Jonathan Harker notes, "[I]t is a wild adventure we are on" (Stoker 309). Yes, Jonathan, indeed it is. With the influx of vampirism among society, adaptations must be made at the collegiate level. However, this change should not be feared. The popularity of vampires outside the classroom only makes their use within courses more timely and interesting to students. One may still ask why vampire literature, and not another type of fiction, best serves Writing for the Sciences. While vampire literature is now particularly timely and therefore relatable, vampire literature has much to offer in a science-writing course. In the above examples one can see that vampire literature is typically framed as a reliable and scientific account. As a result, the prose that follows is most relatable to the composition that students of Writing for the Sciences produce in their science courses. Vampire literature offers a perfect balance, well-suited for Writing for the Sciences students, and for those enthralled with starry-eyed Bella and Edward.

Bibliography

LeFanu, J. Sheridan. *Carmilla*. London: Bibliolis, 2010. Print.
Richardson, Mark. "Who Killed Annabel Lee? Writing About Literature in the Composition Classroom." *College English* 66.3 (2004): 278–93. JSTOR. Web.
Rodabaugh, Wendy L. "Teaching Gothic Literature in the Junior High Classroom." *The English Journal* 85.3 (1996): 68–73. JSTOR. Web.
Shelley, Mary Wollstonecraft. *Frankenstein*. London: Penguin, 1992. Print.
Stoker, Bram. *Dracula*. Ed. Nina Auerbach and David J. Skal. New York: W.W. Norton, 1997. Print.

Fangs in the Cornfields:
Teaching Vampire Literature
to Nontraditional Students
in the Composition Classroom

Vicky Gilpin

Often, people who fantasize about teaching about vampires in the college or university setting tend to imagine a course devoted solely to vampire literature, vampires in popular culture, or other aspects of the vampiric presence through multiple cultures and generations. A perfect example of such an excellent and rigorous course devoted to vampires is Dr. Sue Schopf's "The Vampire in Literature and Film" through the Harvard Extension School.[1] However, students are not required to gain credits in "vampire studies," and many institutions, particularly community colleges, do not have the ability to offer an endless number of elective courses even if those courses involve intense literary analysis, as does the study of vampire literature. Therefore, many educators seek creative ways to weave their favorite topics, genres, or themes within common required courses, especially composition courses. Some institutions encourage this type of niche or genre emphasis, particularly for lower-level courses, because it provides an automatic focus for students and introduces them to the examination of a theme as they master the goals of the course. Some students, particularly non-traditional students, can find non-thematic composition courses too open-ended, so they spend more time worrying about what they should focus on in order to demonstrate their reading, writing, and research skills rather than honing those skills; a thematically-focused course is perfect for these students because the theme provides structure for inquiry. However, one cannot merely deposit a whole-cloth exploration of vampire literature through all time directly on top of a pre-constructed course with its own goals and requirements for student success; instead, teaching courses through a vampiric lens requires pre-planning, consideration of multiple aspects of the teaching process, and a willingness to improve planned assignments, discussions, and reading requirements through the semester by carefully noting and incorporating the needs of the students.

Teaching vampire literature in the composition classroom can be simultaneously rewarding and challenging, often because of the diverse mix of students required to take composition courses as well as the goals inherent in such courses. I had two options of where to launch a vampire-focused course. As a teacher at a private liberal arts university as well as a community college in central Illinois, I was determined to teach a course empha-

111

sizing vampire literature, but I knew that the approach for doing so at each campus would be different because of the needs of the students and the goals of the course into which I would inject the vampiric themes. As the Dean of the Communications, Education, Humanities, and Fine Arts (CEHFA) department at Richland Community College had mentioned an interest in promoting themed English 101 courses, I decided to incorporate vampires into the community college schedule first. Unlike teaching a course solely focused on vampire literature as an academic field of study, melding vampires into a pre-established course can validate vampire studies as a theme rather than a *raison d'être*, which relieves the pressures on teachers in introducing vampire literature to some institutions. Because English 101 at the community college is an established course with predesigned goals and requirements, the question of whether or not vampires would be a rigorous enough topic for students was not a concern; in fact, the more pressing concern was about meeting the English 101 goals with a vampire emphasis without overtaxing the students through excessive reading and writing beyond the normal academic rigor of the community college course.

Although composition courses may be fairly standard across the country on most campuses, teachers take different approaches to the material in regard to in-class activities, outside writing expectations, and how students are required to meet the goals of the course based on multiple factors. In order to develop a successful community college composition course centered on a specific genre or themes, one must be aware of the potential students. Knowing the students requires a combination of recognizing the different types of students within the region and institution as well as developing a working knowledge of the individuals during the course itself in order to cultivate multiple avenues from which to approach the course content and vampiric themes.[2] My students at the community college had various needs to be considered in order to make the course accessible for them in a way that would encourage them to be successful, not only in English 101, but also in the next course, English 102.

For teaching the vampire-themed English 101 course at Richland Community College, different factors were important to the development of the class. Community college students can be an exceptionally diverse mix of ages, socio-economic groups, ethnicities, and academic backgrounds. Evening courses increase the potential variety of the student body because that is when students who work full- or part-time tend to take classes. According to the *Richland Community College Institutional Data Book 2009–2010*, sixty-five percent of the students were enrolled part-time, the average age of evening students was thirty-one, and sixty percent of the total students were considered non-traditional, as they had not entered the college directly after high school. In addition, although Richland Community College is technically located in Decatur, Illinois, a city of 109,000 people, it is surrounded by cornfields and gains many students from local rural high schools. Therefore, the students are an interesting mix of people with urban experiences as well as those with rural backgrounds.

Students within this particular class, which met from 7–8:15 P.M. on Monday and Wednesday, were varied, not only in age, socio-economic, ethnic, vocational, and academic backgrounds, but also in regard to their familiarity or enthusiasm for the topic. No matter what type of institution or what kind of theme one teaches, the enthusiasm for the topic will vary, and that variety can alter the way the educator must approach the curriculum. Two nontraditional male students were taking the course simply because it was the only late evening English 101 section offered that semester, and they had not been exposed to vampire literature, but they were adamant that they wanted vampires to be monsters and not romantic heroes. Several nontraditional female students had read three or four works of vampire literature and were familiar with some popular movies; one nontraditional female student was well-versed in vampire literature and movies, had been drawn to the course by a publicity activity I had arranged in the fall, and had already emailed me a few times about vampire literature and themes prior to the start of the course; most of the rest of the class, a mix of traditional and nontraditional female students, were only familiar with the *Twilight* franchise and the *True Blood* television show. Knowing where the students were coming from in their familiarity with vampire works was an important aspect of developing the course, so the students would get the most exposure to differing perceptions of vampiric representations while successfully meeting the goals of the course. I promised those looking for monsters that there were plenty to be found, and I also promised the Twi-hards that we would discuss how the roots of the vampire as romantic hero, or at least sympathetic character, are older than Stephenie Meyer's imaginings. On the second day of class, I brought the hard-core vampire fan an extended reading list, which she proceeded to devour and use as a guide to alternate sources to support her writings in the course.

In addition to knowing the students and their skill levels, teachers must also be able to work with, rather than against, the goals for the course into which they are incorporating the vampire-related themes and elements. Many goals and outcomes of the composition classroom align with the topics, themes, and readings one might desire in a course about vampires, as do the ones for Richland Community College's English 101 courses:

Students will exit the course —

Being able to develop essays appropriate for academic audiences through a process of invention, planning, drafting, and revision;

Being able to choose and use the appropriate variety of written English given topic and purpose, with particular attention to acceptable standards of grammar, punctuation, and diction usage;

Being able to distinguish between the writer's attitude and his/her reader's probable reaction;

Being able to understand and work with an effective relationship between generalizations and details;

Being able to structure paragraphs and paragraph sequences with thesis statements and topic sentences;

Being able to use several types of organization and persuasive strategies in accordance with the purposes of academic writing assignments, in particular the proposal and defense of an argumentative position with logic and evidence;

Being able to write clearly, concisely, and coherently;

Being able to apply critical and analytic thinking skills to a variety of texts.

Although the reading and writing goals may align well with how one might approach teaching a vampire course, instructors must remember that they are not teaching two courses, one vampire course and one composition course, so they must ensure that the assignments meet multiple needs; otherwise, a common error is to end up doubling-up on the work required of the students, an unfair tactic that can lead to lack of student success, both with the vampire information as well as the goals of the course. We have to remember that most students need the skills produced by the course more than they need to know whatever fascinating tidbits we adore about vampires in literature.

A way to ensure that each activity not only forwards the students' engagement with the vampire themes but also emphasizes the course outcomes is through the use of a simple chart noting the desired activities and what goals or outcomes connect to each. For example, the English 101 course traditionally consists of several essays with multiple revisions and a final revised portfolio of the essays. The essays for the vampire-themed course included one involving the perspectives of a normal scene that becomes permeated with vampiric tropes, an analysis of a short story, an exploration of two vampire movies in conjunction with two vampire-themed songs, an examination of an approved vampire text not on the syllabus, and a final argument paper. The chart on the syllabus indicated how the essays met the goals and kept me focused on the larger picture of ensuring the students had opportunities to achieve the skills necessary for successful completion of English 101. For example, the short story and novel analyses emphasized reading comprehension skills about authorial tone, while the argument paper focused on writing structure, drafting, revision, and persuasive strategies, among other goals. Many institutions require this type of format in the syllabus in order to demonstrate how hands-on artifacts associate practically to the abstract goals required for success in each course; this format is doubly important for teaching about vampires because when one has a passion for a topic, and vampires certainly inspire passion, particularly in classroom discussions, one may need support in staying focused on the course goals with student activities. In addition, keeping the goals of the course at top-of-mind throughout each class meeting encourages excellent time management. My course was an hour and fifteen minutes long twice a week. Although I usually entered the room half an hour early for informal conversations with students, I felt like the course should have been about three or four hours a night to cover everything I would have really liked to cover or to have the intense discussions we only barely previewed; having the syllabus open to the course goals for every class meeting was an excellent reminder of the purpose of the course and kept me focused on the students' long-term needs.

All students require multiple entry levels into their subject matter, often created through differentiated instruction strategies, but nontraditional students have needs different from those students just out of high school. For example, some nontraditional students may have low lexile levels because of a lack of familiarity with scholarly reading material. Traditional students also often have difficulty with scholarly material because of the lexile gap between high school and college reading requirements, but nontraditional students may feel even more overwhelmed. Lexile levels indicate reading and comprehension ability or a text or type of text's level of difficulty. For example, magazines and blogs often have low lexile measures, while academic journals are usually ranked as higher levels. This is where the plethora of vampire short stories can be an effective tool: I often paired a scholarly article about aspects of vampire literature with a short story demonstrating some element discussed in the article. This pairing encouraged students to make connections between the two works, emphasized critical reading skills, and appeared less overwhelming than the scholarly material alone. One pairing involved Matheson's short story "Drink My Red Blood" combined with De Marco's "Vampire Literature: Something Adolescents Can Really Sink Their Teeth Into." Using short stories in combination with scholarly writing can work at many institutions to meet the needs of students with various reading comprehension skills.

Another challenge, for traditional and nontraditional students alike, is a dearth of effective note-taking and study skills. Composition courses require a lot of information, and much of that comes from modeling appropriate essay construction. Outside of class, students have to read literature and articles, remember important themes, and construct their own writings. Some students may have to juggle jobs and families while others are immersed in the technological multi-tasking age; this can cause problems with coming to class on time, reviewing in-class information, and writing coherent papers. These are situations that can require more than mere words in order to make a point. As students walked in at the start of each class, I would play a snippet of vampire music, a vampire movie, or someone reading vampire literature. The YouTube vampire parodies were particularly popular, and another favorite was David Tennant (one of actors who have played television's Doctor Who character) reading a selection of vampire stories. This fun but relevant activity drew their attention toward the front and led straight into modeling of note taking through the chalkboard and smartboard while also encouraging students to be on time; this course had the least problems with timeliness of any English 101 course I have taught.

However, I also used other supplemental vampiric materials to encourage positive out-of-class scholarly behaviors. On the class before the first essay was due, I asked the students to write a paragraph summary of their potential essay. As they were writing, I turned on the final fight scenes of *The Lost Boys*, played Concrete Blonde's "Bloodletting" in a different part of the room, had another teacher read the start of *Dracula* at the door, and blew up their cell phones with text messages about Nina Auerbach's themes of a vampire for every age. After about two minutes of this, at which point I thought some of my students were going to revolt, I had them continue writing in silence. The activity did not require much explanation afterward: I just reminded them that perhaps they should write their assignments for the class with their text, social networking, and at least one noise-producing object off in order to have the most effective thought processes.

Even with a topic as rich and multi-layered as vampires, some students may take the themed composition course solely because it is required or fits into their schedules. They may have little interest in the topic and therefore find the course challenging. Knowing the demographic of the class is important for this reason; if someone has an interest, there is probably a vampire story or work that references it! In order to find out as much about my students in a limited amount of time, I had them do an in-class writing on the first day about their interests in general, purpose for taking the class specifically, and previous encounters with vampire-themed books, movies, or music. This information not only helped me hone how to fashion my in-class discussions or examples to use, it also allowed me to understand how to help students throughout the semester by constantly connecting vampires to their non-vampire interests.

In addition to constant checks for student understanding of the materials, a willingness to talk to students through email, text, or in the hallways outside of class helped me continue to help students engage the material. One of my students was concerned about an essay assignment, one in which students had to use the reading comprehension and writing skills they had been building to analyze a novel of their own choosing in regard to the vampire themes we had been discussing in the course. He did not know what to pick to read, as he did not enjoy fiction, and he did not want to read about what he called "fluffy, girly, sparkly vampires." After chatting for a while about the type of movies he liked, I brought in several vampire novels that are more action/adventure-style, and he happily read and analyzed Farnsworth's *The President's Vampire*. He particularly enjoyed that the work was interesting beyond merely the vampire elements and that the vampire was valuable to the government for its traditionally lethal characteristics rather than for reasons involving paranormal romance.

Teaching about vampires in a rural area has its own challenges. I also teach at a very small high school that sends a large portion of the graduating seniors to Richland Community College. Several years ago, when I directed Tim Kelly's interpretation of Rymer's

Varney the Vampire at the high school, some family members of students refused to attend because of stereotypes about vampires and vampire literature being perceived as evil. Because I knew that was a prevalent feeling in the area surrounding the college, and I also wanted to make sure to be able to discuss the erotic elements of vampire literature within the course, I included this caveat in the syllabus:

> This English 101 Course uses literature, film, music, and art about vampires as its theme. The student must be prepared to explore this theme and must be willing to read extensively. This course focuses on topics related to vampires as an outgrowth of literary and other popular cultural expressions. Some of the subject matter may be considered "adult," so you want to gauge your own reaction to the material and maturity level.

As I expected, no one dropped the college's course because of the evil nature of vampires or the racy lectures, but I did note to the students that I had alternate works available in case someone was uncomfortable with anything we read. Happily, that was not the case. In fact, a few of the English 101 students read Laurell K. Hamilton's *Anita Blake, Vampire Hunter* series in its entirety during the semester, leading to some lengthy post-class discussions in the hallways, and another student read a fairly risqué work for her individually selected novel. Teaching adults in the community college setting allows for an exploration of the sexual themes or supposed sexual themes of vampire literature in a way teaching to younger students might not, but an awareness of students' potential concerns and preparation for those concerns is more realistic than pretending that no one would ever have issues with the sometimes mature content of a vampire-themed course.

Another concern with teaching a vampire-themed composition class is that some potential students may think it will be a "fly" class in which they will not need to work. This is not the usual reaction to the English 101 course, a "gateway" course required in order for students to take many other required classes at the community college, but popular cultural themes are often misconstrued as non-rigorous by people outside of the field. Although those of us who teach vampire studies scoff at the idea of such a rich topic being perceived as some fluff class requiring no dedication to scholarship, it is a common misconception. Transparency is the most effective strategy against having students register for a course for which they are not ready or able to put forth the effort. Although teachers do not want to send potential students fleeing for the hills, they also do not want their courses to be misrepresented. I made sure my syllabus was available before registration opened and, for my first vampire-themed composition course, I sent the syllabus to registered students with the following advice: "read *Dracula* over break; in fact, read as many of the texts as possible over break." Several students said they found that extremely helpful because reading the works early allowed them to review during class rather than try to squeeze thorough readings into their regular semester schedule.

In addition, once we started class, I made sure the students were aware that I would be giving brief daily quizzes over the content of the material to be read for that day, something I do not always do at the college level. They knew that if they read the material, they would do well on the quiz, but that I crafted the quizzes to indicate whether they read the material, not whether they watched a movie, television show, or read a synopsis. This was especially important for quizzes about *Dracula*, *Twilight*, and *Dead Until Dark*. The knowledge of the quiz kept the students up-to-date on their readings, and the discussions after allowed me to determine how much the students had absorbed and understood from the readings. I tend to have several students drop my evening English 101 course, usually because of time management issues or inability to complete the work required. Because of my concern over the incorporation of the vampire elements, I paid special attention to the transparency of my expectations before the course even began. The constant discussion with and feedback from the students about the expectations of the course were beneficial, as I only had a few students decide they could not meet the expectations and drop.[3] Another way to increase the transparency of the course involves displaying even short PowerPoint information that constantly links the past of vampire tropes and English strategies from earlier class meetings, the present of the daily classroom concepts and activities, and the future of the goals and assignments. This benefits not only students whose note-taking foundations may have been shoddy, the large fonts can help nontraditional students who may be hard of hearing or have difficulty viewing presentational styles that rely on smaller type. These strategies are helpful in other institutions, I have learned, as even traditional students in other venues benefit from increased transparency.

Several practical methods exist to help set the foundation for a successful vampire-themed composition class. One strategy is for the teacher to become involved with the PR for the course. Instead of finding one's class the subject of a derogatory "can you believe people take classes in this" article, a shrewd teacher will control the spin early through positive PR. For example, Dr. Schopf did video discussions, interviews, and several articles before her Harvard course began in order to create positive buzz and to demonstrate the potential rigor of a vampire course. Inspired by Dr. Schopf, as part of a grand master plan to guide the vampire course's publicity at Richland Community College, I chose to direct O'Carroll's *The New Kids at Vampire High*, a parody of *Twilight* and other popular vampire works, for Cerro Gordo High School's Fall play; then, I received permission to present the play for a one-time engagement at the community college to promote the vampire-themed English 101 course the next semester. This led to a video interview and local newspaper article, all aimed at not only promoting the course at Richland Community College, but promoting it as a rigorous and exciting one, as opposed to the joke that nay-sayers try to make of vampire studies. As a result, I had a full class of mostly interested and eager students for my vampire-themed English 101 course.[4] In fact, I hope to have another vampire-themed English 101 course at the community college next semester!

Choosing texts wisely is another strategy for a successful vampire-themed composition course. Obviously, teachers would like to have the world of vampire literature at our disposals to discuss as we wish, but students have limited time and limited budgets. In a community college setting, pecuniary concerns may be even more important to the development of the course. Some classics are available at free online sites, and that option can be beneficial, but teachers, particularly in rural areas or places with extreme socio-economic disparity, recognize that some students may not have internet access or computer access that will allow them to read an entire novel online. Noting multiple sources for works, such as online free works, used bookstores, and online book rental companies, can help students in these situations, as can planning with reduction of text purchases in mind. Providing the syllabus, or at least the required text list, early allows students more freedom in making their book purchasing decisions. For my English 101 course with a vampire theme, I required the following works: Ramage, Bean, and Johnson's *The Allyn and Bacon Guide to Writing*, 5th ed., Penzler's *The Vampire Archives Anthology: The Most Complete Volume of Vampire Tales Ever Published*, Williams's *Three Vampire Tales*, Hamilton's *Guilty Pleasures*, Harris's *Dead Until Dark*, and Meyer's *Twilight*. The two anthologies allowed me to pick and choose classic and modern vampire works with a variety of themes at the least expense to the students.

Although I wanted twice as many works, I knew my students would not be able to keep up with that reading workload.[5]

The realization that one cannot teach the end-all, be-all vampire course at all, much less in conjunction with a composition course at the community college without losing important parts of the curriculum necessary for student success, can help educators remember that the vampire aspects of the course are to be used as a tool or a lens to help the students succeed with the goals of the course. This realization also encourages teachers not only to choose required readings and supplemental materials wisely, but also to develop writing assignments wisely and with a willingness to alter assignments based on the needs of the students. I enjoy using in-class writings not only as ways to measure how much the students read or understood about the texts to that point, but also how the students are connecting themes of vampire literature among the texts. Emphasizing how the texts forward themes or ideas or arguments encourages students to develop their abilities to use sources as support; in addition, it provides an easy introduction into appropriate citation practices required in English 102.

At the start of English 101, as part of the important process of getting to know my students and how they write, I like to have them do a bit of creative writing. For my vampire-themed course, I asked the students to develop a scene, like one might find at the start of a vampire novel, story, or film, which appears perfectly normal. They used their skills of description to present the scene as a normal slice of American life. Then, using the vampiric conventions discussed in class as well as their personal knowledge of how the "normal" can become "uncanny," the students provided elements that develop foreshadowing and/or created a space where a vampire might intrude. The short writing encouraged students to reflect on what is "normal" versus "uncanny," as well as what vampiric conventions look like in their own minds. This work allowed me to see how the students approach or see narrative or cinematic scenes as well as gave me an idea of places where the students need to work on their general writing abilities. In addition, it created an entry point to discuss how works featured in the course used foreshadowing or did not to introduce the vampire. The students' works ranged from seemingly harmless homes, forests, and schools that turned dark through over-the-top Gothic elements involving the weather, strange sounds, and uncanny circumstances, to more subtle experimentations with vampire tropes, such as the stranger who both attracts and repulses.

In a course where students may have disparate views on how to perceive vampires in literature, collaborative activities can be beneficial methods of inspiring creative and critical thinking. After discussing how advertising uses pathos, logos, and ethos to focus on particularly cultural demographics in American society and viewing the *True Blood* online PR storm, students worked in groups to create an advertisement aimed at a particular subsection of American culture in the presumed reality of a world with vampires. I chose the groups, so I could place people with differing views together; although homogeneous grouping can be beneficial, nothing produces more discussion than the heterogeneous grouping consisting of those who prefer what they perceive as "old-school monster" vampires with students who support Team Edward. This type of activity is often fun, encouraging students to work together, be creative (something nontraditional students often unknowingly crave), and understand how propaganda or advertising (and we talk about the similarities and differences of those terms) focuses on cultural cues at varying levels. At the time of their video, PowerPoint, or other type of presentation, the students provided a written reflection about how they decided on what to do, other potential choices, and how the elements of wording, sound, and images were chosen to appeal to the demographics in their imagined world. The results were hysterical: vampires were provided with fang enlarging serums, smile brighteners, sanitized coffins, and human attractant spray, to name a few, while vampire hunters could choose from ever-sharp stakes, multi-purpose attack vests, and highly concentrated garlic to put on weapons. Many advertisements explored sexual themes in vampire works with humorous results. Not only were the creations and presentations enjoyable for the class, used differentiated learning techniques, and encouraged investigations into vampire motifs as well as writing to one's audience, the activity gave a concrete learning experience from which to discuss argument and support in scholarly writing. As opposed to in institutions where most of the students are full-time, traditional, and bound to the campus, collaborative work at the community college succeeds more often when some time is given in class for brainstorming and communication within the groups. Students may then communicate through multiple methods, but they will not feel like they have to carve time out of their schedules to try and meet with group members with incongruent schedules.

English 101 required several different types of essays in which the vampire theme is easily incorporated. After we discussed and reiterated how to approach analyses and reflections of cinema and song, the students chose two potentially vampire-based songs and two vampire movies to examine. I provided them with a vast list, but they had the option of choosing something else. The students provided a general summary of the first song (reminded, as always, to use the author/singer's name and the title rather than "the first song I chose") and analyzed word choice, tone, potential audience, musical choices, and other structural and functional elements. Next, the students examined the work in relation to the mood the piece may have attempted to evoke. Then, the students explored the work in regard to the vampiric conventions discussed in the course. The students then followed the same pattern of analysis for the other song and the two movies. Finally, the students explored all four items in relation to each other and vampiric themes, which allowed them to gauge how perception is influenced by connections to other works. In addition, this activity encourages students to look at concepts and themes in different ways, a benefit for literary analysis through synectic metaphor. Some students chose works in which the vampire's character was developed similarly, usually as a lover or monster. Others chose works where the vampire characters were treated differently, an approach that encouraged more intricate analysis beyond "these vampire characters are different." For example, one student analyzed *Near Dark*, a movie about a self-chosen family of murderous southern vampires in which the term "vampire" is never used, *Blade*, a movie with an action-hero half-vampire, "Rest in Peace," a song from the musical episode of *Buffy the Vampire Slayer* from the viewpoint of a sympathetic vampire, and "Emo Vampire," a song from Key of Awesome from the viewpoint of a vampire who cannot get girls because they all want sparkly vampires. He connected the vampires in the works by connecting the themes to different ways people deal with adversity: by destroying it, by discovering solutions to it, by confronting it, and by whining about it.

Another essay focused on the novels the students selected themselves, as opposed to work from the syllabus. They were required to keep layering their perceptions of the novel with other items read in the course, as well as the vampiric conventions. Not only did the students look at authorial choices, potential audience demographics, wordsmithing, where traditional vampiric conventions are followed, broken, or reinterpreted, they had to examine the characters and plot in regard to the author's potential purpose and provided an argument with textual evidence for that proposed purpose, skills that will benefit them when analyzing other works in the future. Most students were excited to delve into different novels and use their newly-acquired prowess at analyzing vampire literature. However, I had to keep ensuring some students did not merely stay within the familiar boundaries of works that inspired television shows or movies or were the next in a series after works that we read in the class. Therefore, I required that the students get their books approved three weeks before the assignment was due. They could change their minds and get the new works approved by me up until a week before, but having the students get approval early meant that they had enough time after choosing a work to get their books read and thought about before the paper was due.

The final essay was the detailed argument, one which allowed the student to argue with scholars, authors, me, other students, or him or herself in an essay with a solid thesis, relevance to and connection with works in the course, and supporting details. The essay emphasized the creation of a solid argument supported by close reading and textual evidence. Because the course was English 101 and not the research-based English 102, I encouraged students to primarily base their arguments on works in the course itself rather than do a lot of outside research. However, the development of the final argument paper was a situation that allowed for that much-emphasized connection to the students. Several weeks before the essay was due, I started conferencing with individual students, so they would be comfortable with the requirements of the essay and their own decisions on what to write. Some students had never done any formal writing until this course, so making the expectations of the essay seem achievable due to the prior work in the course was a very important step. One woman was extremely knowledgeable about vampire literature, had a firm grasp on research and citation methods, and could write solid and intricate arguments. We talked about how she might approach her argument, and she did a fantastic job. Another student had no research experience whatsoever and had valiantly struggled to learn the concepts he needed to succeed in English 101 while also exploring the vampire elements. We discussed what work he found the most interesting and outlined how he might pursue various avenues toward supporting an argument. His resulting paper was a gem of a piece: concise, with great reading comprehension, textual evidence, a solid thesis, and a practically error-free final work. Despite their vast differences from each other, the final works of both students demonstrated success in English 101, success with the vampiric conventions, and an increased learning at the end of the course.

The most important piece of practical advice in incorporating vampire literature into an established composition course is that teachers need to love what they are doing and be prepared to have fun from beginning to end. If developing the syllabus does not thrill you with the limitless possibilities of how to include favorite and interesting works of vampire literature, the course has less potential for success. Loving the vampire mythos, vampire literature, and vampire minutia goes a long way toward a successful course. Students know when teachers are just going through the motions, and nontraditional students have less patience for when they feel their time is being wasted. Being excited about incorporating vampires into a composition course is about even more than setting a strong foundation for students to succeed in the course or even in a college or university. For many students, particularly nontraditional students, seeing someone excited about education and the potential of education may unfortunately be a novelty. Incorporating something you love into a required course that causes a lot of students trepidation alters the way you approach the course and simultaneously alters the ways the students perceive the course. In addition, by infusing a course with something about which one is not only interested in but passionate about, an educator serves as a role model. A matronly academic teaching how to write essays by using vampires and popular culture may feel she has little in common with some of her students; however, each of those students has something he or she feels just as passionately about. By teaching composition through vampire literature, teachers demonstrate that not only can one treat anything in a scholarly manner, demonstrating the worlds of scholarly investigation available, they also provide an example of how passion about even the most unusual topic can be fulfilling and beneficial, an example many students are desperate to see, no matter whether their worlds are lined with skyscrapers or cornfields.

Notes

1. Please see Sue Weaver Schopf's essay, "'Legitimizing' Vampire Fiction as an Area of Literary Study," in this volume.
2. For example, my Fall 2012 course at Millikin University focuses on vampires in the humanities to simultaneously meet the goals of the school's U.S. studies and adolescent literature courses; because the campus has a high concentration of students involved in the fine arts, not only will the examples emphasize literature to focus on the goals of the two courses, many will also come from vampire-themed music, musicals, dance, and art.
3. Because my course at Millikin University is even more intense, being an upperclass course that must meet the requirements for two courses along with the incorporated vampire theme, I have prepared those students in the same way in hopes of a successful semester.
4. For my Millikin University course, I did PR primarily through positive word-of-mouth and ended up with a full class and a ridiculous waitlist, so I have a feeling I will do another section of the course in the future!
5. For my Millikin University U.S. studies/adolescent literature course for upperclassmen, I removed *Dead Until Dark* and the Penzler anthology and added Caine's *Glass Houses*, Gomez's *The Gilda Stories*, Rice's *Interview with the Vampire*, and Lindqvist's *Let the Right One* in to fit the needs of the students and the course requirements.

Bibliography

Auerbach, Nina. *Our Vampires, Ourselves.* Chicago: University of Chicago Press, 1995. Print.
Caine, Rachel. *Glass Houses.* New York: NAL Jam, 2006. Print.
Concrete Blonde. "Bloodletting (The Vampire Song)." *Bloodletting.* IRS Records. 1990.
De Marco, Joseph. "Vampire Literature: Something Young Adults Can Really Sink Their Teeth Into." *Emergency Librarian* 24.5 (May-June 2007): 26–28. *ERIC.* Web. 28 September 2012.
Farnsworth, Christopher. *The President's Vampire.* New York: Putnam, 2011. Print.
Gomez, Jewell. *The Gilda Stories.* Ann Arbor: Firebrand Books, 2005. Print.
Hamilton, Laurell K. *Guilty Pleasures.* New York: Jove/Penguin, 2004. Print.
Harris, Charlaine. *Dead Until Dark.* New York: Ace, 2010. Print.
Kelly, Tim. *Varney the Vampire,* acting ed. New York: Samuel French, 1990. Print.
Matheson, Richard. "Drink My Red Blood." *The Vampire Archives Anthology: The Most Complete Volume of Vampire Tales Ever Published.* Ed. Otto Penzler. New York: Vintage Crime/Black Lizard, 2009. Print.
O'Carroll, Dean. *New Kids at Vampire High.* New York: Playscripts, 2010. Print.
Penzler, Otto. *The Vampire Archives Anthology: The Most Complete Volume of Vampire Tales Ever Published.* New York: Vintage Crime/Black Lizard, 2009. Print.
Rice, Anne. *Interview with the Vampire.* New York: Ballantine, 1997. Print.
Richland Community College Student and Academic Services. *Richland Community College Institutional Data Book 2009–2010. 2011.* Web. 20 May 2012. http://www.richland.edu/sites/richland.edu/files/info/data book/2011databook_web.pdf.
Schopf, Sue. "The Vampire in Literature and Film: A Brief History of the Undead." *FreeThink@Harvard.* Harvard Distance Education. Web. 20 May 2012. http://cm.dce.harvard.edu/1999/01/89003/L03/index_H26 4SingleHighBandwidth-16x9.shtml.

Text Pairing, Setting, and Vampire Literature: Teaching Bram Stoker's *Dracula* and Stephen King's *'Salem's Lot*

Alissa Burger

As literature professors, we often run up against the challenge of making classic works of literature accessible and engaging to our students, especially in introductory-level courses designed for students in their first year or two of college. An approach that has been successful with my students has been getting them to engage with a classic text — in this case, Bram Stoker's *Dracula*— as active, a canonical and familiar tale, though one that is under constant and dynamic negotiation. I employ this in my introductory fiction course, where my class is made up of first- and second-year, non–English major students, many of whom are also first-generation college students, with a generally limited exposure to classic or canonical literature. By bringing Stoker's text into conversation with a more contemporary vampire tale, Stephen King's *'Salem's Lot*, students are able to more readily grasp the resonance between these two texts and the unique evolution of the vampire, the vampire hunter, and the complex and contentious relationship between these two figures over a span of both time and space.

Context and Conversation

The idea of the active text, or the intertexually engaged text, is especially resonant within the Gothic tradition. As John Sears explains, "[t]he Gothic mode is notoriously predicated on varieties of repetition, on the recycling of narratives and forms, on revisiting older, preexistent texts, on labyrinthine texts and spaces, and on the seemingly endless resurrection of an apparently dead, outmoded tradition" (2). Providing students with this larger context of the gothic genre allows them to see Stoker's *Dracula* not as a novel whose meanings and messages are set in stone and nonnegotiable, but instead as one part of a much larger conversation, one that is continuing in the world around them and saturating the literature, film, and popular culture in which they are immersed, including Stephenie Meyer's tremendously popular *Twilight* series and those books' film adaptations, graphic novels like Scott Snyder and Rafael Albuquerque's *American Vampire* series,[1] and television series such as *The Vampire Diaries* and *True Blood*.[2]

To position students within the context of this conversation, before we even open *Dracula*, I have them tell me about vampires: what do they know? What have they seen? What have they read? What are the first images that come to mind when they hear the word "vampire"? In opening up this conversation, students are able to share what they know in an act of cooperative learning, which also helps me establish their frame of reference, so that I can work to connect our class discussions of *Dracula* and the vampire figure with their preexisting backgrounds and interests. This initial conversation takes the form of brainstorming as a large class, asking students what characteristics come to mind when they think of vampires and what vampire representations they already know (and often love) and compiling this list on the board, so they get a visual, as well as discussion-based, sense of the volume and range of their pre-established body of knowledge. Over the course of our extended readings and discussion, we often use this familiar ground as a recurring touchstone, coming back to these examples to see how these contemporary vampires stack up against their traditional counterparts and where those already familiar characteristics came from. This also allows us to identify and address their preconceptions: many of them are confident that they know who Dracula is, what the vampire is like, and how the story goes, even if they have never read the book. Once we have raised the issue of what we expect from *Dracula* and what they already know — or think they know — before opening the book, we are able to delve further into the active negotiation of the vampire figure and the cultural pervasiveness of the Dracula myth.

Whether these preconceptions come from films, such as the classic horror of Bela Lugosi's Count or the melodramatic romance of Francis Ford Coppola, reruns of *Scooby Doo* cartoons, Halloween costumes, or Count Chocula breakfast cereal, identifying these preconceived notions of the vampire serves several purposes. First, it shows students how far-reaching is the conversation in which they are about to participate by reading Stoker's *Dracula*. Second, it scales down this admittedly intimidating scope by showing them how much they already know. Finally, it overtly establishes their expectations as we begin the novel, which can productively segue into an interrogation and critical discussion of those expectations as we discover which ones are fulfilled and which ones are challenged or refuted altogether.

Once we have established what the students are coming to *Dracula* and the vampire figure already knowing, I present them with a more expansive critical context, creating a chronological continuum of texts through a Power Point-presented timeline providing students with a textual and visual historical overview.[3] This positions Stoker's novel more concretely in time and space, as having taken inspiration from his predecessors and having a profound impact on those who followed him. Given that *Dracula* is arguably the most well-known vampire story ever, it should not come as a surprise that many students assume Bram Stoker himself invented the vampire figure, one of those preconceptions that often come up in the aforementioned class discussion and one which must be addressed early on.

So after the initial baseline class discussion, I provide students with a historical overview that includes pre–*Dracula* appearances of vampires in European and American folklore, as well as works of literature, including Heinrich August Ossenfelder's poem "The Vampire" (1748), John Polidori's "The Vampyre" (1819), John Malcom Rymer's "penny dreadful" *Varney the Vampire* (1845–1847), and J. Sheridan LeFanu's *Carmilla* (1872). Depending on time, these texts can be incorporated in several ways. For example, since Ossenfelder's poem is quite brief, we usually read it together in class and then discuss it; images from *Varney* can also be easily projected and discussed in class. In contrast, when asking students to engage with longer texts, such as an excerpt from Polidori's "The Vampyre," this can more productively be assigned as out of class reading in preparation for in-class discussion. Having students work in groups and present their excerpted text to the class can also be an effective and active means of getting students to engage with a fairly wide range of texts in a short period of time, as well as encouraging students to take ownership of their own learning.

In addition to raising students' awareness that Count Dracula is not the first of his kind in Gothic literature, this emphasis on chronology and the ongoing and contested negotiation of the vampire figure also works to further explore how the vampire figure developed its unique characteristics as it was appropriated, added to, and negotiated by a wide range of authors, drawing students once more back to their expectations of the vampire and how those preconceptions have been influenced by more than two centuries of literary engagement. For example, the sexual appeal of the vampire and its illicit temptation are clear as early as Ossenfelder's "The Vampire," while female sexuality and desire becomes of central concern in LeFanu's *Carmilla*. Polidori's Lord Ruthven walks among the elite without his monstrousness being noted, an anonymity that allows for a good deal of horror, much as Count Dracula will ask Harker to teach him how to pass undetected among the British, the very ability that allows Dracula to surreptitiously enter England, with all of the power and horror he wields there.

Varney the Vampire also establishes several visual and thematic characteristics that have come to be associated with the vampire, including "having fangs leaving two puncture wounds, coming through a window to attack a sleeping maiden, hypnotic powers, and superhuman strength. Varney is also the first example of a sympathetic vampire who loathes his own condition but is helpless to stop it" (Laming n.p.). Though time does not permit a thorough exploration of each of these texts in the class, this literary overview works well to provide students with a big picture perspective of the history of the vampire figure in literature, where it came from, and how it developed the characteristics that influenced Stoker and which we have come to expect from our vampires.

Next I work to establish prominent themes in contemporary vampire figures, filling in the gaps of what students already know. I have found grouping representations into themes to be especially useful for the ongoing class discussion. Trying to compile a comprehensive list of vampire representations is not only likely impossible, but tends to overwhelm students and get them too narrowly focused on individual images. Structuring this discussion in terms of theme, on the other hand, encourages students to identify patterns and begin to critically consider why we see vampires represented in certain ways, and provides a larger paradigm within which they can position their own examples and observations. Some of the themes I focus on include science fiction vampires, or more specifically, vampires as a threat of contagion (Richard Matheson's *I Am Legend* and its film adaptation; Guillermo del Toro and Chuck Hogan's *Strain* Trilogy), romantic vampires (Anne Rice's *Vampire Chronicles* series; Meyer's *Twilight* series and its film adaptations), sympathetic vampires (Angel, the vampire with a soul, in *Buffy the Vampire Slayer* and *Angel*), and anachronistic to the Gothic tradition, vampires as humorous figures (*Scooby Doo* cartoons; Mel Brooks' spoof *Dracula, Dead and Loving It*). As with the chronological timeline, a PowerPoint presentation works well for this discussion because it allows me to easily and effectively pair concrete, visual images of the vampire across this spectrum with more abstract overviews of thematic patterns. There is naturally a good deal of overlap between some of these designations, especially between the categories of romantic and sympathetic vampires, and I work to tailor the themes I address based on each individual class's interests and preexisting knowledge.[4] This is an activity that gets repeated over the course of our discussion, first at the beginning of our exploration of the vampire figure and again as we conclude this section of the class.

In emphasizing the ongoing negotiation of *Dracula* I also bring in some intersections with genre as well that point students back to why vampire representations are the way they are, by showing clips from the classic horror film *Dracula* (Tod Browning, 1931), *Bram Stoker's Dracula* (Francis Ford Coppola, 1992), and the aforementioned *Dracula, Dead and Loving It* (Mel Brooks, 1995). We return to this series of films throughout the course of our reading and discussion of *Dracula*, looking at how horror, melodrama, and comedy address distinct features of the vampire myth — such as appearance, sexuality, agency, and destruction — in different ways and how those differences are directly influenced by genre choices. For example, while romance is central to Coppola's melodramatic film, given the horror and comedy genre contexts of Browning and Brooks respectively, it makes sense that the love story of Lucy and her myriad suitors is marginalized, resulting in the elimination of Arthur Holmwood and Quincey Morris from both films. Students respond favorably to this particular activity because in addition to presenting them with a visual representation of what they have been reading and providing a fun departure from Stoker's sometimes staid text, it also encourages them to see from a multiplicity of perspectives. For example, Gabrielle Bogdany reflected, "I believe that the film screenings that we focused on showed us how different people can interpret the same work of art" and James Erwin had a similar insight, commenting that watching the wide range of genre clips made it possible to "visualize how stories change over time, and how the same 'story' can be used for many different purposes."[5] These different takes on the familiar *Dracula* story also encourage some students to develop their own imaginative perspective, like Elizabeth Munoz, who wrote that "having background information to go along with the clips let us explore the characters and storyline a bit more, so I as a reader can feel free to imagine the novels in my way so I would be able to understand it." These screenings also proved more concretely beneficial to some students, such as Cesar Tello, who found them useful in terms of literary recall on the exam, reflecting that the screenings "contributed to better test answers from my part because I could visualize a scene." As these student responses show, the screening of this range of adaptations and the in-class critical discussion of how these representations of the vampire changed as a result of genre perspective provided them with a range of critical tools including visualization, a more concrete understanding of the dynamic negotiation of the vampire figure, ownership of their learning, and more successful recall in testing situations, all of which contribute to increased student success.

I then work to position Stephen King's *'Salem's Lot* in direct conversation with *Dracula* and within the larger context of literary vampires. King began the novel with *Dracula* in mind, starting with the hypothetical question of "what might happen if Dracula returned in modern times, not to London, but to rural America" (Winter 36). In *Danse Macabre*, his critical reflection on the horror genre, King likens his book to a "game of literary racquetball" in which "'*Salem's Lot* itself was the ball and *Dracula* was the wall I kept hitting it against, watching to see how and where it would bounce, so I could hit it again" (25). With this direct influence of one novel upon the other established, we can direct our reading of *'Salem's Lot* to the ways in which King upholds and challenges the vampire as established by Stoker, how the vampire figure changed over the more than seventy-five years between the two books, and the meaning and significance of these shifts. I emphasize this direct connection between the novels twice: first as we begin our unit on vampire literature by establishing the larger conversation both before and after Stoker, and again as we finish *Dracula* and move our reading and discussion on to *'Salem's Lot.*

Finally, to guide our lengthy reading and discussion of *Dracula* and *'Salem's Lot,* I work to direct and structure students' reading with a series of critical questions for each section of chapters. The questions for the next section of readings are presented and briefly discussed at the end of the preceding class period and then updated and added to our online course page following each class, in a constantly evolving PowerPoint file. In addition to guiding students as they read, these questions also form the basis of our in-class discussion of each day's reading, which has proven especially useful as we begin to tackle *Dracula,* which many students find thematically and stylistically daunting at times. In addition to helping students figure out which sections or elements of the reading were particularly significant, students responded that the questions worked to help them focus and to clarify confusing passages. Nicole Kverek commented that because of the extensive scope and wealth of information we encountered in *Dracula,* "the reading section questions were the best and most useful in-class activity.... We talked a lot about the book and it really covered anything that I might not have even picked up on as a reader, or was just generally confused about." For other students, the reading questions acted as a motivation; as Timothy Rosado explained, "the section questions were probably the best because it made me want to answer the questions during class, so that made me want to read. (Not really a fan of reading)." In addition to responding to my reading and discussion questions, students also had the opportunity to write their own questions, focusing on either elements that they were interested in discussing further in class or passages in the text that confused them. Whether the challenge is engaging a reluctant reader or getting students to think and respond critically to what they have read, the reading questions for both books worked to help students focus their reading and prepare for the in-class discussion of that particular section of the text.

Setting

As we begin to draw connections between *Dracula* and *'Salem's Lot,* critical engagement can be productively achieved through a concentrated focus on the setting of each novel, both in terms of time and place, a focus for which the historical overviews and previous discussions have prepared students. While pointing out to students that a key distinction between *Dracula* and *'Salem's Lot* is one of setting may seem initially to be belaboring the obvious, by taking these differences of place and time as a starting point, we are able to engage with more significant differences between the texts, all of which can be traced directly back to the literary element of setting, including issues of characterization, theme, and the shifting representations of the vampire figure and those who hunt him. As Nina Auerbach points out in *Our Vampires, Ourselves,* when it comes to the vampire figure, "each feeds on his age distinctively because he embodies that age" (1). Each individual vampire figure is a reflection of the anxieties of his moment of creation, inextricably linked with the historical context and parrying cultural fears and anxieties that move well beyond fangs and blood. To draw once more on Auerbach, "vampires blend into the changing cultures they inhabit. They inhere in our most intimate relationships; they are also hideous invaders of the normal" (6). This multiplicity of vampires unique to their specific historical and cultural moment makes setting especially significant in discussing *Dracula* and *'Salem's Lot.* Key issues that differ dramatically between *Dracula* and *'Salem's Lot* include the dismantling of the singularly powerful vampire hunter figure, the solidarity and efficacy of a cohesive vampire hunt-ing team, and the addition of the adolescent and popular cultural points of view. Each of these themes has a profound impact on the representation of the vampire and vampire hunters, as well as the way in which the narrative plays out, and each of these themes can be tied directly back to the shift in setting: late 19th century England and Transylvania in Stoker and the 1970s small town America of Jerusalem's Lot, Maine in King.

Stoker's *Dracula* begins by immersing the reader in Jonathan Harker's journal just as he is finding himself engulfed by a new, disorienting, and threatening locale, slipping increasingly further from the "civilization" of England as he passes into the East, through the Carpathian Mountains, and into the very heart of Transylvania and the Count's dan-gerous castle. Taking the tone of a travelogue, Harker describes in detail the food and cloth-ing of the local inhabitants he encounters on his journey, though he becomes most uncomfortable when his sphere collides with theirs, in their superstitions and dire warnings of evil, including "'vrolok' and 'vlkoslak'— both of which mean the same thing, one being Slovak and the other Servian for something that is either werewolf or vampire" (Stoker 16). What is most telling here is that Harker is coming to the realization that he no longer has control or even comprehensive understanding; completely out of his element, surrounded by the unfamiliar, he is at the mercy of this place and unable to control his movement within it, just as he will soon be at the mercy of the Count. As Jason Dittmer points out, "[i]n *Dracula*, as in other literature of the time, Western Europe and Eastern Europe are portrayed as opposing spaces, which together embody a series of dichotomous relationships" (241), the normal versus the exotic, civilized versus savage.

As a quintessential British man, Harker subscribes to this dichotomy without ever addressing this issue directly, with "this process of othering ... rendered invisible by Western Europe's hegemonic economic and cultural power" (Dittmer 241). Considerations of *Dracula* and "the Eastern question," as addressed by Eleni Coundouriotis, Carol A. Senf, Jason Ditt-mer, and others provide a nuanced historical perspective on the cultural position of Eastern Europe, its representation in *Dracula*, and the cultural and colonial anxieties expressed therein. While I believe this would be ideal for discussion in an upper-level literature course, however, most of my students are first- or second-year, non–English major students and this heightened level of theoretical engagement can present particularly obstructive chal-lenges at that level, when my main goal is getting them to critically engage with the text itself. So while I draw on this larger conversation in setting up the context for students, what I emphasize in our discussions are the dichotomous representation of a "civilized" England and "savage" Transylvania, the role of imagination rather than reality in creating this version of Transylvania, and the unsettled state of Stoker's England as a country in transition, torn between the traditional and the modern. I have found that in most cases this gets students engaged with the thornier issues of representation, power, and colonialism without bogging them down in dense literary theory. I address the critical reading of *Dracula* through the lens of Stoker's Irish identity in much the same way, directing students to ques-tion representations of difference, normativity, and the role of national identity rather than featuring theoretical readings, though again this would be a very interesting discussion for an upper-level course.

Just as students come to Stoker's novel with fairly well-established expectations of what the vampire is and how the story of *Dracula* is supposed to go, they also have an image of Transylvania already entrenched in their minds, one "of superstition and horror" (Miller n.p.). While students are reassured by Stoker's descriptions of Transylvania, many of which meet their expectations, they are often surprised to find that Transylvania as Stoker imagined it never actually existed and that Stoker himself never visited the region. As a result, we begin by establishing what kind of place Stoker's Transylvania is through class discussion, mapping, and visualization. We physically trace Harker's route East on a large-scale map of Europe, look at professional and tourist photographs of Transylvania, and even examine advertising and tourist images that "package" Transylvania for *Dracula* fans, playing upon and marketing the aura constructed by Stoker. After this, we are able to take a step back from Stoker's description of this setting and critically engage with what the setting *means*, which is integral to the foregrounding of this literary element in our discussions moving forward through both *Dracula* and *'Salem's Lot*. As Elizabeth Miller explains,

> In [Stoker's] representation of Transylvania, *Dracula* encodes the negative stereotypes that dominated much of nineteenth-century British travel literature, some of which Stoker consulted. Victorian travelers habitually presented their readers with invidious comparisons between Western science and Eastern superstition, between Western civilization and Eastern barbarism.... [Transylvania] assumes the dimensions of myth and metaphor: a land beyond scientific understanding, a part of the "primitive" East, Europe's dark unconscious, a descent into wildness [n.p.].

The imagined Transylvania becomes exclusively Other, primitive and dangerous, the geographic source of the horrors visited upon the intrepid vampire hunters. However, Stoker's Transylvania is a cipher that needs England to stand against; without the dichotomous construction of England's civilization to Transylvania's barbarism, Transylvania, as imagined in *Dracula*, loses much of its meaning.

While England takes on the opposite characteristics of Transylvania — light in the darkness, good struggling against evil — Stoker's England has anxieties of its own with which to contend. As Carol A. Senf explains, Stoker's lifetime was one "in which Ireland and the rest of Europe made the transition from a traditional world to a modern one" (3), a hybrid identity that is perhaps best personified by Abraham Van Helsing's simultaneous embrace of medicine, religion, and superstition as he leads his companions in the fight against Dracula. However, not all characters embrace this hybridity as smoothly as the singularly knowledgeable vampire hunter Van Helsing; while Harker has no choice but to believe in the face of his near-death ordeal, other characters such as Lucy's fiancé Arthur Holmwood are initially resistant, refusing to believe in a supernatural threat in the bright light of the rational and scientific. To overcome this hurdle, Stoker has his characters proceed logically, eliminating all other, more realistic possibilities before facing up to the horrific truth. The scientific is also paired with the experiential: Van Helsing demands that each man, especially Holmwood, bear witness to Lucy's new monstrous state, grant him permission for her destruction, and be present at her execution, knowing there is no other way that they will truly believe and not doubt themselves and their perceptions in the aftermath.

In the face of the irrefutable objective and subjective evidence of Undead Lucy's tomb, the group — with the addition of Harker and Mina — becomes cohesive and mutually supporting, working toward a common goal. One of the core in-class activities that is carried out over several sections of reading is an exploration of these very issues of characterization and group dynamic: we first work in small groups to identify everything we know about individual characters, including their personalities, their strengths, and the abilities that set them apart from one another, combining overall summary and the selection of illustrative close-reading passages by students working in small groups. Students have commented that these characterization exercises often work to make the characters and their motivations more accessible. As Gabrielle Bogdany reflected, "knowing the characters well really helps with understanding the whole plot of the book. And it made the book more interesting knowing certain characters' personalities." Once we have an understanding of each individual's characterization, we can move our discussion on to how these characters work together. Following the staking of Lucy, we return to these character sketches with two central questions: what does each member bring to the group and how are they stronger together than any of the individuals could be on his or her own? With each contributing his own particular perspective, including first-person experience (Harker), logical acumen (Mina), aristocratic mien (Arthur), and unfailing courage and a quick draw (Quincey), all coming together under the expert guidance of that quintessential vampire hunter, Van Helsing, they have a good chance of standing against Count Dracula. In fact, by removing any one of these character's contributions from the group dynamic, we discover that they are in the most danger when they are divided from one another, as when Mina is excluded from the men's conversation and her resultant isolation allows Dracula to prey upon her and force her to drink his blood.

Once the vampire hunters begin working together fairly effectively in their pursuit of Dracula, it becomes possible for them to jettison him from England as they hunt him, pursuing him once more to Transylvania, and destroying Count Dracula in the very place from which he draws his power. As Coundouriotis explains, "[t]o defeat the count, Van Helsing must recontain him geographically, force him back to his place" (155). Only by following Dracula to Transylvania can Van Helsing and his fellow vampire hunters quarantine his hideous power, return their lives in England to safety and normality, and destroy the Count.[6] The value-laden dichotomy between the dual settings of England and Transylvania dynamically pairs setting and characterization, with the battle of good versus evil playing out not only between characters but also reflected in the settings from which each emerges. Senf explains that "*Dracula* resembles a battle of opposing cultures in which the Western European characters associate the vampire with dirt, lack of humanity, darkness, the absence of morality, and predation and pledge themselves to destroy all that threatens their beliefs" (37). The battle, then, is personal, cultural, and geographical, as they must chase Dracula back to Transylvania to contain and ultimately destroy him.

King's *'Salem's Lot* unseats the vampire story from the primitive mystery of Transylvania and the propriety of late nineteenth-century England to small town America in the 1970s, in Jerusalem's Lot, Maine. Rather than building upon the mystique of Transylvania as imagined by Stoker and countless others on page and screen since *Dracula's* first publication, King positions his vampires within the realm of the everyday and the banal, inviting reader's recognition before turning the familiar horrific and plunging this sleepy little town into the realm of the uncanny. Toward the beginning of his novel, King provides a detailed description of the town, separating it into clearly-demarcated quadrants (17–19). We begin our in-class discussion of Jerusalem's Lot and readjust our expectations of the vampire's traditional hunting ground by tying ourselves concretely to what the space of 'Salem's Lot looks like with a mapping and visualization exercise: I divide the class into four groups, each with its own large piece of butcher-style paper and an assigned quadrant to sketch. When these are completed, we tape them together on the wall, giving us a "big picture" sense of what Jerusalem's Lot looks like, with clearly imagined spatial awareness, and each student having a close understanding of at least one segment of the small town.

In playing up the familiarity of this type of setting in our visualization we come to understand that by resituating *'Salem's Lot* in a contemporary time period and small town

America, King "brings to the forefront the idea that supernatural horror is not necessarily something that can occur only in a Gothic castle in Transylvania (as in Bram Stoker's *Dracula*). The undead can exist in the house just down the street, or in our own attics or basements or our neighbors' backyards ... home can be where the horror is" (Wiater, Golden, and Wagner 193). In addition to subverting expectations of the normal, this re-setting also makes the horror inescapable in a new way. While the heroic vampire hunters of *Dracula* could drive the Count back to Transylvania and thereby return London to its previous, comparative safety, the citizens of Jerusalem's Lot do not have that option. Barlow's origin is shadowy and suspect, and unlike Dracula he seems to have no need to remain linked to his homeland to draw supernatural power[7]; with nowhere to drive the vampire back to, and lacking the power to do so in any case, the battle plays out in Jerusalem's Lot, and in the end, running away and becoming placeless themselves is Ben Mears and Mark Petrie's only option for survival.

However, despite the familiar setting it is notable that the horror is not altogether unexpected in Jerusalem's Lot, regardless of the fact that so many of its citizens refuse to believe. Early descriptions situate Jerusalem's Lot within the realm of the familiar and pastoral; upon his return, Ben Mears "was amazed by how little things had changed" (King 5), from the wholesome local dairy farm of his childhood to Spencer's, the old drug store with an ice cream soda fountain, steeping Ben's return — and likely the response of many readers as well — in Americana-style nostalgia. Given the surface description of this setting, readers find themselves experiencing a spark of recognition, that Jerusalem's Lot is just another small town, rural and unchanging, like so many others, with a "well-known landscape and its appearance of wholesome freshness, [which] suggest the American pastoral, a belief in a less complicated life" (Hicks 76). However, this is not the case; as King tells readers, "[t]he town has its secrets and keeps them well" (210) and Jerusalem's Lot "knew darkness. And darkness was enough" (212). It is especially significant that this evil does not begin with the coming of the vampire. Several of the 'Salem's Lot residents are corrupt and degenerate without any supernatural influence needed and in delving below the surface appearance of Jerusalem's Lot's small town simplicity, King "destroys the American pastoral.... Like Norman Rockwell, he depicts small town America with its symbols of home, school, and church; he presents the comforts of friendly companionship and family security; he captures the neighborliness of small town America. Yet he thrusts uncontrollable evil into the midst of Rockwellian America" (Hicks 77). Evil is no stranger to Jerusalem's Lot and the corruption of the people who live there invites further degeneration, first in Hubert Marsten — a child murderer who comes to 'Salem's Lot and dies by his own hand in the Marsten House, a hulking edifice that literally overlooks the town[8]— and then the vampire Kurt Barlow and his companion Richard Throckett Straker.[9]

As in *Dracula*, larger cultural contexts also work to help establish the setting of King's novel and the people we find there. In Jerusalem's Lot, people are isolated from one another, defined in large part by their secrets rather than their solidarity. *'Salem's Lot* exists in the midst of "Nixon's politics of paranoia in the 1970s" (Strengell 170) and as King himself recalls,

> I wrote 'Salem's Lot *during the period when the Ervin committee was sitting. That was also the period when we first learned of the Ellsberg break-in, the White House tapes, the shadowy, ominous connection between the CIA and Gordon Liddy, the news of enemies' lists, of tax audits on antiwar protestors and other fearful intelligence. During the spring, summer, and fall of 1973, it seemed that the Federal Government had been involved in so much subterfuge and so many covert oper-*

ations that ... the horror would never end.... The secret room in 'Salem's Lot is paranoia, the prevailing spirit of [those] years. It's a book about vampires; it's also a book about all those silent houses, those drawn shades, all those people who are no longer what they seem [quoted in Winter 41, emphasis original].

This historical and cultural context provides a productive opportunity for interdisciplinary teaching and reading, reinforcing once more the active nature of the text as responding to what is going on in the wider world at the time of its creation and the ways in which familiar figures, such as the vampire, get appropriated in dynamically different ways that reflect their specific times and places. The settings of Transylvania and England in *Dracula* reflect anxieties of Otherness, the dichotomy of East and West, and the significance of a cultural shift from traditionalism to modernity. Though the vampire threat at the center of *'Salem's Lot* bears many similarities to that of Count Dracula, the setting *means* something different, and carries the vampire story in a new direction unique to its own historical and cultural moment: paranoia rather than progress, evil coming into the familiar space of home rather than retreating into dark, exotic shadows.

The shift of setting in *'Salem's Lot* also positions its characters to respond to the vampire threat in different ways within the more contemporary setting, taking away some powerful means of defense while providing others, though none of these prove infallible. While *Dracula*'s Van Helsing was a renaissance man of vampire hunting, combining expertise in medicine, religion, law, superstition, and folklore as he led his fellow vampire hunters against the Count, there is no singular vampire hunter in *'Salem's Lot* but rather a conglomeration of individuals who bring their own skills— along with an initial reluctance to believe or an inability to cope with the supernatural threat before them — to the fight. Along with the dismantling of the singular vampire hunter, the vampire hunting group in *'Salem's Lot* is fragmented, isolated from one another even as they work together. In fact, the core vampire hunting group — the writer Ben Mears, the teacher Matt Burke, the doctor Jimmy Cody, the priest Father Callahan, the artist Susan Norton, and the child Mark Petrie — are never even all in the same room together. This creates a group that is constantly in danger, in flux, and unable to ever effectively come together as a whole. Repeating a similar discussion and charting exercise centered on characterization and group dynamic as that which we did with *Dracula* and drawing direct comparisons between the charting of these two groups, we discover significant differences in their makeup. In addition to the fragmentation of the group and its members' isolation from one another, this charting highlights the lack of a central Van Helsing-style leader, as well as the elimination of some areas of power and knowledge, with the addition of others, positioning the vampire hunting group and this conflict concretely within the context of its particular time and place.

Two means of response that are significantly compromised in *'Salem's Lot* are those of religion and the law. Father Callahan personifies the religious perspective in *'Salem's Lot*, though he does so imperfectly; as a Catholic priest in the wake of the Second Vatican Council,[10] he has found his authority somewhat marginalized and the great battles of good and evil that drew him into service to the Church in the first place compromised. With his Church's dogma unable to bear his challenge as he finds himself in direct combat with an ancient and supernatural horror, Father Callahan's power fails him and he is forced to drink the vampire's blood, and expelled to wander the world cast out from the Church. Another means of response to the vampire threat that becomes useless in *'Salem's Lot* is that of the law, in the ineffectual Constable Parkins Gillespie. When Ben and Mark turn to Gillespie for help, the hurdle they face is not convincing him of the vampires— he has already reached this conclusion himself—but his apathy and refusal to stand against them. As Gillespie tells Ben and Mark, "I'm leavin' town.... This town will go on without us ... for a while. Then it won't matter" (King 401). The realization that they cannot rely on the law to help them gestures directly back to the paranoia and isolation referred to by King in his reflection on the 1970s cultural climate. There is no guarantee that the ones who wield the power have the strength, courage, or right to do so, and no one is immune from this horrifying realization, least of all Mark, who is deeply shaken when faced with this new and disturbing reality.

However, while religion and the law may not be on their side, King's vampire hunters have a new tool at their disposal that their *Dracula* predecessors did not: popular culture. The popular culture perspective is one with which my students are intimately and enthusiastically familiar, and one which we have cultivated over the course of the semester in our reading and discussion of both *Dracula* and *'Salem's Lot*. As Douglas Winter points out, "'*Salem's Lot* contains a veritable catalog of vampire iconography—from a single, sublime quotation of *Dracula* to a copy of *Vampirella* magazine—with an intent less to instill fear than to reinforce the pervasive recognition and acceptance of the vampire in twentieth-century American culture" (40). It is the young boy Mark Petrie who most fully encompasses this popular culture perspective, with his collection of monster models and his easy acceptance of the reality of the vampires. With Mark, the power of popular culture is highlighted very effectively: he knows the rules that govern the vampires, such as that he must invite Danny Glick into the house (King 240); he can defend himself handily, grabbing the plastic cross from his monster collection to banish vampire Danny (King 241); and he has the acceptance and resilience to more effectively cope with the horror than many of his adult counterparts.[11] Mark's intertextual popular culture-based perspective also closely mirrors that of my students themselves, who often share a similar (though updated) body of knowledge. This means that, in combination with our critical discussions of characterization and setting, as we wrap up this text-pairing, they are able to read and respond to Mark's perspective as a variation of their own, through the newly-developed lens of their own larger understanding of the vampire in Gothic literature.

Learning Outcomes

While the figure of the vampire and his defining characteristics run through both Stoker's *Dracula* and Stephen King's *'Salem's Lot*, the setting of these two books distinguish them in significant ways, both tying each to its unique cultural context and drawing the books into conversation with one another, as well as with the larger discourse surrounding the vampire and its shifting, varied meanings. Pairing these classic and contemporary novels, combined with screening and critically discussing film clips from a range of genre adaptations, extended characterization exercises, and guided reading questions encourages students to engage with the text as active. This approach allows them to see *Dracula* as not simply a concretely canonical and nonnegotiable text to be passively read, but rather as one part of an ongoing discussion that includes not only King's *'Salem's Lot* but more than two centuries' worth of manifestations of the vampire figure in literature, film, and popular culture. Focusing specifically on the literary element of setting with this pairing also works to direct students' attention toward and raise their critical awareness of the ways in which historical and cultural context have an impact on the text, often revealing to readers powerful points of contestation or negotiation during that unique sociocultural moment. Finally, through emphasizing these works as part of an ongoing conversation rather than concrete texts, students are able to more fully appreciate and critically engage with the shifting meanings of the vampire in their own generation, where it has come from, and its expansive capacity for meaning in both the past and present.

Notes

1. Stephen King contributed to the first volume of this series (2011), which repositions the figure of the vampire in the American Old West, reinvesting these creatures with new powers and interrogating the vampire mythology for a new age. The *American Vampire* series has recently finished its fourth volume.

2. The television series *True Blood* is based on a series of vampire novels by Charlaine Harris; the *Twilight* franchise also encompasses a variety of mediums, spanning books, films, and a variety of popular cultural and merchandising manifestations. While I do not assign these particular books in my classes, students' familiarity and comfort with these multi-textual vampires often work to kick-start their critical engagement and appreciation of the vampire figure as one under constant negotiation. It also has the benefit, for many students, of making them feel a bit more comfortable with the larger discussion than they may otherwise, in many cases allowing them to channel their fandom into an expertise that can contribute directly to classroom discussion and allow them to take ownership of their individual learning by connecting it to their outside of the classroom interests.

3. This and all other Power Point presentations and course materials are then made available to students on our online course page as well, so that they can refer back to and continue engaging with this information as our discussion continues to develop.

4. I have taught the text-pairing of Stoker's *Dracula* and King's *'Salem's Lot* in two different sections of my Gothic literature class, each of which had its own unique familiarity with the vampire figure. For example, while only a handful of students in one class were fans of Meyer's *Twilight* series, the other class had several "Twi-hards," so named for their die-hard loyalty to the series and its characters. In my most recent iteration of the course, I paired *Dracula* with the Scott Snyder, Rafael Albuquerque, and Stephen King graphic novel *American Vampire, Volume 1*, which presented its own set of challenges in fostering different types of literacy and guiding students through effectively reading the graphic novel, though their general lack of familiarity with this particular work allowed us to get a fresh look at a new vampire representation, one that was for the most part well outside of many students' pre-existing scope of knowledge.

5. Quotes are taken from student responses to questions of whether they found text-pairing a productive way of engaging with the text, what they found to be the most useful in-class activities, and whether or not they gained a new perspective from the screening and discussion of clips of the three films. Gabrielle Bogdany, James Erwin, Nicole Kverek, Elizabeth Munoz, and Cesar Tello were in the Fall 2012 section of the course; Timothy Rosado was in the Spring 2012 section of the course. My thanks to these students, and the others from those sections, for their feedback and reflections.

6. However, it is true that unless Dracula is destroyed, Mina will continue under his curse, a clear threat to her life, safety, and soul.

7. Barlow and Straker are are established early on as foreign and European. Straker tells Parkins Gillespie that he and Barlow "have worked together in both London and Hamburg" (King 99) and when Gillespie calls the FBI for information on the two, he finds out that Barlow is German by birth though British by naturalization and Straker is British by birth (King 142), but this information seems suspect, especially in regard to Barlow, who — like most vampires — is much older than he appears.

8. The Marsten House and the theme of haunting as explored therein also invites productive text-pairing with Shirley Jackson's *The Haunting of Hill House*, which King quotes in the epigraph to Part One of *'Salem's Lot*.

9. It is revealed in Barlow's letter to the vampire hunters that it was in fact Hubie Marsten himself who invited Barlow to Jerusalem's Lot (King 335), bearing out the idea that evil calls more evil to itself in a self-perpetuating cycle.

10. In addition to the decrease of emphasis on the personified evil — or "EVIL" (King 150) as Father Callahan thinks of it — of Satan, in an attempt to reconcile the traditionalism of the Church with realities of the modern world and contemporary Catholics' needs, the Second Vatican Council (1962–1965) also "underlined the church's solidarity with humanity instead of its separation from the secular world, and this led to a mushrooming of social and charitable activities" (Thavis n.p.).

11. That is, at least until near the novel's conclusion, when even Mark is overwhelmed and descends into

a state of shock after witnessing violent death, including that of his parents, and having come face to face with the reality that in the end, he is largely on his own.

Bibliography

Auerbach, Nina. *Our Vampires, Ourselves.* Chicago: University of Chicago Press, 1995. Print.

Bram Stoker's Dracula. Dir. Francis Ford Coppola. Perf. Gary Oldman, Winona Ryder, Anthony Hopkins, Keanu Reeves, Cary Elwes, Billy Campbell. Columbia, 1992. DVD.

Coundouriotis, Eleni. "Dracula and the Idea of Europe." *Connotations* 9.2 (1999-2000): 143–159. Print.

Dittmer, Jason. "Dracula and the Cultural Construction of Europe." *Connotations* 12.2-3 (2002-2003): 233–248. Print.

Dracula. Dir. Tod Browning. Perf. Bela Lugosi, Helen Chandler, Dwight Frye, David Manners, Edward Van Sloan. Universal, 1931. DVD.

Dracula, Dead and Loving It. Dir. Mel Brooks. Perf. Leslie Nielsen, Peter MacNicol, Steven Weber, Amy Yasbeck, Harvey Korman. Castle Rock, 1995. DVD.

Hicks, James E. "Stephen King's Creation of Horror in 'Salem's Lot: A Prolegomenon Towards a New Hermeneutic of the Gothic Novel." *The Gothic World of Stephen King: Landscape of Nightmares.* Ed. Gary Hoppenstand and Ray B. Browne. Bowling Green, OH: Bowling Green State University of Popular Press, 1987: 75–83. Print.

King, Stephen. *Danse Macabre.* New York: Berkley, 1981. Print.

_____. *'Salem's Lot.* New York: Signet, 1975. Print.

Laming, Scott. "A Brief History of Vampires in Literature." AbeBooks.com. AbeBooks, 1996–2012. Web. 23 July 2012.

Miller, Elizabeth. "Vampire Hunting in Transylvania." *Dracula's Homepage.* Elizabeth Miller, 2008. Web. 23 July 2012.

Sears, John. *Stephen King's Gothic.* Gothic Literary Studies. Series ed. Andrew Smith and Benjamin F. Fisher. Cardiff: University of Wales Press, 2011. Print.

Senf, Carol A. *Dracula: Between Tradition and Modernism.* Twayne Masterwork Studies. Series ed. Robert Lecker. New York: Twayne, 1998. Print.

Stoker, Bram. *Dracula,* 100th anniversary ed. Intro. Leonard Wolf. 1897. New York: Signet Classic, 1997. Print.

Strengell, Heidi. *Dissecting Stephen King: From the Gothic to Literary Naturalism.* Madison: University of Wisconsin Press, 2005. Print.

Thavis, John. "Forty years later, Vatican II continues to reverberate through church." *Catholic News Service.* Catholic News Service, 15 Oct. 2005. Web. 24 July 2012.

Waiter, Stanley, Christopher Golden, and Hank Wagner. *The Stephen King Universe: A Guide to the Worlds of the King of Horror.* Los Angeles: Renaissance Books, 2001. Print.

Winter, Douglas E. "*'Salem's Lot.*" *Stephen King: The Art of Darkness.* New York: New American Library, 1984: 36–44. Print.

Timely ... or Timeless?
Teaching the *Twilight* Saga

Heather Duerre Humann

American author Stephenie Meyer's *Twilight* saga has been wildly popular since 2005 when *Twilight*, the first installment of the series, was originally published. To date, the series has sold over 100 million copies worldwide with translations into dozens of languages around the globe, making the books some of the bestsellers of all time.[1] Film adaptations have been made of all of the books, with the last film installment, *Breaking Dawn: Part II* (a film adaptation of the second part of *Breaking Dawn*), debuting to much hype in November 2012. The series' popularity has prompted some educators (such as myself) to incorporate *Twilight* into the courses they teach at high schools and colleges across the United States. During the spring of 2010, I taught an upper-level special topics course of my design about the *Twilight* saga (designated English 311: Special Topics in Literature). My class was offered as part of the 2010 Interim course offerings in the English Department of the University of Alabama in Tuscaloosa.[2] There were twenty nine undergraduates enrolled in my course; the vast majority of these students were English majors. We examined the four books that comprise the *Twilight* series (*Twilight*, *New Moon*, *Eclipse*, and *Breaking Dawn*) alongside the literary masterpieces that inspired each of the four installments: Jane Austen's *Pride and Prejudice*, William Shakespeare's *Romeo and Juliet*, Emily Brontë's *Wuthering Heights*, and William Shakespeare's *A Midsummer Night's Dream*.[3] In addition to studying these eight literary works for their own sake, we also explored how the themes presented in the canonical literary works—concerns which include these texts' treatment of gender, marriage, family conflicts, and social conventions—are rearticulated and re-emerge in the *Twilight* saga. Teaching *Twilight* reinforced for me the fact that Meyer's series is an easy and enjoyable read for most University students, but the readability of the saga — and the ease with which students in my class were able to engage with the novels— belies many of the more serious lines of inquiry that we undertook to explore during this three-week-long special topics course.[4]

Since the books are so popular, teaching the *Twilight* series, which particularly appeals to young adults, offers educators an opportunity to teach novels that students are already excited about, but importantly the books of *Twilight* saga have assumed cultural significance not only because of their popularity and commercial success, but also since they serve as a locus of inquiry into timely questions related to contemporary values, individual agency, and social conventions. Indeed, when I taught *Twilight*, we considered these and a range of other questions related to canon formation, the cultural and historical forces surrounding and influencing literary works, and the practice of re-imagining and/or retelling classic stories for a contemporary audience (to name just a few of the concerns we addressed in this class). My aims in this essay are twofold: to discuss my experiences teaching *Twilight* and to share pedagogical strategies with others who are considering teaching the series.

In the sections that follow, I will (1) address the controversy surrounding teaching *Twilight*, (2) discuss the *Twilight* series in the context of vampire literature, (3) discuss Meyer's influences and consider the importance of intertextuality with respect to the *Twilight* saga, (4) analyze the series' characters as types with an eye toward comparing Meyer's characters with the protagonists of the canonical works which influenced them, and (5) examine the treatment of gender and gender politics in these literary works. Though it is difficult to distill weeks of teaching into essay form, my hope is that by addressing this range of concerns, I will be able to offer a glimpse into my experience teaching the *Twilight* saga as well as provide insights and pedagogical strategies to other teachers.

Teaching Twilight: *The Controversy*

Although there are examples of vampire literature that date back hundreds of years, Meyer's *Twilight* saga has not been around very long at all. *Twilight*, the first book of the collection, was just published in 2005, so traditionally this series of commercially successful books has not been taught in English or literature courses. Moreover, there is a degree of controversy surrounding whether the series *should* be taught in schools. As soon as these books made their way onto the required reading lists of some high school and college-level courses, a number of media outlets began discussing whether *Twilight* saga was worthy of academic scrutiny. In August 2010, for example (just a few months after I taught my Special Topics in Literature course on the *Twilight* saga at the University of Alabama), Yahoo's *Shine* ran an article that bashed the teaching of the series in college and university classes by suggesting that implementing the books into the curriculum oftentimes constituted "pandering to a powerful market group," the "current generation of college kids [who] are largely responsible for franchise's success" (Weiss).[5] The question of whether or not it is appropriate to teach the *Twilight* books still persists today. In "Majoring in Potterology," her recent Salon.com article, Laura Miller asks, "Are books like J.K. Rowling's popular series and Stephenie Meyer's '*Twilight*' fit subjects for serious scholarship?" As part of this article, Miller considers, "what should literary academics study?" She concludes that "many people believe that academia's job is to ordain great literature and pass on its exalted benefits to students. As for bad literature, the more calumny that can be heaped on it and those who love it, the better!" (Miller). Remarks such as these are just the tip of the iceberg. Without a doubt, the *Twilight* books seem to draw strong reactions from most everyone who has heard of them.

Since there has been (and remains) so much controversy surrounding the series, teachers who are considering making Meyer's *Twilight* saga required reading should keep in mind the degree to which the series has been celebrated, criticized, and heavily debated in many different circles. Rather than shying away from debates about the books, teachers who include these books in their courses could make addressing the many controversies surrounding the teaching of the *Twilight* saga part of the covered material. Certainly, this could offer students another effective vantage point from which to approach the books, since questions about canon formation and debates about (so-called) high culture versus popular culture remain so central to literary studies today. In the course I taught, we incorporated such discussions about canon formation in our classroom conversations. For example, students were particularly interested in learning — and subsequently discussing — how Jane Austen's novels (now considered literary masterpieces and taught as part of the literary canon), received little critical praise during her lifetime despite their popularity.[6]

The Twilight *Saga in the Context of Vampire Literature*

Another lens through which to view Meyer's *Twilight* novels is in the context of vampire literature, a designation that covers a wide spectrum of literary work concerned chiefly with the subject of vampires. Literary tales of vampires date back as far as the 18th century, and within this body of literature there are many recurring motifs including the predatory nature of vampires, as a species.[7] The question "What accounts for the popularity of the *Twilight* series?" can be answered, in part, by addressing a broader concern: "What drives the popularity, adaptability, and distinctive appeal of the vampire figure?" According to Laurence A. Rickels, who explores the history of vampirism and vampire literature in his book, *The Vampire Lectures*, the vampire functions an enduring object of fascination, fear, ridicule, and reverence that can be traced to "a psychohistory of projection" (2). In other words, vampires remain so compelling because of their "identification with some absent (and thus haunting) other" (Rickels 2). What this "other" represents does not remain static; rather, it varies culturally and historically, adapting to different places and times.

To an extent, vampires represent a society's wishes and fears, a point Nina Auerbach emphasizes in her book, *Our Vampires, Ourselves*. Vampires, she contends, have the ability to "stalk and shape-shift" in order to adapt to "changing romantic ideals" (Auerbach 101). Therefore, contemporary vampire literature reveals our recent cultural preoccupations in the same way that early tales of vampires echoed the concerns of previous eras. Although Meyer's representation of vampires (and other supernatural creatures) in the *Twilight* saga departs from the traditional myths, legends, and lore about them in some significant ways, her depiction nonetheless borrows some elements from traditional vampire literature, a genre which is now centuries old.

Because there are both similarities and points of contrast between Meyer's representation and more traditional depictions of vampires, when I taught the *Twilight* saga, one of the first things we discussed was *Twilight*'s place among vampire lore. The students in my class arrived with varying degrees of knowledge and awareness about vampire literature. They all, of course, had heard of Bram Stoker's classic novel *Dracula* (some students had read the book) and HBO's *True Blood* series (many students were fans of the series, which had aired two seasons when I taught my course of *Twilight*), but they tended to be much less familiar with other literary accounts of vampires, including not only 18th and 19th century tales, but also the many notable examples published during the late 20th and early 21st centuries.[8] Given the students' rather uneven knowledge about the genre, I found that spending some class time addressing the history of vampire literature allowed students to consider how Meyer both borrows from and builds upon the genre. We were able to use this discussion as a point of departure to examine Meyer's own take on vampires (and other supernatural creatures) in order to compare and contrast her depiction with the more the traditional mythos.

According to the customary mythology, vampires tend to avoid humans (when they're not hunting them) because of their aversions to garlic, silver, ash wood, and exposure to sunlight, not to mention their fear of a stake to the heart. Because (according to the more conventional vampire mythology) humans have the power to kill them, vampires have traditionally tended to hide away and isolate themselves, since secrecy was so essential to their survival. In contrast, Meyer re-imagines her vampires as sparkly and superhuman. With virtually no weaknesses, her vampires can venture out into sunlight. They also have herculean strength and speed, impenetrable skin, and even unique gifts, such as Alice's power to foresee the future and Edward's ability to read minds. In the same manner in which Meyer re-imagines vampires, she also borrows from and blends elements from the more traditional mythology about werewolves and shape shifters in her creation of Jacob and other members of the Quileute tribe that reside in La Push. In the cases of both Meyer's vampires and the creatures that populate the Quileute tribe, students were able to effectively compare and contrast Meyer's accounts with more traditional legends, thereby enabling them to recognize that though Meyer's books are clearly steeped in a long tradition of vampire and other supernatural literature, they depart from the traditional mythology in significant ways.

We also considered how Meyer's representation of vampires showed the influence of her own personal (and religious) values at the same time as she responds to 21st cultural mores. For example, many have argued that the *Twilight* books seem to promote abstinence.[9] Yet, rather than this detail suggesting that Meyer's treatment of romantic and sexual relations departs heavily from the more traditional motifs in vampire lore, Meyer's treatment may simply offer a new spin on one of the genre's age old concerns: sexuality. As Lev Grossman argues, "it is the rare vampire novel that isn't about sex on some level, and the *Twilight* books are no exception. What makes Meyer's books so distinctive is that they're about the erotics of abstinence. Their tension comes from prolonged, superhuman acts of self-restraint." By the same token, Meyer's novels can also be said to be reflecting her views on recent debates about abortion and marriage.[10] Students were very engaged in the classroom conversations we had about these topics and particularly interested in discussing how Meyer's own, rather traditional views about sex, marriage, and pregnancy were reflected in her novels.

Influences and Intextuality

Including Meyer's literary influences as part of class room discussions about the *Twilight* saga is yet another vantage point through which to consider Meyer's novels. Since Meyer has been quite candid about the variety of, and the degree to which, other literary texts have influenced her writing, it is now well known that each book in the *Twilight* series was inspired by, and loosely based on, a different literary classic: *Twilight* on Jane Austen's *Pride and Prejudice*, *New Moon* on Shakespeare's *Romeo and Juliet*, *Eclipse* on Emily Brontë's *Wuthering Heights*, and *Breaking Dawn* on (another Shakespeare play) *A Midsummer Night's Dream*.[11]

Teaching these canonical works alongside the novels of the *Twilight* series (and including them in discussions about *Twilight*) opens up new avenues to explore Meyer's novels, not to mention raises timely questions about intertextuality and the practice of reimagining classical themes for contemporary audiences. As Hye Chung Han and Chan Hee Hwang argue in their essay, "Adaptation and Reception: The Case of the *Twilight* Saga in Korea," in her *Twilight* novels, Meyer is effective in deconstructing and reconstructing "classical texts such as *Romeo and Juliet, Pride and Prejudice,* and *Wuthering Heights*" (220). Examining the relationship between Meyer's novels and these literary classics allows students to consider the underlying cultural forces at play in the creation of the literary texts in question — and it also gives students an opportunity to consider contemporary views on these older canonical literary works. To be sure, I found in my experience teaching the *Twilight* saga that pairing each of the *Twilight* novels with the books that inspired them encouraged students to make meaningful connections between the themes and plots of Meyer's novels and those present in classic literary works.

In his book-length discussion of *Twilight,* John Granger comments on the similarities between the themes of the *Twilight* saga and those present in classic love stories. He observes, "A love story is, first of all, the 'Boy meets Girl, Boy loses Girl, Boy regains Girl' formula. The friction [...] comes from something conventional [...] that is keeping them apart" (Granger 39). This friction can manifest as a variety of obstacles that stand in the way of happiness for would-be couples. In *Pride and Prejudice,* for example, Elizabeth Bennet and Mr. Darcy must not only move past how off-putting their first impressions of the other were, but they each also must confront 18th century mores regarding marriage, family, and social class. In *Wuthering Heights,* taboo and (later) tragedy keep Heathcliff and Catherine from being together. In both *Romeo and Juliet* and *A Midsummer Night's Dream* (like in many of Shakespeare's other plays), what keeps the smitten couples apart is their families.[12] Of course, in *Twilight,* it is largely the fact that Edward is a vampire and that Bella is human that (at least initially) prevents their being together romantically.

The similarities between the plots, themes, and formulas of these classic literary works and the *Twilight* saga have prompted many comparisons. For example, Granger compares the plot of the *Twilight* books to the "warring Capulets and Montagues," but suggests that *Twilight* ultimately offers a "happier ending for the couple" (39). A striking similarity between *A Midsummer Night's Dream* and the *Twilight* books is that, in each, characters seem to fall for the "wrong people," resulting in a series of complicated love triangles (in the *Twilight* series, the most notable love triangles are those between Edward-Bella-Jacob and Emily-Sam-Leah).

What's more, teaching *Romeo and Juliet* and *A Midsummer Night's Dream* alongside the *Twilight* books brings the question of fate (an old, yet timeless, literary concern) and its importance to the forefront. Studying *Romeo and Juliet* side-by-side with *A Midsummer Night's Dream* provides a nice point of contrast since the two plays so effectively illustrate the difference between comedy and tragedy. In the case of *Romeo and Juliet,* fate and perhaps also a series of bad luck are largely to blame for the play's many tragedies. Fate intervenes most notably in the first scene of Act 5, when Romeo hears false news and mistakenly believes that his love Juliet has perished, yet fate plays a pivotal role in other scenes, as well. Indeed, readers of the play might find themselves asking the sorts of questions that Shakespeare scholar Corinne J. Naden succinctly rattles off: "What if Tybalt hadn't recognized Romeo at the feast? What if Romeo hadn't met Tybalt on the street and refused to fight? What if Mercutio hadn't been so hot-tempered? What if there wasn't an epidemic of plague at the time? What if the letter to Romeo in Mantua had been delivered? What if Romeo had waited a few more minutes before he drank the poison?" (97). In contrast, it is by a stroke of good luck — via the (ultimately benevolent) interference from the fairy realm — that the series of lovers in the comic *A Midsummer Night's Dream* get happy resolutions to their romantic dilemmas. The *Twilight* saga borrows elements from the plots of both of these plays; indeed, Meyer, through characters such as Edward, Bella, Jacob, and Renesmee (not to mention Leah, Sam, and Emily), represents both the tragic and comic possibilities of love.

Beyond creating parallels between her protagonists and characters from these classic love stories, Meyer sets it up so that Bella and other *Twilight* saga characters themselves read, discuss, and reflect on literary masterpieces (including the ones that inspired the series), thereby setting up a meta-narrative about (and offering a meta-commentary on) the nature of love and love stories. As part of her discussion of Bella that appears in her essay, "Girl Culture and the *Twilight* Franchise," Catherine Driscoll points out how, throughout the *Twilight* books, "Bella explicitly learns about love from classic romances, gothic and otherwise, including William Shakespeare's *Romeo and Juliet* (c. 1597), *Pride and Prejudice* (1813), *Jane Eyre* (1847), and *Wuthering Heights* (1847)" (96–97). Tellingly, Bella's impressions of these classic works are shaped by Edward and his reactions to them. As Driscoll puts it, "Edward is Bella's interlocutor for the most important of these readings" (97). In *New Moon*, he insists that "Romeo is a fool"; in *Eclipse*, claims that "Heathcliff is a monster" (Driscoll 97). Resultantly, Meyer's characters seem to learn a lot about love from reading these canonical works. At the same time, Meyer's characters mirror and mimic the struggles the characters from the canonical works faced. This is especially true for Edward, who (though he feels quite above both Romeo and Heathcliff) follows in the footsteps of the literary masterpieces' male protagonists in so many respects.

Character Analysis

In addition to raising questions about influence and intertextuality, reading the novels of the *Twilight* saga alongside *Pride and Prejudice*, *Romeo and Juliet*, *Wuthering Heights*, and *A Midsummer Night's Dream* indeed encourages students to compare and contrast the protagonists from these various literary works. I found that this type of comparison pushes students to think critically, especially about how the characters of Meyer's novel oftentimes function as types.

Comparing *Twilight*'s Edward Cullen to the male protagonists of classic literary works proved to be fertile ground for discussions in my class. We found a particularly fruitful comparison between Edward and the "Byronic Hero" (of which Emily Brontë's Heathcliff is a prime example).[13] A Byronic hero exhibits several characteristic traits, including his rebellious nature. The Byronic hero does not possess heroic virtue in the traditional sense; instead, he typically possesses many dark qualities. As Peter Thorslev describes in his book, *The Byronic Hero: Types and Prototypes*, with regard to his intellectual capacity, self-respect, and hypersensitivity, the Byronic hero seems to be "larger than life," yet "with the loss of his titanic passions, his pride, and his certainty of self-identity, he loses also his status as [a traditional] hero" (187). Thorslev further explains that he is usually isolated from society as a wanderer, or is in exile of some kind. It does not particularly matter whether this social separation is imposed upon him by some external force or is self-imposed. *Twilight*'s Edward Cullen is intelligent, arrogant, and isolated, and his vampirism provides his necessary "dark qualities." Indeed, he has many of the distinguishing features of a Byronic Hero in spades. In order get students to think critically about this comparison, in my class we spent time analyzing Edward Cullen's traits alongside Heathcliff's with an eye toward examining how each conforms to, or deviates from, the notion of a "Byronic hero." I found that, through this exercise, students were able to make meaningful associations not only between *Wuthering Heights* and the *Twilight* saga, but also between those novels' male protagonists.

In the case of *Twilight*'s Bella Swan, students were quick to pick up on connections between her and Juliet, as well as between her and Elizabeth Bennet, which proved to be a good starting point for a discussion about the kind of heroine Meyer is writing about in *Twilight*. We also considered the degree to which the female characters of *Twilight* and the various literary masterpieces we studied ultimately reflect or challenge their respective society's customs, codes, and mores. As Roberts argues, Shakespeare's women reflect the values of their time period, at least to an extent: "the women in Shakespeare's plays are presented primarily as young virgins, like Juliet and Hermia, valued for their marriageability, or as powerless mothers and wives" (Roberts 6). However, characters such as Juliet arguably move beyond such two-dimensionality, for she displays a degree of agency in a number of the play's scenes. According to Roberts, Juliet proves to be the "more active partner in the sudden romance" since she "almost instantly introduces the subject of marriage; she arranges the rendezvous at Friar Lawrence's cell; she renounces her dependence of the nurse when the latter's practicality prevails over passion; and she risks the horrors of awakening in the tomb in order to be reunited with her husband" (6). Thus, Juliet both reflects the limitations of life for women in Elizabethan England at the same time as her character moves beyond any simplistic characterization. The same thing can be argued about Elizabeth Bennet and Catherine Earnshaw — and, for that matter, Bella Swan and many of the *Twilight* saga's other female characters — since they are very much products of their respective time periods, but prove to be complex characters nonetheless.

The Politics of Gender in the Twilight *Saga*

Beyond comparing and contrasting Bella and the *Twilight* series' other female characters with their counterparts from the literary masterpieces that inspire Meyer's saga (which I just discussed in this essay's previous section, "Character Analysis"— and which we covered in the course I taught), considering what messages the series convey about women bears scrutiny. Indeed, an analysis of the *Twilight* saga would not be complete without addressing the issue of the books' gender politics, and specifically the treatment of the novels' female characters, since these constitute some of the more troubling aspects of the story.

To an extent, the *Twilight* books function as products of our time and thus reveal our society's values and attitudes. Our culture has created strict standards about how women should look, act, and conduct their lives, and Meyer's fiction reflects these contemporary gender codes and conventions. Yet, the books also reveal disturbing realities about how many in our society view women at the same time as episodes in the series demonstrate women's subordination, marginalization, and victimization in a patriarchal context.

As many scholars and bloggers have been quick to point out, the theme of violence against women runs throughout the *Twilight* series. Bella, the series' protagonist, is constantly in danger. Not only does she fall for a guy who (for a time at least) can't decide if he wants to feed on her or marry her, but, for Bella, peril seems to lurk around most every corner. Whether in the form of street hooligans or vampires (such as psychotic James and vengeful Victoria, not to mention the menacing Volturi who threaten her!), Bella seems to be always facing jeopardy. Yet, Bella is not alone among the series' female character in confronting violence. As Anne Torkelson illustrates in her essay, "Violence, Agency, and the Women of *Twilight*," examining the many "episodes of violence against Bella in the larger context of violence against other women in the books reveals an imbalance of power relations that extends beyond Edward and Bella to the series' other male-female relations" (210). From relatively mild boundary violations (such as when Jacob gives Bella the unwanted kiss in *New Moon*) to the horrifying gang rape that Rosalie recounts in *Eclipse*, the series is replete with examples of violence against women.[14] Most of the women characters in *Twilight* have been victimized by men at one time or another. Esme and Emily were both abused by romantic partners and Alice, in her human life, was forcibly confined to an asylum where she suffered terrible mistreatment.[15] Taken together, their experiences suggest just how prevalent the abuse of women remains, and thus raises disturbing questions about the degree to which such violence has become normalized. A concern we addressed in my class is whether Meyer's treatment of violence against women constituted an attempt to actively confront and challenge this issue — and thus raise awareness about it — or if her novels merely perpetuated the status quo in terms of depicting women as victims.

This question becomes rather complicated, especially in the later novels of the series, as a closer analysis of the characters Rosalie and Bella will illustrate. Taught by her family that the best she could hope for in life was to "marry well," and then viciously attacked by a group of men (led by her would-be husband, no less), Rosalie's human life highlights the precarious position of women in a male-dominated society. As a vampire, however, Rosalie is able to break "free of the male-dominated power structure when she chooses Emmett for her mate and when she stands with pregnant Bella against the rest of the coven's wishes, acting as her protector" (Torkelson 219).[16] Similarly, as a human, Bella struggles with her own agency and autonomy (not to mention the fact that her life is constantly in danger), but as a vampire, she finally comes into her own. Thus, both Rosalie and Bella represent strong, savvy, confident, and liberated females—characters who are very much in control of their lives— but they only achieve this level of independence once they are in vampire form, thus ultimately complicating the message of the novels with respect to the representation of female characters (and the books' stance on gender equality).

Ultimately, I found that having serious discussions in class about the gender politics in the *Twilight* series really enhanced the students' engagement with the texts. By bringing issues related to women's oppression, abuse, and exploitation to the forefront, we were able to reflect on the mixed messages that the novels seem to impart about contemporary gender relations, which not only aided in our analysis of the novels but also opened up a space to consider literature's more general role in shaping and normalizing how contemporary society views women. Though these topics can be sensitive ones, the students in my class were eager to weigh in on Meyer's treatment of gender, though students' responses to questions about the depiction of female characters in the series varied greatly. The students' responses were mixed in terms of how they viewed Edward and Bella's relationship; some saw him as domineering and controlling while others praised Edward for his commitment to Bella. Several students were troubled by the number of scenes that showed violence against women — and a few seemed particularly bothered by the more graphic scenes (such as Rosalie's gang rape, and James' attack on Bella, from the first book of the series)—but, on the whole, the students in my class tended toward believing that Meyer was merely reflecting the violent realities of our society, rather than promoting (or condoning) violence against women.

Conclusion

Because of the *Twilight* saga's immense popularity, educators who opt to teach these books (which especially appeal to young adults) get to teach literature that many students are excited about, but significantly, Meyer's *Twilight* books have assumed cultural significance not only because of commercial success, but also since they probe timely questions related to contemporary values, individual agency, and social conventions. Whether Meyer's books will stand the test of time or not remains to be seen, but what is clear is that, for today, the series remains not only popular, but culturally relevant because of the timely (and sometimes timeless) issues addressed throughout the series. My approach to teaching the *Twilight* saga by pairing each of the *Twilight* novels with the books that inspired them resulted in a successful class where students were engaged with the material and were ultimately able to make meaningful connections between the themes and plots of Meyer's novels and those present in classic literary works. My hope is that other teachers who are considering teaching these novels will benefit from these pedagogical strategies and my experiences teaching the *Twilight* saga.

Notes

1. According to the 2009 *USA Today* article, "*Twilight* Series Eclipses Potter Records on Best-Selling List," the books have "smashed records" once made by Rowling's *Harry Potter* series (Memmott and Cadden).

2. The University of Alabama's Interim session gives students a chance to earn University credit while offering a more creative approach to learning during three-week sessions. Interim classes take place May of each year; when I taught the *Twilight* saga, the Interim program ran from May 10 to May 28, 2010.

3. We did not read *The Short Second Life of Bree Tanner*, the companion novella to the *Twilight* saga, because *Bree Tanner* had not been released, yet (it was published on June 5, 2010, just a week or so after the Interim course I taught had concluded).

4. All of the students enrolled in my course were familiar with the *Twilight* series and the majority had read at least some of the books in the saga prior to enrolling in my course. Since many of the students were English majors, a number of them had also previously read the other literary works we studied.

5. The article, titled "7 Fall College Courses Based on *Twilight*," was published on August 30, 2010.

6. During Jane Austen's lifetime (1775–1817), her novels brought her little personal fame. Austen published her novels anonymously, though among members of the aristocracy, her authorship was considered an open secret. At the time of their publication, Austen's novels were deemed fashionable by members of high society, but received few positive reviews. By the mid–19th century, however, her novels were admired by members of the literary elite who viewed their appreciation of her works as a mark of cultivation.

7. The literary vampire first appeared in 18th century poetry, before becoming one of the stock figures of gothic fiction with the publication of Polidori's "The Vampyre" (1819), which was inspired by the life and legend of Lord Byron. Bram Stoker's *Dracula*, considered the masterpiece of the genre, was first published in 1897.

8. For example, a fewer number of students number had read Anne Rice's *Vampire Chronicles*, which were very popular during the 1990s (and are still read today), and (disappointingly) none of the students had read Octavia Butler's *Fledgling* (2005), which offers an innovative re-imagining of vampires at the same time as it confronts timely and provocative questions about family, gender, race, and genetic engineering.

9. See, for example, Sarah Selzer's August 9, 2008, *Huffington Post* article titled "*Twilight*: Sexual Longing in an Abstinence-Only World," or the U.K. *Telegraph*'s article "*Twilight* Teaches Teenage Girls That Abstinence Can Be Sexy, Says Robert Pattinson" by Anita Singh, which was published on November 28, 2009.

10. Through both her treatment of Bella's pregnancy and her depiction of Bella's response to her pregnancy, Meyer sends a decidedly pro-life message. Although Bella's pregnancy clearly puts Bella at risk (indeed, her life remains in grave danger for the duration of her pregnancy), she insists on continuing her pregnancy, rather than terminating it, despite the fact that her husband Edward and doctor, Carlisle (who is also her father-in-law), suggest more than once that she abort due to health concerns. Meyer also seems to be advocating abstinence before marriage through characters such as Bella and Edward, who choose to postpone consummating their relationship until after they have said their wedding vows.

11. Meyer has discussed her influences in a number of interviews, including in Karen Valby's frequently cited *Entertainment Weekly* piece (titled "Stephenie Meyer: 12 of My *Twilight* Inspirations"). Meyer has also

said that authors Orson Scott Card and L. M. Montgomery (the author of the *Anne of Green Gables* series) are major influences on her writing.

12. In her discussion of *Romeo and Juliet* and *A Midsummer Night's Dream* from her article "Triple-Threat Shakespeare," Jeanne Roberts comments on how family — specifically Juliet's and Hermia's fathers — attempts to keep the would-be couples apart. She further claims that though both plays represent highly patriarchal societies, in each the "patriarchal father is defeated — tragically in one and comically in the other" (Roberts 6).

13. In his book, *The Brontës and Their Background: Romance and Reality*, Tom Winnifrith discusses the sisters' fascination with the "Byronic hero." He acknowledges, for example, how a "study of the Brontës' juvenilia provides confirmatory evidence of the sisters' preoccupation with the aristocracy, their emancipation from Victorian prudery, and the attraction of the Byronic hero, beautiful but damned" (Winnifrith 4). In this same analysis, Winnifrith examines how they incorporate the figure into their literary works.

14. As Rosalie describes for Bella, before she was turned into a vampire, she was raped and left for dead by her drunken fiancé and his friends. Carlisle found her and, after realizing that she was about to die, he changed her into a vampire.

15. Emily still bears the scars from the time her romantic partner Sam attacked her "on accident." It is revealed via Esme's back story that she stayed in an abusive marriage to appease her family.

16. As Torkelson adds, Rosalie exhibits agency only "after she has gained superpowers," which complicates the message (Torkelson 219).

Bibliography

Auerbach, Nina. *Our Vampires, Ourselves.* Chicago: University of Chicago Press, 1995. Print.

Austen, Jane. *Pride and Prejudice.* London: Penguin, 1996. Print.

Brontë, Emily. *Wuthering Heights.* Ed. David Daiches. London: Penguin, 1985. Print.

Driscoll, Catherine. "Girl Culture and the *Twilight* Franchise." *Genre, Reception, and Adaptation in the* Twilight *Series.* Ed. Anne Morey. Burlington, VT: Ashgate, 2012. 95–112. Print.

Granger, John. *Spotlight: A Close-Up Look at the Artistry and Meaning of Stephenie Meyer's* Twilight *Saga.* Allentown, PA: Zossima Press, 2010. Print.

Grossman, Lev. "Stephenie Meyer: A New J.K. Rowling?" *Time Magazine.* April 24, 2008. Web.

Han, Hye Chung, and Chan Hee Hwang. "Adaptation and Reception: The Case of the *Twilight* Saga in Korea." *Genre, Reception, and Adaptation in the* Twilight *Series.* Ed. Anne Morey. Burlington, VT: Ashgate, 2012. 215–228. Print.

Memmett, Carol, and Mary Caddon. "*Twilight* Series Eclipses Potter Records on Best Selling List." *USA Today.* August 5, 2009. Web.

Meyer, Stephenie. *Breaking Dawn.* New York: Little, Brown, 2008. Print.

_____. *Eclipse.* New York: Little, Brown, 2007. Print.

_____. *New Moon.* New York: Little, Brown, 2006. Print.

_____. *Twilight.* New York: Little, Brown, 2005. Print.

Miller, Laura. "Majoring in Potterology." Salon.com May 25, 2012. Web.

Naden, Corinne J. *Romeo and Juliet.* Tarrytown, NY: Marshall Cavendish, 2009. Print.

Rickels, Laurence A. *The Vampire Lectures.* Minneapolis: University of Minnesota Press, 1999. Print.

Roberts, Jeanne Addison. "Triple-Threat Shakespeare." *Teaching* A Midsummer Night's Dream, Romeo and Juliet, *and* Macbeth. Teaching Shakespeare Institute. New York: Washington Square Press, 1993. 3–7. Print.

Selzer, Sarah. "*Twilight*: Sexual Longing in an Abstinence-Only World." *Huffington Post.* August 9, 2008. Web.

Shakespeare, William. *A Midsummer Night's Dream.* Ed. Stephen Greenblatt. New York: Norton, 1997. Print.

_____. *Romeo and Juliet.* Hertfordshire: Wordsworth Classics, 1992. Print.

Singh, Anita. "*Twilight* Teaches Teenage Girls That Abstinence Can Be Sexy, Says Robert Pattinson." *Telegraph* (U.K.). November 28, 2009. Web.

Thorslev, Peter Larsen. *The Byronic Hero: Types and Prototypes.* Minneapolis: University of Minnesota Press, 1962. Print.

Torkelson, Anne. "Violence, Agency, and the Women of *Twilight*." *Theorizing Twilight: Critical Essays on What's at Stake in a Post-Vampire World.* Ed. Maggie Parke and Natalie Wilson. Jefferson, NC: McFarland, 2011. 209–223. Print.

Valby, Karen. "Stephenie Meyer: 12 of My *Twilight* Inspirations." *Entertainment Weekly.* September 29, 2009. Web.

Weiss, Piper. "7 Fall College Courses Based on *Twilight*." Yahoo *Shine.* August 30, 2010. Web.

Winnifrith, Tom. *The Brontës and Their Background: Romance and Reality.* New York: Palgrave Macmillan, 1988. Print.

A Tale of Three Draculas: Teaching Evolution and Genre Conventions

Murray Leeder

This essay describes an assignment designed for a Film Studies course I taught. It requires students to compare three different adaptations of Bram Stoker's *Dracula*, made in three different countries in three different decades: F.W. Murnau's *Nosferatu, Eine Symphonie des Grauens* (1922; henceforth *Nosferatu*) with Max Schreck, Tod Browning's *Dracula* (1931) with Béla Lugosi and Terence Fisher's *Horror of Dracula* (1958, known simply as *Dracula* in the U.K.) with Christopher Lee. The students were required to trace a single conventional element of their choice through the three versions of *Dracula*, paying attention to how it changes over time and attending to the question of why. It was the first assignment in a second-year Film Studies genre course entitled "Horror Before *Psycho*" that I taught at Carleton University, and it was designed to create an engagement with questions about generic conventions and to encourage the students to address questions about how genres change and develop over time.[1]

Other familiar and frequently revisited texts within the horror genre might similarly serve as case studies: *Frankenstein* or *The Strange Case of Dr. Jekyll and Mr. Hyde*, perhaps. Yet the choice of *Dracula* appealed to me for a variety of reasons. One is that interest of vampires is at a high water mark, and both the *Twilight* fans and its naysayers have reasons to be interested in *Dracula*. Not wanting to go down a sparkly rabbit hole, I limit my references to *Twilight*, like describing Béla Lugosi as the Robert Pattinson of his day (not an entirely facetious comparison, since Lugosi emerged as a sex symbol precisely because of the foreign, transgressive sexuality implied in his characterization of the Count).[2] The other is the way Dracula has reached the point of pop culture osmosis that rivals Santa Claus or Sherlock Holmes, albeit in ways that often obscure the original novel and the older films that made him famous. By the time a student reaches university, the name "Dracula" means something to him or her — often something with only a minor connection to the original 1897 novel by Bram Stoker. Students might have inherited a general familiarity with the iconographies of the character from Count Chocula or *Sesame Street,* even if they have never actually seen a *Dracula* film. If they have seen any film, it would most likely be the Francis Ford Coppola film misleadingly-entitled *Bram Stoker's Dracula* (1992), which is quite tonally, thematically and narratively distinct from the source novel.[3] Only a few students have read the novel. This paradoxical familiarity yet lack of familiarity makes *Dracula* the ideal subject for this assignment. The last, and perhaps most important factor, is the fact that these three films (to say nothing of every other iteration of *Dracula* out there) share core similarities, but are fleshed out in notably different ways. They all tell the story of a young solicitor going on a trip to arrange property purchases for a sinister nobleman who is in fact a vampire, who then relocates into the heart of civilization. Even *Nosferatu*, its story and characters altered specifically to avoid paying copyright laws (unsuccessfully), cannot depart too much from that narrative.

As mentioned, "Horror Before *Psycho*" is a second year Film Studies course at Carleton University, with roughly ninety students enrolled. Only about half of the students are Film Studies majors, with the rest coming from a diverse set of fields including economics, journalism, English, mass communications, psychology, and even a few mathematics, sciences and engineering students. I opted to confine the course to pre–1960 horror films to keep it manageable, and to expose students to some fundamental material they might not otherwise encounter. Despite the high enrollment in genre classes, it is sometimes a challenge to get students to start thinking about genres, since genres almost naturalize their conventions in the minds of their audiences, so stepping back and looking at a genre's classical period is a useful way of forcing a critical engagement that might not be possible with newer texts. To provide some fundamental genre theory, I begin the course with a discussion about genre and genre evolution, and it is here that I find *Dracula* (and the vampire more broadly) invaluable. I introduce the students early on to the significance of genre conventions; thus our explorations of horror are couched within generalizable observations about genre that students might apply elsewhere. The fundamentals of genre theory needed to be taught near the beginning of "Horror Before *Psycho*," before the class scrutinized the classical horror film in terms of race (with *King Kong*, 1933), gender (*Cat People*, 1942), queerness (*The Bride of Frankenstein*, 1935), science (*Dr. X*, 1932), spectacle (*House of Wax*, 1950) and politics (*Invasion of the Body Snatchers*, 1956).

My early lectures emphasize that, as pervasive as genre is, it is often difficult to define (Cherry). Different cinematic genres seem to be defined in very different ways: by a setting (Westerns, science fiction), presumed audience (teen film, "women's picture"), by presumed audience reaction (pornography, horror, melodrama), by style (film noir), etc. Films are sometimes identified with a given genre or subgenre only in retrospect (such as John Carpenter's *Halloween* (1978) with the slasher film) and genres mix, so that it is not always possible to tell where one begins and the other ends. Further, different genres serve different users differently: in horror, a "gore hound" specialist fan may have a very different reaction to a given film than a more casual spectator. The minimum takeaway I want for the first portion of the course is that genres are categories of convention; there cannot be a secret genre we are not aware of, since they exist as much in the minds of audiences as inherent properties of the genre texts themselves.

In an attempt to pin down how we define a given genre, I introduce Rick Altman's influential semantic/syntactic approach to film genre. Even though Altman himself departed from this model in time, it remains quite useful for getting undergrads thinking about how genres function, and especially how genres are located not only within the textual features of a given film text but also within an audience's interpretative capacities. Altman's model borrows from linguistics, with semantic elements as analogous to words and syntactic elements as analogous to sentence syntax. The semantic can include visual motifs, stock characters, familiar settings, props and the like, all constitutive elements identifiable as a given genre. Syntactic elements emerge when semantic elements are combined in such a way as to access cultural meanings, including formulaic plots, conventional character relationships, stock scenes, etc. One stock scenario in the vampire film is a scene in which the vampire is confronted by an expert armed with a crucifix. Different semantic elements (the vampire, the crucifix, the expert) are arrayed in a certain order to produce a conventional meaning. I show them an example from *Son of Dracula* (1943), in which Dracula (Lon Chaney) appears to confront Dr. Harry Brewster (Frank Craven) and is chased off by the crucifix-wielding Van Helsing-surrogate, Professor Lazlo (J. Edward Bromberg). It is a fairly model rendition of this syntax. I follow it with an example from *Fright Night* (1985), in which the designated vampire slayer Peter Vincent (Roddy McDowall) draws a cross on vampire Jerry Dandridge (Chris Sarandon). Dandridge merely laughs and says, "You have to have faith for this to work on me," exposing Vincent as a fake. However, the film's teenage protagonist, Charley Brewster (William Ragsdale), steps in and succeeds in repelling Dandridge, presumably possessing that requisite faith. The sequence thus acknowledges and engages with a traditional syntax of the vampire film (students will soon see its most famous rendition in the Browning *Dracula*) but modifies it, presenting a familiar scene in a new way.

In using the example of repelled-by-crucifix scenes as a recognizable syntax of the vampire film, I am borrowing from Tim Kane's Altman-influenced structuralist take on the vampire film (esp. 7–8). Showing these two sequences together is a useful way of not only dealing with genre syntax, but also of introducing the question of genre evolution, the subject of the new week's lecture. As much as genres are based on stable conventions and audience expectations, they obviously change over time, and indeed need to, both to keep up with shifting societal values and to avoid stagnation. To speak of genre evolution, I draw on the four stages of genre evolution defined by Thomas Schatz: experimental, classical, refinement and baroque (36–41). If the evolutionary model of film genres is contentious and much criticized (not the least its seemingly preordained march from "the not-yet-classical towards the no-longer-classical" (Walton 96), it has pedagogical value for getting students to think about the fact that genres change and asking why. In "Horror Before *Psycho*," the three adaptations of *Dracula* fill the role of the first three stages of the cycle of genre evolution. *Nosferatu*, made somewhat before "horror" was used as a noun, exemplifies the experimental phase, where visual, narrative and formal conventions are just beginning to be established and are not yet tied specifically to a generic frame. An unauthorized adaptation, *Nosferatu* had every interest in distinguishing itself from the novel. It provides a useful vantage not only to see the first use of conventions that would become standard in vampire movies (destruction by sunlight, notably[4]), but also for roads not taken: the idea of the vampire being accompanied by a plague of rats, for instance, or that a woman's pure love can lure a vampire to his death, failed to become conventional. In fact, because *Nosferatu* would spend decades in copyright limbo and was rarely screened, it would only be in the seventies, in Werner Herzog's 1979 remake and the TV miniseries of Stephen King's *'Salem's Lot* that same year, that vampires would begin to resemble the terrifying makeup done on Max Schreck in *Nosferatu*. I raise this point to help reinforce the strange and unexpected circuits that genre conventions often take. Students almost always respond well to *Nosferatu*, in part because of the lasting effectiveness of Max Schreck's performance, and the film's formal ostentation (the use of sped up footage, negative footage, etc.). With the possible except of the films of Buster Keaton, I have found no better film than *Nosferatu* in breaking through the built-in resistance many students have to silent films.

In the classic stage, a sense of equilibrium is achieved; conventions are recognized both by the filmmakers and their audiences. It is a period of stability and, presumably, prosperity. This period tends to be the most valorized by genre historians. Our classical film is Tod Browning's *Dracula*, surely the most influential vampire film of all. From infancy, figures like the Count on *Sesame Street* interpolate us into a certain conceptual visualization of the vampire that stems from it. When one fends off infection by "Dracula sneezing" into one's sleeve, one is unwittingly impersonating Béla Lugosi. From Dracula's first piercing glare into the audience to the creeks of opening coffins and the sensational mad cries of Renfield (Dwight Frye), not to mention the sonorous tones of Dr. Van Helsing (Edward van Sloan) as he delivers immaculate exposition, everything in *Dracula* solidified conventions for decades to come. In contrast to *Nosferatu*, Dracula here is charming and humanlike, of an aristocratic, romantic bearing, and needs to because, I tell them, the source play by John L. Balderston and Hamilton Deane needed to take place in a succession of drawing rooms and other interior locations, and thus needed a talkative, personable Count to place in them. The Count of the novel is ugly, bestial, and absent from huge portions of the novel, much like Sauron in *The Lord of the Rings*, the largely unseen villain. Even its most inveterate fans agree that *Dracula* is stagey and clunky, in part due to Browning's indifferent direction (caused, many say, by his alcoholism), but when students look past this, they gain particular appreciation for Lugosi's icy and commanding performance.

In Schatz's refinement phase, instability is starting to enter the system. Classical conventions are no longer fully satisfying spectators, so filmmakers must attempt new variations in order to maintain an audience. *Horror of Dracula* is an example of refinement-period horror film because it is torn between impulses towards observing the conventions codified in Browning's film and consciously rejecting them. A great example to which I try to point the students is Dracula's first appearance onscreen. When Jonathan Harker (John van Eyssen) arrives in the Castle, we are first shown Dracula in silhouette as three ominous notes sound on the soundtrack. But Dracula steps forward and, rather than attacking his guest or even coming across as the odd, sinister foreigner that Lugosi does, he speaks with an English accent and greets his guest in a friendly, businesslike fashion; this Dracula, we suddenly realize, is less a mysterious foreigner than an articulate country gentleman. Like many refinement horror films, *Horror of Dracula* adds generous helpings of sex and blood. Indeed, the film introduces itself with blood: blood dripping onto the name "Dracula" as it festoons a cold stone crypt. As the first vampire film fully in color, it embraces its new ability to shock the audience with crimson flows; it is also the first time a screen vampire sported fangs, save for *Nosferatu*'s ratlike incisors. Also in prime Hammer fashion, although with more restraint than later films, it sports well-figured women in low-cut dresses and hints at transgressive sexuality, for instance in the sequence where the newly vampirized Lucy (Carol Marsh) tries to seduce her brother. This is also the first film in which Van Helsing (Peter Cushing) is a full-fledged, professional vampire hunter, and in the film's version, Harker is a spy working for him even as he first reaches Dracula's home. The ground is laid not only for *Van Helsing* (2004) with Hugh Jackman, but for all vocational vampire slayers, from Blade to Buffy. One student commented that *Horror of Dracula* was the only film screened in "Horror Before *Psycho*" that felt like a *real* movie to him — a parochial attitude, to be sure, but it speaks to the film's accessibility. Another swore that it is the best vampire film ever made, far above anything from recent decades.

Though they fall outside of the course's temporal limits, I show a few clips from later vampire films to represent the baroque period of the vampire, in which a genre's conventions and values are sharply inverted, mocked or questioned. One is a flat-out parody, *Love at*

First Bite (1979). It starts with the amusing scene of Dracula (George Hamilton) playing the organ in a fog-drenched Transylvanian castle, and then chastising overzealous wolves howling along with a travesty of a famous line: "Children of the night! Shut up!" Dracula is then kicked out of his castle by officials of the communist Romanian government who insist that he "gather [his] aristocratic shit together and leave!" It conveys the point that, by the late 70s, Dracula was an overfamiliar character lacking the ability to scare anyone. I also show a clip from *Martin* (1977), in which the title modern teenager (John Amplas), a serial killer who believes himself to be a vampire, terrorize his Old World relative Tata Cuda (Lincoln Maazel), a particularly backwards Van Helsing figure, while sporting a Lugosi-esque cape and fangs. At the end of the sequence, Martin spits out his fake fangs, mocking his cousin for clinging to such superstitions: "It's only a costume."

In addition to screening these three films, I also provide the students with a short lecture on the history of the vampire, to show that Stoker's *Dracula* did not come from nowhere but that it nevertheless introduced or codified many familiar conventions. Students are surprised to learn that the word "vampire" only enters the English language in the first half of the 18th century, and that the folkloric vampire of the Balkans[5] is a horrible and largely mindless corpse, more like a zombie or a ghoul than the literary vampire that would eventually take shape in the British Isles. The first vampire in English prose was Lord Ruthven in John Polidori's 1819 short story "The Vampyre." A thinly-veiled parody of Dr. Polidori's employer, Lord Byron (a dashing personage with whom students tend to be generally familiar even if they've never read him), Ruthven is a human-like aristocrat, arguably closer to Edward Cullen of *Twilight* or Bill Compton of *True Blood* than the literary Dracula is. Ruthven is vulnerable to knives and bullets, but recovers when placed under moonlight. A special relationship with the moon is also a feature of Varney from the 868-page serial *Varney the Vampyre*, published between 1845 and 1847; this is another example of a once-strong conventional element of the vampire that dropped away over time. *Carmilla*, the classic novella by Irish writer J. Sheridan LeFanu, provided the first literary vampire who could transform into an animal (a cat), as well as the first vampire with fangs (but pointed eye teeth instead of the more familiar elongated canines). Finally, *Dracula* would codify a great many conventions of the vampire in 1897, and is also noteworthy for being the first significant vampire tale set in present times.

I provide students with this brief background about the literary vampire even though this is a film studies class and not a literature one, in part to reinforce the fact that the vampire is an archetype that has changed substantially over time. And Count Dracula himself can signify differently within different national contexts. The readings that accompany the lectures (contained in a coursepack) emphasize the national contexts of each film. A reading from Anton Kaes's *Shell Shock Cinema* (2009) emphasizes *Nosferatu* as a product of the Great War's aftermath and the German culture of mass death, mourning and hysteria, while a chapter from David J. Skal's *The Monster Show* (2001) discusses how the Golden Era of the American horror film, *Dracula* included, would commence during the darkest year of the Great Depression, 1931: "America's worst year of the century would be its best year ever for monsters" (115). Lastly, a reading from Peter Hutchings discusses the reception of *Horror of Dracula*. Hutchings enumerates how many British critics regarded it, not only a bad film, but as a symptom of a sick and de-energized postwar British society. These readings add up to give the students some sense of how nation may interact with historical circumstance and generic convention within a given film.

The full instructions for the *Dracula* assignment are as follows:

Write an essay on the development of the conventions of the vampire film (as a subgenre of the horror film), as seen in *Nosferatu* (1922), *Dracula* (1931) and *Horror of Dracula* (1958). These three films are all adaptations of the same book, but are nonetheless very different, and all play substantial parts in the development of the vampire film's conventions.

Choose **one** convention of the vampire film. Examples might include "the bedroom visitation scene," "the vampire's home," "Dracula's introduction scene," "the Van Helsing figure," "the Renfield figure," "the female protagonist," "the cross," "blood," or anything else you see as a conventional element of the vampire film. Then take this convention and chart it over the course of the three films. In some cases, a given convention may be absent from a film (*Horror of Dracula*, for instance, has no Renfield); it will then be your job to comment on the significance of that absence.

You must discuss all three films. The best essays will be those which do not simply provide a laundry list of similarities and differences between the three films, but comment intelligently on the significance of these changes with respect to the developing conventions of the vampire film.

Please follow the style guide contained in the syllabus.

You must cite at least one published academic source in your essay. Any essay that contains no research will receive a grade of F. This can be one of the course readings, but the following useful books have been placed on reserve at the library:

Bram Stoker's Dracula: Sucking Through the Century, 1897–1997. (Ed. Carol Margaret Davison)

Celluloid Vampires: Life After Death in the Modern World (Stacey Abbott)

Dracula: Between Tradition and Modernism (Carol A. Senf)

Dracula: The Vampire and the Critics (Ed. Margaret L. Carter)

From Demons to Dracula: The Creation of the Modern Vampire Myth (Matthew Beresford)

The Lure of the Vampire: Gender, Fiction and Fandom from Bram Stoker to Buffy (Milly Williamson)

The Monster with a Thousand Faces: Guises of the Vampire in Myth and Literature (Brian J. Frost)

Reading the Vampire (Ken Gelder)

The Vampire Film: From Nosferatu to Bram Stoker's Dracula (Alain Silver and James Ursini)

Vampires: Myths and Metaphors of Enduring Evil (Ed. Peter Day)

The most fun part of teaching, as many of us have discovered, is when students come up with something surprising and original, and I was pleased by how well the *Dracula* assignment delivered in that regard. One student focused on Van Helsing, tracking his rise to a full-fledged protagonist in *Horror of Dracula*, and also noted that, though the character nominally representing Van Helsing in *Nosferatu*, Bulwer (John Gottowt), is narratively inconsequential, Van Helsing's narrative function is fulfilled instead by a tome, *The Book of the Vampires*. Another student perceptively honed in on the absence of the sequence in *Horror of Dracula* in which Van Helsing notes that Dracula does not cast a reflection in a mirror and confronts him with this fact. This sequence is a highlight of *Dracula*, so why is it left out of the latter film? Only because, the student reasons, the 1931 film needs to convince its characters and its audience that the Count really is a vampire, and that need no longer exists to the more genre-savvy audience of 1958. One German exchange student focused on the theme of borders and nationality in the films, arguing with particular care that *Horror of Dracula* is full of World War II imagery that relates Dracula to Nazism (nicely including visuals comparing the eagle statue outside Dracula's castle to Nazi iconography). One of the most successful papers honed in on what the student called "the bedroom visitation scene," the inevitably sexualized sequence in which a supine woman is visited by the vampire in her bedroom. This student charted the progression from Ellen Hutter's (Greta Schröder) self-sacrifice in *Nosferatu* to the passive Mina (Helen Chandler), who is unconscious as Dracula prays on her in *Dracula*, to the much more active Mina (Melissa Stribling) of *Horror of Dracula*, whose scenes with Dracula play as consensual love scenes. The student interpreted Dracula as an agent of Freud's drive, and saw this increase acceptance on the part of his leading ladies as signifying the increasing domestication of death throughout the twentieth century.

Not all papers were that ambitious, but on the whole, the assignment proved quite successful, with many solid essays discussing the different depictions of Dracula's castle, from *Nosferatu*'s desolate ruin to *Horror of Dracula*'s comfortable cottage, or the increasing sexualization of the female characters. The biggest pitfall was when students failed to restrict themselves to a single convention and instead produced nebulous, unfocused papers, or delivered those laundry lists cautioned against in the instructions. The assignment could be reworked to include more films and extended in terms of its timeframe.[6] This assignment could surely be adapted to other purposes, too. One can imagine a class on screen Westerns that would screen three films about Billy the Kid or Wyatt Earp or Jesse James—a common character and a basic plotline holding together a history of variation. Again, the idea is to enable the students to engage with genre conventions and evolution by examining three different iterations of the same story. I have already suggested other familiar texts that might also work in a horror class, and when one student in the "Horror Before *Psycho*" class wanted to do a rewrite, I assigned her three adaptations of Mary Shelley's *Frankenstein*: the 1910 Edison version, James Whale's version from 1931 and the Hammer film *Curse of the Frankenstein* (1957).

Nonetheless, I am reluctant to tamper with the choice of *Dracula* for this assignment. *Dracula* is uniquely familiar and unfamiliar to most students, and this presents an opportunity: they know enough to be interested but not so much that they cannot be surprised. Ken Gelder writes, "What we have is ... not only one *Dracula* but many *Draculas*" (65), and while he is referring to many vastly different interpretations of the novel, his words are equally applicable to its many adaptations. Part of *Dracula*'s lasting appealing is flexibility; there is something in *Dracula* for everyone, and, hopefully, for every student. *Nosferatu*, *Dracula* and *Horror of Dracula* are three films that tell a common story in remarkably different ways, and taken together they provide a succinct case for the twin poles of stability and change on which genre evolution rests.

Notes

1. I am hardly unique in positioning *Dracula* as a kind of pedagogical Rosetta Stone through which a variety of issues can be studied; see Hogle.

2. While hardly an admirer of *Twilight*, I am at pains to explain when asked that it neither invented the idea of heroic nor romantic vampires; one might in fact say that this is has been a significant modes for the vampire since at least the 1970s.

3. One major example is the film's incorporation of the rather slender link between Stoker's *Dracula* and the historical Wallachian *voivode* (warlord) called Vlad the Impaler or Vlad Dracula. After being questioned about this by a few students, I incorporated it into lecture, stressing that Stoker's novel was originally written as *The Un-dead* and that Dracula was originally called "Count Wampyr" before Stoker came across a few references to Vlad and consequently changed the setting to Transylvania (the first draft is set in Styria, as is LeFanu's *Carmilla*). Only a few passages in *Dracula* allude to Vlad, and the connection was not widely known until the 1970s (hence its incorporation both into *Dracula* (1974) and *Bram Stoker's Dracula*). See McNally and Florescu.

4. The convention of vampire being destroyed by sunlight took a while to become standardized, in films like *Return of the Vampire* (1944) and *Horror of Dracula*. Students are frequently incredulous that a convention that now seems so ironclad is of relatively recent lineage.

5. Comparable blood-drinking monsters can be found in mythologies worldwide. Whether or not the word "vampire" is appropriate for, say, the *Penanggalan* of the Malay peninsula — a woman's head that detaches from her body to fly about, entrails dangling, in search of blood of newborns— is a matter of some debate, and may reflect an imperialistic impulse.

6. It could hypothetically include *El Conde Dracula* (1970), *Dracula* (1974) with Jack Palance, *Count Dracula* (1977) with Louis Jourdan, *Dracula* (1979) with Frank Langella, *Bram Stoker's Dracula*, *Dracula: Pages from a Virgin's Diary* (2002), etc., but unless this were a course specifically about adaptations of *Dracula*, it would need to be refrained to three or four adaptations.

Bibliography

Abbott, Stacey. *Celluloid Vampires: Life After Death in the Modern World.* Austin: University of Texas Press, 2007. Print.

Altman, Rick. "A Semantic/Syntactic Approach to Film Genre." *Cinema Journal* 23.3 (Spring 1984): 6–18. Print.

Beresford, Matthew. *From Demons to Dracula: The Creation of the Modern Vampire Myth.* London: Reaktion, 2008. Print.

Carter, Margaret L., ed. *Dracula: The Vampire and the Critics.* Ann Arbor: UMI Research, 1988. Print.

Cherry, Brigid. *Horror.* London: Routledge, 2009. Print.

Davidson, Carol Margaret. *Bram Stoker's Dracula: Sucking Through the Century, 1897–1997.* Toronto: Dundurn Press, 1997. Print.

Day, Peter, ed. *Vampires: Myths and Metaphors of Enduring Evil.* Amsterdam: Rodopi, 2006. Print.

Frost, Brian J. *The Monster with a Thousand Faces: Guises of the Vampire in Myth and Literature.* Bowling Green, OH: Bowling Green State University Popular Press, 1989. Print.

Gelder, Ken. *Reading the Vampire.* London: Routledge, 1994. Print.

Hogle, Jerrold E. "Theorizing the Gothic." *Teaching the Gothic.* London: Palgrave Macmillan, 2006. 29–47. Print.

Hutchings, Peter. *Dracula.* London: I.B. Tauris, 2003. Print.

Kaes, Anton. *Shell Shock Cinema: Weimar Cinema and the Wounds of War.* Princeton: Princeton University Press, 2009. Print.

Kane, Tim. *The Changing Vampire of Film and Television: A Critical Study of the Growth of a Genre.* Jefferson, NC: McFarland, 2006. Print.

McNally, Raymond T. *In Search of Dracula: A True History of Dracula and Vampire Legends.* New York: Galahad, 1972. Print.

Schatz, Thomas. *Hollywood Genre: Formulas, Filmmaking, and the Studio System.* Philadelphia: Temple University Press, 1981. Print.

Senf, Carol A. *Dracula: Between Tradition and Modernism.* New York: Twayne, 1998. Print.

Silver, Alain, and James Ursini. *The Vampire Film: From* Nosferatu *to* Bram Stoker's Dracula. New York: Limelight Editions, 1993. Print.

Skal, David J. *The Monster Show: A Cultural History of Horror.* New York: Faber and Faber, 2001. Print.

Walton, Saige. "Baroque Mutants in the 21st Century? Rethinking Genre Through the Superhero." *The Contemporary Comic Book Superhero.* Ed. Angela Ndalianis. New York: Routledge, 2009. 86–106. Print.

Williamson, Milly. *The Lure of the Vampire: Gender, Fiction and Fandom from Bram Stoker to Buffy.* London: Wallflower, 2005. Print.

Cherokee, Creole and Mormon, Oh My! A Look at Vampire and Religious Representations for the Literature Classroom

Alisha M. Chambers

I stood before a classroom to present my unit plan to the other twenty-three students in my "Teaching Literature in the Classroom" course, a ten-lesson plan entitled: Vampires and Religious Representations in Literature. Most, if not all, of my fellow students, as well as my professor, appeared doubtful over the usefulness of a class devoted to vampire literature. This may have been due to a common misconception I have heard about genre literature as a whole — why waste time teaching inferior "literature" when classrooms already lack the time to teach the classics? The answer is quite simple: reader engagement.

Vampire texts, if chosen properly, contain the very same elements of classic literature in both: writing techniques, such as the skills to create sensory details, believable dialogue, and realistic characters; and theory techniques, such as skills for comprehension and close reading, interpretation, evaluation, and appreciation. The lists are quite extensive. The chosen texts, *Marked* by P.C. and Kristin Cast, *Interview with a Vampire* by Anne Rice, *The Last Vampire* by Christopher Pike, and *Twilight* by Stephenie Meyer, represent current and popular texts that students can relate to as well as to demonstrate modern views on old vampire myths and the transformation of mythos in correlation to cultural transformations; moreover, vampire literature is ripe with religious references that students can utilize for discussion and teachers can use for various assignments.

I presented to the class my first lesson, the one I had hoped would engage students and create a type of dialogue among them concerning how vampires are presented in media and how they are stereotyped in popular culture. Essentially, this lesson will be a demonstration of what the course will entail — a look at religious and cultural stereotypes of each selected text with detailed and structured analytical and creative assessments. The lesson objectives include: to tease out characteristics and themes that the students are already aware of and to compare and build on their knowledge about vampire myths; to begin to draw a connection between popular vampire myths and religion; and to introduce the idea that reading for fun and reading for school can be the same reading.

So where does an analysis of vampire literature begin? It begins with the establishment of a base or working knowledge. For my anticipatory set,[1] I had students work in small groups of three or four to compile a list of vampire representations that they may have been introduced to by novels, short stories, movies, television shows, commercials, and hearsay. Students benefited from small group interactions and began to think about vampire images in a critical way. After five minutes of group discussion, the class regrouped, and we compiled a list on the board. This list covered the top ten vampire myth representations: vampires can fly; vampires are not visible in mirrors or reflective surfaces; vampires prey on virginal women; vampires turn into bats and sleep in coffins; garlic, crosses and religious paraphernalia repel vampires; holy water will burn a vampire's flesh; and vampires can be killed by a stake to the heart, exposure to sunlight, or fire. During this activity, students created smaller networks within the reading and writing community of the classroom.

After the stereotypical attributes of vampires has been established, I showed, via PowerPoint, several iconic media representations, including films *Interview with the Vampire* (1994), *Blade* (1998), and *Twilight* (2008); novels *The Last Vampire Series* by Christopher Pike, the *House of Night Series* by P.C. and Kristin Cast, and the *Anita Blake Series* by Laurell K. Hamilton; and television shows *Buffy the Vampire Slayer* (1997) and *True Blood* (2008). Most students made sounds and movements of acknowledgement as each picture appeared on the screen, and I left them with one last media image, a clip from the show *The Adventures of Billy and Mandy*, where the legendary Dracula dismisses the stereotypical vampire bite with his scrape and lick method.

The clip works as a means to shift discussion. How are these stereotypes created, and where did they come from? The answers to these questions are extensive, thus the students will strive to answer those questions, among others, throughout the unit. As a lead in to the unit, I demonstrated a select nine historical views on where the modern myths of vampires may have stemmed. Nearly every culture around the world has had tales of supernatural beings who consumed blood or flesh, and the notion of vampirism existed in cultures such as ancient Greece and among Mesopotamians, Hebrews, and Romans. The current folklore about vampires originated from early eighteenth-century Central Europe, and most commonly, these vampires were revenants of evil beings, suicide victims, or witches, or were even malevolent spirits that possess a corpse. One could also be bitten by an already existing vampire.

For example, in ancient Greece, the *vrykolakas* were a varied vampiric creature that, in later centuries, had strong holds in the Christian faith. At first, the *vrykolakas* were not feared; instead, they were often seen as the dead returning "to complete unfinished business with a spouse or a family member, or someone close to him or her in life" (Melton 306). Accounts of *vrykolakas* became more and more elaborate, some of which tell of the dead returning to resume their lives. However, the Greek Orthodox Church created the popular belief in the *vrykolakas*, where a curse was placed upon those who were excommunicated to keep the body from decaying and the soul from progressing: "The church developed an explanation, claiming that the devil inhabited the body of the dead and caused it to move" (Melton 307). It is essential for students to understand where lore and current beliefs of vampires come from, but more importantly, students must realize how rich the cultural and religious backgrounds are that underlie vampire literature and that Anglo belief systems are merely a part of the lore rather than consisting of its entirety.

After the anticipatory set and brief introduction to the history of vampire lore, the unit focuses first on the novel *Marked* by P.C. and Kristin Cast as a demonstration of a modern view on old vampire myths. This novel in particular creates an understanding for other cultures and stereotypes with its peculiar take on the vampire. The mother-daughter writing team invents an American mythos by grounding their narrative in Tulsa, Oklahoma, rich with Native American influence and a Cherokee teen, Zoey, as narrator. Therefore, while vampire culture is revealed to Zoey as a new fledgling vampire, the reader receives not only a new take on vampire culture and religion, but the authors also use Zoey's Cherokee, Christian, and teenage perspectives as a filter to challenge common stereotypes.

As I teach college freshmen, expressing one's identity and exploring group affiliations allows one to understand one's place within society as an individual, which the students explore in the Autoethnography essay created by University of Central Oklahoma's Director of First-Year Composition, Dr. Matthew Hollrah.[2] Stereotyping is one of the stages they are urged to explore, and can be examined through Zoey's initial perspective of her new group affiliation. Zoey does not think in depth about what it means to be a vampire until she receives the mark to become one. In the beginning, she stereotypes vampires, which is shown with her description of the tracker as "dead" and "un-human" (Cast and Cast 2). Her friend, Kayla, also cringes away from her mark, signifying she will become a vampire, and refers to them as "things" (Cast and Cast 4). Then, as freshmen discover how their groups influence how they view the world and themselves, they begin a transformation through writing about their group affiliations. Zoey ponders her new group and her place within it:

> Do vampyres play chess? Were there vampyre dorks? What about Barbie-like vampyre cheerleaders? Did vampires play in the band? Were there vampyre Emos with their guy-wearing-girl's-pants weirdness and those awful bangs that cover half their faces? Or were they all those freaky Goth kids who didn't like to bathe much? Was I going to turn into a Goth kid? Or worse, an Emo? I didn't particularly like wearing black, at least not exclusively, and I wasn't feeling a sudden and unfortunate aversion to soap and water, nor I did I have an obsessive desire to change my hairstyle and wear too much eyeliner [Cast and Cast 5].

Here she begins her analysis of a group of people that are typically "othered" and through exploring her initial place within her group, i.e., being a vampire, she breaks down the stereotypes she carries for vampires. This process is important for students to examine and internalize. By using vampires as a group, rather than Christian versus Muslim, black versus white, male versus female, etc., students can apply this process to their own understanding of the groups they are affiliated with and discuss forms of stereotyping and classification openly.

For example, I have the students refer back to the lists we created on the first day in class from our anticipatory set — re-writing that list on the board. Then, I have them create a new list based off of Zoey's stereotypes of vampires. This, too, will be written on the board beside the original. There should be clear parallels and clear differences between the two lists for the students to separate out. Our next step is to discuss: Why might the similar items be consistent? From where do these labels derive? How might Zoey's 21st century perspective change her stereotypes about vampires? From where might these dissimilarities derive? By the end of the discussion, a clear connection can be made: How is this comparison similar to or different from the way stereotypes are created and perpetuated about your groups?

The stereotypes in the novel continue, generally surrounding the belief that vampires are synonymous with monsters. This is first mentioned on page five, then on page six, the readers witness Zoey battling with the idea that she will now become one of them: "I was turning into a monster" (Cast and Cast 6). The key terms in this part of the process include the common rhetorical strategy of defining groups in terms of *us* versus *them*, showing how a common belief within a culture can create a good side and a bad side and, therefore, demonize those referred to as *them*. Again, vampires are described as being avoided like they "had the plague," which aids young readers, more specifically college-aged students, to see how hateful stereotypes can be formed and, hopefully, can aid in transforming their views on how they judge others and how they are perceived or "othered." Since students typically latch onto the idea of being stereotyped and othered in the Autoethnography, giving them a frame of reference or a rhetorical strategy to aid in their analysis can also help them understand why groups are separated out as they are.

Finally, by the end of page six, Zoey brings the most prominent issue to a head: choice. In several assignments for my freshman classroom, their main goal is to analyze rhetorical choices of others, but most importantly in their first assignment, they must analyze whether or not they have a choice in their own group affiliations. So there is a clear connection for the readers when Zoey contemplates her own choices: "The problem, of course, was that turning into a monster was the brighter of my two choices. Choice Number 1: I turn into a vampyre, which equals a monster in just about any human's mind, Choice Number 2: My body rejects the Change and I die. Forever" (Cast and Cast 6). For some students, this is also true; they cannot help many of the physical or biological aspects of themselves. I, for example, cannot help that I am a Caucasian female with bushy Italian eyebrows and thick lips. Sure, I can pluck and tan and have a surgeon reshape my mouth, but the fact is, these attributes define me without my consent, and students also have an already formed understanding of how humans judge by appearance.

The use of Zoey's internals here engages the young reader due to his or her familiarity with identity battle, but the style is also used to define Zoey as a rhetorical vehicle. Thus, placing the young narrator before freshmen, or older students, gives students their first of two types of assignments. Strictly analytical and composition-based assignments may include an Autoethnography, an essay about group affiliation, stereotypes, and self-definition, or variations thereof. In this essay type, a comparison between the student and Zoey should be clear, but it also exposes students to well-written expression in which they can imitate, such as writing style, voice, and word choice. Also, a creative piece can demonstrate a student's development and comprehension of self in juxtaposition to fiction. A short fiction or poem must display both creative techniques and how Zoey's vampirism can be paralleled with their character's struggle with identity. Finally, the last option is a combination of the two, or a variation/adaptation, an assignment also created by Dr. Hollrah of UCO.[3] This type of assignment requires a creative work that interprets key aspects of Zoey's story. But the student must also write a short reflective essay in which the student must explain how his or her creative work analyzes the original through interpretation. Essentially, why did the student choose certain aspects to focus on over others, and how does leaving those aspects out change the meaning of the story?

Since the Adaptation/Variation assignment requires both self-analysis, which *Marked* is well suited for, and the analysis or interpretation of others' work within a cultural context, the text allows students practice with textual interpretations of common cultural beliefs. Most prominently, *Marked* focuses on Christian religion and Cherokee culture. The beginning of the novel heavily relies on the opposition between Christianity and vampirism. Zoey's mother and stepfather create this divide more so than any other in the novel; however, Christian hate groups are prevalent throughout the series. Her description of her stepfather sets the tone and foreshadows further religious representations:

> He was an Elder of the People of Faith, a position he was oh, so proud of. It was one of the reasons Mom had been attracted to him, and on a strictly logical level I could understand why. Being an Elder meant that a man was successful. He had the right job. A nice house. The perfect family. He was supposed to do the right things and believe the right way. On paper he should have been a great choice for her new husband and our father. Too bad the paper wouldn't have shown the full story. And now, predictably, he was going to play the Elder card and throw God in my face. I would bet my cool new Steve Madden flats that it irritated God as much as it annoyed me [Cast and Cast 22–23].

Because of the stepfather's brief role in the book, the representation of Christianity is negatively stereotyped and brings forward commonly viewed representations of Christian extremists in the media. He quotes phrases such as "Get thee behind me, Satan!" and "God's knowledge surpasses science, and it's blasphemous for you to say otherwise" (Cast and Cast 22–23). The mother also contributes to this skewed view by saying, "'What will the neighbors say?' Her face paled even more and she stifled a sob. 'What will people say at Meeting on Sunday?'" (Cast and Cast 23). These small snippets of dialogue show a duality of typecasting; first, the belief that Christians blindly believe in God over science, and second, the belief that the perceptions of their church people are more valued than their family crisis. Both of these views are then countered later in the novel by the addition of Damien, a gay, Christian vampire, although his parents also perpetuate the typecasting that Zoey's parents do by their involvement in the People of Faith, their disownment of their son for being gay, and their "narrow-minded, 'our way is the only right way' ideas" (Cast and Cast 95). Unfortunately, there is little redemption for the Christian faith in the first novel. The People of Faith as a religious denomination is separated from other less extreme Christian denominations and believers as the novels progress. However, by using the People of Faith instead of a mainstream denomination, students could more readily share about their own religious experiences and discuss their beliefs about religion versus science and possibly about homosexuality through the use of the novel's characters, again creating a safer environment to discuss sensitive topics such as these. Since these are sensitive topics, students are asked to free-write for five to seven minutes on the ways they have been exposed to the binaries presented above; however, I ask them to write in the third person, even when their examples are about themselves, to steer them towards objectivity.

Some prompts I may provide students with include: What types of debates or arguments have you been exposed to over the clash between science and religion? Are the two mutually exclusive, as Zoey's stepfather believes? What do both have to say about homosexuality? Why do you believe their perspectives on homosexuality differ? How does Damien promote or undermine homosexuality in the novel? Before discussion begins, I remind my students that we are to be objective and analytical when discussing these topics rather than arguing about whether someone's view on these topics are right or wrong. We merely want to explore where these perceptions come from to better understand why authors write about these subjects the way that they do.

Finally, the Cherokee culture and religion aids the Cast team in redeeming the idea of faith and belonging for their narrator and readers, as well as gives the use of vampirism as a rhetorical vehicle more merit. Zoey is given several physical representations of each of the groups: Vampire, Christian, and Cherokee. Zoey's grandmother is her Cherokee symbol. Throughout the entire novel, and series, Grandma Redbird signifies strength in character, in faith, and in understanding, and in turn, she gives Zoey the strength to embrace each part of herself:

Grandma Redbird understood people. She said it was because she hadn't lost touch with her Cherokee heritage and the tribal knowledge of the ancestral Wise Women she carried in her blood. Even now it made me smile to think about the frown that came over Grandma's face whenever the subject of the step-loser came up (she's the only adult who knows I call him that). Grandma Redbird said that it was obvious that the Redbird Wise Woman blood had skipped over her daughter, but that was only because it had been saving up to give an extra dose of ancient Cherokee magic to me [Cast and Cast 33–34].

Grandma Redbird is a continuing source of support for Zoey. She preaches acceptance and self-love to her granddaughter, which melds well with the vampire-goddess Nyx's welcoming of Zoey. On page thirty-nine, Nyx greets Zoey by using the Cherokee word for daughter, continues to speak in Cherokee to Zoey, and refers to several Cherokee traditions, such as the realm of the *Nunne 'hi* or the spirit people. The vampire goddess also begins the process of Zoey's identity transformation by complimenting what her grandmother has taught her: "You are a unique mixture of the Old Ways and the New World — of ancient tribal blood and the heartbeat of outsiders" (Cast and Cast 39). In the end, Grandma Redbird's reassurances coupled with Nyx's gifts brings Zoey peace over her mixture of blessings — the power of her vampirism, her Cherokee background, and her faith in something more than herself.

In contrast to *Marked*, the second and third texts analyzed during the unit, in combination, show a strikingly different view of the vampire and religion. Comparing the film *Interview with the Vampire* with the novel *The Last Vampire* by Christopher Pike allows a more traditional look into the mythical vampire. Ideally, each text's point of view allows students to analyze technique and characterization as they also compare the cultural and religious references threaded through each text. Comparing these two narrators may help students understand that stereotypes can be based on truths and that not all members of their groups have to be or are indistinguishable from each other, assuming the use of the aforementioned essays — the Autoethnography, the creative piece of fiction, or the Adaptation/Variation.

Although the use of first person point of view is not uncommon in the vampire genre, like Bram Stoker's *Dracula*, J. Sheridan LeFanu's *Carmilla*, or P.N. Elrod's *Vampire Files*, the narrators of both texts create interesting insights into their genres. *Interview with the Vampire*'s narrator, Louis, is a two-hundred-year-old vampire — not ancient in the realm of vampires but old enough to warrant a shift in perspective that many readers cannot readily share. Louis, as he narrates his story to the reporter, often comments on his journey with Lestat, showing his age in retrospective thoughts, such as his brief conversation with Lestat: "Louis: We belong in hell. / Lestat: What if there is no hell? Or they don't want us there? Ever think of that?" and his voice-over: "But there was a hell. No matter where we moved to, I was in it" (*Interview with the Vampire* 29:26–29:38). Throughout the movie, Louis refers to himself and the other vampires as evil and violent creatures, creating a parallel between the view of his species and common elder views of humanity. This and his "lingering respect for life" also characterize Louis in a likeable way, a common attribute of a protagonist.

Likewise, *The Last Vampire*'s narrator, Sita, has collected five thousand years and, thus, has an outlook that reaches further beyond what many readers can initially comprehend. For example, when Sita became a vampire, she left her family to ensure their safety, and in the present of the novel, she finds the reincarnation of her husband as a teenager named Ray and ponders the words of Krishna to Rahda about love: "'*Time cannot destroy it. I am that love — time cannot touch me. Time but changes its form. Somewhere in some time it will return. When you least expect it, the face of a loved one reappears. Look beyond the face and ... you will see me'"* (Pike 66–70; Pike's italics). Remembering these words momentarily changes Sita's approach for seducing Ray because she fears her evil nature, as a vampire, will soil the light inside of him. Again, this returns to the parallel between humanity and vampires, and the ability of both to choose their actions.

Briefly, students begin to formulate a commonality between the two narrators— their extended existence on earth and the acceptance of their evil natures as vampires. From these commonalities, they experience the world in similar ways: drinking blood, striving for companionship, and fighting what they both see as their natures. Strikingly enough, both narrators have influential backgrounds and lose their families near the beginning of their stories. This creates protagonists who have little to lose and yet remain prominently good. Potentially, the goodness in these two characters is in direct correlation to the degree of their loss, or it may be the heavy weight of their responsibilities, or both. Students can certainly make an argument for each. To encourage this conversation, I ask my students to provide two examples from each text to support this type of analysis with the following prompts: In which circumstances have Louis and Sita refrained from evil merely based on their beliefs or morality? What is their rationale? Do they repeatedly reference their past or their losses when their choices between good and evil present themselves?

Other similarities of their character can be attributed to their physical attributes. Aside from their overall pale, Aryan appearances, a remarkable number of their vampire traits are similar as well. Simply listed, they keep to several of the older myths: they must drink blood, they grow stronger as they grow older, they exhibit exceptional speed, strength and heightened senses, and alcohol has no effect on them. Both combat the myths in similar ways as well, with the narrators drinking from animals to survive, both having reflections in the mirror, and both able to look upon and hold religious items. On the contrary, Louis explains to his reporter how he cannot walk in the sun, although he enjoys light, and that a stake to the heart will not kill a vampire. For Sita, the sun merely weakens her, for she has a tolerance she has built up over five millennia, and a stake to the heart has a slim chance of killing her. And finally, the most differential vampire aspect for the two is that Louis has fangs, and Sita does not. Again, comparing these two nearly identical vampires aids students with the understanding that stereotypes may be based on truth and that not all members of their groups have to be or are identical with each other.

Contrasting these texts gives students the chance to see how each vampire text is rich with culture and religion even as they adhere to their own, larger group culture. Beginning again with *Interview with the Vampire*, Rice chose Louisiana for both personal background reasons, and for the different cultures that have occupied the state, and their mixture makes Louisiana, or more precisely New Orleans, a prime setting for exploring the issues of difference that analyzing vampire literature allows: "The purpose ... is to relate the particular history and culture of Louisiana to Rice's ... choice of it as a setting for [her] novels and to analyze the figure of the vampire as representative of the fears towards what is different and may pose a challenge to the established values of a particular society" (Alonso). Louis is Creole, demonstrating a rich and important part of his culture, both as a human and as a vampire. Although Louisiana has been associated with slavery and discrimination, the Creoles "offered mulattoes and free people of color an important role in the society," as can be seen by the respect Louis' slaves give him on his plantation (Alonso). Even though the culture does not play a heavy hand in the movie, a student given the knowledge could give several examples of Louis' French-Creole descent and action, and more readily give examples of their influence on Louis' later actions as a vampire and his respect for life. This respect for life may have another cause that is not heavily alluded to, i.e., religion and his worries over his damned soul and his deserved place in hell.

However, *The Last Vampire*'s culture is heavily weighted in religion, especially in extended chapters of flashback that allow the reader to experience the birth of the first vampire and of Sita's initial experiences as a young vampire. Sita's narration begins with excellent literary technique — exposition that sets the scene, gives necessary background, creates a more in depth character, and uses precise metaphor:

> We were the original Aryans — blond and blue eyes. We invaded India, before there were calendars, like a swarm of hornets in search of warmer climates. We brought sharp swords and spilled much blood. But in 3000 B.C., when I was born, we were still there, no longer enemies, but part of a culture that was capable of absorbing every invader and making him a brother.... I was there at the beginning, and had as a friend the mother of all vampires.... She was a good woman [Pike 42].

Sita's original culture resembles Louis', but in the next few pages, Sita's vampire twists the ancient Indian vampire, the *rakshasas*, into the demon or cause for the birth of the vampire in the novel. An Aghoran priest blames the *rakshasas* for the disease that plagued Sita's people, saying that the demon took offense to their worship of Vishnu, which as she describes it, was blasphemous for her people. Yet, due to the plague, her people perform a ritual on a dead pregnant woman, Sita's friend, calling the *yakshini* to eat the *rakshasas*. During the ritual, the dead child becomes reanimated and is cut from the womb, birthing Yaksha, the first vampire. Once again, the vampire is created from blasphemous practices and demonic creatures, as is often the case with vampire lore.

The Last Vampire continues to present the reader with Hindu beliefs by characterizing Krishna in chapter nine when Yaksha, Sita, and their offspring seek out Krishna — both a prophetic/enlightening experience and a violent one. There are several characterizations of Krishna in this chapter: "We began to hear stories about a man many said was the Veda incarnate. A man who was more than a man, perhaps Lord Vishnu himself," "It was said this man, this Vasudeva — he had many names — was capable of slaying demons and granting bliss," and "He was not a blue person as he was later to be depicted in paintings. Artists were to show him that way only because blue was symbolic of the sky, which to them seemed to stretch to infinity, and which was what Krishna was supposed to be in essence..." (Pike 136, 140). The chapter is filled with Hindu representations and other Hindu deities, providing a springboard for students to delve into this religion and the ability to begin comparing the beliefs and cultures represented in other vampire texts. Once again, this allows for the safe exploration of culture and religion for students in the classroom. Here, my goal for students has more depth than previous discussion. I implore them to explore Hindu traditions and beliefs, possibly comparing them with their own beliefs or other cultural representations of Hinduism. A short assignment or presentation over a particular deity may also aid in comprehension and to allow for analysis over the representations of culture in texts.

As the last three texts demonstrate, vampire literature and film are ripe with literary technique and cultural and religious references that students can utilize for discussion and teachers can use for various assignments. *Twilight* demonstrates a bit of an adverse criteria for analysis. Where *Marked, Interview with the Vampire,* and *The Last Vampire* can generate assignments that allow mimicking, *Twilight*'s literary technique lacks; however, the novel is an important asset for comparison. But most importantly, students are already familiar with the text, either from a previous encounter with the book or the movie. This allows for deeper analysis of techniques such as character and plot, and it initiates students into analyzing the world in which they already exist, giving the use of this text several favorable outcomes. I chose this text to analyze last so that students would have the appropriate exposure to vampire "literature," but the text can be used first to create a familiarity with the genre and its mythos.

Beginning with *Twilight*'s downfalls seems most appropriate, since the text does maintain undeniable value for a course that uses more than one vampire text. The saga's character development and plot are the most discerningly lacking in technique. *Twilight*'s opening paragraph cements the type of character the narrator will be — a superfluously flat and undeveloped character. In the first four lines, Bella tells the reader that she is being driven to the airport, that Phoenix has a normally perfect blue sky, and what she's wearing. Firstly, using clothing as descriptors for the narrator and having her describe herself through her clothes is shallow and bland character development, who doesn't amount to more than how she dresses herself, or her outward appearance, and this does not seem to change throughout the course of the novel. More specifically, the language used in this first person narration remains monotonous. For example, on page 78, "When I got home, I decided to make chicken enchiladas for dinner. It was a long process, and it would keep me busy. While I was simmering the onions and chilies, the phone rang. I was almost afraid to answer it, but it might be Charlie or my mom," uses telling action and emotionless language, but ultimately, her senses are absent and her voice dull (Meyer). Bella Swan's ordinary characterization can also explain the prominent focus on Edward's good looks, genetic make-up, and misogynistic nature — his need to control and protect Bella from herself and his constant struggle to not kill her, which he would then blame on her for arousing such passion in him. Frequently, Edward's eyes, chiseled beauty, and perfect face are commented on in order to overshadow the basic structure of his abusive relationship with Bella, seen by his controlling nature and his isolation of her from her friends, among other evident signs (Rainchild).

Twilight's plot also leaves much to be desired. There is very little content in the five-hundred-page book; most of the conflict happens in the first few pages and the last few pages, leaving the rest of the novel for Bella and Edward to flirt with each other. However, Meyer stretches out the smaller elements she does possess so that they have absolutely no impact, for example, the reveal of Edward's vampirism. Finally, the last chunk of the book provides an abrupt conflict to bring the plot to climax; unfortunately, these outsiders that attack and attempt to eat Bella have no foreshadowing and seem to work merely as a plot device.

Writing technique aside, the religious representations create interesting interpretations for the genre. Dracula, in Francis Ford Coppola's film version, for example, was once a human crusader for the church but renounces the church when he comes home from battle to find his wife dead and her soul unsavable. In this version of the movie, he pierces a large, stone crucifix, makes it bleed, and drinks the blood as he renounces his faith and promises his revenge. The crucifix, therefore, repels Count Dracula. In the novel, Dracula's personal history is much more mysterious, and thus, the repulsion by a crucifix is attributed to merely warding off evil. Meyer, however, transformed this ruthless creature into a cold, hard, glittery Mormon. In fact, the sparkling of the vampires' skins in the sunlight can be a reference to the Mormon angels and their glory. Edward's insistence on marriage before copulation and the "unique Mormon teaching is that marriages are 'sealed' for eternity; spouses are referred to as eternal companions and eternal partners" (Aleiss). The Cullens also represent the ideal familial bonds and contrasts sharply with Bella's friendly divorced parents, and Bella quickly picks her vampire boyfriend's perfect family over either of her parents (Petro and Mehta).

One of the strongest themes Meyer perpetuates in *Twilight* is the Mormon belief in overcoming the natural man or overcoming sin through redemption, hence Edward's over-powering desire to consume Bella, which is literally "carnal and carnivorous," and his rejection of the vampire's natural way of life (De Groote). Edward "strives through willpower to live a good life against his nature," and as he learns to live completely for Bella, he is transformed, and his self-control throws off the natural man (De Groote). Through this, Edward challenges and supports more recent representations of protagonist vampires or what can be categorized as the more heroic vampires.

In truth, not all vampire literature is created equal. However, all literature has its uses—either for deep and substantial literary and cultural analysis, like *Marked*, or for juxtaposition and comparison, like *Twilight*. In either case, vampire texts serve the literature and writing classrooms by creating a safe environment in which to discuss more delicate aspects of humanity — race, gender, religion, and cultures— through a filter to allow students a fuller exploration of each subject. Most importantly, the use of vampire literature conquers the most difficult aspect of teaching literature in the classroom, student and reader engagement, and of course, the understanding that all literature has influence and backgrounds that pertain to plot, character, and culture. Ultimately, popular media and cultural analysis is prevalent in each assignment I present to my students; they need to be aware of the influence popular media has on their lives. The ability to break down each message into pieces in order to understand a text in its entirety allows them to gain a more complete view of the world they live in, thus better equipping them with the tools to understand the opinions, backgrounds, and actions of others as well as of themselves.

Appendix A: Autoethnography
Created by Dr. Matthew Hollrah

Part of the process of becoming more of who we want to become includes understanding our place among others and how we enter into dialogues with other people through language. Because language is a major way, perhaps the major way, that we express our identities, a written exploration of our group affiliations should also lead us to a deeper understanding of ourselves as individuals who are, in part, made by our connection to and avoidance of others. The purpose of this assignment, then, is for you to analyze and explain how one such cultural or group affiliation has affected your sense of who you are, but you need to do this with some depth, using two outside sources. Here are some things you may want to consider and address as you write this essay.

- Analyze and explain the extent to which your identification with a particular group has contributed to you being "othered." By "othered," I mean how you or your group has been excluded or separated or made to seem strange or at odds with other groups.
- Along with giving your perception of how your group has been perceived, you should also include the actual perceptions of others as expressed through their writings or through interviews with individuals about your group.

- What stereotypes exist about the group you identify with? Where do you find these stereotypes? TV? The hallways? Textbooks? Websites? Be specific.
- Explain what it means to you to be a part of this group. Address how belonging to this group has influenced how you view yourself, the way you view the world, the way you view other people not part of the group.
- Investigate the history of this group. How did it get started? What were its founding principles? Are those founding principle still endorsed and practiced by most followers? By you? Have the principles changed? Why? Are there less than positive aspects to your group's history that bother you as a member of this group?
- If this is a group you chose (rather than chose you,) how do your reasons for belonging to this group cohere with the major tenets of the group?
- Can anyone be a member of the group? Why or why not? To what extent did you choose to belong to this group and to what extent were you born into it?

Keep in mind that your audience will most likely include those not identified with your group. Therefore, your voice and tone, as it encounters the voices and tones of your sources, will need to take these members of your audience into consideration.

Restrictions:

You may NOT write about the following groups: Religion, Race, and Gender (with few exceptions, i.e., a specific group within the religion, race, or gender, ask me for specifications). If your paper is written on one of these subjects, I will not accept it. I would prefer you to be creative and think outside the box.

Requirements:

This essay should be 1200 to 1500 words long, typed, double spaced, and should follow MLA Style for general formatting and the documentation of sources. You should have at least two sources. If you do interviews, one interview can count as a source. In other words, both of your sources cannot be interviews, but you may do as many interviews as you like.

Appendix B: Variation or Adaptation of a Text
Created by Dr. Matthew Hollrah

For this paper, we will analyze texts through the process of creating variations or adaptations. Through the process of variation or adaptation, we should come to a deeper understanding not only of what a particular text means, but how it means, and how we develop interpretations in general. In fact, what we will find is that any variation or adaptation is also an interpretation of the original work. This assignment comes in two parts—(1) the variation or adaptation, and (2) a commentary.

OPTION 1: VARIATION

Take any relatively complex but short text and write a variation of it. In writing a variation, the trick is to keep key aspects of the original text while making the new version of it your own. To an extent your variations will also reveal your interpretation of the original text through the choices you make about what aspects of the original to keep in your newer versions of it and what you decide to change. The aspects of the original that you decide to keep are up to you, but your readers should be able to tell somehow which text you are doing a variation of. You may try a serious or a humorous variation. Humorous variations often take the form of parody, which is a variation that exaggerates certain aspects of the original in order to make some point about it. All good variations, though, whether humorous or serious, reflect a thorough understanding of the original text, so you will want to read it several times.

Option 2: Adaptation

An adaptation is a variation, but it is primarily a variation in form. If you choose this option, you will adapt a text into some other form. I will not restrict this art form to the written arts, so you can change from print text to visual text, stationary text to moving text, hard copy to something interactive and web based, reading to performance, language to music, etc. The challenge here is a bit different than the variation because the change in form will naturally create differences to be explained. In moving from a short story to a play or screenplay, for instance, you move from a text with a narrator to one without a narrator. This makes a big difference in the way your adaptation will be understood by an audience.

Again, I want you to take this seriously. I don't want and will not accept stick figures scribbled on notebook paper as an adaptation of a poem into the visual arts. Effort counts. If you want to do a group project with other members of the class for either a film or dramatic presentation, I am open to that as well. Just let me know before hand who is in your group and what responsibilities each group member has. Also, if you choose to do a performance you would do it on the day the paper is due.

The Commentary

Regardless of the option you choose, you will also write a 1,200 to 1,500 word reflective essay, explaining how your variation or adaptation reveals your interpretation of the original text and what you wanted to accomplish with your text.

This part of your assignment is the most crucial and will carry the bulk of your evaluation, but a poorly executed variation or adaptation will not give you much to write about either. Thus, both parts of the assignment are important. Here are some things to think about when writing your commentary:

- what you changed and why
- what you kept the same and why
- the extent to which your imagined audience affected the changes you made
- how your changes affect meaning — i.e., what your text means verses what the original means
- your intentions or what you wanted your text to do. (Be specific here. Simply saying that you wanted to write a funny poem does not give your reader any insight into why you thought a humorous variation ought to be written at all.)
- the extent to which your work is its own work separate from the original

Assignments:
Exercises from Matt Hollrah, *So What:* Great River Technologies, 2012. Web. Reprinted by permission of Great River Technologies.

Notes

1. The anticipatory set refers to an activity to focus the students' attention, provide a brief practice and/or develop a readiness for the instruction that will follow. It should relate to some previous learning. If successful, the anticipatory set should help the student get mentally or physically ready for the lesson (Combs).

2. See Appendix A for the Autoethnography.

3. See Appendix B for the Adaptation/Variation.

Bibliography

Aleiss, Angela. "Mormon images abound in *Twilight*." *Religion News Serve*. OregonReport. 25 June 2010. Web. 29 Jan. 2012. http://oregonfaithreport.com/2010/06/mormon-images-abound-in-twilight/.

Alonso, Irene Sanz. "Why Do Vampires Prefer Louisiana?" *NeoAmericanist* 5.2 (2011–2012): n. pag. Web. 10 Aug. 2012. http://www.neoamericanist.org/paper/why-do-vampires-prefer-louisiana.

Cast, P.C., and Kristin Cast. *Marked*. New York City: St. Martin's Griffin, 2007. Print.

Combs, H. Jergen. "Lesson Plan Design." *Lesson Plan Design*. 2008. Web. http://www.edulink.org/lessonplans/anticipa.htm.

De Groote, Michael. "Book editor points out religious symbolism." *Deseret News*. 8 April 2009. Web. http://www.deseretnews.com/article/705380539/Book-editor-points-out-religious-symbolism.html?pg=2.

Hollrah, Matthew. *So What? Inquiry, Interpretation, Rhetoric, and Composition*. Dubuque: Great River Technologies, 2012. Web.

Interview with the Vampire. Dir. Neil Jordon. Perf. Tom Cruise, Brad Pitt, Antonio Banderas, Stephen Rea, Christian Slater, and Kirsten Dunst. Warner Home Video, 1994. DVD.

Melton, J. Gordon. *The Vampire Book: The Encyclopedia of the Undead*. London: Visible Ink Press, 1999. Print.

Meyer, Stephenie. *Twilight*. New York: Little, Brown, 2005. Print.

Petro, Anthony, and Samira K. Mehta. Big Vampire Love: What's So Mormon About *Twilight*?" *RD Magazine*. Religion Dispatches. 4 Dec. 2009. Web. 29 Jan. 2012. http://www.religiondispatches.org/archive/culture/2052/big_vampire_love%3A_what's_so_mormon_about_twilight.

Pike, Christopher. *The Last Vampire*. New York: Pocket Books, 1994. Print.

Rainchild. "*Twilight*: A Critical Literary Analysis." War on You. Web. 10 Aug. 2012. http://waronyou.com/forums/index.php?topic=15861.0.

National Literature to RPGs:
Vampires in the Polish Classroom

Michał Wolski

Although the stereotypical image of a vampire in popular culture comes from the titular character of Bram Stoker's 1897 novel *Dracula*, vampirism itself seems to be as old as human culture. At the same time, the turn of the 20th- and 21st-centuries saw the motif become so widespread that it started to serve as a basis for reflection on various phenomena observable in the culture of the West, both on a grander scale — as a diagnosis of the condition of modern humanity based on rampant consumerism — and in regard to individual matters, such as a fear of minorities, an apotheosis of loneliness, a vivisection of toxic personalities, and so on. All these issues of social, cultural, historical, or even political nature can be inscribed into a literary discourse (among others) that uses and transforms the traditional vampire image.

From the point of view of a literary critic interested in vampirism, the evolution of the vampire will be of the most interest, as well as an attempt to contrast the image with stereotypes functioning in the collective consciousness. This approach seems just as sensible from the point of view of didactics. Students — given the richness and constant transformation of vampire literature — expect a sensible, well-considered selection of motifs significant to a holistic and relatively up-to-date understanding of vampirism in culture. Therefore, while planning a course dealing with the vampire image, one should not only include the vampire's strong roots in literary tradition — especially one's national literature — but also didactically appealing interactive works of culture which transform and redefine traditional concepts. A comprehensive class presenting the various aspects of how vampires are imagined should include cinematic versions of vampire stories, which add to the visual aspects of vampirism, as well as selected video games and RPGs.

When it comes to references to tradition, concentrating on them in the teaching process has — beyond the obvious cognitive value — an additional goal. It allows the students to develop awareness of a process in literary history that governs the vampire image. It is important to show if and when the foremost works of national literature took inspiration from folkloric and literary roots of vampirism. The point is to go beyond the Dracula stereotype and uncover its inspirations, also those absent from Stoker's novel. This way students can discover surprising connections and analogies based on the vampire image but hitherto absent from the narrative of literary history.

This can most probably be illustrated by any European canon of literature, but the Polish canon proves to be an especially useful example. Even though the stereotype is to search for the genesis of the modern vampire in Romania, where Transylvania now lies, many ethnologists and anthropologists (like Erberto Petoia) point to the fact that the undead who rises from the grave to drink the blood of the living is of Slavonic origin. The folk tales of vampires (in Polish: *upiór* [*uh-pyuhr*], formerly *upir* [*uh-pyhr*], transformed into the modern *wampir* [*vam-pyhr*]) sneaked into high literature in the age of Romanticism, which transformed Europe's artistic sensibilities and was often inspired by folklore, rural morality and—most importantly—folk demonology. Polish Romanticism additionally put much more emphasis on patriotism and national liberation than its European counterparts, mostly because the partitions by Russia, Austria and Prussia wiped Poland off the map in 1795.[1] This marriage of folk motifs, strongly accentuated spirituality and sensibility, and national issues led to a unique reworking of traditional images.

The main precursor and foremost author of Polish Romanticism was Adam Mickiewicz (born 1798, died 1855). His works are discussed at almost every step of education in Poland, which means students usually know him and are able to connect certain themes and motifs to proper literary contexts and episodes in the writer's life. One can therefore say that among secondary school pupils in Poland, Mickiewicz is a well known figure. However, academic interpretations of his art usually follow the patriotic or pious-national route, marginalizing or outright omitting folkloric threads. This not only obscures the connections between Polish and European Romanticism, but also ignores the theme of folk demonology strongly accentuated in Mickiewicz's writing. The best example of this is the author's flagship work, *Dziady*, a drama mixing folk and patriotism and an obligatory reading in secondary schools. Rarely do students realize, however, that the protagonist is a vampire.

Dziady was a drama divided into four parts, written out-of-order in various intervals. Part One is often omitted in analyses as a not very believable, almost baroque scene in the lives of two lovers that might — but does not have to—connect to the whole. Parts Two and Four, the so-called Vilnius-Kaunas *Dziady* (named after the places of their creation), concentrate on folk customs meant to help the spirits of the dead achieve salvation. There is, however, one ghost — or *upiór* — named Gustaw, whose death resulted from tragic love and who, despite the congregation's efforts, fails to find his way into the afterlife. In Part Three, the Dresden *Dziady*, this Gustaw becomes Konrad, a man possessed by Satan and imprisoned by Russians for acting towards Polish independence. The prisoner proclaims inspired but haunting poems about his own and Poland's fate, which cease when a friendly priest exorcises him.

The story sketched above is known to secondary school pupils in Poland, but questions are rarely asked of why Gustaw becomes Konrad, or why he is alive in Part Three if he was a ghost in Part Two. Meanwhile, evidence can be found in the text itself, in a part called Konrad's "small improvisation":

> My song was already in the grave, already cold–
> It smells blood — peers from underneath the earth–
> And rises hungry for blood like a vampire:
> And demands blood, demands blood, demands blood....
> And the song says: I'll go in the evening,
> First I must bite my kinsmen,
> Whose soul my blood touches
> Must like me become a vampire....
> We'll go then, drink the enemy's blood.
> His body we'll hack with an axe:
> His hands and feet we'll pin with nails,
> So that he doesn't rise as a vampire[2] [Mickiewicz 46–47].

The solution to this incongruence lay in Mickiewicz's lectures on Slavonic demonology at Collège de France in Paris. They prove that the writer was well aware of the Slavonic concept of double heart, or double soul, which was the foundation of the belief in vampirism; when one soul — the human soul — died, another — the vampiric one — awoke. The analogy between this notion and the transformation of Gustaw into Konrad was traced by the distinguished researcher of Polish Romanticism, Maria Janion, in her book *Wampir: Biografia symboliczna* (*Vampire: A Symbolic Biography*). In his lectures, Mickiewicz "claimed that 'the vampire is born with a double heart and double soul.' Initially, he lives 'unaware of his being,' but soon 'recognises kindred creatures' and meets them 'at secret gatherings,' plotting how to destroy humans. In another lecture, Mickiewicz calls these gatherings 'sabbats.' In the vampire, the negative soul or heart takes hold, thus developing and fulfilling a destructive drive.... In this view, the duality of the vampire's existence is similar to the Romantics' other dualities of human existence, the bifurcations of personality that interested them" (Janion 129–130). Thanks to Janion's discovery pupils — and later students — who know *Dziady* might unexpectedly discover that Mickiewicz's vague and now very outdated drama is in fact a vampire story woven into a specific historical context. This sort of revelation is usually met with surprise on the part of students who had not known those facts before. They also admit to finding this new perspective more appealing and more sensible than the canonical interpretation of the play. Discovering such references to vampirism in the Polish literary canon might inspire one to seek out other vampires in the field, which is already a visible educational success.

The search itself will not be fruitless, because vampiric themes exist in Polish literature, though not always — as in Mickiewicz — hidden in plain sight. One example is a poem by a Polish left-wing poet, Władysław Broniewski. "Dubbed 'Broniewski's most enigmatic text' (by Artur Sandauer), 'The Ballad of Theatre Square' uses all the ambiguity of the *upiór*-vampire being, at once the shadow and the doppelgänger. The poem, full of historical references to the revolution of 1905, to the independence manifestations and 1st of May marches on Theatre Square in Warsaw, reflects the poet's tangled relationship to Romantic literature embodied by the figure of Piłsudski"[3] (Janion 132), the years-long leader of Inter-bellum Poland. Another example is a lesser known novel by Polish Nobel Prize laureate, Władysław Stanisław Reymont. Thirteen years before his prize-winning portrayal of animistic relationships in the Polish countryside in 1924, he wrote *The Vampire*, a novel in the vein of Victorian horror stories, strongly influenced by satanic, spiritualistic and vampiric themes. And though Daisy — the titular creature — is closer to the vampires of Goethe or LeFanu than to Gustaw/Konrad from *Dziady*, she exists as evidence of a strong link between Polish literary tradition and European culture, meaning that she can be used to trace vampiric threads in that period's literature.

The thematic range evoked by literary texts belonging to the given tradition could naturally be complemented by works of authors writing about vampires in the given language, taking into consideration specific geographical and cultural backgrounds, characteristic for users of this language. In Polish literature these will be stories about the self-made exorcist and vampire hunter Jakub Wędrowycz, written by Andrzej Pilipiuk, as well as the author's *Kuzynki* (*Cousins*) trilogy, modeled like a realistic novel of manners with elements of fantasy. It is also important to mention Magdalena Kozak's action novels about vampires in the Polish intelligence agency, who live on artificial blood and fight with evil, degenerated bloodsuckers. Making use of the abundance of Polish academic literature on the topic of vampirism, intended for readers familiar with Polish culture, could also prove fruitful. The cognitive tools developed by Polish and European literary criticism are well suited to describe vampires in literature, and the subject itself is not alien to local academia.

It is worthwhile to remember that Polish texts classified as vampire literature serve only as an example of a specific didactic approach to the discussed subject, which is in great part transgressive and indeterminate. Nevertheless, it is a safe assumption that Polish literary vampires are not an exception. It may be possible to find texts in other national literatures never before approached from a vampiric angle, or ones that had no impact on the canon of vampire texts, but could be used to track general literary themes in a given period. Starting from known canonical literary works and moving towards more universal vampire stereotypes seems like a legitimate and productive method of designing classes on this topic.

An academic course on vampire literature cannot, however, be limited only to literary texts, mainly because of the importance of visual representations in shaping the vampire stereotype. Besides, considering the weight of multimedia in modern culture, films, graphic novels or video games using the vampire motif should be treated not as a complement or addendum to vampire literature, but — if it is justified — as equal works of culture. It is often that one medium better than another consolidates some aspects of the vampire, contributing to the evolution of its general image. What is more, Polish creators can be said to have added to the overall vision of vampirism (as in the case of Roman Polański's *Fearless Vampire Killers*), which proves that a more general analysis of the vampire in culture can also be conducted through the lens of national culture.[4]

Interactive works of culture — meaning video games and RPGs— are of particular interest. They tend to transform and systematize known literary and iconic vampire images and, through playing vampiric roles, allow the various aspects of vampirism to be deeply understood on many levels. Some titles could provide material for a whole academic course on their own, which would allow for not only learning about the cultural diversity of vampires, but also analyzing them thoroughly. Because of length limitations, I will narrow this focus to a role-playing game from White Wolf Publishing titled *Vampire: The Masquerade*.

The Masquerade, like other games of its type, can be approached in two ways in class. First, as a text it is ostensibly post-modern, given its openness, dependence on the audience, the emphasis on endless variability (while sketching the background in minute detail), self-irony, etc. Second, it is a compendium of stereotypes and vampiric themes alive in Western culture. For the sake of narration and the setting's consistency, these themes were transformed and unified, which led to a kind of critical treatment. At the same time, *Vampire: The Masquerade* belongs to popular culture and, as such, tends towards universality, selectively and one-sidedly using literary tradition and folklore, holding its own coherence paramount.

The world of *Vampire: The Masquerade* is based on the premise that humanity is being manipulated by thirteen species (or clans) of vampires engaged in eternal struggle. Each of the clans has its own character, abilities and preferences, which in many cases reflect existing vampire stereotypes. Whereas their variety is so vast that it is possible to plan a course about vampirism on *The Masquerade* itself, a much more interesting perspective is to have the students compare and contrast their vampiric knowledge with its treatment by the authors of the game. One can, for instance, examine the relationship between folkloric vampire images in Slavonic lands and the Slavonic roots of clan Tzimisce that comes— in *The Masquerade*'s reality —from those very lands: "In nights past, the Tzimisce was among the most powerful clans in the world, dominating much of the region now known as Eastern Europe. Potent sorcerers, the Fiends dominated the region's mortals as well, in the process inspiring many of the horror stories about vampires" (Rein·Hagen 86). One sees at a glance that the game does not include the concept of two souls, popular in that region, because it did not fit the general, very gnostic nature of the setting. A more thorough analysis, however, reveals certain analogies, like attributing fiendish characteristics to Slavonic vampires or — just as interestingly — trying to rewrite Polish history with the inclusion of vampiric interventions, such as the influence of the undead on the political climate in the time of the Partitions. In a sourcebook set in the 19th century, one of the vampires—calling themselves "Kindred"— mentions Poland in these words:

> Warsaw itself is the capital of the "Kingdom of Poland" (an amusing title, considering that it was a "kingdom" under Russian rule), though ever that distinction has been all but forgotten since the Russians fully absorbed the region after the insurrection of 1863. The city lies in the center of what was Poland, bisected by the Wisła River. Multiple bridges, including several modern iron ones, span the river, connecting the historical and mercantile sectors of the west bank with the residential areas of the east. The city, particularly on the west, is home to multiple castles and cathedrals that date back to medieval times. The Kindred of Poland seem to me to be at least as conflicted as the mortals around them and exist in a state of continuous struggle that is, in my experience, far more vicious than in any other Kindred city that does not lie directly between Camarilla and Sabbat [the names of two opposing vampire sects] territory [Achilli et al. 153].

Simplifications aside, the socio-political situation of Poland as sketched in this paragraph is true to historical sources.

Drawing those kinds of analogies could be more productive in the case of other vampiric stereotypes whose historical and geographical roots could be traced, and thus used to identify the folk tales and images of popular culture which served as inspirations for the game's creators. In this way, students can not only learn about the distinctive features— whether derived from folklore or modern popular culture — of various vampiric images, but also, more importantly, examine their vitality and validity in Western culture.

It is also possible to reverse this way of thinking: how would the vampire's folkloric image fit into *The Masquerade*'s reality? Modern popular culture often aims to create a feeling of coherence between texts that shape or modify certain images. Hence, the rules of *The Masquerade* offer a complete and relatively consistent system unifying the sometimes contrary views of vampirism, and might serve as a basis for their comparison. The proposed method would involve thoroughly analyzing the vampiric images implied by various (traditional or other) works of culture and comparing them to the vampire systematic as described in the game. This would require much involvement and creativity on the part of the students, as they would need to not only research and specify the vampires' supernatural abilities— which serve as distinctive features for *The Masquerade*'s clans— but also analyze their behavior, characteristics, passions, weaknesses and goals. It is important for the students to use their reading experience to decide a given protagonist's affiliation, role and demeanor. Results need not and should not be predetermined; the students' analytical process, though moderated by the professor, should be as liberated as possible.

Going back to the Konrad from the third part of *Dziady*: his origins, abilities and goals within *The Masquerade*'s system would all be enigmatic and debatable, his clan affiliation being just one example. Konrad's closeness to humans and his imprisonment would situate him among the Caitiff, but his love of poetry and uncommon improvisational skills would be more appropriate for a Toreador. Projecting one's own shadow, as Konrad does in Parts Two and Four, is the domain of the Lasombra, but dealings with the Devil are characteristic of the Baali. Finally, the region where the action takes place suggests belonging to the Tzimisce. Naturally, that is just one of the problems the students will face, and their perceptiveness while reading will determine their eventual conclusions and their understanding of Mickiewicz's Romantic drama. RPG systematics, particularly from *Vampire: The Masquerade*, can be used as the basis of description for most, if not all, scenes from *Dziady*. This is especially true of the exorcisms conducted by the character of Father Piotr, the dream-visions of Eva and the Senator, who see heaven and hell respectively, or the instances of black magic use throughout the plot, as in a scene where one of the characters is killed by lightning. Konrad's motivation and his transformation into a vampire, which made him exchange romantic love for patriotic love, may also be described in *The Masquerade*'s terms. Other examples are plenty, although they touch different aspects of the drama, thus only indirectly connecting to vampirism. Seeking out references to mysticism and folk demonology, however, may result in new readings and interpretations of a work that is traditionally regarded as first and foremost a patriotic manifesto.

This approach is obviously not without its flaws. First of all—just as any other systematic—it limits the students' perception to features favored or underlined by the overriding work of culture that is *Vampire: The Masquerade*. It could disrupt student attempts to absorb without bias any texts which use an image of the vampire unfitting to or incoherent with the one implied by the RPG. This could touch creations conventionally detached from *The Masquerade*'s setting, like the British television series *Count Duckula*, as well as the titular vampire from Bram Stoker's famous novel—a character nearly constitutive to the image of the bloodsucker in popular culture, but also incompatible with the system (though the game tries to suggest differently). Secondly, the attractive feature of interactivity and the aforementioned uniformity of *Vampire: The Masquerade* aside, there are a few reasons why this particular work of culture and its variations should be the prism through which other texts referring to the vampire image are examined. A course based on *The Masquerade* might therefore be considered too arbitrary. Lastly, the variations of *The Masquerade* in different media use different codes of interaction, meaning they are not one hundred percent coherent. A different set of rules applies to the setting of the RPG, to the reality of the TV series based upon it, titled *Kindred: The Embraced*, and to the worlds of *Vampire: The Masquerade—Redemption* and *Vampire: The Masquerade—Bloodlines*, two video games set in the discussed universe. Disparities between them stem largely from the differences between their media, so using *The Masquarade*'s systematic could be subject to criticism on this ground as well.

That said, besides its semantic value, *Vampire: The Masquerade* presents another possibility that is tempting but scarcely used in academic contexts: the drama, generally meaning the opportunity to play the roles of self-designed vampires. University settings rarely allow for guiding the students through a believable RPG session, but it is not the point to acquaint them with the rules of the system, but to use said rules for cognitive purposes. It is wise to remember, however, that "a role-playing game will not be successfully conducted by teachers who cannot quickly react to changing situations and introduce new plot points ad hoc. The very attempt to keep track of various plot threads and quickly moving from one group to another might be too taxing for many. Nevertheless, a well-prepared plot and a good choice of roles and goals for the pupils allow to transcend these obstacles, which are, by the way, common to all modes of class activity" (Szeja 218). The forerunner of RPG studies in Poland, Jerzy Szeja, proposes dividing pupils (he refers to his own experience teaching secondary schools, but it seems his methods might be applied to literature courses at university) into groups portraying characters—in our case vampires—functioning within a specified narrative and a pre-made setting based on other works of culture. Verifying experience gained in such sessions would need to involve creative assignments connected with play, such as discussing potential plans and character actions, describing character relations, or just summarizing the game.

It is worth noting that these kinds of methods could also be used to talk about other works of culture, or about the same texts as proposed, but with emphasis on a different set of aspects and contexts.

> An example illustrating the above considerations might be theatrical role-playing game *Senator Wasylew's Feast*, which I based on a few scenes from the third part of *Dziady*. Playing the game helps students understand the atmosphere of those times. When the lack of independence and the servility of a large part of society (especially the aristocracy) towards the victors (Russians), and the hot blood of young patriotic Romantics clash with everyday motivations, the setting of Mickiewicz's masterpiece becomes at least partly as understandable for as it was for its first audience. Those people knew the times and conditions, and often people similar to the characters from the play, while the modern pupils are given a chance to become such characters for a few hours. That way even the ones who do not read acquire basic receptive competence, increasing the probability of not only their reading the play, but also of understanding its complex nuances, prometheisms, messianisms, visions, dreams, and secrets [Szeja 222].

Naturally, games of this type may seem time-consuming, and their introduction into the flow of academic classes carries the risk of limiting the attention paid to other topics. Additional preparations on the part of the teacher are also required.[5] Class time assigned for the game should only include the mechanics and models of character action, and introduce only basic plots and conflicts, which the students will build further narration upon by playing outside of class. The method proves more efficient in secondary schools, where the teacher's contact with pupils is longer and more intense. Furthermore, the pupils prefer this form of learning as being more active and creative, able to—partially, of course— replace the at times monotonous readings of source material. At universities, where close reading is a must, Szeja's method is better suited as a tool to complement given texts and make them more attractive.

To summarize, if one were to gather all the proposals and weave them into one consistent and relatively comprehensive university program for teaching vampire literature and culture, the effects would be interesting. It is important to remember that no project presented herein is final, and everything can be heavily modified with regard to both the range of materials and the individual topics. Examples of Polish vampires can also easily be replaced with bloodsuckers from the pages of other nations' literature. It is the methodological approach that is important. Whether one chooses to use *Vampire: The Masquerade* as a compendium of vampiric lore, a semantic basis for analyzing individual works of culture, or a methodological foundation, the rules can serve as a kind of "escape" for systematizing the students' knowledge and impressions of the undead. In the Polish higher education system, the normal course is one semester long, consisting of fifteen meetings, ninety minutes each, so it is assumed a part of this time—about 15–20 minutes—should be devoted to less important works whose rank or form make it impossible to analyze them through *Vampire: The Masquerade* (this means especially music, poetry, short animation, collectible card games, etc.). The remaining time may be divided into meetings conducted according to one of the three didactic paths proposed. Here is an example of the thematic range of individual classes:

1. Introducing the setting and chosen rules of *Vampire: The Masquerade*.
2. Traditional vampires: from antiquity to Enlightenment.
3. Vampires in Polish culture and literature of the 19th century (including chosen works of the early 20th century).
4. The vampire as result of Victorian fascinations with Gothicism: Stoker's Dracula, Reymont's Daisy.
5. The vampire parodied (from the Polish perspective, it would be wise to mention Roman Polański's *Fearless Vampire Killers*).
6. The vampire as collective, thoughtless evil: horror fiction and slashers (it is worth mentioning the influence of Richard Matheson's *I Am Legend* on cinema's zombie fascination).
7. Deconstructing vampire myths: Anne Rice and others.
8. The image of vampires in the 1980s.
9. Vampiric horror and alternative realities.
10. The vampire in Japanese culture: from tradition to anime.
11. The modern Polish vampire in works of Andrzej Pilipiuk and Magdalena Kozak.
12. The vampire in comics: Dracula, Blade, Vampirella.
13. Interactive vampires: from *Bloodrayne* to *Legacy of Kain*.
14. The literary vampire and modern cinema.
15. Paranormal romance: mutation or evolution?

Requirements and rules of assessment remain to be established by individual professors. It is important, however, to reward individual students' creativity and ability to work in groups. The professor also needs to determine whether the students' familiarity with given texts is accurate.

The proposed system can certainly be modified according to the needs of a particular class. Interesting results can be achieved by telling the students to draw a vampire at the beginning and at the end of the course. Moreover, the themes and issues present in vampire-related texts are broad enough to allow student creativity in selecting and commenting individual works, which is greatly encouraged. As has been shown, the search of vampiric concepts in national literature can lead not only to a discovery of interesting sources of vampire stereotypes, but also to a reinterpretation or redefinition of the entire canon of such literature. The Polish example is merely a model — parallel examples are sure to be found in literatures of other nations as well. Being educated on the relationship between the vampire stereotype and known literary canon opens students up to new readings and methods of interpretation. The best illustration of this is referring to the RPG formula, both as a means of describing the settings in literature (and other works of culture), and as a means of exploring — sometimes literally — the literary world. This allows one to offer the students new means and areas for interpreting and utilizing vampire literature.

Notes

1. It is a good idea at this point to introduce some information regarding Polish history. In the 18th century, the Kingdom of Poland functioned as the Polish-Lithuanian Commonwealth and was the largest country in Europe, hailing democratic ideals. Its internal weakness, however — brought upon by ineffectual monarchs

and short-sighted gentry, as well as numerous wars—caused Poland to grow gradually weaker, to the benefit of its rising neighbours: the Russian Empire, the Kingdom of Prussia, and the Holy Roman Empire of the German Nation (commonly known as Austria). In 1772, the first partition of Poland between the three states took place. This caused the growth of Enlightenment movements and the adoption of the Constitution of May 3, 1791 (second after the American). Prussia and Russia did not take kindly to the emergence of modern democracy in Poland, and a war was waged over the constitution, resulting in Polish loss and a second partition. After an armed uprising against the invaders in 1794 (dubbed the Kościuszko Uprising after its leader, Tadeusz Kościuszko), Russia, Prussia and Austria finally partitioned the remaining territory of Poland in 1795, wiping it off the map for 123 years (until the end of the Great War).

The fall of Polish governance coincided with the decline of Enlightenment tendencies in Europe. The Poles' last hope, the imperial expansion of Napoleon Bonaparte — a grave enemy of Prussia and Russia — was extinguished in 1812. It was then that the generation of May Constitution defenders moved aside, making way for the young idealists raised on Goethe, Schiller and Macpherson. One of them was Adam Mickiewicz, whose writings were a most effective mix of European Romanticism and youthful rebellion realised as a need to strike against the architects of partition and re-establish Polish independence. Many among the young intelligentsia shared these sentiments, and thus came another insurrection, the November Uprising of 1830. The resulting Polish-Russian war of 1831 ended in defeat and forced the surviving revolutionaries to emigrate. One of such emigrants was Mickiewicz who was not involved in the combat himself, but compelled, partially by guilt, to uphold the fighting spirit of his compatriots through his art. Hence emerged his demonic, semi-mystical work that is *Dziady*.

The failure of the November Uprising meant that Poland was largely unaffected by the Spring of Nations—the string of revolts and insurrections throughout Europe, meant to topple absolute monarchy in favor of republican rule. Many of those failed as well, but they nonetheless resulted in the birth of nation-forming mechanisms whose goal would be to transfer power in a given country to the citizens thereof. In the case of Poland, this nation-forming process had come earlier, during the Kościuszko and November uprisings, but failed to change the political situation. An effort to fix this was the January Uprising, brought about by the second generation of Polish Romanticists, and marking the final failure of Polish intelligentsia, who were virtually wiped out in the aftermath. Adam Mickiewicz did not live to see this moment; in 1855 he tried to mobilize Polish troops to aid Turkey in the war against Russia, but died of cholera en route to Constantinople.

The January Uprising of 1863 saw the death of Poland's finest intellectuals. Survival belonged to those who preferred educational work and economic growth as pathways to independence. It was not until the next generation, coming of age in the 1890s, that Romantic traditions regained their followers. Among these were social activists and military personnel the likes of Józef Piłsudski and Roman Dmowski—vastly different but equally dedicated to the rebirth and well-being of a free Poland. Using first the Russian Revolution of 1905, and later the turmoil of the Great War, the Poles managed to regain independence on November 11, 1918.

2. All Polish texts—unless stated otherwise—translated by Łukasz Buchalski.

3. Władysław Broniewski was a left-wing poet, whose writings centred around themes of war, uprising and revolution. This made him one of the most notable and popular poets of the Polish interbellum. During World War II, he found himself on USSR–occupied lands, where he was arrested and eventually drafted into the Soviet-formed Anders' Army. After the war, he wrote propaganda poetry, which branded him as a Stalinist poet. At the heart of most of his poetry, however, was an honest patriotic message. "The Ballad of Theatre Square" refers to the happenings on May 1, 1905, when a bloody skirmish broke out between revolting workers and Russian military (at the time, Warsaw was under Russian rule). The clash was part of the Russian Revolution of 1905–1907, which brought the end of tsarist rule in Russia, therefore ushering in the USSR.

4. And the other way around—the aforementioned *The Vampire* by Reymont, although undoubtedly Polish, is directly descended from Western traditions, the knowledge of which is crucial in understanding the novel.

5. Szeja describes the role of RPG in didactic efforts as follows:

> The organiser: describes the roles of participants (often supplementing them during the game, or asking for unwanted elements to be abandoned); sets the scene of the events; decides the success of actions that might help players to achieve goals contrary to the goals of another (i.e., determines the way of testing whether an assassination attempt of a high-ranking tsarist official has been successful); settles conflicts or provides the rules for settling them; introduces and describes things happening outside of player participation (i.e., announces that a burning shed on Solec can be seen through the ballroom window, and that a thirty-person squad of the tsarist guard has just entered said ballroom); describes the passing of time (i.e., informs the players that the ball is one hour from ending and that this means 20 minutes of real time for the players). The goal of the GM is for the activities to be fun for as many participants as possible, so he influences the ongoing game, making the goals harder to reach for some, and easier for others. For this purpose, he introduces non-player characters (NPC), played by himself or his helpers, and tries to control the flow of key information [223].

Bibliography

Achili, Justin, Kraig Blackwelder, Brian Campbell, Will Hindmarch, and Ari Marmell. *Victorian Age: Vampire.* Stone Mountain, GA: White Wolf, 2002. Print.

Janion, Maria. *Wampir. Biografia symboliczna.* Gdańsk: Słowo/obraz terytoria, 2008. Print.

Mickiewicz, Adam. *Dziady. Część III.* Ed. By J. Wieczerska-zabłocka. Wrocław: Zakład Narodowy Imienia Ossoli skich, 1984. Print.

Rein•Hagen, Mark. *Vampire: The Masquerade. A Storytelling Game of Personal Horror.* Stone Mountain, GA: White Wolf, 1992. Print.

Szeja, Jerzy Zygmunt. "Teatralne i narracyjne gry fabularne jako aktywizuj ce metody nauczania." *Homo Ludens* 1 (2011): 215–235. Print.

Team Edward! Team Eric!
Team Critical Thinking!
Teaching the New American Vampire
to First Year Undergraduates

Candace R. Benefiel and *Catherine Coker*

First Year Seminars and Teaching New Students

For four years now, we have taught a course on vampires in popular culture for the First Year Seminar program at Texas A&M University. Designed to introduce freshmen students to the academic arena through courses on popular topics in a small class setting, the FYS program focuses on high impact learning. It particularly emphasizes teaching critical thinking and other skills that will be useful in both college-level courses and life outside the college campus. The purpose of our class, titled "Twilighters and Moonlighters: Fan Studies and the New American Vampire," is to introduce students to academic discourse through the interdisciplinary realm of Fan Studies. (See the appendix for a modified syllabus.) Students read critical essays on works such as *Twilight* and *Buffy the Vampire Slayer* and other texts on vampires; they attend film screenings to learn how to critically discuss multimedia; they are challenged to think both creatively and critically of both source texts and the fan works based on them. In sharing our experiences with teaching a first year seminar, we hope to highlight the ways in which we are drawing students into critical thinking about a subject they might assume has no academic importance. Our class teaches students that they can study subjects about which they are passionate. Using the lens of fan theory and studies, they become aware that academic study is a discourse, a conversation in which many topics are acceptable, and divergent opinions are welcomed.

The First Year Seminar (FYS) program is one of many such programs established in recent years at college campuses across the country. As discussed by White, Goetz, Hunter, and Barefoot, such initiatives "should be understood not as single events, but as processes that should be linked programmatically" rather than the traditional, singular experience of orientation prior to classes starting (33). At Texas A&M, the seminars themselves are weekly, one hour credit courses taught voluntarily by faculty and staff across the University, thus providing a multitude of subject areas and viewpoints. The University is a large one, with a total undergraduate population of over 50,000 students in the fall of 2012. Of these, some 8150 are in their first semester of college, and it is from these that the students for the FYS classes are drawn. There is a perception that students at Texas A&M University are predominantly from rural backgrounds (after all, the school began as an agricultural college), but in recent years, the balance in the student body has shifted to urban and suburban areas within the state, as more students are attracted to programs in the sciences and engineering. Nonetheless, over a quarter of the entering freshmen are first generation college students who still tend to be from smaller communities.

The First Year Seminars are designed as a corrective to the drop-out and flunk rates that beset first year students— particularly those who are the first in their families to go to college. The transition from high school to undergraduate is a tense, fraught one for any student, but even more so for those who have had no tools to prepare them for this life change. As such, the FYS Program provides some shielding in the first semester: small course size (the local cap size is twenty), an emphasis on discussion and participation rather than passive lecture attendance, a "fun" topic rather than the requisite course distributions. Both the number of people involved and the self-selecting nature of the group's participants ensure an atmosphere of scholarly inquiry — even if some students don't realize that's what they are doing.

Teaching new students through this framework has its own challenges, separate from those of a traditional three hour credit course. For instance, we have to be mindful of workload with regards to assignments. Given the weighting for grades, the logical student will prioritize traditional coursework over seminar work. At the same time, the students must be made aware that we do have expectations for both attendance and the work that is turned in. This is a delicate line to walk, but thus far we have been fortunate with our students: again, because they are a self-selecting group, they are genuinely interested in the material and willing to follow through on their academic responsibilities. For this particular course, we have generally had the maximum enrollment as classes started, although usually two or three students drop the class after the first day for a variety of reasons.[1] Overall, the course has provided an extensive learning experience both for the students and their instructors.

Exploring the New American Vampire

Repetitively teaching a class focused on a specific element within contemporary popular culture may seem daunting. How to keep the material new and relevant? Will students even be interested this year? And of course, perhaps the question we are most frequently asked "Isn't everyone *over* vampires yet?" As it happens, people have *never* been "over" vampires. A vibrant and consistent literature marks the vampire's fictional evolution from 1819 (John Polidori's "The Vampyre") to the present (see *The New York Times* Bestseller List). Each year we have updated the course to respond to the current trends in both popular culture and in fandom. For instance, in the fall of 2009, the second season of *True Blood* had just concluded, *The Vampire Diaries* began airing on the CW, and the second film in the *Twilight* saga debuted. We were able to draw each of these programs into weekly discussion as well as hosting an anthropological expedition to a midnight showing of the latter.

One aspect that we find key to our class's success is in maintaining an atmosphere of collegial respect and academic inquiry that we call the "safe space." A safe space indicates both intellectual and physical protection; within our classroom, students are invited to voice their thoughts, opinions, and concerns openly and without fear. Such a space is already constructed just by virtue of the majority (and in some years, the entirety) of the class's participants being young women.[2] However, because it is a diverse campus and we do live in interesting times, the safe space necessitates both some ground rules as laid down by the syllabus and on the first day in class, as well as their occasional reinforcement. The rules are simple: the students are to treat one another with respect and to use respectful language with one another at all times; the use of derogatory language aimed at other students, individuals, or groups is not tolerated.

While we seek to stimulate intellectual discussion pertinent to the readings, we do acknowledge that some topics in fandoms have the potential to cause offense, particularly to youths from predominantly conservative, Christian backgrounds. (Evidently, the attraction and popularity of *Twilight*, and more recently, *The Vampire Diaries*, is sufficient to overcome what might be otherwise seen as an unusual interest in vampires. The vampire, for good or ill, has been mainstreamed, and a sparkling, chaste, 'vegetarian' Edward Cullen, worrying about the state of his soul, overcomes the long Gothic/supernatural tradition of the vampire genre.) For example, one of the subjects discussed in the assigned textbook is slash fiction, a somewhat controversial genre that focuses on gay and lesbian romances. The week that this is the topic of discussion, we ask that any student who doesn't want to participate in class due to moral objections may abstain without penalty so long as they notify us in advance and still turn in the assigned reading response for that week. It is perhaps worth noting that in four years of teaching, although several have voiced concerns, only twice has a student ever chosen to skip that session. Above all, we find that, when the students are genuinely interested in the topic under consideration, their willingness to learn and to confront the unknown is amplified; in short, they become true scholars.

Fan Studies

The past few years have seen an increasing awareness in mainstream media of fans and fan activities. Even before the recent publication of the bestselling *Fifty Shades of Grey* trilogy (which began life as a *Twilight* fan fiction novel) provoked debate over the adaptation of fan works for publication, pundits and bloggers were commenting on the explosion of fan fiction on the internet, and the ramifications that this sort of informal and open publishing process might have on traditional publication practices. Essays such as author Cory Doctorow's "In Praise of Fan Fiction," see fan fiction as a means of extending the audience of a given work, while Bryan Thomas Schmidt's blog entry, "Why I'm Not a Fan of FanFic," takes the opposite viewpoint of fanfiction as inherently disrespectful to the author's creative process and intellectual property; such discussions continue to proliferate. On a more objective note, John Sutherland pondered in 2009 the topic of "How Fan Fiction Took Over the Web," commenting that in the field of fiction, the trend toward fan fiction is "perhaps the biggest trend in the two decades since the world became web-connected," although he puts, perhaps, more emphasis on the sensationalistic furor surrounding slash. The high-profile public dialogue regarding *Fifty Shades* will doubtless extend the mainstream interest in fan fiction, and there is some indication that for-profit publication of fan fiction "with the serial numbers filed off" will become even more prevalent in the foreseeable future. In fact, James Bridle, writing in *The Observer*, contends that publishers will soon be actively mining fan fiction for lucrative properties. That trend is off and running, with the recent publication of another re-titled Twi-fic, *Gabriel's Inferno*; tellingly, the words *National Bestseller* were already emblazoned on its cover the date of its release.

All of this attention provides a convenient springboard to attract students' interest, particularly given the enthusiasm and vitality of fan communities which have coalesced around *Twilight* and other vampire franchises, such as *True Blood* and *The Vampire Diaries*, in the early twenty-first century.[3] Many of the students who sign up for the course are already ardent readers of the *Twilight* saga, and have followed the story from page to screen with keen interest. They range from those who have been fans, in the narrowest sense of the word — actively involved in web communities and producing fan works on their own — to students who have only tangentially been involved as casual readers. In fact, the first year the course was offered, we had one student who wandered in under the misapprehension that the course was on a totally unrelated topic. He stayed and quickly became one of the most engaged students in the class.

One of the emphases at the beginning of the course is to inform students of the wide variety of vampire narratives, beginning with a brief history of the vampire in literature and film. This takes the form of an hour-long lecture, which discusses the development of the vampire as a literary trope, starting with Polidori and continuing through the most current manifestations on television and film. Along the way, there is some discussion of the vampire in folklore, particularly those aspects of vampirism present in most vampire narratives. As the course progresses, in addition to essays on works such as *Twilight* and *Buffy the Vampire Slayer* and other texts on vampires, students are required to read two vampire novels they have not read before: one from the plethora of available young adult vampire texts, and one from the romance/chick lit end of the spectrum. While we provide a short list of suggestions, it is intended as a starting point, and we have had students read a wide-ranging selection of materials. Many of the students have little familiarity with the vampire beyond the *Twilight* saga, and most are surprised at the sheer volume of vampire stories currently available. The vampire is such a pervasive trope in contemporary Western culture, it is educational to them to discover that the concept has a much broader background than they might previously have known.

Discussion of the vampire on television comes with assignments to view selected episodes of several vampire series, including *Buffy the Vampire Slayer*, *Angel*, *Forever Knight*, and *Moonlight*. Viewings and screenings are followed by in-class discussion of how the vampire has been used on television, and an overview of their associated fandoms— particularly *Buffy*, which has spawned a great deal of scholarly interest in past years. Students have been fascinated to learn of the scholarly attention that has been directed toward Joss Whedon's television work; it is often the first they have heard of popular culture being the target of academic study.

As a part of the class, the students are also encouraged to attend film screenings, although these are not mandatory. We have selected feature films and documentaries (such as *Twilight in Forks* and *Ringers*, a documentary on *Lord of the Rings* fandom) which are targeted to stimulate discussion of fans and fan activities. For example, *Galaxy Quest*, with its overt parody of both *Star Trek* and of fan conventions, is counterpointed with both an episode of *Star Trek: The Original Series*, and a screening of the 2009 *Star Trek* "Reboot" film. *Vampires Suck* is a more pointed deconstruction of both *Twilight* and *Twilight* fandom. Halloween gave us the opportunity to host a *Supernatural* marathon, which we weighted with episodes that showed the series' awareness of fan activities,[4] and the heavily "meta" episodes that showed the series' willingness to wink at the viewer and play with the knowledge that they know that we know that they know *Supernatural* is a television series.[5] While the screenings are great fun, they are also used to guide discussions in class. The documentaries often give an insight into fans and fan practices; the feature films and television episodes can be used to highlight topics. The screening of the Star Trek reboot offers a start for discussions of the "alternate universe," and also can be useful in illustrating the slash subtext in a popular media franchise.[6] Each of these activities helps the students learn how to critically discuss multimedia. They gradually see over progressive viewings—documentaries to film texts—that all media compose a social discourse of critique, reference, and reaction which is filtered back into both their readings for class and contributions for discussion.

In addition, readings in fan studies are covered, particularly scholarly discussions of fan fiction and other creative manifestations of fandom. Discussions of fan artwork are accompanied by a PowerPoint slideshow of representative fan works; the class on fan vids usually involves showing a number of pieces on YouTube. Every year, during this process, the students have participated by suggesting favorite fan videos they have discovered. One of the videos we always show is rebelliouspixels's "Buffy vs. Edward: Twilight Remixed," which makes creative use of footage from the *Buffy* television series intercut with scenes from the first *Twilight* movie. It makes a useful point of how Edward Cullen, the brooding protagonist of *Twilight*, displays stalkerish tendencies, and how Buffy, arguably a more liberated young woman than Bella Swan, might react to his behavior outside the context of "fated romance."

We do spend a large portion of class time discussing the uses and creation of fan fiction, perhaps the most popular of fan activities. This includes readings in Sheenagh Pugh's *The Democratic Genre: Fan Fiction in a Literary Context.* Pugh addresses fan fiction not in the vein (as so many others have done) of questioning the psychological makeup of the creators of fan fiction, or the legality of the transformative work from a standpoint of copyright law, but simply as a medium of expression. She concentrates not on why, but on how — discussing what authors are doing as they extrapolate scenes in the silences of their most beloved books, movies, and television series, and also explaining how fan writers use their fiction to analyze the original media sources. We have found a wide variety of experience level among our students; some are familiar with the concept of fan fiction, some are completely new to the concept. This has led to lively class discussion, with some students feeling that the whole idea of fan fiction is derivative and "stealing" from the original authors.

The discussions on "Slash Day" have been particularly intense. Many of our students are prone to find the slash paradigm, which makes what is often a homoerotic subtext in media franchises much more explicit, to be troubling. One frequent response to the idea of taking characters from their canonical setting, where any homoerotic content is at best subtext, and making it the focus of a story, is that fan fiction writers are somehow changing the characters, and presenting them as they were never intended to be; this is seen as more of a literary offense than a moral lapse. As mentioned above, we do offer students who find the idea of same-sex relationships problematic an opportunity to avoid participation in this particular class session; this seems to be comforting enough to their sensibilities to enable them to attend. In addition, this session is far enough into the semester that a level of trust has built up which enables students to feel comfortable in expressing their viewpoints, in the knowledge that they will not be mocked or criticized by the instructors or their classmates.

Literary interpretations of sexuality are, coincidentally, one of the preoccupations that arises in the criticism of both vampires and fan studies. For example, Christopher Craft's seminal 1984 essay, "Kiss Me with Those Red Lips," brought the idea of homoeroticism in *Dracula* into the mainstream of vampire criticism, with his assertion that "the novel's opening anxiety, its first articulation of the vampiric threat, derives from Dracula's hovering interest in Jonathan Harker; the sexual threat that this novel first evokes, manipulates, sustains, but never finally represents is that Dracula will seduce, penetrate, drain another male" (109–110). The current of same sex attraction and pairing in other vampire novels has been explored in Benefiel's "Blood Relations: The Gothic Perversion of the Nuclear Family in Anne Rice's *Interview with the Vampire*," which discusses the domestic arrangements of the vampire characters Louis, Lestat, and their adopted child, Claudia. As the author posits,

> Even the establishment of a vampire family is a subversive twist on the more normal biological reproduction of children. As the vampire turns its lover into its child, the relationship is oddly incestuous, a configuration that carries over into the portrayal of the vampire family. In the bulk of vampire fiction, a master vampire functions as father, mother, and husband, with other younger vampires as children/lovers. No biological mother is necessary, and the vampire "family," isolated from human society by its extreme longevity and its essential otherness, becomes an intensely inwardly directed unit, and the blurring of normal familial relationships creates unnatural tensions. The vampire family, incestuous and blurred as it is, presents a subversive alternative model to the nuclear family [263].

Further attention is drawn to the alternative sexualities of Rice's vampires by Wasson, "when blood becomes the fulcrum of desire, it can begin to represent other intensities, other sexual delights: it draws the eye out to the limits of the human body" (205). Through reading about and studying the sometimes perverse, but ultimately more accessible, depictions of vampire sex and sexuality in fan fiction, students are prepared to understand the more subtle expressions of this in more canonical works of vampire fiction.

In order to establish a ready resource for class information, we set up a LiveJournal page to give easy access to other online fan communities. While there are readily available online class resources (such as Web CT) in use at TAMU, we deliberately chose a non-academic platform for hosting the class syllabus, links to various web resources, bibliographies, announcements, and so on, in order to give the students a closer view of the typical fan-related web presence. The syllabus, as per Texas state law, is posted on the university's website, but we decided that putting it on LiveJournal was more in the spirit of the class itself: a user-friendly portal to the wider world at large.

Towards the end of the semester, we usually have a course session titled, "A Very Special Class," where we invite in several colleagues who are active in fandom. Texas A&M University has long been the home of one of the largest student-run science fiction conventions in the nation, AggieCon. Our special collections library on campus, Cushing Memorial Library & Archives, houses a Science Fiction Research Collection that is one of the largest collections of its kind in the country. In addition, we have scholars on campus who are active in the field of fan studies, including one who has been engaged in scholarship on *Buffy the Vampire Slayer* and fan reactions to the series. Drawing from these resources, we are typically able to schedule a panel for one class period in which several people to speak about how they have been involved with organized fandom, in some cases over many decades. We also usually can bring in artifacts from the Science Fiction Research Collection, such as copies of zines and other fan memorabilia, to provide a graphic introduction to the material side of fandom.

In addition to regular class meetings, the class has culminated for two years in an anthropological field expedition to midnight film screenings of *Twilight* saga movies. Students were encouraged to take notes on fan activities, observing the crowd while waiting for the screening and examining such attributes as clothing (costumes versus franchise t-shirts), behavior, and the general composition of the audience. All of this became the basis for part of their reports on the screening. They were encouraged to offer their own reactions to the films: how the adaptation related to the original, whether the changes in the material worked well, and so on. We have also considered the class field trip as another means of providing students with an opportunity to bond. While we do provide the tickets for the screening (and typically buy a few tubs of popcorn to share around), we leave transportation issues to the students, and have found that they are well capable of arranging car pools to get to the theatre.[7] In light of the recent tragedy in Aurora, Colorado, however, we may have to re-think the midnight screening field trip. While long-term reactions to this are yet to emerge, it may be that we will need to re-schedule the event to a more conventionally timed screening, perhaps the Friday evening of the opening weekend. If theatres ban costumes, as has already been reported (Shyong), the fan exuberance may be subdued. The *Twilight* movies, perhaps fortunately, have not lent themselves to the wearing of masks, although "Team Edward," "Team Jacob" and even "Team Carlisle" shirts have been observed at previous midnight screenings.

Students are generally quite eager to participate in the midnight screening field trip, and have not only used it as an opportunity to see a new movie in which they are interested, but also as a bonding experience with their classmates. They have commented in responses to the screenings, concerning the demographics of the audience, the attire and demeanor of fans at the screenings, and the film itself. Not a few have offered extensive commentary on the comparison of their close reading of the book with the screen adaptation. In the end, whether at midnight screenings, or online, by observing fan practices and communities, students come to appreciate the idea of viewing a subject in which they are already interested, through an academic lens.

Conclusions

Response to the class and the FYS program in general has been uniformly positive, with students declaring at the end of the semester that they have learned not only about the broad history of popular vampires but also how to view popular culture in general with a critical eye. One of the major projects for the class has been to create an original fan work. Students were not restricted in their choice of fandom, and we have received works related not only to the various vampire fandoms, but also *Harry Potter*, *Doctor Who*, and Disney musicals. We have also encouraged students to use their creativity in responding to the assignment, thus, while some students have written fan fiction, others have produced such varied offerings as a vampire *Jeopardy!* style trivia game, presented in PowerPoint format; a detailed consideration of where the main characters of the *Twilight* saga would be placed, in Dante's version of Hell; a video recap of the Harry Potter movies; an imagining of what the corkboard in Bella's room would look like, during her romance with Edward; a live duet with guitar of Oasis' "Wonderwall" with a *Twilight* themed re-write of the lyrics; and a fan video where costumed students re-enacted key moments of most of the major Disney animated movies.[8] As a part of the experience, students present their fan works to the class in a showcase, spanning one to two class sessions.

Originally, we scheduled the fan work to be done partway through the semester, and followed it with an assignment to write a more serious academic paper on some aspect of fan culture. This approach, while it did produce some thoughtful scholarship, seemed like a heavy burden to put on students in a one-hour credit class, and we modified the syllabus to eliminate the paper, placing more emphasis on the creative fan work. In the context of educating students in fan culture and practices, the project provides them with an impetus to participate not just as academic observers, but in an artistic and creative capacity. The fan work becomes a laboratory exercise, and has encouraged students to begin to learn skills like video editing, which they might find useful in other endeavors.

Teaching this class has been rewarding and educational for us, as well as the students. The decision to teach a combination of vampires and fan studies has worked well, as the vampire fandoms currently give such a good cross section of fan activities. It would be easy, of course, to limit the course to either a study of the vampire in literature, or to a broader emphasis on fan studies generally. The cross between the two, however, and the fact that many of the students are already familiar with some of the more popular contemporary manifestations of the vampire in popular culture, give us a "hook" into their interests, and allow us to introduce them to the field of fan studies, as well as teaching that the vampire has far more presence than the *Twilight* saga. In any institution that offers First Year Seminars, the ideal course is one that has a topic popular enough to appeal to a number of students, but is also structured to provide an introduction to a more scholarly investigation of that topic. By combining the widely-known vampire, and teaching the history and variations of the vampire theme, with introducing the varieties of topics covered in studies of fan practices, students are made aware of the idea that scholarly study can encompass a far wider range of subjects than they had previously known.

Vampire narratives are pervasive in modern American popular culture, continuing to appear in most media, and attracting a following. Using the popularity of the vampire, particularly the *Twilight* saga books and movies, to draw in students, and introduce them to academic study of popular culture, has been successful for several years. We expect that, while the general vampire fad may wane over time, that the vampire has established a presence in the American landscape that will continue to draw the interest of students.

Appendix

Syllabus — Twilighters & Moonlighters: Fan Studies and the New American Vampire

UPAS 181-520

Fall 2011

Course description: The purpose of this course is to introduce students to academic discourse through the realm of "Fan Studies." Students will read critical essays on works such as *Twilight, Moonlight, Buffy the Vampire Slayer*, and more. Students will also view segments of media to learn how to critically discuss multimedia.

Learning outcomes: Students should become familiar with critical literary and media discourse appropriate to the undergraduate college level.

Instructor information: Catherine Coker, Assistant Professor,
                                          Candace Benefiel, Associate Professor,
                                          Office hours by appointment.

Textbooks and required materials: Students will be expected to purchase or otherwise have ready access to:

1. Two novels of your choice (see below).
2. *The Democratic Genre: Fan Fiction in a Literary Context* by Sheenagh Pugh (ISBN 1854113992)
3. *The Vampire Archives* Otto Penzler, ed. (ISBN 0307473899)
4. A stapler.
5. The Internet. We have a class community online at http://upas-fanstudies.livejournal.com/ with additional material for your reference and entertainment. Checking this page should be a weekly part of your participation in the class.

We want you to select two books to read from the following lists, one from each category. We suggest books be purchased online at Amazon, Powells, or Abebooks. We are open to suggestions for additional novels, which we encourage you to share with the class via the listserv. However, we expect your reading choices to be books you **have not read previously.**

Young Adult	Chick Lit/Romance
The Twilight saga / Meyer	Sookie Stackhouse series / Harris
Twilight	*Dead Until Dark*
New Moon	*Living Dead in Dallas*
Eclipse	*Club Dead*
Breaking Dawn	*Dead to the World*
The Morganville Vampires / Caine	*Definitely Dead*
Glass Houses	*All Together Dead*
The Dead Girls' Dance	*From Dead to Worse*
Midnight Alley	*Dead and Gone*
Feast of Fools	*Dead as a Doornail*
Lord of Misrule	Undead series / Davidson
The Mortal Instrument series / Clare	*Undead and Unwed*
City of Bones	*Undead and Unemployed*
City of Ash	*Undead and Unappreciated*
City of Glass	*Undead and Unreturnable*
The Blue Bloods series / Cruz	*Undead and Unpopular*
Blue Bloods	*Undead and Uneasy*
Masquerade	*Undead and Unworthy*
Revelations	*Undead and Unwelcome*
The Vampire Diaries /Smith	Anita Blake series / Hamilton
The Awakening and the Struggle	*Guilty Pleasures*
The Fury and Dark Reunion	*The Laughing Corpse*
The Return: Nightfall	*Circus of the Damned*
The Vampire Academy series / Mead	*The Lunatic Café*
Vampire Academy	*Bloody Bones*
Frostbite	*The Killing Dance*
Shadow Kiss	*Burnt Offerings*
Blood Promise	*Blue Moon*
Spirit Bound	*Obsidian Butterfly* [...]
House of Night / Cast	Black Dagger Brotherhood series / Ward
Marked	*Dark Lover*
Betrayed	*Lover Eternal*
Chosen	*Lover Awakened*
Hunted	*Lover Revealed*
Standalones	*Lover Unbound*
Jessica's Guide to Dating on	*Lover Enshrined*
the Dark Side /Fantaskey	*Lover Avenged*
Sucks to Be Me/Pauley	*Lover Mine*

Etc. Etc. Also, a **highly recommended text** is *Bitten by Twilight: Youth Culture, Media, & the Vampire Franchise* (ISBN 9781433108945) which contains critical essays on the phenomenon and fan culture of the *Twilight* saga.

List of assignments:

Weekly reading response papers. Each week you will be responsible for writing a short 300–500 word paper discussing the readings/viewings from your assignments. Reading response papers are due by noon on the day of class, and should be submitted to the instructors via email.

Monthly film screenings. Every month, date TBA, we will host a Tuesday night film screening of movies/documentaries/television episodes relevant to the course. Screenings will be in the library, and run from 5:30 to approximately 8 P.M. Attendance is not mandatory, but you will receive credit for participation, and this will enrich your course experience.

Extra credit readings. For up to 3 points of extra credit, you may choose a story from *The Vampire Archives*, read it, and write a brief response, 150–200 words, which may be attached to your weekly response paper, or emailed separately to the instructors. You may do this up to five times over the semester, for a possible total of 15 points. All extra credit readings must be completed by two weeks before the end of the semester.

Field trip! We are going to go to the midnight showing of *Breaking Dawn, Part 1* on November 18. We will be buying the tickets and snacks: your assignment is to movie-watch ... and people watch. Aside from cons, midnight releases are the highlights of fan culture. At the following class meeting we will discuss the film and our observations of the fan presence. Your response paper for that week should include notes on your experience.

Final project. Your final project will be an original, creative work of your choice. Works can include, but certainly aren't limited to: a substantive piece of fiction, a fanvid, artwork, musical work, or other original work of your choice to be approved by us in advance.

Grading policies: Grades are based on points earned for assignments, attendance, and participation. We will be meeting thirteen times during the semester. Attendance for each class is ten points and participation (talking during discussions) is five points, for a total of 195 points. Your weekly writing assignments will count as ten points each, for a total of 100 points. Your final project will count for fifty points. There will be an optional class field trip or gathering during the semester which will be worth an additional five points. Grade breakdown will thus be as follows:

325–350 points = A
300–324 = B
250–299 = C
200–249 = D
Less than 199 = F

Attendance policy: It is expected that all students will arrive to class prepared and on time. Students are allowed one unexcused absence. Any additional absences must have an approved excuse such as a doctor's note, religious holiday, etc.

Late policy: Assignments have one week to be turned in late with a ten point penalty. Assignments turned in after one week will accrue penalties of ten points plus one point per day late.

Class atmosphere and participation: This class is meant to be a bit different than other classes at A&M. Classes will generally involve more discussion than lecture. Therefore, we want all students to be comfortable and willing to participate in class. Here are some ground rules:

1. This is an academic atmosphere. We ask that all students treat each other respectfully and with respectful language in the course of our discussions. Derogatory language aimed at fellow students, individuals, or groups will not be tolerated.
2. This is a small class. Contribution to the conversations and activities is important. If you are usually shy, this is the best place to overcome your shyness: surrounded by friendly colleagues! Likewise, if discussion turns to sensitive topics, we ask that all discussion be conducted in an academic, objective, and respectful manner.

Expectations and how to succeed:

1. Students should arrive to class prepared and on time.
2. All assignments must be typed and printed in 12-point Times New Roman font with 1" margins. Papers with multiple pages must be stapled together.
3. Assignments submitted via email should be in an attached Word document, formatted as specified above.
4. All cell phones and other electronic devices not being used for classwork should be turned off during class time.
5. This class comes with a significant reading load. Because knowledge from the readings are necessary for discussion to take place, we do expect you to keep up with your readings. Any student who does not come prepared to speak will lose participation points for that class session.

➤In short: If you come to class and turn your work in on time, you will be fine.

Additional Resources: You!

If you come across an article, website, or other source that you think is interesting and would add to the discussion, please share it with the class. The class listserv email is cs-ugst 181520-fall2011@groups.tamu.edu. **Please note: by submitting email to this address you are sharing with everyone in the class, not just the professor.** Please plan your post accordingly.

Online Media

Hulu.com: Legally streaming videos of *Angel*, *Buffy the Vampire Slayer*, *Forever Knight*, and more.

TV.com: Yet more legally streaming videos of popular television shows.

Americans with Disabilities Act (ADA) Policy Statement

The Americans with Disabilities Act (ADA) is a federal anti-discrimination statute that provides comprehensive civil rights protection for persons with disabilities. Among other things, this legislation requires that all students with disabilities be guaranteed a learning environment that provides for reasonable accommodation of their disabilities. If you believe you have a disability requiring an accommodation, please contact the Department of Student Life, Services for Students with Disabilities, in Cain Hall or call 845–1637.

Academic Integrity Statements

AGGIE HONOR CODE

"An Aggie does not lie, cheat, or steal or tolerate those who do."

Upon accepting admission to Texas A&M University, a student immediately assumes a commitment to uphold the Honor Code, to accept responsibility for learning, and to follow the philosophy and rules of the Honor System. Students will be required to state their commitment on examinations, research papers, and other academic work. Ignorance of the rules does not exclude any member of the TAMU community from the requirements or the processes of the Honor System.

For additional information please visit: http://www.tamu.edu/aggiehonor/

CALENDAR

Date	Topic	Reading/Viewing	Discussion	Assignment
August 30	"Introduction to Fan Studies"	"Fangtastic" (handout)	Overview of the course.	n/a
September 6	"History of Vampires in Literature and Media" "Introduction to Fan Works"	"In Praise of Fanfic" by Cory Doctorow (handout)	Presentation by Professor Benefiel: Vampires in popular culture and their reception.	Reading Response #1 due.
September 13	"Young Adults with Fangs: *Twilight* et al." "Fanfiction"	*The Democratic Genre* Chapter 1 & 2 Recommended reading: *Bitten by Twilight* Chapter 10	The multitude of young adult novels with vampire protagonists; the popularity of vampire narratives in fan work.	Reading Response #2 due.
September 20	"Team Edward vs. Team Jacob: *Twilight* Fandom" "Canon and Mary Sues"	Begin reading Book 1 (Young Adult) "150 Years of Mary Sues" http://www.merrycoz.org/papers/MARY SUE.HTM	Meyer's *Twilight* saga. How does Meyer conceptualize the vampire? How do Twilight fans conceptualize the characters in fanfiction?	Reading Response #3 due. Tentative film screening: *Twilight in Forks; Ringers*
September 27	"Blue Bloods, The Morganville Vampires, and The Mortal Instruments Series" "Non Canon: AUs and More"	Continue reading Book 1 (Young Adult) *The Democratic Genre* Chapter 3 "The Cassandra Claire Plagiarism Debacle." http://www.journalfen.net/community/bad_penny/8985.html.	How do fan writers respond to the original texts? What happens if a fan goes "too far"?	Reading Response #4 due.
October 4	"Vampire Chick Lit: *True Blood*"	Begin reading Book 2 (Chick Lit/Romance) *The Democratic Genre* Chapter 4	The HBO series based on Charlaine Harris's Southern Vampires series.How does a series of novels aimed at one audience change into a TV series aimed at a different audience?	Reading Response #5 due.
October 11	"Vampire Chick Lit: Mary Janice Davidson and Charlaine Harris" "Slash"	Continue reading Book 2 (Chick Lit/ Romance) *The Democratic Genre* Chapter 5	The vampire romance — a genre unto itself.	Reading Response #6 due. Tentative film screening: *Star Trek Night*

Date	Topic	Reading/Viewing	Discussion	Assignment
October 18	"A Very Special..." "Fans as Community"	Continue reading Book 2 (Chick Lit/ Romance) *The Democratic Genre* Chapter 6	Fandom and Academia panel: Guest speakers. (TBD: Some possibilities include: Hal Hall, Bill Page, Sarah Gatson, Robin Anne Reid.) Fan-scholars will discuss the history of fandom.	Reading Response #7 due.
October 25	"The Vampire Crime Procedural: *Moonlight, Forever Knight,* and *Angel*" "Fanfic and Profic"	*Moonlight*: "No Such Thing as Vampires" and "Fever" And *The Democratic Genre* Chapter 7	The vampire detective as television trope. Discussion of *Moonlight*'s creator and fans.	Reading Response #8 due.
November 1	"The Vampire Crime Procedural: *Moonlight, Forever Knight,* and *Angel*" "Fanvids and Narrative Methods"	*Angel*: "Somnambulist" And *Forever Knight* "Dark Knight" (Episodes may be viewed online, or in the library's media center; the DVDs will be on reserve.) *The Democratic Genre* Chapter 8	How does retooling a set of tropes change its meanings, particularly in film?	Reading Response #9 due.
November 8	"Slayers Unite: Girl Power!" "Narrative Methods and Fan Voices"	*Buffy the Vampire Slayer* : "Welcome to the Hellmouth" *The Democratic Genre* Chapter 9 Twilight/Buffy Remix Vid	The presence of female protagonists in popular vampire fiction; *Buffy the Vampire Slayer* as mega-text. After last week's discussion, how do you view the remix vid?	Reading Response #10 due. Tentative Film Screening: Once More with Feeling; Moonlight Paley Panel
November 15	"Anita Blake, Vampire Hunter" "Fan Art" "Fanzines"	*The Democratic Genre* Chapter 10	"A good reader also creates"—fan texts throughout the twentieth century.	Final Project proposal due. Last week to turn in extra credit reading responses.
November 17	*Field trip!*	*Breaking Dawn, Part 1*	*Midnight showing to see the newest film.*	*Organizing carpools, etc.*
November 22	"*Breaking Dawn Part 1* Post-Film Review"	n/a	Fan culture in person: What did you see?	Field-trip write-up.
November 29	"A Very Special..." Fan Creations Symposium, Part 1	n/a	Presenting your projects	Final project due.
December 6	"Fandom and You: A Fan Creations Symposium, Part 2"	n/a	Presenting your projects!	

Notes

1. It is not known, in most cases, what motivates students to drop the course, although some surmises may be made. Some students are apparently dismayed at the idea that some actual work (i.e., reading and

writing) is involved in the class. Several male students have dropped before ever attending a class meeting, apparently discomfited by the perceived gender imbalance. Still others decide that the time commitment required is too great.

2. We surmise that the gender imbalance has to do with a perceived idea that the class is mainly geared to fans of the *Twilight* saga, and that these books (and films) appeal primarily to young women. Most (although certainly not all) contemporary vampire literature is marketed towards women, with a strong emphasis on the "forbidden romance" dimensions of the vampire narrative, rather than the horror/terror aspects. Although some of the students are drawn by the prospect of studying fandom from an academic viewpoint, it cannot be denied that the majority of the students draw their interest in vampires from popular romantic versions of the theme.

3. One need only visit fanfiction.net to see that many of the vampire series have attracted actively involved fans. In addition, there are active fanboards for Laurell K. Hamilton (http://www.laurellkhamilton.org/category/fanclub/), J.R. Ward's *Black Dagger Brotherhood* (http://z13.invisionfree.com/The_Cell/index.php?), *The Vampire Diaries* (http://vampirediariesonline.com/; http://forums.vampire-diaries.net/), *True Blood* (http://www.trueblood-online.com/; http://truebloodnet.com/), *Twilight* (http://bellaandedward.com/; http://twilight-fans.net/), and *Moonlight* (http://www.moonlightaholics.com; http://www.moonlightforever.com/forum/), to list but a few.

4. In "The Monster at the End of This Book," Sam and Dean discover not only that someone has been writing supposedly fictional books based on their lives, but also that fans of the books are creating slash fanfiction (usually known within the fandom as "Wincest"). In "The Real Ghostbusters," the boys are tricked into attending a fan convention, where the presence of an actual ghost makes the live-action role playing into something more real. "Live Free or Twi-hard" shows real vampires using the internet, and the devotion of teenage girls to a popular vampire series, to troll for victims.

5. "Monster Movie" features a shape-shifter who is re-enacting what he sees as the noble plots of old black and white monster movies, while the mind-bending episode, "The French Mistake," has the "real" Sam and Dean Winchester thrown into an alternate universe where they are mistaken for Jensen Ackles and Jared Padelecki—actors who play characters "Sam" and Dean "Winchester" in a television series called *Supernatural*.

6. Unilke the original *Star Trek* series, where the primary slash pairing was Kirk/Spock, in the reboot, there is considerable canonical evidence to suggest a Kirk/McCoy pairing.

7. Public transportation is not an option, and the local theatre is far enough from campus that walking or biking would be ill-advised. Most students, however, even freshmen, do have cars.

8. The video, found on YouTube at http://www.youtube.com/watch?v=6Cp3WO505G8, includes such moments as the presentation of Simba, recreated with a stuffed animal; and a spirited version of "Kiss the Girl" from The Little Mermaid, performed in a small inflatable boat on a local pond.

Bibliography

Angel: Season One. Prod. Joss Whedon and David Greenwalt. Perf. David Boreanaz, Charisma Carpenter, Elisabeth Rohm. Twentieth Century–Fox Home Entertainment, 2003. DVD.

Benefiel, Candace R. "Blood Relations: The Gothic Perversion of the Nuclear Family in Anne Rice's *Interview with the Vampire*." *The Journal of Popular Culture* 38.2 (2004): 261–273. Print.

Boog, Jason. "Sylvain Reynard Lands 7-Figure Deal." Galleycat. 31 July 2012. Web. 1 Aug. 2012.

BreakingProscenium. "A Dream Is a Wish Your Heart Makes." YouTube. 22 Oct. 2009. Web. 1 Aug. 2012.

Bridle, James. "Fan Fiction Promises to Be a Rich Vein for Publishers." *The Observer*. 5 May 2012. Web. 1 Aug. 2012.

Buffy, the Vampire Slayer: The Complete First Season on DVD. Prod. Joss Whedon, Perf. Sarah M. Gellar, Alyson Hannigan, Nicholas Brendon, David Boreanaz, Anthony S. Head, and Charisma Carpenter. Twentieth Century–Fox Home Entertainment, 2001. DVD.

Craft, Christopher. "'Kiss Me with Those Red Lips': Gender and Inversion in Bram Stoker's *Dracula*." *Representations* 8 (1984) 107–133. JSTOR. Web. 22 Sept. 2010.

Doctorow, Corey. "In Praise of Fan Fiction." *Locus Magazine*. 16 May 2007. Web. 1 Aug. 2012.

Forever Knight. Prod. Richard Borchiver. Perf, Geraint W. Davies, John Kapelos, Catherine Disher, Nigel Bennett, and Deborah Duchene. Columbia Tristar Home Entertainment, 2003. DVD.

Galaxy Quest. Dir. Dean Parisot. Perf. Tim Allen, Sigourney Weaver, Alan Rickman. DreamWorks Home Entertainment, 2000. DVD.

James, E L. *Fifty Shades of Grey*. New York: Vintage, 2012. Print.

Meyer, Stephenie. *Twilight*. New York: Little, Brown, 2005. Print.

Moonlight. The Complete Series. Prod. David Greenwalt, et al. Perf. Alex O'Loughlin, Jason Dohring, Sophia Myles. Warner Home Video, 2009. DVD.

Polidori, John William, Kathleen Scherf, David Lorne Macdonald, and John William Polidori. *The Vampyre: A Tale; and Ernestus Berchtold, or, The Modern Oedipus.* Peterborough, Ontario: Broadview Press, 2007. Print.

Pugh, Sheenagh. *The Democratic Genre: Fan Fiction in a Literary Context.* Bridgend, Wales: Seren, 2005. Print.

rebelliouspixels. "Buffy vs. Edward: Twilight Re-Mixed." YouTube. 19 June 2009. Web. 1 Aug. 2012.

Ringers: Lord of the Fans. Dir. Carlene Cordova. Perf. Dominic Monaghan. Sony Pictures Home Entertainment, 2005. DVD.

Schmidt, Bryan Thomas. "Why I'm Not a Fan of FanFic." Bryan Thomas Schmidt.net. 22 Aug. 2011. Web. 1 Aug. 2012.

Shyong, Frank. "Some Costumes Banned at AMC Theaters After 'Dark Knight' Shooting." L.A. Now. 20 July 2012. Los Angeles Times. Web. 1 Aug. 2012.

Star Trek. Prod. Jeffrey Abrams, Roberto Orci, Alex Kurtzman. Perf. Chris Pine, Zachary Quinto, Karl Urban. Paramount Home Entertainment, 2009. DVD.

Star Trek, The Original Series: Season One. Prod. Gene Roddenberry. Perf. William Shatner, Leonard Nimoy, DeForest Kelley. Paramount, 2004. DVD.

Supernatural: The Complete First Season. Prod. Eric Kripke. Perf. Jared Padalecki and Jensen Ackles. Warner Home Video, 2006. DVD.

Sutherland, John. "How Fan Fiction Took Over the Web. *London Evening Standard.* 8 June 2009. Web. 1 Aug. 2012.

Texas A&M University. "Fall 2012 Fingertip Facts." 7 Sept. 2012. Texas A&M University. Web. 1 Oct. 2012.

True Blood. The Complete First Season. Prod. Alan Ball. Paquin, Anna, Stephen Moyer. Perf. Home Box Office, 2009. DVD.

Twilight. Dir. Catherine Hardwicke. Perf. Kristen Stewart, Robert Pattinson, Taylor Lautner. Summit Entertainment, 2009. DVD.

Twilight in Forks: The Saga of the Real Town. Prod. York Blair, Jason Brown, and Stephenie Meyer. Summit Entertainment, 2010. DVD.

Vampires Suck. Dir. Jason Friedberg and Aaron Seltzer. Twentieth Century–Fox Home Entertainment, 2010. DVD.

Wasson, S. "'Coven of the Articulate': Orality and Community in Anne Rice's Vampire Fiction." *The Journal of Popular Culture* 45 (2012): 197–213. Print.

White, E. R., J. J. Goetz, M. S. Hunter, and B. O. Barefoot (1995). "Creating Successful Transitions Through Academic Advising." *First-Year Academic Advising: Patterns in the Present, Pathways to the Future.* Ed. M.L. Upcraft and G. L. Kramer. Columbia: University of South Carolina, 1995: pp. 25–34.

Luring Online Students
with the Power of the Vampire

Anne Daugherty and *Jerri L. Miller*

The intersection of popular culture, vampire literature and films, "inquiry-guided learning," and digital storytelling affords students in online classes a unique and rewarding opportunity to explore social issues. The vampire, evidenced in the folklore of many world cultures, historically conveys an image of a rat-like creature with long nails and fangs able to suck the life out of humans, striking fear into the hearts of literary and cinematic audiences. Recent popular culture manifestations of the vampire represent him or her as largely misunderstood, desirous only of acceptance into the community. Coupled with the dark, sexy, brooding nature of the new wave of vampire struggling against his or her innermost desires, the result is an irresistible creature as personified by Edward from the *Twilight* saga, Angel from *Buffy the Vampire Slayer*, or Bill and Eric from *Dead Until Dark* (adapted into the HBO series *True Blood*). Vampire literature and films provide rich potential for study, particularly in the online classroom, inviting engaging opportunities for analysis of gender roles, social issues, and the implications of the division of power in our culture.

Online courses pose a unique challenge for student engagement. Baker University, a small liberal arts college in the Midwest, pioneered the course "Gender Roles in Vampire Literature and Film" in 2009, and repeated it in 2010, 2011, and 2013. Each time the course attracted 18 students, the maximum number allowed in online courses. Many students erroneously perceive online courses to be easier than traditional classes and the temptation of plagiarism is more readily accessible in online classes. Whereas traditional classes require the student to interact with the instructor and his or her peers to discuss the subject matter during class meetings, the online student typically contributes to discussions in a written rather than oral format. Because students are already online, many succumb to the temptation to search the Internet for a few poignant comments, which are easily copied and pasted as their own responses to discussion fora. The challenge for online instructors, then, is to fully engage students in the learning experience. Vampire literature and films provide interesting and appealing material for such engagement.

The ability to draw conclusions about gender roles, humanity, and power from literary and cinematic material typically categorized as fantasy helps students think beyond the surface, to develop analytical reading, thinking, conversation, and writing skills essential to enhance an understanding and appreciation of literature and the world around them. To that end, "inquiry-guided learning" and digital storytelling offer students unique methods to explore fundamental aspects of society and their role within it. Classic and contemporary vampiric literature, film, and television series illustrate these learning experiences, including *Dracula*, *Shadow of a Vampire*, *Interview with the Vampire*, *Buffy the Vampire Slayer*, and *Dead Until Dark*. These vampire stories provide the student exposure to classic and contemporary literature.

Count Dracula and "Traditional" Vampires

Deciding which works to include in an online vampire literature course is not without its challenges. From the ever-growing plethora of available novels, three key eras of vampire literature emerge, as represented by Bram Stoker's *Dracula* (1897), Anne Rice's *Interview with a Vampire* (1976), and Charlaine Harris's *Dead Until Dark* (2001).

Bram Stoker's *Dracula* may not be the first or even the best-written vampire novel of its time, yet it is arguably the most well-known piece of vampire literature and the inspiration for many vampires since. Far from the sexy, brooding vampire beloved by contemporary teens and frustrated housewives, Stoker's Dracula is a tall man with sharp teeth, pointed ears, long sharpened nails, and hair on his palms. Recognizing the elements of the Gothic novel (as epitomized by *Dracula*) establishes a baseline for students' understanding of literary works featuring vampires.

To that end, Robert Harris's list of ten elements of the Gothic novel provides a useful taxonomy for students to catalogue and comprehend the common features of the traditional vampire novel. According to Harris, the Gothic novel includes the following: set in a castle; an atmosphere of mystery and suspense; an ancient prophecy; omens, portents, and visions; supernatural or otherwise inexplicable events; high, even overwrought emotion; women in distress; women threatened by a powerful, impulsive, tyrannical male; metonymy of gloom and horror; and vocabulary of the Gothic. Understanding these "traditional" features provides an effective springboard for analysis of later works and their variation from the established norm of the original vampire's world.

Likely the trickiest part of including *Dracula* in an online literature course is encouraging the students to actually read the novel. Most students have at least passing familiarity with the name Dracula through various cinematic renditions of the Count by Bela Lugosi in 1931, Christopher Lee in 1958, and especially Gary Oldman in 1992. Easy access to these films may lure students away from reading the novel, thinking they can glean what they need from watching the movie. Yet reading the novel is rewarding not only because it exposes students to a literary classic, but also for its unique format. Reading the novel potentially fosters critical thinking skills because students have to piece together the story from the various narrative threads, which, at times, are particularly stretched.

Providing students with a specific task to accomplish as they read — and holding them accountable for that task — helps ensure a close reading of the novel. One method is to ask students to read against the accepted interpretation of the novel. Typical readings of Dracula usually reference sexual metaphors and Victorian era repression. A deeper reading might align Stoker's novel with the nascent suffragette movement, reading the character of Dracula as metaphor for women's rights.

Dracula was first published the same year as the formation of the National Union of Women's Suffrage. The novel's female protagonist, Mina, addresses the suffrage movement in her journal, joking, "Some of the 'New Women' writers will someday start an idea that men and women should be allowed to see each other asleep before proposing or accepting"

(Stoker 205). The women's suffrage movement, along with Mary Wollstonecraft's *Vindication of the Rights of Woman* (1797) and John Stuart Mill's *The Subjection of Women* (1869), birthed what theorists call "liberal feminism." These early feminists maintained the primary cause of women's subordination to men is a set of "social norms and formal laws that make it hard for women to succeed in the public world" (Haslanger, Tuana, and O'Connor). Clearly, Mina does not have the same opportunities as the men in *Dracula*. Indeed, in their attempts to protect her, the novel's male characters actually leave Mina more vulnerable to attack from Dracula. Reading the Count's lure over Mina (and Lucy) as a rallying cry to shun societal norms and achieve their full potential urges careful critical thinking to ascertain where the theory holds and where it falls apart. For example, as the newly emancipated Lucy spreads her message of freedom to children, perhaps her "bite" spreads her message to demand equality.

Through the use of primary sources (albeit fictionalized) in the form of letters, journal entries, and press releases designed for newspaper articles, *Dracula* lacks an omnipotent voice explaining the action. Instead, the reader must infer meaning from the parcels of information provided by the characters. As they piece together the story from the various narrative threads, readers have to evaluate the truth behind each parcel. Would a journal (or blog) genuinely contain whole strings of dialogue? Asking students to read against the surface level of the text requires mature critical thinking skills. Can the author be trusted? What biases does each character hold? Are the news articles completely factual?

Assigning tasks to assess students' understanding of the novel also presents a significant challenge. Students lead busy lives and essays on *Dracula* are readily available for purchase on the Internet. One method to help students avoid plagiarism in literature classes, particularly online, is assigning creative tasks employing inquiry-based learning techniques. Rather than assigning formal essay questions, proponents of inquiry-based learning encourage students to ask questions and seek answers. An inquiry-based approach "is more web-like in how students pursue knowledge, as opposed to the linear, vertical and compartmentalized structure of traditional education" ("Intro to Inquiry Learning"). Clearly, this web-like approach is ideally suited to students in online classes who must be actively engaged.

One model of active learning, articulated by L. Dee Funk, suggests that all learning activities involve some kind of experience or some kind of dialogue. The two main kinds of dialogue, according to Funk, are with self and others, while the two main kinds of experience are observing and doing. To dialogue with others in traditional literature classes, students gather together to discuss a novel. Skilful facilitators engage the students, ascertaining their level of understanding and deepening it. Online discussions require careful design to ensure students actively engage with the novel and authentically participate in discussions.

One facilitation approach involves beginning with broad open-ended questions. This strategy deliberately seeks to draw students into the conversation by not honing immediately into specific questions. Leaving the questions broad allows freedom for students to develop the conversation along lines of interest to them. A typical discussion of *Dracula*, for example, might begin with only four questions: (1) Did you like it? (2) Discuss the role of class, gender, and sexuality in the novel. (3) How is the vampire a metaphor in the novel? (4) Which Gothic symbols emerge?

Most students need structure to understand what is required of them. Rubrics help students understand the required number of posts and the quality of those posts. Rubrics might also constrain students to only complete the required number of responses, rather than contributing fully to the conversation. Typically an over-arching instruction proves effective: "Please respond to the following questions. Each person should contribute a **minimum** of ten (10) entries, with a 100-word response (about half a page) per question." Another significant guideline for students is when to post. If the course opens on Monday morning, for example, requiring students to post their first comment by Thursday affords them reading time to prepare for the conversation while also allowing ample time for the conversation to develop over the remaining days of the week.

Finding a balance between responding and keeping quiet is paramount for a good online facilitator. Many students forward the discussion threads to their email, so it is important to address students by name when replying to their posts. Building on the comments of the students provides an effective means to follow up on comments and push them to think a little deeper. A balance of chatty banter and provocative questions helps foster student engagement and build interest to check the conversation and contribute to it.

A lively discussion of *Dracula*, and in particular the concept of vampire as metaphor, sets the stage for deepening the students' interaction with the novel. An inquiry-based student assignment related in some way to the novel requires students to explore textual and sub-textual information as it relates to the novel. Discussing the vampire as metaphor for the suffrage movement (which may be quite a stretch for some) potentially frees students to explore an inter-disciplinary project of interest to them. Requiring students to work in pairs (or threes) holds each student accountable for the quality of product created.

Suggested topics for inquiry-based learning as part of the study of *Dracula* are seemingly endless. While the actual research topic should emerge from the student's interest rather than the instructor's suggestion, instructor approval early in the process ensures students remain on track to achieve established and agreed-upon goals. Stoker's writing references any number of geographic, political, and medical issues, all worthy of exploration. Examples include the biochemistry of blood, the history of blood typing, the geography of Europe in 1897, vampire bats, women's rights, and psychotherapy. Requiring a polished and shareable presentation holds students accountable for the quality of their research. Further, requiring students include a reflection statement with their inquiry-based assignment may help hold them further accountable for their work. This reflection might include: (1) two or three important things the student learned from investigating the topic, (2) the student's research strategy and the methods employed locating sources, and (3) the most challenging part of the assignment or the part of the assignment that garners the most pride. Establishing a set format for peer-reviewing projects also holds students accountable for viewing and evaluating each other's work.

Shadow of the Vampire

Dracula's epistolary format allows readers to experience the innermost thoughts and feelings of the novel's characters, except those of Dracula himself. This lack of voice is but one device employed to demonize the Count as the ultimate villain. The film *Shadow of the Vampire* (2002), a fictionalized "behind the scenes" examination of the making of the classic horror film *Nosferatu,* adds another dimension to our understanding of the Count. Accentuating the "humanity" of Dracula (who is named Orlock in the film) affords students a unique insight into the concept of the "gradients of evil."

F.W. Murnau's expressionistic silent film *Nosferatu* (1922) modified the Dracula story by omitting several characters (Van Helsing, for example) and changing geographical locations. Unable to obtain the rights to the novel from Bram Stoker's estate, Murnau superimposed a few changes in nomenclature — vampire becomes Nosferatu and Dracula becomes Orlock — then stole the storyline. This curious backstory of *Nosferatu* provides an interesting opportunity for discussing plagiarism.

Shadow of the Vampire recreates the making of *Nosferatu* with John Malkovich as director F.W. Murnau and Willem Defoe as "method actor" Max Schreck playing Count Orlock. Claiming to be part of an elite acting company, Schreck will only appear to the others in character, in full make-up, and at night. The uneasy feeling he causes in his fellow actors and the audience is soon explained; Schreck is a vampire. Murnau and Schreck enjoy a mutually beneficial bargain. Murnau believes he will create the best vampire movie of all time; Schreck gets Greta, the lead female actress, for lunch. At the movie's close, Schreck bites and ultimately kills Greta, then feasts his way through the rest of the crew. As Schreck feeds, Murnau continues to run the camera, shouting direction to the vampire saying, "If it is not in frame, it doesn't exist" (Merhige). Who, then, is the real villain?

Comparing the characters of Schreck and Dracula and aligning their attributes with Harris's list of Gothic elements provides effective synthesis and evaluation tasks. Students can work together in the online environment to create a matrix comparing and contrasting the characteristics of the vampires. Requiring students to work in pairs to creator their matrices ensures they discuss their ideas with another person before posting them to the whole group. Students might begin examining the physical representations of the central characters as the first point of comparison between Stoker's novel and Merhige's film. Schreck physicalizes the Count as bald, beady-eyed, and fond of clicking together his long, claw-like fingernails. While Dracula aligned with wolves, Orlock is more akin to rats. He also has a softer side. He watches film footage of sunshine and longingly reaches out to touch it. He pitifully asks Murnau, "Tell me how you can harm me, when even I don't know how I can harm myself" (Merhige). His tone and body language convey his longing to end his existence trapped in the body of a vampire.

This humanization of the vampire affords students the opportunity to critically think about ethical behavior. Do serial killers or pedophiles express similar remorse, for example? *Shadow of the Vampire* provides a critical glimpse of humanity and humans' willingness to overlook the real value of human life in the pursuit of personal goals. The movie's focus on the humanity within Schreck almost urges a sympathetic response from viewers. In *Dracula*, the Count is portrayed only as evil, lacking humanity, ruthlessly killing people. Identifying the villain in *Shadow of the Vampire* is less obvious. While the vampire does the killing, the director allows the situation to unfold. Schreck follows his nature (cf. Aesop's tale "The Scorpion and the Frog"); Murnau sacrifices his crew for personal gain.

A Marxist reading of the subtext of the film suggests a strong indictment of capitalism and the idea that producing a leisure activity is more important than individual lives of the masses. As with *Dracula*, a possible student assignment for *Shadow of the Vampire* might explore the primary source as a springboard for critical and creative thinking. Current media events provide effective sources for discussion of media ethics, particularly when compared to the central characters of *Shadow of the Vampire*. For example, in December 2012 two Australian radio personalities placed an on-air prank phone call to a hospital in London treating the Duchess of Cambridge for morning sickness. Pretending to be the Queen, one DJ asked for information regarding her granddaughter's condition. British nurse Jacintha Saldanha committed suicide after allegedly putting the call through to a nurse who provided medical information to the media pranksters. The ensuing outcry caused shares in the radio station's parent company to tumble, all the while provoking water-cooler conversations about media ethics and the desperate need for public titillation at whatever cost. Newspapers and television news programs capitalized on the devastated lives of the Saldanha family and the two radio announcers, whose media careers likely ended that day. Comparison between Murnau and the Australian radio announcers (or another current media event) establishes an effective parameter for critical analysis. Who is at fault for feeding the voracious appetite of public amusement, which, not unlike that of a vampire, seems insatiable and particularly fond of blood?

The causal relationships within *Shadow of the Vampire* demonstrate the power broker manipulates his talent inappropriately in order to titillate the audience. The director literally preys on the foibles of his star to create entertainment for his own personal profit and/or glory. These interactions align with the Australian DJs who preyed on the vulnerability of the Duchess of Cambridge to create an entertaining moment. The stunt was only seen as reprehensible when someone died. A similar parallel might be drawn between the relationships in any number of reality television shows. The student assignment aligned to the film is to identify a popular culture artifact or current event that mirrors the causal relationships in *Shadow of a Vampire*, whereby person A manipulates person B in a public manner. By sharing their findings in a public forum, students discuss the merits of each case and its effective alignment to the film.

The Brooding Vampire

Anne Rice's *Interview with the Vampire* (1976) introduces the first of a new generation of vampires, the "brooding" vampire, Louis, who recounts his story to an interviewer known simply as "the boy." Rice's novel extends analysis of the vampire beyond the confines of gothic horror. Deeply personal and told using an oral format, Louis' first-person narrative, completely opposite from how we come to know Dracula, draws readers to him. As students grabble with the meaning of Louis' life and what it conveys about the natural tendencies of humans and the consequences of human actions, it is appropriate they turn a similar lens to their own lives. Digital storytelling provides an effective method for critical reflection as students posit their place in society.

Digital storytelling conveys short personal digital narratives, typically less than three-minute multimedia movies, employing a combination of photographs, video, animation, sound, music, text, and narration. Described as "an active process that teaches students to fully engage in a multi-step project, which helps them to develop skills in management, critical thinking, problem-solving, and collaboration," digital storytelling affords students the opportunity to work on creative curricula projects, which are published to YouTube (Frazel 9). The accountability of publication typically enhances the quality of student work. Digital storytelling boosts two skills in particular: taking on a particular viewpoint and asking a dramatic question.

Louis' oral format and first-person narrative provide the parameters for the assignment. Students must first identify one key element Louis shares of his life, perhaps a relationship, or his place in society, or a life choice he made. Using Louis' narrative as a guide, students create a digital story of one aspect of their own lives, ensuring they address the seven elements fundamental to good digital storytelling as detailed by Lambert and the Center for

Digital Storytelling: point of view; dramatic question; emotion, feelings, memories; voice; the soundtrack; economy (compact, brief, fast moving); and pacing (rhythm, tempo, rate, speed, interest).

Students post their digital stories to youtube.com and mark them unlisted, enabling only class members to view and evaluate the stories. One week after the assignment due date, students may remove their stories, or change the youtube.com listing to private. This strategy is important because it addresses student concerns about privacy and avoids copyright infringements. Fair use covers works of educational purpose that are not publicly posted.

Buffy the Vampire Slayer

The shift from vampire as villain to vampire struggling to find purpose in life takes a further leap in Joss Whedon's *Buffy the Vampire Slayer* (1997–2003). The title character, Buffy, an adolescent female superhero, keeps her community safe from vampires while exploring the complexity of desire, love, and sex with her vampiric paramours Angel and Spike. The former proves himself a hero while an invasive medical device controls the latter, ensuring he maintains socially acceptable behavior.

Personable and attractive, Buffy does not look much like a superhero. She continually struggles with her professional duties, her attraction to men others perceive as villains, and trying to keep some sort of normalcy in her life. Buffy's struggle mirrors that of many young women. In her everyday humanness, Buffy typifies the average American teenager. Young women want to be independent and strong, but they also need to belong. That she slays vampires in the evenings seemingly sets her apart, until the viewer recognizes the vampires Buffy slays as an effective metaphor for the various angsts that plague teenagers. Buffy's clueless single mother, her circle of friends who support her, and the one adult figure who helps guide her path are all common elements of many American teenagers.

If Mina in *Dracula* provides a blueprint for the "New Woman," Buffy is the realization of the dream. An iconic liberal feminist, Buffy protects her community, supported by her friends Willow and Xander, and her watcher. Often labeled a troublemaker by the authority figures in her community, Buffy always manages to save the day. She never falters in doing what is right, even if that means taking the hard path. Of the two schools of thought that generally represent the hero — the utilitarian view of doing what is best for the greater good (e.g., Bentham) and doing the right thing based on one's beliefs regardless of the outcome (e.g., Kant) — Buffy follows the second. She will not take a human life even if it means more work to save the world from evil. Alsford, in *Heroes & Villains*, claims Buffy cannot sacrifice humans as the means to an end, even if it is for the greater good (28).

Produced at turn of the twenty-first century after the sexual revolution, the vampires in *Buffy the Vampire Slayer* are sensual, sexual, bad boys. And unlike Lestat and Louis, they show interest in women. Buffy describes Angel (her first love) as dark and gorgeous. A hero in a villain's body, Angel is a sexy, dangerous, brooding vampire. He helps Buffy and her friends fight off the vampires and other demons that invade their hometown, Sunnydale. Meanwhile, the sexual tension between Buffy and Angel builds throughout the first season.

Buffy and Angel consummate their physical attraction in season two and it ends badly. In this act of pure happiness, Angel's soul is taken away and he returns to his former evil self — surely one of the greatest warnings against the dangers of premarital sex since the "slasher" films of the 1980s! By season five, Buffy's absolute disregard for patriarchal norms is apparent. Spike, a seemingly nasty vampire with working class dress, actions, accent, and personality suggestive of punk rock, is Buffy's second love interest. The quintessential rebel, he smokes, drinks, and sings songs by the Ramones. A chip in his brain prevents him from committing the evil deeds he longs to mete out on society. Buffy and Spike develop an uneven relationship. Spike loves Buffy; she takes advantage of those feelings. This act of Buffy's might be her least heroic trait.

The chip in Spike's brain restrains him from acting on his urges and desires. His chemical restraint mirrors the societal restraints on Mina in *Dracula*. Mina's true gifts were held in check by accepted traditions of the time. In order for Spike to assimilate into society, he has to deny his true nature. The change in Buffy from loving Angel to a casual sexual relationship with Spike indicates a significant transformation in both the girl and the sexual mores of the time. While both love interests are vampires and thereby bad boys, a different guiding force controls each relationship.

Particularly confusing, however, is the scene, where, purportedly in an effort to make her care about him, Spike attempts to rape Buffy. The action ends their relationship and sends him off seeking redemption. However, the rape is never addressed. Buffy does nothing about it, not even tell her friends. Statistics reported by the Rape, Abuse and Incest National Network indicate 44 percent of victims are under age 18 and 80 percent are under age 30. Fifty-four percent of sexual assaults are not reported to the police, 97 percent of rapists will never spend a day in jail. Someone known to the victim commits approximately two-thirds of assaults and 38 percent of rapists are a friend or acquaintance (RAINN.org).

At the conclusion of the show, Buffy throws her power to all women, saying:

> In every generation, one Slayer is born, because a bunch of men who died thousands of years ago made up that rule. They were powerful men.... I say we change the rule. I say my power ... should be *our* power.... From now on, every girl in the world who *might* be a Slayer, *will* be a Slayer. Every girl who *could* have the power, *will* have the power, *can* stand up, *will* stand up. Slayers ... every one of us. Make your choice. Are you ready to be strong?

The rallying cry to stand up for equality suggested as a counter-reading in *Dracula* is now a blatant call for action. Given feminism is an unconcealed premise of *Buffy the Vampire Slayer*, what are the subtexts? Typical questions for students to pursue while studying *Buffy the Vampire Slayer* include: (1) How do we reconcile the idea of a hero in a traditionally evil presence? (2) Why humanize the vampire? (3) Does Buffy's overt "girlyness" cloud the viewer's judgment of her as hero? Is she a hero? (4) Does her attraction to dangerous men weaken her standing as feminist hero? (5) What is upshot of Buffy not reporting her rape?

Because of the sensitive nature of these questions, concern for how to handle the discussion may hamper instructors from exploring important questions. Yet the online classroom affords an excellent environment for tackling difficult questions, as long as adequate groundwork has set the stage for interaction. Indeed, the online classroom may actually enhance the potential for well-thought out, on-topic discussions. Discussion in a traditional course might quickly dissolve into the something the instructor has trouble controlling. Online, the students have time to think about their responses before sharing them and many understand the need for respect and intellectual discourse. In the event the instructor deems comments inappropriate, most Learning Management Systems (LMS) allow the instructor to delete the post. The instructor should always contact the student to explain why the comments are improper.

Good discussions are not possible without establishing an effective learning community. It is easy to dehumanize the individuals in the class when there is no face-to-face interaction. Students need to feel comfortable in their learning environment to feel safe enough to participate in discussions, much like in a traditional classroom. Digging into sensitive social issues about Buffy sets the stage for discussing controversial social issues in *Dead Until Dark* by Charlaine Harris. While the novel again features a strong woman who desires a sexy, reformed bad boy, Harris employs the vampire as metaphor for another key contemporary social issue.

Dead Until Dark

While vampires in *Buffy the Vampire Slayer* might be interpreted as a metaphor for teenage angst, the subtext of Charlaine Harris' novel, *Dead Until Dark*, is a thinly veiled allegory demanding equal rights for the gay community. The protagonist, Sookie Stackhouse, falls in love with a Civil War veteran turned vampire named Bill, who attempts to mainstream into the community thanks to a new synthetic blood product called "True Blood."

Neither all humans nor all vampires agree with mainstreaming. As Bill explains to Sookie, "our life is seducing and taking and has been for centuries, for some of us. Synthetic blood and grudging human acceptance isn't going to change that overnight — or over a decade" (Harris 72). Just as the humans in *Dead Until Dark* cannot accept vampires, so, too, many in American society express displeasure at mainstreaming non-conformists. Same-sex marriage, for example, is legal only in seven states. The issue remains heated, with referenda slated on a number of state ballots in 2012. The opening credits for *True Blood* (the HBO series based on Harris's Sookie Stackhouse novels) features a sign reading "God Hates Fangs," mirroring those made by members of Westboro Baptist Church in Topeka, Kansas, led by Pastor Fred Phelps. The group's most favored catch phrase, "GOD HATES FAGS" (also the URL for the church's website — godhatesfags.com), expresses their belief that the bible says homosexuality is a sin. When Chick-fil-A president Dan Cathy publicly stated his company's stance against gay marriage, the issue quickly spread to social media. Celebrities expressed their discontent on Twitter and friends reported their stance on Facebook. Suddenly eating or not eating a certain brand of chicken became politicized.

Dead Until Dark is the first novel in what Harris calls "The Southern Vampire Mystery Series." The mystery driving the plot of *Dead Until Dark* is the serial killing of residents of the town of Bon Temps, Louisiana, the setting of the novel. Many of the townspeople express the opinion that a vampire is responsible for the killings — it is the obvious choice. However, the killer is revealed as René Lenier, a human, who killed to express his disgust of women who bed vampires. This novel provides rich material for discourse but requires careful vetting of critical thinking practices. Only after students carefully evaluate their own lenses, including beliefs, values, and biases can they employ critical thinking to construct arguments on both sides of the issue before deciding upon a thesis.

Genuine critical thinking may cause personal confrontation between what students know and believe and something different, new, or contrary. Hatcher and Spencer write that critical thinking "attempts to arrive at a decision or judgment only after honestly evaluating alternatives with respect to available evidence and arguments" (1). Urging students to honestly evaluate alternatives provides a challenge, particularly if the alternatives challenge long-held beliefs.

Student discussion should begin by recognizing the author's bias in writing the novel. As Harris says, "Gay rights is just one of the social issues I'm interested in. I think that people might be less tense about it if we would all accept the fact that not everyone is wired the same way" (Solomon). Rene dislikes assimilation so intensely he kills those who support a belief he abhors. He expresses his bigotry by taking the lives of others. If we consider Rene as representing one side of the argument, we also have to separate out that he is mentally unstable. Not all people who support his side of the argument are serial killers.

One method to ensure students genuinely evaluate alternate positions is to provide a matrix for students to complete in pairs or small groups. An example matrix requires students to complete three carefully considered arguments for and against the topic as they explore parallel controversial allegories about issues such as gender equality; gay rights; terrorism; racial tensions, including Muslims in America; and immigration. The resulting investigational presentation, completed in pairs, addresses one possible current political/sociological issue explored in *Dead Until Dark*. The components of the project include two articles on both sides of the argument, general research about the topic, and the student's viewpoint concerning how effectively the topic is presented within the novel.

One model, provided by Hatcher and Spencer, details a complete thesis statement as including a position statement, reasons for the position, and major objections or alternatives to the stated position. An example matrix might include (1) the introduction to the issue, (2) the thesis statement (student's judgment on the issue), (3) supporting arguments and evidence for the judgment, (4) objections to the thesis or arguments or alternative views worth considering on the issue, including replies, and (5) a summary.

A generic sample thesis statement about vampire novels, then, might read:

> While some critics claim the implausibility of the central characters makes novels about vampires nothing more than fantasy, others argue the vampire novel offers an effective metaphor for the human condition by effectively addressing issues of homo-sexuality, sexually transmitted diseases, and drug and alcohol addiction.

This thesis could then be expanded into the following matrix:

1. Vampire novels help readers address the human condition.
2. While some critics claim the implausibility of the central characters makes novels about vampires nothing more than fantasy, others argue the vampire novel offers an effective metaphor for the human condition by effectively addressing issues of homosexuality, sexually transmitted diseases, and drugs and alcohol addiction.
3. Supporting arguments and evidence for the judgment
   a. The vampire novel provides an effective metaphor to address the treatment of homosexuality in our society.
      i. Evidence...
      ii. Evidence...
   b. The vampire novel provides an effective metaphor to address the issue of sexually transmitted diseases.
      i. Evidence...
      ii. Evidence...
   c. The vampire novel provides an effective metaphor to address the issue of drug and alcohol addiction.
      i. Evidence...
      ii. Evidence...

4. Objections or alternative views
   a. The implausibility of vampirism makes novels featuring vampires nothing more than fantasy.
      i. Evidence...
      ii. Evidence...
   b. Rebuttal to fantasy argument.
      i. Evidence...
      ii. Evidence...
   c. The novels are not related to real life.
      i. Evidence...
      ii. Evidence...
   d. Rebuttal to real life argument.
      i. Evidence...
      ii. Evidence...
5. Summary of arguments and evidence.

The deliberate rigidity of the matrix may provide an effective structure to guide students' thinking as they grapple with sensitive and controversial issues. Perhaps the most difficult part of critical thinking is honestly considering the opposite side of an argument, particularly in cases where deep-seated beliefs might be questioned.

Conclusion

Book sales and cinematic attendance quantify the popularity of vampires. While the brooding, sexy vampire of contemporary popular culture gets hearts pumping in many individuals, vampires garner attention both when they struggle to be good and/or allow their evil nature to take over. The study of vampires affords a ready opportunity to explore many facets of humanity and human desires. It provides an outlet for excitement and fear within the safe confines of a book, movie, or television series. History proves vampires fascinate us, so why not harness this fascination to engage students in a close examination of the culture in which we live? The long-standing attraction of the vampire readily lures students. Interactive methods of online learning, such as "inquiry-guided learning" and digital storytelling, engage students to creatively explore the impact of gender roles, social issues, and the implications of the division of power in our culture. Vampires and online learning provide an exciting opportunity for student learning with bite!

Bibliography

Alsford, Mike. *Heroes & Villains*. Waco: Baylor University, 2006. Print.
Frazel, Midge. *Digital Storytelling: Guide for Educators*. Washington, DC: International Society for Technology in Education, 2010. Print.
Harris, Charlaine. *Dead Until Dark*. New York: Ace, 2001. Print.
Harris, Robert. "Elements of the Gothic Novel." *VirtualSalt* 22 Nov. 2010. Web. 5 July 2012.
Haslanger, Sally, Nancy Tuana, and Peg O'Connor. "Topics of Feminism." *Stanford Encyclopedia of Philosophy*. Stanford University, 2011. Web. 5 Aug. 2012. http://plato.stanford.edu/entries/feminism-topics/.
Hatcher, D. L., and L. A. Spencer. *Reasoning and Writing: From Critical Thinking to Composition*. Boston: American Press, 2000. Print.

Hu, Elise. "Chick-Fil-A Gay Flap a 'Wakeup Call' for Companies." *All Things Considered.* NPR. 27 July 2012. Web. 2 Aug. 2012.

"Into to Inquiry Learning." Youth Learn Education Development Center, Inc. 2012. Web. 5 July 2012. http://www.youthlearn.org.

Lambert, Joe. *Digital Storytelling Cookbook.* Berkley: Digital Diner Press, 2010. Web. 7 July 2012.

Merhige, E. Elias, dir. *Shadow of the Vampire.* Perf. John Malkovich and Willem Dafoe. Lionsgate, 2000. DVD.

Palloff, Rena M., and Keith Pratt. *Building Online Learning Communities: Effective Strategies for the Virtual Classroom.* San Francisco: Jossey-Bass, 2007. Print.

Poole, W. Scott. "Why Historians Should Be Vampire Hunters." *Huffpost Arts & Culture.* 20 June 2012. Web. 14 Aug. 2012. http://www.huffingtonpost.com.

Rice, Anne. *Interview with the Vampire.* New York: Ballantine, 1976. EPUB file.

Solomon, Deborah. "Once Bitten." *The New York Times Magazine.* 30 April 2010. Web. 2 Aug. 2012.

"Statistics." *Rape, Abuse, & Incest National Network.* RAINN 2009. Web. 15 Aug. 2012. http://www.rainn.org/statistics.

Stoker, Bram. *Dracula.* 1897. New York: Back Bay Books, 2005. Print.

Trueman, Chris. "The Suffragettes." History Learning Site. Web. http://www.historylearningsite.co.uk/suffragettes.htm.

Blood, Lust and Transformation:
Vampires in the Community
College Classroom
Leslie Ormandy

Students love vampires. Vampires are an integral element of popular culture, especially in these post–*Twilight* days. In this fascination with vampires, our students follow in the footsteps of authors such as Byron, Shelley, Gautier, Southey, Keats, Coleridge, and Poe, among others, who were equally fascinated with this seminal supernatural character who found a transformed life beyond death, purchased through ingesting blood. I spend a fair amount of time reminding deans and the Board of Education of the long list of perfectly respectable canonical authors who have written in this subset of the popular culture genre. I talk about the ways watching the transformation of the vampire as it passes through time and cultures tells us as much about ourselves as it does about the vampire. I talk about the ideas of blood, life, eternal life, and salvation all related to vampires. Like my students, I have a love affair with vampires.

"Vampires in Literature" came to my rural Oregon community college in 2008; it took me two years to design the class. Designing the class was actually the easy part; learning to run the class with the quite diverse student body who signed up for it was much harder. There has been a learning curve. Experience has taught me that the most important part of designing a Vampires in Literature class for a community college classroom is an understanding of the students the class will attract; the selection of clear objectives that bear those students in mind comes later. The objectives require a careful choice of texts and textual themes that support teaching not only about vampires, but how to read analytically, how to discuss texts both orally and in writing, and how to write a college level paper that displays an understanding of the topics discussed. To shorten your learning curve, included in this essay is a variety of exercises which have proven successful in melding the diverse student body into a cohesive class; and including some sample Student Learning Outcomes and Course Objectives for the 100-level and 200-level class since both sections will be need to be included in the Course Outline. I am suggesting texts and online resources which have proven their worth in freshman and sophomore level classrooms. This essay includes only exercises meant for the development of either a face-2-face class (a traditional class in which teacher and students gather in one location synchronously) or a hybrid class (a mixture of face-2-face and online time); I do not address the needs of an online class.

I have chosen to run the 100-level class as a free-ranging survey class, with the students allowed great leeway to move the discussion away from my own planned destination. For instance, I recently planned a discussion of the vampire as the representation of outsider surrounding the reading of the manga *Dance in the Vampire Bund* by Nozomu Tamaki. Instead, discussion diverted to the question of pedophilia and vampires—a discussion that continued for the rest of the term. The students cared passionately about these discussions, and the discussions acquired a depth which a forced return to my planned destination would, perhaps, have lacked. A 100-level class usually asks students to read around one hundred pages per week (depending on complexity), features texts that are less demanding lexically, and asks for shorter papers and no more than one or two presentations. In the 100-level section below you will find some first day suggestions that work for both levels, such as Vampire Bingo, Vampire Characteristic Brainstorming, and suggestions regarding a writing diagnostic.

The 200-level class can be a much more demanding class, with more pages and more linguistically demanding text selections. Students can be asked to present larger and more involved presentations, and asked to design key pieces of certain classes. Students are encouraged to delve deeper in discussions and support their observations with textual support. My own 200-level class focuses closely on vampire literature in the Victorian period, vampires as they appear in other cultures, and the interaction of science and vampires.

No matter what your own choice for focus and underlying theme is as you design your course, understanding the diverse types of students Vampires in Literature classes at a community college will attract is the key to holding successful classes. In my experience over the past four years, I have learned that these often are not the same students who would sign up for a traditional, canonical class. The typical Vampire in Literature class at my college will blend Goths, atheists, agnostics, witches, Christians who expect to be allowed to evangelize, students who belong to costumed role-playing groups (Cos-players), such as *Vampire: The Masquerade*,[1] all mixed with a smattering of academics. Some of the students already have read and watched a wide variety of vampire media, while others are present only because it sounds like more fun than an American Literature class and carries transferable English credit. Most of these students are enthusiastic, but often untrained for the academic terrain; they are unfamiliar with analytical reading, researching using scholarly sources, writing papers that do more than summarize the plot, and the basics of sentence structure and grammar are often missing. This diversity makes teaching Vampires in Literature at the community college a commitment to not only discuss vampires as they are represented in literature, but it is also a commitment to teach basics of college level reading and writing since a larger than normal number of the students will not have yet taken College English Composition (at the transfer level), meaning while interest in the topic, vampires, is high, analytical reading skills and basic essay writing might require some remediation for both levels as will some components of grammar. Preventing a tiered, classist system in which students who are already schooled in the rules of academia receive the great grades and lord it over the less prepared students is essential if a cohesive class is desired. It requires effort on the teacher's part; a willingness to treat every individual as though their ideas are equally worthwhile.

When emphasis is placed on creating a cohesive whole from the wildly diverse students, basic economics need to be addressed. At my own college, a majority of the students are on financial aid of some sort. This means that for either level, minimizing obvious economic disparities between the students is necessary; to this end, planning early assigned readings around texts which either are internet available, or handouts, is recommended. Many of the students are attending community college for financial reasons and are thus at-risk students. They often will not be able to purchase the texts until mid-week two after their financial aid has been disbursed. Structuring the reading away from texts they have no ability to access is easy enough to do, and a silent, hidden method of preventing simple economics from destroying class-building efforts.

With the diversity of students my classes on Vampires in Literature attract, the importance of class-building cannot be overstressed. At a community college, you often have no control over students having actually met prerequisites; a few simple tools can help form the diverse social groups into a cohesive class: a grammar lecture and the instigation of kindness points. The first tool might seem silly at first glance. But a lecture on basics of sentence structure is one of the best time investments I make in my classes. It levels the knowledge playing field and creates a common language. It is also self-serving since I read the papers students produce. This lecture should cover the basics of sentence types: simple, compound, and complex sentence structures, and the flaws which emerge when these sentence formats are not done correctly: fragments, fused sentences, comma splices, broken complex sentences, and run-on sentences. The lecture can be quite basic; mine runs just under an hour. This short lecture enables the use of short-hand that means something to students; they will understand that fragment (frag) means that one of five possible sentence pieces is missing, and they will understand how to avoid making the same mistake in future papers. This basic discussion of grammar not only helps students produce less hair-raising papers, it begins the process of turning twenty or thirty disparate student types into a cohesive class unit through giving students a common language. It is recommended that the students be informed only of the self-serving purpose. They respect honesty.

The second tool that assists in forming a cohesive class is kindness points. Kindness points are extra-credit points offered to students which are earned only via student to student kindness. Kindness points create a very civilized Vampires in Literature class environment because they are only earned by students reaching across traditional social divides which exist naturally between people of differing belief structures with an aim of helping. Students receive one or two extra points for each instance of helpfulness to another student up to a pre-set total, and they are earned by both participants in the kind act: the giver and the receiver. Kindness points can be earned during class-time when one student explains a concept to a struggling student with a good attitude; an example in a recent class was one student explaining what a soul was to another student in the 100-level class. Not one student in the class even rolled his or her eyes. Kindness points can also be earned during peer reviews by reviewing an extra paper, or outside class when one student renders extra assistance to a classmate with research, preparation for a presentation, or a paper. It is important that students understand that kindness points are only issued for kindnesses which rise above normal classroom expectations, so examples and suggestions are a necessity. Noting one or two class instances and issuing on-the-spot kindness credits early in the term enforces the ideas of expected classroom interactions and subtly reinforces your own authority as both the instructor of the class, and as someone who appreciates, recognizes, and rewards kindness.

The 100-Level Class

It is impossible to generalize the skill level incoming students bring to this class. At my college it has varied from graduate students to students who have never read a complete book before, but an interest in the figure of the vampire connects them all. Again, given the more than normally disparate student types, class building is essential from day one. The following are standard day one exercises in my face-2-face class: Blackout Bingo, vampire characteristic brainstorm, and a writing diagnostic.

Blackout Bingo is a game designed to introduce students to each other. In this variant, students are required to get a signature on a traditional bingo card with squares that include: "own a black cape," "has dressed as a vampire," "is part of Team Edward," "does not believe vampires sparkle, ever," and other traditionally vampire interested behaviors. It is an effective method to begin the process of getting students acquainted with each other, reinforcing the shared interest in vampires that overrides their own social assignment as Goth, Christian, etc. It also allows an instructor to acquire some idea of the basic interest level of each student. Day one most students are strangers to each other, so merely introducing them to each other through Blackout Bingo works. It is a good idea to include yourself in the game, getting acquainted personally with each student and encouraging the idea that a teacher is both accessible and human.

Vampire characteristic brainstorming is an exercise that seamlessly follows Blackout Bingo. The question to be answered is "What do we know about the characteristics of vampires as they are represented in media?" The characteristics are differentiated into two categories: classic and modern, with a center area between them in which characteristics that fit both categories are placed; for instance, cannot cross running water is classic, sparkles is modern, shape-shift is in the center. When possible, I ask students to say which work sparked this particular thought for them. This class brainstorming session works several ways: first it is a subtle, informative method of slipping the idea of brainstorming a large topic to discover smaller topics to students who might never have been introduced to the idea of brainstorming, without embarrassing them on their lack of existing knowledge. Second, it makes it clear to students that they are expected to be active participants in their own education instead of mere vessels to be filled; they can also learn from each other as well as from the instructor. Third, it allows the instructor to assess how many participatory students are present in the class: who speaks, who doesn't. Finally, it provides the instructor an idea of the existing student knowledge base. Later in the term, it might be necessary to occasionally call upon the quieter class-members to participate in some way; I privately request the more outspoken class-members to wait occasionally before answering to allow the quieter members to interact.

The final activity for day one is the collection of a writing diagnostic which will allow an overview of what writing levels are present. Ask for a short essay—no more than two pages—in response to one of two questions, one of which is an essay response to a very short vampire themed reading, and one of which is a personal response to a question such as "Are vampires real?" or "What is your favorite vampire, vampire book, or vampire movie?" Responses to vampires being real make an interesting read with the most offered proof being that man has not discovered everything, and why would vampires want to reveal themselves to us if they were real? The favorite vampires are usually Stoker's Dracula, Rice's Lestat, or *The Vampire Diaries'* Damien and the reasons are always fascinating. It is not recommended that a fictional story option be used. Writing a fictional story requires different skills than writing an essay. Not only will the student responses demonstrate what each individual student's strengths and weaknesses are, it suggests which students are more academically comfortable. The students who are more academically comfortable will usually choose to write a short academic response. Basic knowledge is also readily shown in the responses: who knows how to form paragraphs, who knows how to use sentence variety and correct grammar? Future remediation of missing knowledge will stem from this activity. The diagnostic works the same way for the 200-level class, and although returning students might want a fiction option, blending the students works best without having two layered options: one for new students and one for returning students. Again, being upfront and explaining to students why this writing assignment runs the way it does usually clears up all resentment and makes it clear that you have one class and you expect everyone to belong to that one class.

As the class continues, some training in reading analytically can occur through asking leading questions that engender the desired outcome. During this training period, it is often necessary to combat the negative habit some of your students will possess of not reading the assigned material. This is one reason to assign no more than fifty to one hundred pages of text at the 100-level. Gradually increasing the difficulty of the reading is essential in encouraging the students to practice reading analytically, and to get students in the habit of actually doing the assigned readings. While it adds to the instructor's workload, asking for a weekly 200 — 300 word paper responding to one or more specific aspects of the assigned text encourages students to actually read the assigned text and gives them an angle to examine it from. For instance, the directed question in my 100-level class asks students to postulate what moral is being taught children by the child's comic, *The Little Vampire*, by Angela Sommer-Bodenburg et al. By asking for interaction tackling one specific guided facet of the text, students are introduced to the idea of reading critically, and gradually develop an ability to pull one specific strand out of a text for discussion. But still, it is highly recommended that you have a plan in place to deal with the inevitable day when none, or only one or two, of the students have read the assigned text meant for discussion that particular day. Having a point bearing pop quiz on hand is a reminder that this is a college class that has the expectation that students will do their readings. Note that the pop quiz covering the text can be structured in such as way as to reward the one or two students who have done the reading. It is easy to build the pop quizzes into the class point system, and any quiz points which are not used by quizzes are gifted to the students as free points towards their graded total at the end of the class. This encourages students to read the assigned readings so that they can have the free points. Please remember that although both are very tempting options, letting everyone go early for the day, or putting on a movie to watch, rewards the negative behavioral pattern. It only takes one "class read" of a story such as John Polidori's "The Vampyre," in which every student is required to read segments aloud to ensure that positive reading habits replace the negative ones.

Offering a direction for class discussions surrounding each text is recommended during the first few weeks of the 100-level class, at least until students get a sense of what is expected of them during discussions. Many of the students have learned through high-school experiences that speaking in class is a risk with unknown consequences. Thus, a class structure which encourages each person to participate in some way in their own education with only positive results is necessary, and kindness points encourage that all attempts are met with positive results. My own students are perhaps overly familiar with my "what is the take-away?" question. Every student is strongly encouraged to state publicly what they believe was the main point the audience for the text was supposed to learn from it. All answers are encouraged, and often their answers lead to vigorous discussion, such as the take-away for *Cirque Du Freak* by Darren Shan, in which the morality of lying was hotly debated. Students also are sharing the experience of being on the hot-seat and shared experiences grow community.

English 126:16 "Vampires in Literature"

My own choice has been to run the 100-level class as an age specific and genre-based survey class. It is designed to examine the ways in which the genre of the book, poem, or movie, and the age of the intended audience alter the representation of the central vampire figure, and the ways in which the portrayals interact. A literary genre class provides a multitude of options for texts which allow the students to discuss the ways character, settings, plots, and language choices create the "horror" of the vampire work.

Age specific is used here to describe a focus on the age of the intended audience: from picture books through adult novels/media. Picture books, such as the *Little Dracula* series (Martin Waddell) or *A Vampire Is Coming to Dinner: 10 Rules to Follow* (Pamela Jane), offer little variance within their own genre, but a selection of picture books featuring vampires is easy, and fairly inexpensive, to accumulate and share with students early in the term, before they might be expected to have purchased the other required texts. Discussion of the picture books can occur in discussion groups (with at least one of the more talkative students per group); they then come together to share and visually graph their discoveries. Comics, manga/anime, middle school easy-readers, 'tween novels for both males and females, as well as novels authored by/for adult women or novels authored by/for men are possible features for this particular approach (suggested texts in all these categories will follow). There are a few modern anthologies that allow the wide range of genres to be affordable for students. Inclusion of Matthew 26.17–29 allows a discussion of the Christian usage of blood which only adds to the student understanding of vampires. One movie is added to liven the reading, along with various snippets of media which match the assorted book choices. Certainly a selection of vampire themed YouTube clips, songs, role-playing games, games, and artwork can also find a place in the class, usually as student projects in which they are asked to discuss their choice in carefully selected ways. Actual textual choices will depend in large part on what themes you wish the discussions to include, and what the specific Objectives and Student Learning Outcomes are for your class. A specific list of texts used in the 100-level class and what discussions grow from them will be covered later in this essay.

Interaction of Course Objectives and Suggested Texts

To teach a class on Vampires in Literature the preparation of a class outline is necessary and it will need to include a list of suggested texts. The course objectives will stem from your selected texts. To merge your suggested texts and your objectives, it is necessary to first choose an approach and a level. At the 100-level, if a genre approach is chosen, what specific genres will be covered? Are anthologies going to be used or full texts? How does each text add to the page count assigned each week? At the 200-level, the texts assigned and the course objectives and student learning outcomes can be more demanding and nuanced. With book choices, expense can play a role. Anthologies such as *Blood Thirst* (Leonard Wolf, ed.) or *Vampires: Dracula and the Undead Legions* (Ulanski & Anderson, eds.) which cover a variety of specific genres are less expensive and can cover a wide range of genres within the one cost. Novels give a more fully nuanced plot and character development, often simply through their length. If a themed approach is chosen, what is your theme? What texts will be used? It is possible to offer a critical theory approach to one novel (an inexpensive option on the student pocketbook, and it combines composition theory with literature nicely)? Remember that while your suggested texts can be swapped out for others at the actual class level, the course objectives will be permanent. They need to be global enough to embrace changing texts.

What are course objectives? Objectives are easiest to define if thought of in teacher-centered language: Objectives are ideas the instructor gives to, and discusses with, the class. Thus they are expressed in terms of: introduce, present, explore, and discuss. For instance, any vampire media will lead to questions such as: Do vampires represent outsiders, people who are different from the dominant culture? Are vampires still within the bounds of human? If vampires are not human, should they be held to human morality regarding killing? Does the changing representation of the vampire ability to day-walk reflect changing mores on souls? This is a 100-level class, so the expression of the objectives should reflect the level. The question "Does the vampire character represent the outsider?" is reformed, and expressed in the list as:[in this class students will:] discuss the vampire character as a representative of outsider.

The formal objectives for my own 100-level class include:

- Present the ideas of life, death, and the undead life in relation to literature about vampires.
- Present the vampire myth and how it shifts with genre.
- Explore ways in which the myth shifts depending upon religious ideas and cultural norms prevalent in the times in which any particular vampire literature is written.
- Explore the uses of figurative language and the ways it is used to produce the tones inherent in each genre.
- Explore cultural ideas of morals as they are presented to various age groups in vampire novels.
- Explore the ideas of literary genres by seeing how the figure of the vampire fits the characteristic genre requirements.
- Explore ideas of pedophilia and vampires in literature.
- Explore ideas of Gothic and how it is represented and/or created within vampire literature.
- Explore the relationship between the Christian Eucharist and the blood that sustains a Vampire.
- Discuss the ways in which vampire literature fits within a horror genre.

You will note that the objectives are both narrow enough to provide rigor and great discussion while being wide enough to be accomplished via a wide variety of texts or other media. The actual class discussions move well beyond those objectives as the students grapple with characteristics and basics of horror literature, and a genre that encompasses gender representations, ideas of pedophilia, ideas of necrophilia, ideas of self-image, and worship of youth among endless other ideas. Before suggesting texts, a discussion of student learning outcomes, both for the course outline and the syllabus, is in order.

Student Learning Outcomes

Student learning outcomes (SLOs) are the reverse of course objectives; in teacher-centered teaching terms, they are what students can be expected to have done or produced at the end of the course. At the 100-level, a recollection that these SLOs are meant for community college freshmen, who are also learning how to read analytically and to respond to literature in college-level essays, is essential. At the 200-level, most students should have at least the basics of college composition, and SLOs should be more rigorous. SLOs are expressed in terms of students having accomplished the outcome wished for. The section begins with "Students should be able to," and the verbs used to express the actions are: demonstrate, discuss, evaluate, or write for each item of the itemized list. SLOs will also enumerate the form of the item which will be assessed and graded. For example, the objective above was "Discuss the vampire character as a representative of outsider." The SLO will be expressed as "[The student should be able to:] [bullet point] Discuss their understanding of the vampire as representative of an outsider through production of an essay analysis of a vampire themed media.

Formal student learning outcomes for a genre-based 100-level class might read thusly: Students should be able to:

- Demonstrate their understanding of the role of figurative language in creating tone within the vampire genre in short essays or discussions of specific examples through production of an essay analysis of a short story or poem.
- Discuss the ways vampires have become a literary metaphor (for instance the metaphor of the banker as a vampiric blood-sucker) and demonstrate their understanding through production of an essay, picture, short story, or visual presentation such as a short movie or cartoon.
- Evaluate the ways in which vampires are presented to different age-groups and the ways the presentation affects societal behavioral expectations. They should be able to express this both verbally with specific examples, and in written form. (For instance, what happens when Count Chocula intersects with *Thirty Days of Night?*)
- Write a paper analyzing the relationships between the presentation of the modern vampire and the social cultural construction of the vampire.
- Have begun to wrestle with ideas of life, death, and un-death in relation to vampires, and be able to lucidly discuss their ideas.
- Have at least some understanding of the role of religion and its place in authorial creation and presentation of vampires and their slayers.

TEXT SUGGESTIONS FOR THE 100-LEVEL

There is a plethora of vampire themed media to choose from, and each choice made leads toward different discussions. But community college reality is that students will want to purchase their books used, they will want to sell their books back to the bookstore, the bookstore will only buy back a text it has an expectation of the class reusing in the future, and your department also will want to limit the ongoing expense of purchasing copies of the text to have available in the library for student use. This means that while it might be tempting to swap out most of the texts to keep up with the newer works being published; at least half of your choices should be pretty permanent. Those used consistently in my Vampires in Literature classes are as follows:

Picture books: I suggested that these be purchased and owned by the instructor to control the range of vampire characteristics and plots, and to increase the number of differing texts. This does not have to a be a major expense since a collection can be built though borrowing from the library (order in advance and place holds on those needed for class), or from purchases made at garage sales, library book sales, thrift stores, Amazon, etc. Picture book vampires are those aimed at the youngest readers, and usually purchased by family. In discussion, remind the student that an adult has chosen this particular text for his or her child, and will be participating in the reading. Picture books enable discussion about what a society tells its children, what reality society wants children to believe in and what morals society wishes to impart. Questions, among others, include:

- How are the vampires constructed to make the audience not fear these fearsome creatures?
- Why is not fearing an outsider—clearly represented by the usual green color of the vampires in these texts—an important moral to teach children?
- Is it a good thing to not fear outsiders?

My own set of picture books include *Little Dracula at the Seashore* and *Little Dracula Goes to School,* by Waddell & Wright and *A Vampire Is Coming to Dinner! 10 Rules to Follow,* by Pamela Jane, among others.

Early reader comic: *The Little Vampire,* by Joann Sfar, is a short and easy read for students. It continues the discussion of what society tells its children while introducing ideas of culture and acceptable representations (the author is French). Its major themes include desire for schooling and friendship, cheating and punishment, environmentalism, bullying, and medical ethics which are represented alongside ideas of diversity and otherness—all in comic form and occurring on differing levels for differing readers. *The Little Vampire* also allows for discussion of the ways comics are *read* by varying age groups. It would be a good choice for a recurring text.

Child vampire (movie): *Interview with the Vampire,* director Neil Jordan, shows the section with Claudia in which she is turned into a vampire through her destruction for being a child vampire. This segment is used for discussion on the issues of maintaining always the appearances of a child while the mind, personality, and emotions mature with time.

'Tween male: *Cirque Du Freak,* by Darren Shan, offers a coming of age adventure geared for middle-school[ish] age males. It offers a very different view of vampires, and includes non-standard characteristics and myth. It is useful as a comparison to the fare offered 'tween girls.

'Tween female: *Never Bite a Boy on the First Date,* by Tamara Summers, presents young (in appearance) mainstreaming vampires who attend high school with mortals and live in family units. This particular novel mixes elements of mystery as the protagonist, a young female vampire must solve the mystery of what vampire has fallen off the no-human- blood wagon and begun murdering humans to consume their blood.

Young adult: *Twilight,* by Stephenie Meyer. This novel has a few advantages for college freshman. First, it is a very easy read, and most students have read it before which makes the fairly large page count doable even in short term classes. Second, it is rich in possible discussion angles and topics, including May–December romances, pedophilia, vegetarianism, interspecies romances and relationships, feminist issues, free will and suicide, etc. This novel is used as an alternative to the 'tween novel. There is a wide range of critical texts available which discuss this text.

Graphic novel: *Tales of the Vampire,* an anthology collection bookended by Joss Whedon. It features comics by Ben Edlund, Jane Espenson, and Brett Matthews among others. This is recommended as a permanent placement for the class reading list. The world views and presentations of the various vampire mythos are rich with topics to discuss, and more discussion of the form of comics and graphic novels can occur.

Manga: *Dance in the Vampire Bund*, by Nozomu Tamaki, offers the opportunity to discuss people's expectations of vampires, as well as offering opportunity to discuss the age factor in relationships the students as the lead character, Mina Tepes, who appears eight years old although she has ruled the vampire empire for four-hundred years, attempts to seduce the sixteen-year-old werewolf pledged to protect her. There are companion anime pieces available online and on Netflix, which allow students to discuss both how, and why, the text changes to accommodate the form it is presented within.

Adult: This choice depends upon your personal preference for theme. Currently classes at my college are using the anthology, *Dracula and the Undead Legion*, featuring stories by authors L. A. Banks, Elaine Bergstrom, P.N. Elrod, C. J. Henderson, Nancy Kilpatrick, Paul Kupperberg, Bill Messner-Loebs, Martin Powell, J. C. Vaughn, Dan Wickline, and Ken Wolak for its inclusion of romance, gothic elements, detective fiction, humor, vampire animals, really funny slayer stories, coming of age stories, framed by stories of Dracula. We have also used *Blood Thirst*, an older anthology (1997) out of Oxford University Press. Its editor, Leonard Wolf, has sectioned the stories into genres: The Classic Tale, Psychological Vampire, The Science Fiction Vampire, The Non-Human Vampire, The Comic Vampire, and The Heroic Vampire. A fun discussion of the gendered view of vampires can be provided by use of one of Mario Acevedo's novels, such as *X-Rated Blood Suckers*, written by a man for male readers. Text choice will control the themes discussed in class and the student outcomes and objectives for the class. Remember that once the students read a text, even if it features behaviors normally considered gross, aberrant, or almost pornographic, it will need to be discussed, so choose texts with themes you are willing to discuss.

The 200-Level Class

If your college permits students registering for classes out of sequence, the students in the 200-level Vampires in Literature class will include not only those who have taken the 100-level class and have some grounding in the media and an understanding of the class expectations, but your class will also include new students whom you have not yet trained. Blending this range takes more effort since a larger number of students are trained and at level. The instructor has two basic options: ignore the difference and run the class as though all students were fully prepared for a 200-level class, or acknowledge the difference in preparedness and work some gentle remediation into the discussions and assignments.

With proper preparation, blending the class into a coherent unit is possible. Preparation begins on day one with the exercises described in the 100-level section which clarify for students what the class expectations are regarding their commitment. Stressing kindness points helps to enforce a friendly blending of student types. If you choose to use them, clarify for students that each instance of kindness is worth a set number of points, and that points work both directions; the person doing the assisting receives points, and the person receiving assistance receives points. The dual directionality encourages students' willingness to admit that they need help. Kindness points help the instructor as well since the papers, presentations, or whatever the expected outcome, will be better since it will be more informed. Including a class grammar discussion, perhaps allowing the continuing students to teach sections, and earn kindness points, will again allow a familiar and shared class language.

CLASS DESCRIPTION

The second part of the Vampires in Literature series, the 200-level, can explore a full spectrum of more advanced ideas. My own 200-level includes a look at Victorian vampire literature, vampires of other cultures, and the intersection of science and vampires. Other options for the class can explore the social and cultural aspects surrounding the representation of the vampire figure within both the dominant culture and the subculture, looking at the representation when authored by different cultures and aimed toward differing audiences. It can examine the historical changes of the vampire mythos as it moves from folklore to modern media, with a heaping of both historical vampires such as Vlad Dracul and Elizabeth Báthory, and modern vampires such as Don Henrie and Sarah Lester, who appeared on the *The Tyra Banks Show* October 2008 (available on YouTube). A 200-level class can cross the bounds of Western culture and explore the representation of the vampire within other cultures, such as the Chinese hopping vampire and the Mexican *chupacabra*, among others. It could focus on the theological construction and underpinnings of the vampire character within story, folklore, and film when authored within our culture and others as the cultures producing the media become more secular. It can examine the science behind vampires including discussion of how the human body would have to change in order to become a vampire and discussion of the Vampyre clans of Sanguinarians, psychic vampires, and living vampires; a discussion of the intersection of Goth and Steampunk subculture with the Vampyre culture fits well here. A 200-level class about vampires in media can be run as a second, higher level survey class as well, and provide students an overview of the themes above. A plethora of media can be used to further discussions at the 200-level, such as film, music, advertisements, games; in fact, unless you have a multi-lingual classroom, vampires written for Spanish, Russian, or Chinese culture can only be readily accessed in media such as film.

CLASS OBJECTIVES

As with the 100-level, the 200-level class objectives and SLOs are dependent upon the texts and themes which are selected. For instance the objectives could include a look at vampires in other cultures in which students research, discuss, and present the other culture's vampires, and this choice would be reflected on the course outline and course syllabus as: Introduce students to vampire myths as they appear in other cultures.

In a blended 200-level class which includes anyone who wishes to sign up for the class, a survey class which continues where the first class left off is a safe bet. For a survey 200-level class, objectives might include:

- Introduce students to historical vampires: Elizabeth Báthory, Vlad Tepes, Slobodan Milošević.
- Explore ways in which the myth shifts depending upon religious ideas and cultural norms prevalent in the times in which any particular example of vampire literature is written.
- Discuss the possible existence of vampires through discussion of the physiological changes necessary for the transition to occur.
- Explore the relationship between the Christian Eucharist and the blood that sustains a vampire.

- Explore the differences between the vampire story written for the economically disadvantaged and published serially (Varney the Vampire), and those written for a more educated readership such as Polidori's, "The Vampyre," or Byron's, "The Giaour."
- Explore the vampire myths when authored by African Americans such as the novels of LA Banks or Octavia Butler.

STUDENT LEARNING OUTCOMES

Recall that SLOs are the flip side of course objectives, so while objectives are discussions you plan upon holding, SLOs are statements of what the student should have learned upon successful completion of the class from discussions and other class material. Remember too that an SLO should state the assessment tool you will use for grading. The SLO for the outcome: Introduce students to vampire myths as they appear in other cultures would be to "summarize the main vampire myths as they appear in other cultures either orally or in writing."

For the survey 200-level class, SLOs might include: Upon successful completion of this course, students should be able to:

- Summarize the content of a given vampire text and explain its major themes orally and in writing.
- Discuss the physiological changes which would need to take place for a human to transform to a vampire in class discussions.
- Discuss historical "real" vampires and their relationship to the creating cultures orally and in writing.
- Demonstrate in writing, online, and in class discussions an understanding of how the vampire myth in literature (story, film, and poetry) defines, redefines, and critiques the authoring culture in terms of religious and cultural expectations.
- Analyze, orally and in writing, a specific vampire in relation to its place in the vampire mythology.
- Evaluate differing presentations of the female vampire in prose and poetry dependent upon gender of the author orally and in writing.
- Evaluate the differences in vampires when they are written by authors of other cultures in class discussions.
- Explore the progression of characteristics and abilities of vampires as they have developed in prose and poetry in their relationship to social constructivist ideas in a short evaluative essay, creative short story, or presentation.
- Discuss the ways in which economics impact the presentation of the vampire in class discussions.

TEXT SUGGESTIONS FOR THE 200-LEVEL

Science and vampires: *The Science of Vampires,* by Kathleen Ramsland. This is the only text available which discusses the ways in which the human body would have to change to become a vampire. She also discusses some possible reasons for the morphing of the myth as it came forward in time, serial killers with vampire connections, and vampires in the age of DNA. Her "Everything You Ever Wanted to Know About Vampire Sex but Were Afraid to Ask" chapter is guaranteed to spark discussion.

Worldwide vampires: *Vampires: A Field Guide to Creatures That Stalk the Night,* by

Bob Curran and Ian Daniels. This text provides a nicely inexpensive, although brief, over-view of the different vampires of selected cultures. While not comprehensive enough for higher level courses, the language is accessible for undergrads.

Vintage: Easily accessed online or via anthology. "Der Vampir" Ossenfelder; "The Vampire" Kipling; "Lenore" Göttfried August Bürger; "The Vampyre" Polidori; "Augustus Darvell" Byron; *Carmilla* J. Sheridan LeFanu. A wider selection of prose or poetry can be easily added.

Varney the Vampire: or; The Feast of Blood by James Rymer. It is a rarely read classic serial novel which leads to discussions on differing mythos of vampire characteristics such as day-walking, revivification, and what happens when a vampire tries to mainstream in a small English village.

African American: *Fledgling*, by Octavia Butler, will spark discussions of aging and pedophilia. This excellently written novel is, occasionally, sexually explicit. The anthology *Dark Thirst* which includes stories by Omar Tyree, Donna Hill, Monica Jackson and Kevin S. Brockenbrough can be used, but it features some heavily sexualized stories, so remember if it is assigned, there will be discussion of some fairly hard-core sex scenes. Either will raise the question "Why are African American vampire characters so sexualized?"

Hispanic American: *X-Rated Blood Suckers* by Mario Acevedo does double-duty since it also is written by a man for men (rare these days). It will surprise the students in having very few actual sex scenes.

Films can also be used to introduce varying cultures' ideas of vampires since so few foreign language texts are translated into English. The following list is not meant to be comprehensive, but the films have proven interesting.

Mexico: *El Santo y Blue Demon contra Dracula y El Hombre Lobra* (1973) can be found in translation or subtitles.

Cuba: *Vampire en La Havana* (1985) has the advantage of being funny and mafia related.

China: *Mr. Vampire* (1985 or the 1992 version). The Chinese hopping vampires are mixed in with ghosts and Kung Fu in this really funny film.

Websites are useful too:

"Our Vampires Are Different" TV Tropes.org, http://tvtropes.org/pmwiki/pmwiki. php/Main/OurVampiresAreDifferent. This website focuses on television, movie, role playing, and game vampires.

www.shroudeater.com — European vampire research, http://www.shroudeater.com/ main.html. This site provides an overwhelming amount of research on European vampires from a variety of sources.

"Montague Summers' *Guide to Vampires*," abridged by Nigel Suckling, http://www. unicorngarden.com/vampires.htm#vampires. This is the classic text by Summers which is made more student friendly by Suckling for who has provided translations Summer's non-translated sections.

The mythos of the vampire pervades the culture around students, and students who are not normally interested in the more canonical classes offered by English Departments are interested in learning more about the nature of the vampires appearing in the media surrounding them. They are interested in all the various media containing vampires, and they crave discussions about the ideas embedded within the media. Students want discussions about life and death, and the vampire's un-death. They are excited at spending hours learning and discussing the intersection of vampires and the cultures that spawn them. Through understanding the vampire they gain a greater knowledge about themselves; they are transformed into more mature students. Teaching them how to read more analytically, how to express themselves in class discussions, how to write more academically, how to research vampires effectively in an internet age, how to present their findings to the other students appropriately, and perhaps how to write a vampire story or poem are all side benefits the class offers the students. After four years and eight classes covering two levels of Vampires in Literature, my love affair with the vampire is ongoing, a love shared by my diverse students. The question is not so much why vampires, a popular culture icon, would not belong in serious academia given their embedding in all cultures, but why they would not. Any other single figure that allows such breadth of discussion from life and death and salvation to the mores inherent in a culture simply does not exist. While the 100 and 200-level classes might often need to include some training for less-academically trained students and might not embrace the rigor a graduate survey class offers, popular culture embraces all strata of society and students. Simply put, vampires belong at the community college.

Note

1. Please see Michał Wolski's essay in this volume, for a discussion of this RPG.

Bibliography

Acevedo, Mario. *X-Rated Blood Suckers*. New York: Rayo, 2007. Print.

Brautigam, Rob. Shroudeater.com. Ed. Rob Brautigam. N.p., 2008. Web. 15 Aug. 2012. http://www.shroud eater.com/main.html.

Butler, Octavia E. *Fledgling*. New York: Grand Central, 2005. Print.

Curran, Dr. Bob. *Vampires: A Field Guide to the Creatures that Stalk the Night*. Franklin Lakes, NJ: New Page, 2005. Print.

Delgado, Miguel M., dir. *Santo y Blue Demon vs Drácula y el Hombre Lobra*. 1976. Cinematográfica Calderón S.A. DVD.

Jordan, Neil, dir. *Interview with the Vampire*. Perf. Tom Cruise, Brad Pitt, and Antonio Banderas. 1994. Geffen Pictures. Web. 15 Aug. 2012.

Lau, Ricky, dir. *Mr. Vampire*. Writ. Ricky Lau and Barry Wong. 1985. Golden Harvest Company. DVD.

Meyer, Stephenie. *Twilight*. New York: Little, Brown, 2005. Print.

Our Vampires Are Different: TV Tropes. TV Tropes.org, n.d. Web. 15 Aug. 2012. http://tvtropes.org/pmwiki/ pmwiki.php/Main/OurVampiresAreDifferent.

Padrón, Juan, dir. *¡Vampiros en La Habana!* Writ. Ernesto Padrón and Juan Padrón. 1985. Instituto Cubano del Arte e Industrias. DVD.

Ramsland, Katherine. *The Science of Vampires*. New York: Berkley, 2002. Print.

Rymer, James. *Varney the Vampire: or; The Feast of Blood*. (Any version of print or online.)

Sfar, Joann. *The Little Vampire*. New York: The First Second, 2008. Print.

Shan, Darren. *Cirque Du Freak: A Living Nightmare*. New York: Little, Brown, 2002. Print.

Stoker, Bram. *Dracula*. Print or Web. I am listing this here with a caveat; it is a heavy read for most 100-level or 200-level students.

Suckling, Nigel. "Montague Summer's Guide to Vampires." Abridged Text. UnicornGarden.com, n.d. Web. 15 Aug. 2012. http://www.unicorngarden.com/vampires.htm#vampires.

Summers, Tamara. *Never Bite a Boy on the First Date*. New York: Harper Teen, 2009. Print.

Tamaki, Nozomu. *Dance in the Vampire Bund*. Los Angeles: Seven Seas, 2006. Print.

Ulanski, Dave, and Garrett Anderson, eds. *Vampires Dracula and the Undead Legions*. Sarasota: Moonstone, 2009. Print.

Whedon, Joss, Ben Edlund, Jane Espensen, Brett Matthews, and Sam Loeb. *Tales of the Vampires*. Milwaukie, OR: Darkhorse Books, 2004. Print.

In the Cultural Shadows: Insights from a Media and Culture Studies Course
Rita Turner

Across multiple centuries and cultures, narratives about vampires have offered compelling and unsettling material for readers, listeners, and viewers of folk stories, poems, novels, films, and countless other forms of media. Carmilla, Dracula, Lestat, Miriam, Angel, Edward, Eli, and perhaps even Lilith herself — all offer the audience characters full of mystery, power, sin, passion, conflict, and dangerous appeal. But, as the growing body of scholarship on vampire narratives makes clear, these stories don't speak to us simply because they offer glimpses of glamour, sex, death, and the promise of eternal youth; they hold our attention because of the nuanced cultural information they convey, constitute, and question.

For this reason vampires are a rich subject for analysis in classrooms; the narrative events, structures, characters, and imagery of these stories provide not only artistic interest, but they can reveal much about a culture's accepted and contested values and behaviors. Guiding students through an analysis of vampire narratives can help them develop greater insight into cultural structures and ideologies, and also equip them with greater skills for analyzing other artifacts of popular culture. Students who examine vampire texts have the opportunity to develop wide-ranging insights about the symbolic and conceptual systems in which they are embedded, including new understandings of the ongoing social construction and negotiation of gender, class, sexuality, ethnicity, and ideals of family, community, and love.

In this essay I explore the value of teaching a course that examines vampire narratives from the perspective of media studies and cultural studies. I suggest that these bodies of scholarship can contribute an invaluable array of theoretical frameworks that help position students to directly examine the ways that vampire narratives not only manifest particular cultural attitudes, but also authorize, naturalize, and at times contest beliefs, norms, behaviors, and social frameworks. Below I describe a vampire-themed course I designed that utilizes this scholarly tradition.

About the Course

I created my course, titled "From *Dracula* to *Twilight*: Vampire Narratives in Media and Culture," as an upper-level special topics offering within the Media and Communication

Studies Program at the University of Maryland, Baltimore County. UMBC is a mid-sized local university with a relatively diverse, though still majority white and middle-class, student population. Academic skill level varies among my students, although those entering this class are fairly well-prepared. As an advanced course, my class is generally taken by students who have already fulfilled other media and cultural studies course requirements; most are juniors and seniors who have some familiarity with conducting media and literary analysis from other courses. The material I include in my course ranges in its degree of difficulty; for students with less background in media and cultural studies some of the readings would be quite challenging, but much of the course content is very accessible for students of differing skill levels and backgrounds.

I teach the course using a seminar-style format informed by critical pedagogy and sociocultural theories of learning (i.e., Freire; Gallimore and Tharp; Vygotsky; Wenger). I focus heavily on close discussion of readings and viewings and I require students to do regular analytical writing, share analysis of texts in class, participate in a weekly online discussion board, and give individual presentations on relevant films and topics not covered in the course materials. The course features weekly readings and screenings of vampire narratives from mythology, literature, history, film, and television, arranged in chronological order from earliest to most recent. Interspersed with these materials are readings by theorists and scholars in the traditions of media studies and cultural studies, intended to provide perspective and conceptual tools that students can apply to their analyses of the vampire texts.

As I describe these readings and viewings below, I will at times include quotes and close paraphrases of student writing from the class, to illustrate common reactions and analyses my students have demonstrated. I've marked all comments excerpted from my students, whether direct quotes or close paraphrases, by placing them in quotation marks.

Texts Explored in the Course

I present students with a range of vampire-themed texts from a broad period of human history, touching on pieces from early mythology to contemporary literature and film. By exploring vampire narratives from such diverse eras students are able to identify features these stories share in common and features that have shifted over time, allowing for the development of interesting insights into aspects of cultural reasoning that have remained quite consistent as well as aspects that have been reformulated or challenged in different time periods.

We discuss each text in depth, thereby building a shared analysis of the themes, structures, stances, and attitudes manifested in each narrative. This analysis is expanded through response papers that students write and post to a discussion board within our online learning platform. I require students to read and reply to their classmates' posts, extending the discussion of the texts beyond available class time. However, I prioritize in-class discussion time for those texts that I find are either challenging for students to analyze or provide particularly rich material for discussion. I highlight some of those key points of discussion in my overview of the texts below.

We start our exploration of vampire narratives by reading selections from and about ancient mythology. We read selections from *Lilith's Cave: Jewish Tales of the Supernatural*

(Schwartz), exploring the figure of Lilith from post-biblical, rabbinic, and folk stories. Lilith is described in these stories as Adam's original companion, who was not satisfied to live subservient to Adam and eventually left or was expelled from Eden, living outside of the human world as a proto-demon, taking the souls of babies, seducing men, and populating the world with demons. Schwartz's text also offers stories of other characters with demonic features from the Jewish tradition, including a demonic princess who kills the man who betrayed her by drawing his breath from him in a kiss, and a vain young woman who falls under demonic influence by too often gazing into a mirror that serves as a gateway to Lilith's realm. Students are struck by these stories, and quickly begin to explore the gender relations within them. One student notes, "I see some sexist themes in these early vampire stories. The evil deeds of Lilith and the other women have specifically feminine aspects, like seduction. The men are often portrayed as 'innocent,' seduced by demonic women. This may show us something about the creators of these stories." Another states, "The reader assumes that Lilith turned into a vampire because she refused to accept the traditional female roles in society. Society seems to be saying to women that they'll become vampires if they aren't subservient to men."

Students also read summaries of folk stories from a number of ancient cultures that feature vampire-like creatures. These include information about demonic female figures from Mesopotamian lore such as Lilitu, Lilith, and Lamashtu; figures from ancient Greece including the Empusa, striges, and Lamia; creatures known as vetalas in Indian lore; Asian figures such as the mandurugo of the Philippines or the Penanggalan of Malaysia; and the adze and ramanga in Africa (see Bunson; Burton; Graves; Hurwitz; Marigny; Thompson). We touch only on brief descriptions of these mythologies; my goal is not to achieve complete historical depth, but to expose students to the existence of such stories in ancient cultures, and to give them a glimpse into some of the sorts of content these stories contained. Students find the features of these figures from ancient folklore fascinating, noting the many similarities among mythological traditions, as well as the many traits held in common with modern vampires.

As one example of common traits, many of the mythological figures described in these articles are said to have become demons or vampires by breaking some cultural taboo, and are portrayed as threatening to draw other members of the community into breaking taboos as well. This can be seen in descriptions of Mesopotamian, Greek, Slavic, Romanian, and Romany traditions, among others. Early vampire-like figures are also often described as rising from the grave in shadow-like or non-corporeal form, or as a walking corpse, then slowly drawing life energy from others to restore their bodies. Lore from a number of regions also features a dangerous female figure who is semi-demonic, and who can sometimes change form, becoming a bird or other animal. These elements are described in Mesopotamian, Greek, Slavic, and Asian tales. Echoing — and often historically linked to — the story of Lilith, these female figures often draw out the life force of men, kill babies, or target pregnant women (Bunson; Burton; Graves; Hurwitz; Marigny; Thompson).

In their discussion of these mythological figures, students draw strong links to the tales from *Lilith's Cave*. They comment that within much of this lore, "one of the themes is the evil found in female characters." They note that the figures described in these myths and seen in the ancient Jewish tales are depicted as "lustful" and "bloodthirsty." One student states that "the causes of vampirism seem to vary by gender." Another student notes, "These stories would be used to keep people in line and provide a threat for bad behavior." And another posits, "These tales are tools to control women and force them to act in stereotypically female ways." Already noting the symbolic and communicative power of the texts, students begin to notice patterns, common values, and normative attitudes conveyed and reproduced within these narratives.

In order to explore additional early stories, students also read short selections from *The Testament of Solomon*, a text described by Schwartz as supplying the earliest version of the Lilith legend and perhaps the earliest compendium of demons, and which also contains an early vampire figure (Schwartz 7, 14–15). Students also read selections from *King Vikram and the Vampire* (or, as it is sometimes titled, *Vikram and the Vampire*), Sir Richard Burton's translation of a series of Hindu legends, the *Baital-Pachisi*. The legends contained in this collection aren't themselves about vampires; rather, a Baital, a vampire-like character, actually serves as the narrator for the bulk of the text, telling stories to the hero, King Vikram, and offering him both guidance and challenges as he seeks to conquer an evil magician.

Students are intrigued by the vampire figure in this tale. They make comments like, "The male vampire from King Vikram is clever and powerful, and he saves the King's life. He also never attacks anyone and only seeks revenge for his own murder. This is an odd and sort of positive image of a vampire compared to the female vampire characters." Other students add that the Baital in the story is portrayed as a "good guy" or they comment that he has "humanistic qualities," making him a more sympathetic character than many other early vampire figures.

The course next moves into historical overviews of beliefs about vampires as they develop in later centuries. This includes selections from *Legends of Blood: The Vampire in History and Myth* (Bartlett and Idriceanu), including chapters which explore the vampire epidemics of the seventeenth century and the historical symbolism of blood in religion, mythology, and popular culture. In addition to these pieces, students conduct reading online to learn about the historical figures of Vlad Dracula and Elizabeth Báthory, both of which have amassed a reputation for "blood-thirsty" practices derived from a mixture of verified and rumored behaviors.

As they read this historical background, students are struck by the legendary and lasting image that has been created surrounding these real figures and events. Many are amazed at the story of Elizabeth Báthory, a member of the Hungarian nobility who was accused of luring young women to her palace with the promise of work or education and then torturing them, draining their blood, and bathing in it. My students quickly note the many similarities to literary and mythological vampire figures found in accounts of Báthory's actions. They remark, for example, "her victims were young women and children, like in a lot of the stories we've seen." One student points out, "She deceived families into sending their daughters to her — she had a draw and there was a lack of suspicion about her because of her nobility." They also comment on the fact that Báthory is purported to have believed in a connection between youth and blood, bathing in it to preserve her beauty. They point out that this connection is not so different from the link drawn between blood and immortality in many vampire stories. Students carry their observations from these historical accounts forward as we progress through our readings, finding literary works that share a number of commonalities with the tales of Vlad Dracula and Báthory.

Moving to vampire narratives from more recent centuries, students next read selections from classic 19th- and 20th-century literature, including Lord Byron's *Fragment of a Novel*, John Polidori's "The Vampyre," J. Sheridan LeFanu's *Carmilla*, and selections from works by Bram Stoker. They also read excerpts of Montague Summers' 1928 text *The Vampire, His Kith and Kin*, a volume intended by Summers as a scholarly and factual account of the nature, origins, and behavior of vampires. Many of these classic texts are available online through Sacred Texts (a project collecting sacred and religious works in open-access electronic format) and through other various electronic repositories of literature, as well as through print compilations of vampire literature (e.g., Ryan).

One of the first things students notice in these pieces of classic literature are the features of vampire characters that have become foundational to modern narratives. Students make comments like, "Lord Ruthven is an example of many important elements of the archetypal male vampire." They note traits of the vampire characters in these texts such as their connection to "high society" and "European nobility," and they describe them as "mysterious," "inviting," and "smooth talking." They also note that these characters are portrayed as dangerous outsiders, who often tempt innocent young women only to lead them to their doom. One student comments on this pattern as it relates to Carmilla, saying, "Carmilla has close sexual relationships with young women, and because of this she falls outside of what society would consider normal. Her vampirism may be a warning against these sorts of relationships. Nontraditional sexual relationships are shown as dangerous, and characters who give in to temptation face death and tragedy." As their knowledge of vampire texts deepens and broadens, students develop increasing perspective into the features and methods of meaning-making these texts engage in, a perspective they demonstrate well in their analyses.

From here students go on to explore 20th- and 21st-century vampire texts, including films and television series such as *Nosferatu*, *Dracula*, selections from the original *Dark Shadows*, *The Lost Boys*, *Bram Stoker's Dracula*, *Interview with the Vampire*, *Blade*, *Underworld*, *Let the Right One In*, *Twilight*, selections from *Buffy the Vampire Slayer*, and selections from *True Blood*. To make sure all students get a chance to see key films and television episodes, whenever possible we watch them in class in their entirety, although in a few cases we skip some scenes for the sake of time. In addition to the films watched in class, I also have students choose and watch an additional film outside of class and write an analysis comparing it to a text from the course (which they then present in class). I offer a list of options but am open to diverse proposals from students as well — selections have included *The Hunger*, *Fright Night*, and *Blacula*. This assignment expands the number of films students get a chance to view beyond just those we screen during class, and when students hear one another's analyses they get a chance to learn the details of even more films.

After screening films and television episodes we discuss each one, and students also conduct analysis through their response papers posted to our online discussion board. I make sure to spend plenty of time in class on films like *Nosferatu*, *Dracula*, *Bram Stoker's Dracula*, and *Interview with the Vampire* in order to make sure students identify certain points I consider essential to analyze, including the gender roles in each film, the distribution of agency and power, and the degree of "othering" applied to the villain. We also spend a good deal of time in class discussing episodes of *Buffy the Vampire Slayer* and the first *Twilight* film, exploring their varying constructions of teen female identity, love, and power, among other topics.

Students find much to explore in all of these films, and do an excellent job of relating them to the earlier texts. They note shifts that occur in the portrayal of vampire characters over time, making comments like, "the characters here are different from earlier narratives; this may demonstrate changes in society's attitudes over time."

One change students promptly identify is an increase in character development and depth among vampire figures, and they are eager to explore the inner life of these new vampires. My students note elements of "inner struggle," "sadness," and "nostalgia" in vampire characters who mourn for the life they've lost. They also point out recurring elements of "lost love." They also suggest that the violence committed by vampires in these later texts is sometimes depicted as a misguided "act of love," rather than simply as a heartless attack. Students reflect that some vampire characters in these texts are to be pitied, not feared and hated. They describe characters like Angel from *Buffy the Vampire Slayer* (and the spin-off *Angel*) as "the ultimate tragic hero."

One of the texts in which students first mark these changes is the original television version of *Dark Shadows*. Of the vampire character Barnabas Collins, one student notes, "His interest in recreating his former life shows us he feels a sense of loss. We learn that he never chose to become a vampire. This humanizing opens the door for recent stories where the vampire is the hero." Another student suggests, "This time the audience knows the motives and internal conflict of the vampire character."

Students comment of many modern vampire narratives that even characters who are shown to kill humans for centuries can still gain sympathy from the audience. They note that these characters often seem to wrestle with their "lingering human morality" and to actively wonder over difficult questions of life and death. They also note the weight of immortality showing in many characters, and a common theme of longing for human life. Speaking of Claudia from *Interview with the Vampire*, one student remarks, "being trapped as a child for so long would have a huge psychological impact. We see her character change from being impulsive to being a tiny poetic woman, aware of her situation and capable of strong hatred and strong love." Speaking of the character of Count Dracula, another student posits, "he obsesses over his long lost love, but it's not just her he wants—he also seeks to recapture the time in his life when he felt most happy: when he was human."

Reading and viewing this progression of vampire narratives through history offers students valuable perspective. With this context in mind, students are able to note changes in the construction and positioning of "hero," "villain," and audience, and thereby identify important shifts in the features of vampire characters, and the societies that create them, over time.

Conceptual Vocabulary for Analyzing Vampire Narratives

Interspersed with these readings and viewings we also explore scholarly essays to enhance students' conceptual vocabulary and to more fully equip them to engage with the vampire texts. We read a range of authors including Will Wright, Roland Barthes, Louis Althusser, bell hooks, Janice Radway, and others. I include this particular selection of theorists in order to give students a variety of different analytical strategies and concepts to apply to their exploration of the texts, drawing from wide-ranging scholarly traditions including structuralism, semiotics, cultural studies, literary theory, feminist theory, and psychoanalysis. Exposure to these diverse approaches and theories gives students a broader set of tools for considering the texts from many angles. As my course is an advanced Media Studies class, I expect students to enter the class equipped to read and apply rather dense theory, so some of these readings are more suitable for advanced students, but others are accessible to students at diverse skill levels. I'll outline some of these essays here and discuss the tools that each provides students for better engaging in critical analysis.

One piece that provides an extremely useful set of theoretical frameworks for students to utilize is *The Structure of Myth and the Structure of the Western Film* by Will Wright.

Wright draws on insights from Kenneth Burke and Claude Lévi-Strauss, merging them to formulate a theory about the social function of myth and then applying this theory to an analysis of Western films. Although this piece doesn't deal directly with vampire narratives, it outlines and illustrates valuable tools that are broadly relevant to vampire texts and other genres.

Wright contends that myth "orders our experiences" and that it uses a particular structure to communicate social concepts and attitudes to members of society. He states that the narrative structure of events, as well as the attributes of characters and what they do, "presents a model of appropriate social action" (273). Referring to Kenneth Burke's work to support and elaborate on this idea, Wright states:

> Interaction — such as conflict or sexual attraction — is never simply interaction between individuals but always involves the social principles that the characters represent. Thus, a fight in a narrative would not simply be a conflict of men but a conflict of principles— good versus evil, rich versus poor, black versus white [271].

This conceptual approach is very useful for students. The tools Wright lays out can guide students' attention toward determining the social principles, roles, and attitudes that vampire figures and other characters in vampire narratives represent. Once students have analyzed these roles, they can work to identify what attitudes the audience is positioned to hold toward each character, which then illuminates the attitudes the narrative is establishing toward the larger "social principle" as well. In my class students readily and astutely identify a number of social principles represented within each text, often forming insightful conclusions about how the text is directing audience members to feel about these principles. Some of the social principles, values, and behaviors that students in my course have identified as represented by vampire characters include a rejection of dominant religion or of mainstream gender roles; sexual promiscuity or liberality; a "foreign" or "unknown" element outside of the accepted community; participation in nontraditional family structures; homosexuality; a desire for immortality; undying love; temptation; greed; and a range of departures from social norms. As my students put it, "Frequently vampire myths influence society to abide by hegemonic norms and they dictate what a proper relationship should and shouldn't be like." And, "The characters are acting out a social order. The struggle between a vampire and a victim is a struggle between the nontraditional and the traditional."

Will Wright also makes use of Lévi-Strauss' structural analysis of myth in developing his discussion. He points out Lévi-Strauss' argument that, in myth, an image comes to represent a concept because of the differences between it and the "image or character it is opposed to" (271). This, too, helps students think about their own analysis, as they explore the idea that we can often identify the concept a vampire character represents by noting what character is placed as structurally opposite to the vampire within the narrative, and identifying what this character represents. Structural oppositions in vampire narratives differ vastly among texts and over time periods, but each is illuminating. Lilith and Eve, Carmilla and Laura, Dracula and Jonathan, Lestat and Louis, Edward and Jacob — these and other character binaries can be extremely revealing when examined in this light. Students comment, "Viewing the characters as opposing pairs, and as an interplay not just between people but between values and ideas, opens up new interpretations."

Supplying a related conceptual approach is Roland Barthes. Barthes formulates the notion that myth is a "type of speech," a particular manner of conveying a message. He argues that in myth, writing and pictures are both signs that are used to signify another layer of meaning beyond what they convey at face value. Barthes contends that myth conveys messages to us through forms that seem like "facts," thereby naturalizing a concept, taking a socially constructed idea and making it seem natural and eternal. This notion is also quite useful, as it helps students identify ways that vampire narratives may operate to naturalize certain attitudes. Students often note that when socially taboo traits are paired with the obvious dangerousness and monstrosity of a vampire character, those taboo traits become wrapped up with the overall picture of evil and are naturalized as "obviously" wrong, bad, or harmful. As such, when "dangerous" vampire characters display traits of homosexuality, sexual appetite, or non-normative gender interactions, for example, these traits are presented as "dangerous" as well. The "truth" that these qualities and behaviors are unacceptable and destructive becomes a given within the text, hiding the socially constructed nature of such assumptions and beliefs from view.

We next connect Barthes' formulation to concepts offered by Louis Althusser. Althusser asserts that dominant social forces exert power through ideology, which they disseminate through various cultural products as well as repressive institutions. The ideologies that are communicated through these products and institutions act to make certain things seem obvious, right, and true. Ideology establishes or constitutes us each as individual subjects. Althusser says that we "find our place" as subjects through and in ideology (or ideology "places" us, positions us in relation to society). These notions further bolster students' analysis of the role of vampire narratives in shaping, communicating, legitimizing, or shifting ideology.

Providing another analytical tool is Slavoj Žižek, who argues that fantasy "stages" desire. Žižek states, "through fantasy, we learn how to desire" (335). He tells us that narratives operate to construct, position, and reproduce desire, suggesting that "fantasy space" is an empty space into which we can project and articulate our desires. As such, it can reveal the "psychic reality" of our desire (343). According to Žižek, the boundary between our real desires and our everyday reality is necessary for sanity. Students use this theory to point out that vampire narratives allow society to explore desires that would otherwise be deemed improper, unacceptable, or scandalous, such as homosexuality, and to some extent sexuality in general.

In order to offer a somewhat related perspective on the notion that narratives can reflect subconscious desires, I also have students read a short piece by Sigmund Freud, *The Dream-Work*, conveying his argument that in dreams, features like allusions, images, and structural elements can all represent thoughts in our subconscious. According to Freud, objects and acts in dreams can stand in for similar or related things, for abstract words or concepts, or for their opposites. For our purposes in class, we extend this notion, translating dreams to stories or narratives and broadening the subconscious to include society's collective subconscious as well as the individual subconscious mind. Students apply this idea by suggesting that, "In narratives, the images can be symbols of subconscious thought, and can reveal the human desire for the other."

For further theoretical insight we explore essays from the collection *Blood Read: The Vampire as Metaphor in Contemporary Culture*. This volume offers a number of excellent analyses, ranging in approach from discussions of vampires and consumerism, to vampires and homosexual desire, to vampires and disease, to vampires as models for positive relationships with the *other*, to vampires as postmodern challenge to social identity (see Carter; Hollinger; Jones; Latham; Nixon). I won't summarize each essay we read from this volume individually here, but I will share as an example the details of one of these essays, titled *When Hollywood Sucks, or, Hungry Girls, Lost Boys, and Vampirism in the Age of Reagan*, by Nicola Nixon. Nixon first explores the link between vampire characters and the idea of "infection," tying this to AIDS through an analysis of 1980s vampire texts. She then goes on, through a discussion of the films *Near Dark* and *The Lost Boys*, to propose links between vampire narratives and traditional models of family structure, focusing in particular on Reagan-era U.S.–American ideals of "family values." Nixon comments of these two films, "Both ... envision vampires not as sophisticated, sexy, charismatic, lone predators, but as dysfunctional families" (120). She argues that, in both films, dysfunctional family units are presented as the primary threat to society, and especially to "the good American boy," who becomes "tempted to stray" through contact with these "anti-families" (122). Meanwhile, traditional nuclear families are offered as the only salvation, the one thing that can keep America's young men from ruination and corruption.

Students find Nixon's essay quite valuable. Drawing on Nixon's arguments in a discussion of *The Lost Boys*, one student says, "This film is a thinly veiled message about the destructiveness of rebellion and the safety and protection offered by a traditional life — a theme through many vampire stories." Students make connections between Nixon's work and other texts, as well. They link the piece, for example, to *Interview with the Vampire* (which Nixon herself mentions briefly), finding an analysis of the family dynamics within that text to be extremely fertile ground. Other students point out that Nixon's analysis can offer interesting insights when applied to the *Twilight* series, as well. In this series one can see a "good" nuclear family of friendly, benign, even protective vampires, who are opposed to other, non-nuclear groupings of vampires that are more dangerous. One could also explore the implications of the way that Bella becomes "adopted" into this nuclear family, leaving her own "split" family behind.

Another selection of essays provides insights from feminist film theory. Carol Clover discusses gender roles in slasher films and the function of the Final Girl, the "female victim-hero" who survives to the end (235). Barbara Creed discusses horror narratives as expressions of the fear of female sexuality and the male conception of its "monstrousness" (252). And bell hooks discusses the role of the black female spectator in interrogating representations of race and gender in film and television. Students make fascinating use of these essays in their analyses of such narratives as *Buffy the Vampire Slayer*, of which they note, "Buffy takes the tradition of a male vampire hunting and killing an innocent girl and turns it on its head."

Offering another take on film theory, Walter Evans provides an interpretation that links "monster movies" to issues of youthful human sexuality. Evans argues that classic horror films and gothic literature explore the fear and confusion of adolescent sexuality, articulating its seemingly mysterious, uncontrollable, tempting, and frightening urges. My students immediately point out the potential of Evans' theory to help explain the enduring appeal of vampire narratives among adolescents and the phenomenon of the *Twilight* series, and they also note the "coming of age" thread present in many vampire stories that feature characters transitioning from youthful innocence to maturity.

We follow this up with Janice Radway, who offers a very useful conceptual framework for exploring gender, sexuality and the construction of romantic relationships in narrative. Through close ethnographic research, Radway explores the reasons that many women read romance novels. She examines some of the major narrative features of typical romance novels and then proposes arguments about what purpose these features serve for the women who read the novels, even in the case of features that seem misogynistic or negative. For example, Radway suggests that in many romance novels the hero behaves coldly, cruelly, or even violently toward the heroine before eventually acknowledging his love for her; she argues that this allows women to explore their fears that men are cruel or can't give them the fulfillment they're looking for, but by then demonstrating that the hero's bad behavior was actually motivated by the depth of his love for the heroine, the novels reinforce the culturally normative notion that a relationship with the "right" man really is what a woman needs to be happy (140–141).

Radway's framework is particularly useful for considering vampire narratives that feature a human female and a male vampire in a romantic relationship, and is extremely relevant for students as they analyze *Twilight*, which follows many of the structural conventions of romance novels. Students note that in *Twilight*, hero Edward treats heroine Bella badly at first, acts coldly toward her, avoids her, and threatens her. However, the audience is eventually led to understand that he is behaving this way because he feels strongly for her and is trying to protect her. The audience is positioned to immediately forgive and sympathize with Edward, who is portrayed as tortured by his love for Bella, thereby (supposedly) justifying his bad behavior. As one student puts it, "The audience forgives Edward, blaming his actions on passion." Some students also note that in this storyline Bella locates her existence as solely about her love for Edward, thereby constructing her identity as "self-in-relation," a concept explored by Radway (147). Radway also provides a chart of the narrative structure of typical romance novels (150)—it's interesting for students to consider how many of the features here align with *Twilight* and other vampire narratives.

Students also read two contemporary articles that engage in direct analysis of *Twilight*. Alisa Valdes-Rodriguez offers political and religious-spiritual perspective in *The Politics of Wizards and Vampires,* comparing the Harry Potter series to the *Twilight* series. She suggests that Potter reflects a worldview that is progressive, portraying humans as primarily good, socioeconomic status as an oppressive construct, and cooperation with and respect for nature as positive. Meanwhile, she argues that *Twilight* reflects the conservative Mormon background of its author and portrays humans (and vampires) as primarily sinful and only good when they actively — and with great difficulty —choose to be so. Further, she suggests that the series reinforces Christian hierarchies of humans over other species, presenting nonhuman animals as "inferior," and she also points out that the text frames lead female Bella's only function in life as to love Edward.

Meanwhile Latoya Peterson interrogates the racial dynamics of the *Twilight* novels, suggesting that "people of color are exoticized and sexualized — and often dangerous," that whiteness and paleness are often linked to beauty, and that characters of color, like Jacob, are presented as "noble, long suffering, [and] never in need of anything that would inconvenience Bella."

I find this particular mixture of essays very helpful in supporting and equipping students for their own exploration of vampire texts. Each essay contributes a distinct perspective, and students are able to try out the different approaches, focusing on those they find most compelling or applicable for any given text. I find that my students make quite effective use of all of these essays, though some they utilize with more frequency than others. Pieces they cite most often include Wright, Clover, Evans, and several essays from the collection *Blood Read* (particularly Carter, Jones, and Nixon). Although these essays are academically challenging, my students find them accessible and engaging. For less advanced classes, eliminating the more abstract readings (such as, perhaps, Barthes, Althusser, and Žižek) in favor of some of the contemporary pop-culture oriented pieces would still provide useful variety and help students gain new analytical and conceptual tools for exploring vampire texts.

All of these essays together help arm students with the concepts and frameworks to conduct critical analysis. They suggest to students that narrative can reflect personal and cultural fears and desires, can create the impression that certain attitudes and assumptions are natural and historically consistent, can constitute and maintain gender roles and expectations, can position audience members to align with or reject particular values, and that they can also break down habits of exclusion, can provide a "safe" venue for exploring non-normative interests and desires, can challenge the marginalization of certain practices and groups, can protest conventionalization, and can either vilify or exalt transgression and either re-inscribe or dissolve othering.

Insights from Students

I find myself very impressed and pleased with the range of insights my students derive from all of these materials. Students pick up on many of the key points made by the above theorists and effectively apply these points to the narratives we read and view in class. They also raise a number of fascinating original insights. To conclude I'll review a brief selection of some of the points my students have made in their writings and in class discussions, to further provide a sense of the effect of the materials and approaches I utilize.

A central insight that emerges among students throughout the course is the link between vampire characters and socially transgressive or non-normative behavior. Students note that whatever is most taboo in a given culture at a given point in time will often be the quality associated with the vampire. This taboo act may be rejection of the dominant religion or participation in pre-marital sexual activity in tales like some of those from ancient folklore, or homosexuality in stories like Lord Byron's and LeFanu's, or hints of incest and pedophilia, as some students have astutely unearthed in texts like *Interview with the Vampire* and *Let the Right One In*. In general, students unfailingly point out endless variations of the common message in many vampire texts that deviance from normative practices leads to destruction.

At the same time, as they move from reading ancient mythology toward more contemporary texts, a number of students observe a progression from more "monstrous" to more humanized vampire characters. They ponder the idea that cultural shifts may have led audiences to be more intrigued than afraid of transgressive behavior and of the other, making comments like "society seems to be more tolerant of deviant behavior than in past generations."

Students also focus strongly on issues of gender dynamics in vampire narratives. Many note the frequent presence of dominant, aggressive, sexually aware, or socially subversive females that are portrayed as inherently dangerous and sinful, drawing connections to Lilith, Carmilla, and Bram Stoker's character of Lucy, among others. They also comment on the prevalence of vampire tales that seem to support hegemonic models of ideal relationships, both romantic and familial, some pointing out the potential for salvation presented by traditional romantic relationships in stories like *Dracula* and *Blade*, among others.

Some students have also noted that male vampire characters may offer a unique "fantasy man" figure, possessing conflicting traits that could never be combined in human characters (as characters that are dangerous, powerful, protective, wealthy, educated, cultured, taboo, and at the same time offer emotional depth, sexual skill, and the promise of eternal love and possibly eternal youth and beauty). Others suggest that vampires are the new "bad boy," replacing other marginalized groups (such as men of another race or socioeconomic status) who have become increasingly socially accepted and therefore no longer provide the same rebellious cachet for teenage girls.

Students also remark on vampire narratives' role in exploring the dark side and dangers of love and obsession, and in exploring fear of the unknown (students sometimes link this to historical hysteria over vampire epidemics) and fear of abnormal behavior. Some students link vampiric "thirst" to consumerist impulses, as well as to exploitation and sexual objectification by the powerful.

The range of insights students have shared with each other and with me, of which this outline just starts to sketch, makes the course an immensely satisfying, and often thought-provoking, experience for me. I'm gratified to see students leave the class thinking deeply about the values our culture holds and the assumptions it makes, and actively interrogating the process through which those values and assumptions come into being. To see vampire narratives, and other narratives and cultural artifacts, as sources of insight into cultural structures and as arenas for questioning, contesting, and shifting collective attitudes is to take a powerful step toward cultural reflection and positive reformulation. I believe such reflection and reformulation is vital, for as all vampire stories clearly demonstrate, what remains buried just below the surface might not stay buried, and those left lurking in the shadows may prove more dangerous than those who are invited into the light.

Bibliography

Alfredson, Tomas. *Let the Right One In*. 2008. Film.

Althusser, Louis. "Ideology and Ideological State Apparatuses." *Cultural Theory and Popular Culture: A Reader*, 4th ed. Ed. John Storey. Harlow, England: Longman, 2009. 302–312. Print.

Ball, Alan. *True Blood*. 2008–present. Television series.

Barthes, Roland. "Myth Today." *Cultural Theory and Popular Culture: A Reader*, 4th ed. Ed. John Storey. Harlow, England: Longman, 2009. 261–269. Print.

Bartlett, Wayne, and Flavia Idriceanu. *Legends of Blood: The Vampire in History and Myth*. Westport, CT: Praeger, 2006. Print.

Browning, Tod. *Dracula*. 1931. Film.

Bunson, Matthew. *Vampire, the Encyclopaedia*. London: Thames & Hudson, 1993. Print.

Burton, Sir Richard. "Vikram and The Vampire: Classic Hindu Tales of Adventure, Magic, and Romance." Ed. Isabel Burton. 1870. Web. 3 Aug. 2012.

Carter, Margaret. "The Vampire as Alien in Contemporary Fiction." *Blood Read: The Vampire as Metaphor in Contemporary Culture*. Ed. Joan Gordon and Veronica Hollinger. Philadelphia: University of Pennsylvania Press, 1997. 27–44. Print.

Clover, Carol. "Her Body, Himself: Gender in the Slasher Film." *Feminist Film Theory: A Reader*. Ed. Sue Thornham. New York: New York University Press, 1999. 234–250. Print.

Coppola, Francis Ford. *Dracula*. 1992. Film.

Creed, Barbara. "Horror and the Monstrous-Feminine: An Imaginary Abjection." *Feminist Film Theory: A Reader*. Ed. Sue Thornham. New York: New York University Press, 1999. 251–266. Print.

Curtis, Dan. *Dark Shadows*. 1966–1971. Television series.

Evans, Walter. "Monster Movies: A Sexual Theory." *Popular Culture: An Introductory Text*, 1st ed. Ed. Jack Nachbar and Kevin Lause. Bowling Green, OH: Bowling Green State University Popular Press, 1992. 463–475. Print.

Freire, Paulo. *Pedagogy of the Oppressed*, 30th anniversary ed. Trans. Myra Bergman Ramos. New York: Continuum, 2000. Print.

Freud, Sigmund. "The Dream-Work." *Cultural Theory and Popular Culture: A Reader*, 4th ed. Ed. John Storey. Harlow, England: Longman, 2009. 246–254. Print.

Gallimore, Ronald, and Roland Tharp. "Teaching Mind in Society: Teaching, Schooling, and Literate Discourse." *Vygotsky and Education: Instructional Implications and Applications of Sociohistorical Psychology*, 1st paperback ed. Ed. Luis C Moll. Cambridge: Cambridge University Press, 1992. 175–205. Print.

Graves, Robert. *The Greek Myths*. Harmondsworth: Penguin, 1990. Print.

Hardwicke, Catherine. *Twilight*. 2008. Film.

Hollinger, Veronica. "Fantasies of Absence: The Postmodern Vampire." *Blood Read: The Vampire as Metaphor in Contemporary Culture*. Ed. Joan Gordon and Veronica Hollinger. Philadelphia: University of Pennsylvania Press, 1997. 199–212. Print.

hooks, bell. *Reel to Real: Race, Sex and Class at the Movies*. New York: Routledge Classics, 2009. Print.

Hurwitz, Siegmund. *Lilith the First Eve*, 3rd rev. ed. Einsiedeln, Switzerland: Daimon Verlag, 2009. Print.

Jones, Miriam. "The Gilda Stories: Revealing the Monsters at the Margins." *Blood Read: The Vampire as Metaphor in Contemporary Culture*. Ed. Joan Gordon and Veronica Hollinger. Philadelphia: University of Pennsylvania Press, 1997. 151–168. Print.

Jordan, Neil. *Interview with the Vampire: The Vampire Chronicles*. 1994. Film.

Latham, Rob. "Consuming Youth: The Lost Boys Cruise Mallworld." *Blood Read: The Vampire as Metaphor in Contemporary Culture*. Ed. Joan Gordon and Veronica Hollinger. Philadelphia: University of Pennsylvania Press, 1997. 129–150. Print.

LeFanu, J. Sheridan. "Carmilla." 1872. Web. 3 Aug. 2012.

Marigny, Jean. *Vampires*. London: Thames and Hudson, 1994. Print.

Murnau, F. W. *Nosferatu*. 1929. Film.

Nixon, Nicola. "When Hollywood Sucks, or, Hungry Girls, Lost Boys, and Vampirism in the Age of Reagan." *Blood Read: The Vampire as Metaphor in Contemporary Culture*. Ed. Joan Gordon and Veronica Hollinger. Philadelphia: University of Pennsylvania Press, 1997. 115–128. Print.

Norrington, Stephen. *Blade*. 1998. Film.

Peterson, Latoya. "Running with the Wolves—A Racialicious Reading of the *Twilight* Saga." *Racialicious— The intersection of Race and Pop Culture*. 26 Nov. 2009. Web. 3 Aug. 2012.

Polidori, John. "The Vampyre." 1819. Web. 3 Aug. 2012.

Radway, Janice A. *Reading the Romance: Women, Patriarchy, and Popular Literature*. 2d ed. Chapel Hill: University of North Carolina Press, 1991. Print.

Ryan, Alan, ed. *Vampires: Two Centuries of Great Vampire Stories*. Garden City, NY: Doubleday, 1987. Print.

Schumacher, Joel. *The Lost Boys*. 1987. Film.

Schwartz, Howard, ed. *Lilith's Cave: Jewish Tales of the Supernatural*, 1st ed. San Francisco: Harper & Row, 1988. Print.

Stoker, Bram. "Dracula's Guest." 1914. Web. 3 Aug. 2012.

Summers, Montague. "The Vampire, His Kith and Kin." 1928. Web. 3 Aug. 2012.

Thompson, Karen. "The Mythology of the Vampire." Web. 15 Aug. 2012.

Valdes-Rodriguez, Alisa. "The Politics of Wizards and Vampires." *Racialicious — The Intersection of Race and Pop Culture*. 11 Dec. 2008. Web. 3 Aug. 2012.

Vygotsky, Lev S. *Mind in Society: The Development of Higher Psychological Processes*. Ed. Michael Cole, et al. Cambridge: Harvard University Press, 1978. Print.

Wenger, Etienne. *Communities of Practice: Learning, Meaning, and Identity*, 1st ed. New York: Cambridge University Press, 1999. Print.

Whedon, Joss. *Buffy the Vampire Slayer*. 1997–2003. Television series.

Wiseman, Len. *Underworld*. 2003. Film.

Wright, Will. "The Structure of Myth and the Structure of the Western Film." *Cultural Theory and Popular Culture: A Reader*, 4th ed. Ed. John Storey. Harlow, England: Longman, 2009. 270–284. Print.

Žižek, Slavoj. "From Reality to the Real." *Cultural Theory and Popular Culture: A Reader*, 4th ed. Ed. John Storey. Harlow, England: Longman, 2009. 332–347. Print.

Blogging the Undead: Information Literacy and Vampire Literature in an Honors Seminar

Lisa A. Nevárez

As part of the Halloween and vampire paraphernalia I have accrued over the years, one proved particularly useful as I met with my seminar students for the first time in the bitter January cold of the Spring semester. Clutching my black-cloth Halloween candy basket, complete with purple-lined pointy ears, dot eyes, and a thread smile garnished with two white, pointy teeth, I entered the classroom, eager to meet my "vamps." Inside there was no candy, but instead there were white slips of paper, which would provide my students with the start of their research projects.

This course, "The Vampire," was an Honors seminar I designed and subsequently taught at my institution, Siena College, which is a Liberal Arts institution in the Franciscan tradition, and is located in upstate New York. This particular Honors seminar was under the purview of the English Department and was designated as such, although the students enrolled were not all English majors. While Honors seminars, capped at twelve students and meeting once weekly in a two-hour block of time, readily lend themselves to intense discussion and dialogue, I wanted something more into which the students could, well, sink their teeth. Thanks to an Information Literacy grant I received in 2011, I was able to design a framework for "The Vampire" that engaged students in a learning process outside of the traditional discussion-based seminar format.[1] In this essay, I will share my assignment for "blogging the undead" and take the reader through my design of an Honors seminar on vampire literature.

While I have twice before taught courses on the horror novel, which included sections on vampire literature, this was my first outing with a course solely dedicated to vampire literature. Where to start? Where to go? In anticipation that I would be shaking up the traditional seminar format, I selected a range of texts to represent a range of vampire literature, based in the Western literary tradition. The main overarching question in this Honors seminar was How/why/when/where has the figure of the vampire evolved in literature? I aimed to cover the canonical, or more classic, vampire texts and then move on to more contemporary works.

Our readings for the seminar covered a wide span of time (c. 1800–2011) and jumped from country to country and explored different permutations of the vampire, albeit maintaining a focus on Western European/North American traditions. After beginning with some historical background on the history of the vampire, we opened with John Polidori's "The Vampyre" (1819) and continued with a greatest hits compilation of the classics: J. Sheridan LeFanu's *Carmilla* (1872), Bram Stoker's *Dracula* (1897), Stephen King's *'Salem's Lot* (1975), and Anne Rice's *Interview with the Vampire* (1976). We then continued with more recent texts: John Ajvide Lindqvist's *Let Me In* (2004), Marta Acosta's *Happy Hour at Casa Dracula* (2006), and Stephenie Meyer's *Twilight* (2005). We concluded with a class session devoted to vampire-themed children's literature, such as the book series featuring the vampire rabbit, Bunnicula, by Deborah and James Howe, which first appeared in 1979 with *Bunnicula: A Rabbit Tale of Mystery*. Given that this was an upper-level seminar, students were responsible for a novel per week, save for *Dracula* and *'Salem's Lot*, which I divided over two class sessions. With the seminar format, these longer texts worked very well, and gave us concrete blocks of text for each meeting.[2] For this particular vampire outing I opted not to include a film component, although on occasion we viewed a film clip that related to the text under discussion.

As is customary at my institution for Honors courses, students applied for permission to enroll, and I had a dozen or so more applicants than I could accommodate. Many of the seminar participants already had a strong interest in vampire literature, albeit largely confined to the non-literary sources, such as the television series *True Blood* and *The Vampire Diaries*. They all were familiar with the *Twilight* saga; if they had not read a novel or seen a film, they at least had heard of the saga and, as I learned, had strong opinions for and against it. My challenge was channeling and honing these select students into a cohort who could apply their acumen to a study of vampire literature, thus balancing their out-of-class interests with rigorous literary study, as is expected in an English Honors seminar at my institution. This class is hardly alone in this goal, as the other essays in this volume attest. I found the selection of novels, versus short fiction and poetry, to be particularly effective as far as pushing these students to grapple with a full-length text and engage with an intense reading experience. They also neatly suited our two-hour sessions: we could cover a novel and carry on a sustained discussion.

For the literature under discussion, I sought to balance the canonical texts with the contemporary ones, and in the latter half of the semester, as the above mentioned reading list demonstrates, the classics of vampire literature —*Carmilla*, *Dracula*, and others— segued to more recent texts. Aside from *Twilight*, which as mentioned above the students were already familiar with, the two texts I included were the Swedish *Let Me In* and the novel by Marta Acosta which focuses on a Latina vampire seductress/slayer, Milagro de los Santos. With these two novels, students were able to take their knowledge of vampires into new directions, and explore other cultures and ethnicities, and then compare them with the earlier texts. This was a fruitful endeavor, for the following reasons.

The inclusion of *Let Me In* allowed the students to analyze a child vampire, Eli, and situate him/her[3] in an entirely different context from our previous readings. In addition, given both the Swedish and American film versions, there existed a ripe opportunity to screen clips that depicted a certain scene, in this case when Eli reveals his/her identity to Oskar (Swedish) and Abby to Owen (American). They were simultaneously fascinated and horrified by *Let the Right One In* and its depiction of a child vampire entirely unlike the fearsome Claudia of *Interview with the Vampire*, which we had discussed earlier in the semester. Students were taken aback by her ruthless nature, as she voraciously preyed on humans and plotted the murder of her maker, Lestat.

In contrast to the intensity of *Let the Right One In*, *Happy Hour at Casa Dracula*, which is the first novel in the series of *Casa Dracula* books, is a more light-hearted read. It permitted students to engage with an ethnic divide set in the United States, albeit in an unnamed city. The Latina Milagros finds herself intertwined with the Caucasian — and vampire — Grant family after Oswald Grant bites her at a book party. The novel is marketed as a romantic comedy, with a blurb from *Booklist* on the cover of the paperback that reads: "A fun, snappy read for romantic fantasy fans." The humor dwells in part with the contrast between the "fiery" Latina and the "cool" Caucasians as Milagros must choose between the vampires Oswald and Ian. Several students proclaimed *Happy Hour at Casa Dracula* to be their favorite text, citing the humor and romantic tension between Milagro and Oswald, and Milagro and Ian.

Both of these novels allowed us to loop back to several texts, and primarily to *Dracula*. We were able to discuss otherness and both the ethnic outsider and the foreign vampire, as well as amplifying our discussion of critical articles addressing this, such as Stephen Arata's pivotal essay. Students were able to compare Dracula and his presence as an "other" in Victorian England with the two abovementioned texts. The Latina Milagro and her presence in the Caucasian Grant family in a present-day setting provided a more contemporary depiction of cross-cultural relations. The *Dracula* framework assisted students in grappling with our collective experience as "outsider," e.g., American, readers for the Swedish novel and its culture. The students responded enthusiastically to these two texts. Given the students' interest in the theme of the outsider, in the future I will include Octavia Butler's novel *Fledgling* (2005), which contains themes related to race and genetic engineering.

The culminating reading, the inclusion of children's literature, was something the students enjoyed very much. They could then see how the vampire emerges with humor in not only the aforementioned Bunnicula, but also in *Dear Vampa* (2009) by Ross Collins and *Vampire Boy's Goodnight* (2010) by Lisa Brown, and in other texts. Tony Fonseca's entry on "Children's Vampire Fiction" in S.T. Joshi's Encyclopedia of the Vampire (2011), provides an excellent starting point. The inclusion of the children's literature also added a lighter note at the end of the semester, when the students were even more actively engaged in the final stages of the research project. During this class we even had "story time" with *Dear Vampa*.

But before we delved into the picture books, we needed to first discuss the primary texts for the course. First, the not-so-novel method for encouraging discussion of the abovementioned texts: divide and participate. I divided the students into two groups of six, Group A and Group B. Each group alternated being seminar "leaders" for a class session. Each individual in the designated group was responsible for writing a short, one- to two-page essay that resulted in a question for the class. For instance, a student writing on *Let the Right One In* crafted a paper that ended with a series of questions regarding the "child" vampire, Eli. This student asked: "To what capacity does Eli, the child vampire, have the ability to mature and develop mentally and emotionally? Is her mind actually trapped somehow in the developmental stages of her twelve-year-old body?" These short papers provided me with the opportunity of seeing the students' writing early on in the semester, so as to suggest improvements prior to the final research paper. And, the questions provided a ready avenue for students to enter the class conversation.

The in-class discussion was only a part of "The Vampire" seminar. One of my primary goals in developing the blog assignment and information literacy component, as will be discussed shortly, was to get the students to interact and engage with each other. In a seminar, which is discussion-based, students have plenty of opportunities to participate in a class conversation. An Honors student is often self-selecting, and is, generally speaking, quick to raise a hand to offer an insight. However, I wanted them to take that same caliber of discussion outside of our classroom and into the online world, as well as refine their in-class sharing of ideas. Further, I wanted them to further develop their already strong research skills. The students enter an Honors class prepared to conduct research, but many times I found that synthesizing and processing the sources and thinking "outside the box" with researching popular culture topics to be lacking. These were the two goals I hoped to address.

Happily for my goals, what got the students talking the most was the blogs. Courtesy of Blackboard, the online education platform my institution utilizes, I was able to set up an individual blog for each student, titled by name. These can best be defined as a "bound-aried community," as defined by Nancy White. To this end, access to these blogs was restricted to my students, Siena College Librarian Catherine Crohan, and me. My aim behind setting up the blog component was to catch my students inside their technological comfort zone, where they could write and share in a mode of communication that "spoke" to them, and in a comfortable space restricted to the seminar. Students had the ability to include images and links in that blog space. Through the "comments" section, the idea process behind the project became more collaborative in a medium that went outside of the class-room. Jean Burgess observed with the use of weblogs in her own courses, "If we give students a voice, they will most certainly use it" (110). My experience was similar: my students down-right enjoyed, they reported to me, utilizing the blog format.

My concern in setting up these blogs lay in a concern for diminishing the level of in-class engagement and discussion. After all, an Honors seminar thrives on a discussion among these very sharp students. Happily, the blogs only augmented our conversation, and did not hurt it in any way. Tony Reeves and Phil Gomm draw upon research by Farmer, Yue, and Brooks on the pedagogical use of blogs, observing that "although the individual act of adding information to a blog might be seen as being in opposition to the communal act of participating in an online community, bloggers share personal information and opin-ions via their blog as a means to encourage others to comment, thereby providing a basis for interaction and discussion" (55). This proved to be the case, as students relied on the first person voice to expound upon their research, to be discussed shortly.

The one pitfall of using the blogs in the manner in which I did is that the blogs were very assignment-driven which, according to Marcus O'Donnell, can lead to students posting on their blogs in order to garner a high grade, instead of working more holistically to craft a network of learning and communication between their peers (Reeves and Gomm 56). For instance, I required my students to post blog entries by certain due dates, and most followed that instruction quite rigidly and did not post outside of those specifications.

All this is where the vampire Halloween basket came into play. Inside that basket were twelve slips of paper, each ready to be plucked by an eager student hand. I selected these topics because these are themes that run throughout vampire literature — and notably in our course readings — as well as in popular culture. My goal was to provide the students with a broad enough topic, so they could then focus their individual research. The twelve topics inside were:

- Animal transfiguration (bats, wolves, etc.)
- Children (as vampires or as victims, or both, or children's literature)
- The historic Dracula (Vlad the Impaler)
- Homosocial or homosexual relationships

- Heterosexual relationships/marriage
- Tween/young adult audience
- Vampire hunter/slayer
- Female victim or vampire
- Male victim or vampire
- Ethnicity and race
- Interaction with zombies, werewolves, etc.
- Setting (geographically or other, ex: Transylvania, castles, nature)

Each student selected a topic by reaching a hand into the basket. While I could have sent around a sign-up sheet, I chose instead to maximize the level of surprise with this random selection. Instead of conducting an internal debate between choosing "ethnicity and race" or "zombies and werewolves," a student instead could focus on the project, with the topic in hand, right off on the first day. There was some grumbling as individual faces registered receiving a treat (a topic s/he liked) or a trick (a less desirable topic, to him/her). But at the end, each student was truly an "expert" in his/her "field."

Each student was charged with answering the following question by the end of the semester: "How has this topic evolved over the course of vampire literature/history?" They were free to focus and refine the topic in consultation with me, and they understood that they would be using the class texts as part of this process. At the end of the semester they were each responsible for presenting on the topic in class, writing a research paper, and presenting a posterboard at Academic Celebration Day, a culminating end-of-year event at Siena College that showcases student projects. Ultimately, they shared their work with me, with their classmates, and with the college community. I included a checklist of several research components that were required to "prove" the evolution of the topic. Students were responsible for: engaging with at least two course readings; utilizing six critical sources at minimum (ex: peer-reviewed article); and including four popular culture references (such as from film, music, television, magazines, celebrities, etc.).

In order to facilitate the research process, each student was required to meet with Librarian Catherine Crohan at minimum one time over the course of the semester; some students met with her more often. This interaction with Catherine proved to be extremely valuable. With some of these more wide-ranging topics that relied on popular culture, she opened their eyes to a world of resources they wouldn't even have considered. Instead of the "standard" MLA or JSTOR searches as with a traditional literary research paper, my students found themselves in multiple databases and exploring all sorts of reference works via Connect NY (our local library consortium) and Interlibrary Loan, not to mention consulting the Siena Library's collection.

While this section of the assignment honed their research skills, an additional piece of the assignment was sharing and synthesizing their newly-found sources. To this end, students were each responsible for posting on their individual blogs at least six times over the course of the semester, by dates posted on the syllabus. As well, they were required to comment on each other's blogs; I required them to post at least two comments on each of their classmates' blogs, so 22 comments. I posted some comments, as did Catherine. I found this to be an overwhelmingly positive part of the course for several reasons.

One, I found that students, once they knew they had an audience, truly did synthesize and sum up their sources and could pass judgment on them. Again and again they wrote about what a source discussed and whether it would be useful for their project, and posted this judgment on their blogs. Second, the students responded to each other's narratives of their research strategies, and did so in a productive yet rigorous and focused manner, as will be discussed shortly. The instructions were as follows:

> Your blog update should frankly assess where you are at in the research process, and update the class as to where you are in answering the over-arching question. Your update should include reference to at least one of the check-list items, and explain how/why you will use it. And, share your thoughts on the project at these various stages. Do you agree — or disagree — with many of the critics? Are you frustrated that a particular source didn't pan out? Are you finding so many sources your head is spinning? Finally, in your update you should explain what your next step is, going forward.

Here are some examples.

> *Hello Everyone!*
>
> *As you can plainly tell from my title, my topic is centered around Vampires and their interaction with other beings such as werewolves, zombies and the like. Pretty interesting stuff, huh? To be honest, this is probably the most excited I've ever been for a project/paper, and that's saying something. I haven't done an extreme amount of research yet, but I am definitely looking forward to it. I will most likely include references to many pop-culture/modern instances of vampires, werewolves and Zombies, such as the Underworld and Twilight Series (Yes ... Twilight will make a ... ahem ... shining example) as well as things like Being Human and True Blood. All of these and more are swirling around my head and I can't wait to start putting my thoughts down on paper (or, more likely, Here). Feel free to give me any ideas that you may have, as I'm always open for a helping hand (as long as, you know, there's no stake in it). I shall see you all later, and I look forward to our discussion on those fanged fantasies that are, VAMPIRES.*

In the above entry, I was pleased to see the student already outlining a research strategy and thinking of which texts would best apply. This is an example of conversational tone the blogs all took: they were truly research "diaries."

Another first blog entry, and the student has started the research and met with Catherine.

> *The overarching topic that I will be tackling for the remainder of the semester is "Homosocial or homosexual relationships" regarding vampires. I am going to be dealing with homosexual relationships and the vampire because I feel that it would be more interesting to learn about.*
>
> *To be honest, upon receiving this topic I felt a little dumbstruck.... I could not recall any instance of homosexuality between two vampires or between a vampire and it's victim in any book that I had read or any movie or TV show that I had seen.*
>
> *At least that was until I read the required novel for this week. Carmilla by LeFanu expressed many instances of homosexuality between the protagonist, Laura, and the vampire, Carmilla. The highly sensual scenes that existed between Laura and Carmilla were something that I had never read in a vampire novel between two people of the same sex. And so, I was provided with some very valuable information to eventually use. Yes!*
>
> *Today I scheduled by first meeting with Catherine since I have been absolutely lost on where to begin the actual research part ... especially since as an "x" major the extent of my research has involved scientific papers. However, Catherine was able to provide me with a plethora of options to use! I have two books on the way here through Connect NY as we speak, Our Vampires, Ourselves by Nina Auerbach and Blood Read: The Vampire as Metaphor in Contemporary Culture edited by Joan Gordon and Veronica Hol! I'm super excited to see what these books are going to contain! Catherine was also able to provide me with a few articles and some books that were in the library on campus. Who knows what I'm actually going to find in all this stuff but we'll find out soon enough! Wish me luck!*
>
> *I'll let you all know how this goes! :)*

Here I saw that the student was able to get the research process off to a good — and early — start and used strategies new to her/him.

The virtual interaction with each other allowed these Honors students, already well-versed in the level of discussion contingent with a seminar, to take that discussion elsewhere.

Here for instance, is a student's blog entry, detailing where s/he is at with the research:

> *Hey guys,*
>
> *So I assume by now you guys know what I'm doing with my thesis. To put it simply, I'm examining the evolution of the vampire as a natural creature (like an animal) versus one that is more human or superhuman.*
>
> *In one of the texts I'm working with* The Science of Vampires *I found a very interesting section on the "crime scene." To summarize, it states that in modern literature the vampire often cleans up after himself as though he were a criminal, while in more classic literature, the vampire acts as a natural predator. I think this is absolutely something I will contrast when I select the two pieces (I'm going to pick a "classic" vampire tale and a more modern one) I'm working with.*
>
> *I definitely want to talk about the vampire as a member of a food pyramid where humans are not on top, but I was also thinking of discussing them in terms of a parasite. The idea came to me when I was contemplating living victims. This would also make a valid parallel to the drinking of blood.*
>
> *I'm still trying to figure out what I'm going to say about vampires interactions with the sun. I feel like in a lot of classic literature you don't see what happens to vampires in the sun, you just know they don't go out into it. I think I might use this to present them as nocturnal. In modern literature you often see the effect of sunlight on the vampire. For example, Edward sparkles, vampires in Morganville burn, and vampires in Let Me In get very sick and tingle. That, to me, seems much more supernatural.*
>
> *One section of the book* The Vampire in 19th Century Literature *is titled "Myth Becomes Metaphor." This section has a lot of really great examples of how the vampire has become a lot less tangible as an actual entity, and I think that this idea will relate to the "naturalness."*
>
> *The Natural History of the Vampire* gives two definitions of "lycanthropy." One is the psychological state of a human believing they are an animal, the other is the actual transfiguration between human and animal. I think this fact might highlight and reiterate my last point. Myth becoming metaphor seems related to psychosis versus actuality.*
>
> *What do you guys think so far?*

His/her peers responded rapidly to this update and question. The responses, here and elsewhere, were full of praise for their peer's efforts — the praise could have been toned down — and also offered suggestions for where to go with the research. Some student responses to the above blog are:

> *I really like your ideas of setting up the vampire as at the top of the food chain. The part with the sun I think you may be able to use as something like the vampire's only "natural" predator if you are going along the lines of looking at it like a food chain, like the food chain webs that we used to look at it school. For example: Sun — — >Vampire — —>Human — —> ext. I don't know if this is along the lines of what you were thinking about, but hope it help.*
>
> *I actually just suggested this movie to [student] also, but I really really think it would be worth your time to watch the movie 30 Days of Night. These vampires are most certainly predators at the top of the food chain as well as completely nocturnal. The whole film revolves around the idea of these vampires invading a town in Alaska that experiences 30 days of night (which does actually happen in Alaska due to the way the sun revolves around the Earth). However, since the town is in total darkness for so long you can really see how these vampires function as killers. I believe that there is also a graphic novel that the movie was made from so that might be worth a look as well if you can find it.*

I like your idea to put vampires at the top of the food chain. I think they are really the only creature that can go above humans. Are you going to focus more on vampires like the ones from Let Me In and Salem's Lot where they have to feed on humans or will you talk a little about vampires like the ones from True Blood who have found ways to avoid feeding on humans? I know you want to talk about vampire as being more animal like, but there seem to be a lot of vampires out there that are more like humans and have found ways to avoid killing. You may be able to argue that even though they don't feed directly off humans, they still need blood, but I think you may want to address those vampire who are not purely animalistic.

(There were three other comments posted.)

This demonstrates the kind of interaction in which I wanted students to create: they were candid about research frustrations and had ideas to share, and their classmates chimed in, offering ideas and support and feedback.

Because of the interactive nature of the blogs, I think the seminar had an additional layer of participating and sharing. Seminars by nature permit a free flow of conversation, but in "The Vampire" I found the students to be especially respectful, helpful to their classmates, and free to offer insights. The final projects were all very engaging, in part because the groundwork for the research allowed them, truly, to research and "blog" the Undead. They frequently referenced their projects in our class sessions, and seemed to enjoy forging connections with the texts under discussion.

The final outcome of the course was threefold. It began with a seminar presentation (many students opted to use PowerPoint or Prezi, and/or bring in their posterboards). Students were then able to share, in our circle, about their projects. At the aforementioned Academic Celebration Day posterboard session, students presented their research to the campus community. With the structure of that event, students stood by their posterboards and fielded questions from community members as they circulated around the room. Finally, students wrote a final research paper on the topic. The paper was based off of the research and was a minimum of eight pages, recapping the results— and answer to— the overarching question. With these three areas for assessment, students were able to share their ideas orally, visually, and in writing, in both a "protected" space and in a public/community space.

The primary focus in the seminar was on conversation and discussion and, with the intimate number of students, led to a more candid, in-depth class session than I find in larger-sized classes; in this respect, one can see overlap with a First Year Seminar experience.[4] Moving the conversation off the seminar table and into an online venue assisted students in accessing a form of technology that they are comfortable with and, I think, that increased comfort assisted in creating a more dynamic in-class setting. The challenge, in some ways, lay in my own admitted not as up to speed technological skills. The Blackboard system, though, is quite user-friendly.

All this allowed us to share ideas about these texts in a way that only enhanced our understanding of, and appreciation for them. The texts became more dynamic, and the topics assisted us in navigating through different centuries and authors, all through identifying their designated themes. The topics became our touchstone for the entire semester's conversation. The topics also provided us with moments of levity and the formation of seminar-specific "inside jokes." For instance, students would frequently connect the day's reading to his/her topic with overdramatized — and humorous— responses. And, since we were all "in" on the joke, they could point out references to their classmates. We had an amusing time talking about "nature" in *Twilight*, for example. However, to share those asides here would not be nearly as funny an experience for the reader as it was for me, sitting in a classroom with my snickering seminar students.

Of course, thrilled as I was that the blog and process worked in this seminar, there is room for improvement. Next time around, I would like to make the blogging process even more interactive, and have the students share—in class—their updates. Then, the loop is more continuous: class discussion to blog to comments and back to class. With my ever-increasing knowledge of Blackboard and other online sites, it could be useful to move other parts of the research project online as well.

My vampire Halloween basket worked its "trick" that January day. Even though some students—they admitted—were less than thrilled with their topics, they grew into liking them. Seeing them pull together their ideas at the end of the semester in their threefold means of presenting them was fascinating, and it was rewarding to see them bond together. As one student commented in the course evaluation, "I absolutely loved the discussions that took place every class. I felt like in the end our class formed a kind of family.... It was like an awesome book club with higher thinking. LOVED coming to this class every week!" And my "treat" was to enjoy an Honors seminar on a topic I am passionate about and, with the research assignment, the students and I were able to access the information in a new and technologically innovative way.

(I extend a special thank you to my wonderful "vamps" in the seminar, who have graciously permitted me to share their blog posts and other assignments. Thank you also to Librarian Catherine Crohan for all her work with the students.)

Notes

1. Information Literacy is defined as follows: "Information literacy is a set of abilities requiring individuals to 'recognize when information is needed and have the ability to locate, evaluate, and use effectively the needed information.'" American Library Association, *Presidential Committee on Information Literacy. Final Report* (Chicago: American Library Association, 1989), retrieved from http://www.ala.org/acrl/standards/infor mationliteracycompetency on Jan. 16, 2013.

2. In my seminars on "The Horror Novel," students, in pairs, were responsible for leading a seminar meeting, including posing discussion questions and incorporating critical sources. For instance, those who discussed Rice's *Interview with the Vampire* not only prepared information packets for the students on Rice's biography and influences, but also included excerpts from critical sources, and then requested that students respond to those insights. In future semesters in "The Vampire" I may incorporate a similar assignment.

3. In the novel, Eli begins life as a male and is castrated, and then presents him/herself as female. The Swedish film captures this to a certain degree, by showing Eli with no sexual organs. The American film sidesteps this, and Abby is very obviously a female, with no past trauma related to a castration.

4. In this volume, see the essays by U. Melissa Anyiwo and Candace R. Benefiel and Catherine Coker which discuss those learning environments.

Bibliography

Acosta, Marta. *Happy Hour at Casa Dracula*. New York: Pocket Star, 2006. Print.

Alfredson, Tomas. *Let the Right One In*. 2008. Film.

Arata, Stephen. "The Occidental Tourist: Dracula and the Anxiety of Reverse Colonization." *Victorian Studies* (Summer 1990): 627–34. Print.

Burgess, Jean. "Blogging to Learn, Learning to Blog." *Uses of Blogs*. Ed. Axel Bruns and Joanne Jacobs. New York: Peter Lang, 2006. Print.

Fonseca, Tony. "Children's Vampire Fiction." *Encyclopedia of the Vampire: The Living Dead in Myth, Legend, and Popular Culture*. Ed. S.T. Joshi. Santa Barbara: Greenwood, 2011. Print.

Reeves, Matt. *Let Me In*. 2010. Film.

Reeves, Tony, and Phil Gomm. "Blogging All Over the World: Can Blogs Enhance Student Engagement by Creating a Community of Practice Around a Course?" *Increasing Student Engagement and Retention Using Online Learning Activities: Wikis, Blogs and Webquests*. Ed. Charles Wankel and Patrick Blessinger. Bingley, U.K.: Emerald, 2012. Print.

White, Nancy. "Blogs and community — launching a new paradigm for online community?" http://www.full circ.com/2007/12/20/repost-blogs-and-community-launching-a-new-paradigm/#more-91. Retrieved Feb. 21, 2013.

About the Contributors

U. Melissa **Anyiwo** has a Ph.D. from the University of Wales, Swansea, where she wrote on "Mammy" and "Jezebel" figures from the sixteenth century to the present. She is an associate professor of politics and history and is the coordinator of African American studies at Curry College. She has published articles on vampires and edited *Buffy Conquers the Academy: Conference Papers from the 2009/2010 Popular Culture/American Culture Associations*.

Candace R. **Benefiel** is an associate professor and humanities librarian at Texas A&M University, and a Ph.D. student, focusing on the vampire in literature. She has an M.L.I.S. from the University of Texas at Austin and an M.A. from West Texas State University. She wrote *Reading Laurell K. Hamilton* (ABC-Clio, 2011) and has published articles in the *Journal of Popular Culture, Wilson Library Bulletin*, and *College and Research Libraries*.

Crystal **Boson** is a Ph.D. candidate at the University of Kansas in the American Studies department. She has an M.A. from Texas A&M University with a focus on black postmodern literature and has been published in *PANK, Callaloo* and *The Project on the History of Black Writing*. Her two collections of poetry, *The Icarus Series* and *The Queer Texas Prayerbook*, are with Seven Kitchens Press.

Alissa **Burger**, Ph.D., is an assistant professor of English and humanities at SUNY, Delhi, where she teaches Gothic literature, women in literature, women's studies, and a seminar on Stephen King's fiction. She has done a number of active text pairings with literature of ghosts and the undead, as well as vampires, the last with Bram Stoker's *Dracula*, Stephen King's *'Salem's Lot,* Scott Snyder et al.'s *American Vampire* series, and multiple film adaptations.

Alisha M. **Chambers** holds an M.F.A. from the University of Central Oklahoma, where she teaches freshman composition courses. She is an avid lover of the vampire, and writes articles and essays for her blog.

Neena **Cinquino** received an M.A. in English from The City College of New York. She teaches composition and literature courses at the collegiate level, at both two- and four-year institutions. Her research interests include 19th and 20th century Gothic literature, with a focus on the female Gothic. She is a graduate student at New York University.

Catherine **Coker** is pursuing a Ph.D. in English literature at Texas A&M University. Her research interests focus on women in popular culture and in print history.

Heide **Crawford**, Ph.D., teaches German language and literature in the Department of Germanic and Slavic Studies at the University of Georgia. She has published articles and book chapters on the cultural history of the literary vampire, fairy tales, the German Gothic tradition and the true authorship of the popular German vampire story "Wake Not the Dead!"

Anne **Daugherty**, Ph.D., is a professor of education at Baker University. A native of Australia, she holds degrees from the University of Newcastle, Australian Catholic University, and Florida State University, where she was an International Rotary Foundation Scholar. Her research interests include online teaching, women, and film.

Vicky **Gilpin**, Ed.D., is a high school and post-secondary teacher in Illinois. Her publications include "Attempting to Dominate Objectification: Sexual Power Exchange in Strindberg's Miss Julie" in *Artefact* and "Vampires and Female Spiritual Transformation: Laurell K. Hamilton's Anita Blake, Vampire Hunter" in *The Undead and Theology* (Pickwick, 2012). She is researching *Varney the Vampyre* for a thesis for Harvard University's Extension School.

Jean R. **Hillabold** has taught English courses at the University of Regina in Saskatchewan, Canada, for more than twenty years. She writes erotica, blog posts and reviews under a pen name. She is co-editor (with Wes D. Pearce) of *Out Spoken*, an anthology based on presentations from the faculty speakers series at the University of Regina Queer Initiative which includes her work on Radclyffe Hall's novel *The Well of Loneliness*.

Amy **Hodges**, Ph.D., is a graduate of the University of Arkansas, and is a postdoctoral research associate at Texas A&M University at Qatar. Her research focuses on how personal and cultural attitudes toward literacy impact identity construction.

Heather Duerre **Humann**, Ph.D., is an instructor in the Department of English at the University of Alabama where she teaches a range of writing and literature courses. Her articles and book reviews have appeared in *African American Review*, *Children's Literature Association Quarterly*, *South Atlantic Review*, *Studies in the Novel* and elsewhere. She is also on the editorial board of *Margaret Atwood Studies*.

Lisa **Lampert-Weissig**, Ph.D., is a professor of English literature and Katzin Chair in Jewish Civilization at UC San Diego. She is the author of *Gender and Jewish Difference from Paul to Shakespeare* (University of Pennsylvania Press, 2004) and *Medieval Literature and Postcolonial Studies* (Edinburgh University Press, 2010). Her teaching and scholarship on vampires and other monsters is an extension of her work on marginalized figures in medieval literature.

Murray **Leeder**, Ph.D., holds a doctorate from Carleton University and teaches film studies at the University of Manitoba. He is the author of the entry on John Carpenter's *Halloween* for Auteur Press's *Devil's Advocates* series, as well as the author of numerous articles, mostly on ghosts and vampires in cinema.

Seri I. **Luangphinith**, Ph.D., is a professor of English and chair of the Humanities Division at the University of Hawai'i, Hilo. Her recent work includes service as the accreditation liaison officer for UH Hilo, which is part of a group helping the Western Association of Schools and Colleges (WASC) pilot new accreditation guidelines that encourage core competency and graduation proficiency assessment.

Jerri L. **Miller** holds an M.A. in liberal arts with a concentration in literature from Baker University. She is an adjunct online instructor at the University of Phoenix and Baker University where she looks for ways to better engage students and make their learning experience relevant.

Lisa A. **Nevárez** has a Ph.D. in comparative literature from Vanderbilt University and is an associate professor of English at Siena College. Her research and teaching interests include British Romanticism and Latino/a literature, in addition to her work on vampires, horror fiction, and the Gothic. Her recent work has included essays on Matthew "Monk" Lewis' *Journal* *of a West India Proprietor*, Lady Maria Nugent's *India Journal*, and Stephenie Meyer's *Breaking Dawn*.

Leslie **Ormandy** teaches "Vampires in Literature" classes at an Oregon community college. She also teaches remedial and college-level composition. Three of her short stories can be found in audio format on *Favorite Vampire Stories: Tales with Bite*, editions 1 and 2. She has presented vampire-focused papers at PCA/ACA, as well as at Open Graves, Open Minds: Vampires and the Undead in Modern Culture (U.K., 2010) and TV Fangdom (U.K., 2013).

Sue Weaver **Schopf**, Ph.D., is an associate dean, the director of the Master of Liberal Arts program, and research advisor in the humanities in Harvard's Division of Continuing Education, where she has also taught a variety of writing-intensive literature courses for more than 25 years. A specialist in 19th and early 20th century literature, she has published scholarly articles on various literary topics.

Rita **Turner**, Ph.D., is a lecturer in the Media and Communication Studies Program and the American Studies Department at the University of Maryland, Baltimore County. Her research focuses on educational design for cultivating critical social and environmental consciousness. She has published articles in *Environmental Ethics* and *Sustainability*.

Michał **Wolski** is a Polish philology and journalism graduate, and a Ph.D. candidate at the University of Wrocław, where he also teaches. His research focuses on vampires as modern antiheroes. He is also interested in theoretical and practical aspects of typography and the reception of "superhero movies" in Poland.

Index

www.ingramcontent.com/pod-product-compliance
Lightning Source LLC
Chambersburg PA
CBHW080551270326
41929CB00019B/3268